The
SANTA FE & TAOS
Book

A Complete Guide

THE
SANTA FE & TAOS
BOOK
A Complete Guide

BRANDT MORGAN

with Keith Easthouse and Ramona Gault

Berkshire House, Publishers
Stockbridge, Massachusetts

ON THE COVER AND FRONTISPIECE

Front Cover Landscape — *View of Santa Fe and mountains from I-25, south of the city, Murrae Haynes; Inset — Skiers at Taos Ski Valley, Ken Gallard;* Die Agyptische Helena *at Santa Fe Opera, Bayard Horton, courtesy Santa Fe Opera; Taos Pueblo, Ray Lutz; Maria Ysabel Restaurant, Santa Fe, Murrae Haynes.*

Frontispiece — *Silver jewelry inspired by petroglyphs, Murrae Haynes, courtesy Ross LewAllen Jewelry.*

Back Cover — *Zozobra; Santa Fe chamber Music Festival; Kiva at Pecos National Monument, all by Murrae Haynes.*

ISBN 0-936399-13-9
ISSN 1056-7968 (Series)

Editors: David Emblidge, Virginia Rowe
Design of original text for Great Destination series: Janice Lindstrom
Cover design: Jane McWhorter

Berkshire House, Publishers
Box 297, Stockbridge, MA 01262
Manufactured in the United States of America

First Printing 1991
9 8 7 6 5 4 3

The GREAT DESTINATIONS Series

- The Berkshire Book: A Complete Guide
- The Santa Fe & Taos Book: A Complete Guide
- The Napa & Sonoma Book: A Complete Guide
  (Fall 1991)

Contents

CHAPTER ONE
The Dinosaurs to the Present
HISTORY
1

CHAPTER TWO
Getting Here, Getting Around
TRANSPORTATION
18

CHAPTER THREE
The Keys to Your Room
LODGING
31

CHAPTER FOUR
What to See, What to Do
CULTURE
72

CHAPTER FIVE
Pleasing the Palate
RESTAURANTS AND FOOD PURVEYORS
134

CHAPTER SIX
For the Fun of It
RECREATION
197

CHAPTER SEVEN
Antique, Boutique and Untique
SHOPPING
237

CHAPTER EIGHT
Practical Matters
INFORMATION
263

Acknowledgments

This project embodies the energies and talents of more than a score of friends and associates. One of the most helpful of those friends was Murrae Haynes, Santa Fe's photographer for all seasons, who somehow managed to shoot or acquire almost all the photos for this book while juggling about a dozen other assignments. Two others were Keith Easthouse and Ramona Gault. With considerable legwork and meticulous attention to detail, Keith researched and wrote the *Transportation, Lodging* and *Information* chapters. Ramona, with an eye for particulars and a strong background as an arts editor, researched and wrote the *Culture* and *Shopping* chapters.

I would also like to thank my team of restaurant reviewers, without whom I would still be eating and taking notes (not an unpleasant occupation, by any means, but definitely time as well as food consuming). Gourmet researchers and writers include Keith Easthouse, David Emblidge, Gigi Espinoza, Ramona Gault, Miriam Jacobs, Bob and LaDonna Mayer, Sharon Niederman, John Villani (who continued to eat and write even after the budget was cut in half), Josef Tornick, Gail Vivino, Michael Winkelhorst, Annie Woods and Teresa Wright.

A big thanks to Brian Epp for his excellent and timely mapwork and to my friends at *The Santa Fe Reporter* for their assistance with maps and photographs — especially Lisa Burnett, Joy Rae and Wendy Walsh. Another big thanks to Orlando Romero at the Museum of New Mexico History Library and to former State Historian Myra Ellen Jenkins, for reading and critiquing the *History* chapter and suggesting worthy titles for the Bibliography. Also, thanks to Orlando for his willingness to answer perplexing questions at the most inconvenient times.

Another thanks to the principal suppliers of photographs: Murrae Haynes, Leslie Tallant, Wendy Walsh, Mark Nohl, the Museum of New Mexico (especially Art Olivas in the Photo Archives division) and Don Laine at the Taos County Chamber of Commerce. The names of the many others who donated photographs are indicated along with the photos themselves. I am also grateful to the countless people who so generously supplied information, whether in personal interviews, by phone or in printed material.

Finally, a special thanks to John Biethan at Bear & Company for repeatedly bailing me out of sticky computer problems; to John Villani for fact checking; to Fr. Miguel Baca for his help with the glossary; to Jan Roby for copyediting; to David Emblidge and the staff at Berkshire House for their advice and support; and to Teresa Wright for her research and fact checking as well as her patience and love.

Introduction

License plates in these parts have an intriguing subtitle: "Land of Enchantment." I didn't think much of the label before I came here, except that it seemed like a good marketing ploy. However, my opinion changed when I laid eyes on the wide-open land and sky of New Mexico in the winter of 1984, and my impression continued to grow as I became more deeply attached to this place and its people.

Now I realize that the label is appropriate and true. Here is a landscape both ancient and modern — a landscape with a wild and primal spirit. You can hear it in the wind sifting through piñon pines or fluttering through aspen leaves in the high country. You can sense it in the distant roar of whitewater on the Rio Grande — or better, as your raft suddenly descends into a chaos of foaming waves. Afternoon thunderstorms can shake you to the core, as can hailstones pelting like pebbles onto the windshield of your car. Perhaps most impressive of all is the haunting mix of drums and voices at the pueblos, where Native Americans gather to dance their prayers into the earth.

People have been enchanted by the Santa Fe–Taos area since time immemorial. For at least 12,000 years, Native Americans have honored the spirits of nature here. Four hundred years ago Spanish conquistadors gave up dreams of gold to become farmers and ranchers in the Rio Grande Valley. Traders, trappers and mountain men left their wanderings to become family men. In the early 1900s, artists and writers flocked here like pilgrims to the light, seeking new perceptions. And much like modern tourists, traders have been buying jewelry and textiles here for centuries.

It is not surprising that Santa Fe and Taos have become such popular centers of tourism in recent years. The reasons go well beyond the blazing sunsets and the rugged land, and far deeper than all the trendy hype over "Santa Fe Style" and other gimmicks that are used to market the area. There's a striking sense of cultural continuity here. I never tire of looking at the adobe architecture — particularly the mission churches and other old structures. Buildings, places and people here sometimes seem like beads on a thread reaching back hundreds, even thousands of years. You can sense this while sitting inside an ancient ceremonial *kiva* at Bandelier National Monument, while driving the High Road to Taos through still-quiet farming villages or, best of all, by slowing down and talking to people whose families have lived here for generations.

Much of this continuity is preserved in wonderful detail in numerous museums. The rest of it lives in the time-honored traditions of many cultures, from Feast Days at the pueblos to fiestas on the plazas to myriad expressions of the visual and performing arts that have flowered here. It also lives in local restaurants where you can still get "home-cooked" New Mexican meals. And if you're entranced by the timelessness of nature, there's no end of wild adventure, from ski runs and hiking trails to river floats and fishing trips.

The lure of the Santa Fe–Taos area is a little different for everyone — probably as different as the perceivers themselves. My hope is that this book will lead you to new attractions and perceptions in the Land of Enchantment, whether they spring from landscape, weather, food, culture or some unusual combination thereof. I hope you will let this book serve as your personal guide — as a sort of companion offering a deep and detailed look at an ancient and fascinating area. May you enjoy it, as well as the land and people it celebrates, whether you've come for a short visit or lived here for many years.

Brandt H. Morgan
Santa Fe, New Mexico

THE WAY THIS BOOK WORKS

This book is divided into eight chapters, each with its own introduction. If you are especially interested in one chapter or another, you can turn to it directly and begin reading without losing a sense of continuity. You can also take the book with you on your travels and skip around, reading about the places you visit as you go. Or you can read the entire book through from start to finish.

If you're interested in finding a place to eat or sleep, we suggest you first look over the restaurant and lodging charts in the appendix (organized by area and price); then turn to the pages listed and read the specific entries for the places you're most interested in.

Entries within most of the chapters are arranged alphabetically under four different headings: "Santa Fe," "Near Santa Fe," "Taos" and "Near Taos." The first two headings refer to the area within the city or town limits. "Near Santa Fe" and "Near Taos" mean within a 30-mile radius of these two centers. (Look at the map on page 24: all points within the two circles are less than an hour — and frequently not more than a few minutes — from Santa Fe or Taos.) And for those "don't miss" places in parts beyond, we've included another category called "Outside the Area."

Some entries, most notably those in the lodging and restaurant chapters, include specific information (telephone, address, hours, etc.) organized for easy reference in blocks in the left-hand column. The information here, as well as the phone numbers and addresses in the descriptions, were checked as close to publication as possible. Even so, such details change with frustrating frequency. When in doubt, call ahead.

For the same reason, we've usually avoided listing specific prices, preferring instead to indicate a range of prices. Lodging price codes are based on a per-room rate, double occupancy, in the high seasons (summer and ski months). Low season rates are likely to be 20–40 percent less. Once again, it is always best to call ahead for specific rates and reservations.

Restaurant prices indicate the cost of an individual meal including appetizer, entree and dessert but not including cocktails, wine, tax or tip. Restaurants with a *prix fixe* menu are noted accordingly.

Price Codes

	Lodging	*Dining*
Inexpensive	Up to $50	Up to $10
Moderate	$50 to $80	$10 to $20
Expensive	$80 to $120	$20 to $30
Very Expensive	Over $120	Over $30

Credit Cards are abbreviated as follows:

AE — American Express	DC — Diner's Club
CB — Carte Blanche	MC — Master Charge
D — Discover Card	V — Visa

There is one telephone area code for all of New Mexico: 505. For all numbers in the 505 area, we cite local exchanges only.

The best sources for year-round tourist information are the **Santa Fe Chamber of Commerce** (983-7317; 333 Montezuma, Santa Fe, NM 87501) and the **Taos County Chamber of Commerce** (1-800-732-TAOS; P.O. Drawer I, Taos, NM 87571). For specific information on activities near Taos, contact the **Angel Fire/Eagle Nest Chamber of Commerce** (1-800-446-8117; Angel Fire, NM 87710) or the **Red River Chamber of Commerce** (754-2366, 1-800-348-6444; Red River, NM 87558).

TOWNS IN THE SANTA FE–TAOS AREA

Though we focus primarily on Santa Fe and Taos, many other towns in the area are worth a visit. Within the circle to the south of Santa Fe, for example, you'll find Golden, Madrid, Galisteo and Lamy, all old towns that retain some of their Wild West flavor. A few minutes north of Santa Fe you'll find the quiet little village of Tesuque, a favored suburb of Santa Fe with the Shidoni Gallery and some excellent restaurants. To the west is Los Alamos, home of the Los Alamos National Laboratory and the birthplace of the atomic bomb.

Scattered up and down the Rio Grande are 11 different Indian pueblos — not towns, but separate nations — all are unique in their own ways, from ceremonies and dances to crafts and cooking. On the way to Taos via the Rio Grande on N.M. 68, you'll pass through the little farming and orchard villages of Velarde and Embudo (with Dixon and La Chiripada Winery a quick side trip east). And if you take the High Road via N.M. 76 and N.M. 518, you'll cruise through more than a half dozen old villages — Chimayó, Truchas, Peñasco, Vadito and others — that offer everything from wonderful crafts shops to looks at quieter times.

North of Taos are the old mining towns of Questa, Red River, and Angel Fire, today all hubs of outdoor sports and backwoods places with wild and rustic flavors. West of Taos is Ojo Caliente, home of the famed mineral springs spa. And if you go out as far west as Abiquiu (outside the area), you'll find the home of famed artist Georgia O'Keeffe. One look at the landscape with its pink and red cliffs is enough to explain why she was so entranced with northern New Mexico, and why her work seems so inspired.

The
SANTA FE & TAOS
Book

A Complete Guide

CHAPTER ONE
The Dinosaurs to the Present
HISTORY

Courtesy Pecos National Historical Park

Kiva and ruins of 18th-century Spanish church at Pecos National Monument.

The history of northern New Mexico — more specifically that of Santa Fe and Taos — is one of turbulent change. From the hot, crushing forces that originally shaped the land to the often violent social movements that mold its present-day mix of cultures, the area has been embroiled in flux since prehistoric times. The story of Santa Fe–Taos is one of an enchanting land and its varied peoples: of ancient hunter-gatherers and modern Pueblo Indians; of Spanish conquistadors and colonists; of American mountain men, merchants and adventurers; and more recently of artists, tourists, sportspeople and spiritual seekers.

Today this landscape and mix of cultures continue to evolve. The Pueblo Indians not only perform ancient ceremonies and make handcrafted jewelry but also hold key positions in business and government. Hispanics with surnames of the conquistadors, many of whom continue their rich religious and folk traditions, populate both the statehouse at Santa Fe and the quiet little farming villages of their ancestors. Anglo–Americans (or "Anglos," as they are called in these parts) today migrate in droves to Santa Fe and Taos, which their ancestors saw only as trade centers on the great trail west.

Due in part to vigorous promotion and national media attention, both Santa Fe and Taos have become burgeoning centers for recreation and the arts. Each year such attractions as the Santa Fe Opera, the Chamber Music Festival, the Desert Chorale, the Indian Market and Spanish Market, the Taos Summer Jazz Festival, and a plethora of shops, museums, galleries and world-class ski slopes draw more than a million tourists from all over the world. Understandably, many who come to visit decide to stay.

1

Today both Santa Fe and Taos find themselves embroiled in battles over expansion and development. As condominiums and expensive houses creep inexorably up into the pine-studded foothills, locals worry about overcrowding and loss of traditions. Meanwhile, government continues both to promote tourism and to search for ways to make the economy less dependent on it.

The largest portion of the area's income comes from tourism. In addition, about 40 percent of all working Santa Feans are employed by city, state or federal government; a large proportion of Taoseños work in the Molycorp molybdenum mines near Questa; and many people from both towns commute to the Los Alamos National Laboratory or other defense-related industries. At the same time, most of the Santa Fe–Taos area is undeveloped, offering thousands of wooded acres and some of the most entrancing sunsets in the world. Not surprisingly, people tend to be very protective of the land and very outspoken in defense of the environment, whether the issue is recycling, nuclear waste disposal or logging in the national forests.

Overall, Santa Fe–Taos continues not only as a modern playground and showcase of the past, but also as a cauldron of change. In some ways that cauldron is bubbling as briskly today as it was thousands of years ago.

NATURAL HISTORY

If we could compress two billion years into a few minutes, we would see the New Mexico landscape being shaped and reshaped like putty in the hands of a master sculptor. The invasion and retreat of inland seas, the rise and fall of great mountain ranges, the shifting of subterranean plates, the cracking of mantle and crust, exploding volcanoes, seeping magma, shifting sands and continual erosion by wind and water — each of these forces has left its mark on the modern landscape.

Time, too, has left its mark. During the Mesozoic era, more than 100 million years ago, great dinosaurs roamed the land, as evidenced by skeletons on display at the Ghost Ranch Conference Center near Abiquiu. At the same time, colorful sands and silts from the ancestral Rockies formed pink and red cliffs, and volcanoes spewed ash over the landscape. As the modern Rockies rose to the north, the dinosaurs mysteriously disappeared, giving way to the mammals, including the ancestors of modern-day camels, horses, cats and bears.

To the east of Santa Fe–Taos, the Sangre de Cristo Mountains began to rise near the end of the Mesozoic. Later, about 30 million years ago, an upwelling in the earth's mantle created a pair of massive fault lines, and the land between them caved in. The result was the Rio Grande Rift, a trench up to five miles deep that neatly bisects the entire state. Even as it formed, the rift filled with debris, and water from the mountains created a long chain of basins within it. Finally, about 2.5 million years ago, the Rio Grande became a continuous river flowing all the way to the Gulf of Mexico. Thereafter, vol-

Rio Grande Gorge and Taos Plateau with Sangre de Cristo Mountains in background.

Murrae Haynes

canic activity on the west side of the Rio Grande created basaltic mesas and broad volcanic tablelands, including the present-day Taos Plateau.

The Jemez (pronounced HAY-mess) Mountains west of Santa Fe are the remains of a composite volcano that geologists believe was once almost as high as Mount Everest. About a million years ago the volcano blew its top and caved in. The explosion, 600 times more powerful than the 1980 eruption of Mount Saint Helens, left a crater 15 miles wide and buried much of the land with ash up to 1,000 feet thick. Later, some of that volcanic tuff became home to the Anasazi Indians, whose cave dwellings still pepper the bases of canyon walls at Bandelier National Monument.

During the recent Ice Ages, lava seeped in the foothills and glaciers scoured the mountains. Heavy snows and rains formed lakes and created wide, sloping foothills. As the weather warmed, these areas sprouted new vegetation, from scrub brush and small pines in the lowlands to lush aspens and evergreens in the mountains.

Such was the landscape discovered by the first human inhabitants of the Santa Fe–Taos area some 12,000 years ago. Today it is essentially the same: the wide, fertile Rio Grande Valley flanked by spectacular sets of mountains. To the east lies the Sangre de Cristo range, a modern ski paradise that stretches

SANTA FE – TAOS TOPOGRAPHY

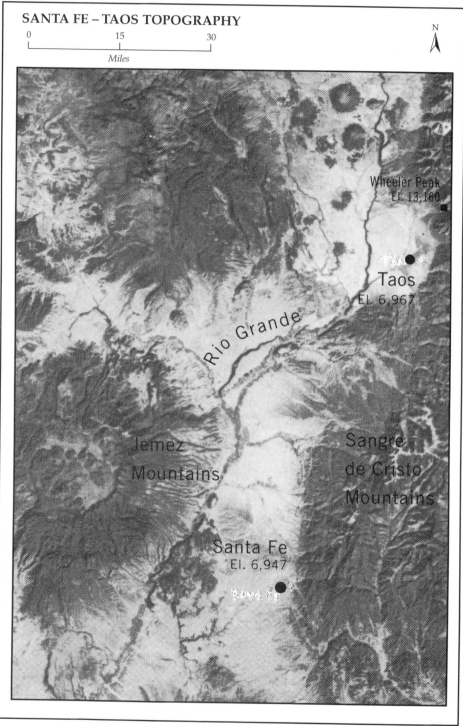

N

0   15   30

Miles

Wheeler Peak
El. 13,160

Taos
El. 6,967

Rio Grande

Jemez
Mountains

Sangre
de Cristo
Mountains

Santa Fe
El. 6,947

north to the Colorado Rockies. To the west lie the volcanic Jemez, now a setting for human-made explosions created by the Los Alamos National Laboratory.

From north of Taos the Rio Grande rushes through a 50-mile stretch of basalt, the gorge providing excellent winter fishing and summer thrills and chills for white water enthusiasts. Likewise the Chama River, flowing north of the Jemez into the Rio Grande, offers some of the most spectacular wild and scenic excursions in the state. Flowing south through the fertile farms and orchards of Velarde, the Rio Grande slows down, eventually meandering quietly through the ancient Pueblo lands north of Santa Fe and the hills and valleys to the west.

Elevations in the area range from under 6,000 feet in the valley to 13,161 feet at the top of Wheeler Peak, the highest point in the state. The air is clear and dry, with sunny skies 300 days of the year. A 14-inch average annual rainfall leaves a desert like setting in the lowlands, while winter storms dump up to 320 inches of snow a year on lush mountain areas such as the popular Taos Ski Valley.

These factors make for a diversity of life zones and an especially rich flora and fauna. Santa Fe and Taos have wonderful shade trees, the most prominent being the giant willows and cottonwoods that grace the municipal plazas and downtown areas. Juniper and piñon pines dominate the dry, lower elevations, giving way to scrub oak and thicker forests of ponderosa pine and finally to high alpine forests with a spectacular mix of fir, aspen and spruce. Spring and summer wildflowers, especially in the mountains, range through a colorful spectrum, from Indian paintbrush and woodland pinedrops to buttercups and alpine daisies.

Northern New Mexico is also a haven for animals large and small. The *arroyos* (dry gullies or washes) and foothills are dominated by mice, prairie dogs, jackrabbits and cottontails, and by the coyotes and occasional bobcats that feed on them. Muskrats and beavers still thrive in some rivers and streams, and even signs of river otter can be found on secluded parts of the Rio Grande . Some sure-footed bighorn sheep still roam parts of the Sangre de Cristo, and pronghorn antelope are common on the plains. The mountains are home not only to snowshoe hares and various species of squirrels, but to herds of mule deer and elk and a fair number of black bears. There have even been occasional mountain lion sightings in these parts.

Birds fill every available avian niche, from seed-eating finches and bug-eating swallows to breathtakingly beautiful mountain bluebirds and a variety of large winged predators. Eagles and hawks soar above canyons, while quail, doves, and roadrunners (the state bird) skitter through the brush below. Lowland wet and marshy areas play host to myriad ducks, geese and shorebirds, and the mountains are home to a wide range of species, from ravens, jays and nuthatches to grouse and wild turkeys.

SOCIAL HISTORY

EARLY HUMAN INHABITANTS

The first human inhabitants of the Santa Fe–Taos area were Stone Age hunters who followed herds of giant bison and mammoth more than 12,000 years ago. As the centuries passed, they became less nomadic, gathering fruits, nuts and greens in the lowlands, hunting deer and elk in the mountains and trapping small game. By around 5,500 B.C., these hunter-gatherers were living seasonally in the Santa Fe–Taos area, mostly in caves and other natural shelters. Soon afterward they began to plant corn and other crops, and to make baskets. Eventually they constructed circular pithouses, which centuries later gave way to above-ground dwellings of stone and adobe. Around 200 B.C. they began making pottery.

From A.D. 900–1300 great Anasazi complexes (*Anasazi* is a Navajo word meaning "ancient strangers") flourished at Chaco Canyon and Mesa Verde to the west and north. These centers were marked by extensive roadways and huge, multi-tiered complexes of stone. The people performed sophisticated ceremonies, irrigated extensive farmlands and accurately predicted the movements of sun and moon. Another group of Anasazi developed a similar complex in Frijoles Canyon about 30 miles northwest of Santa Fe, in what is now Bandelier National Monument. However, by A.D. 1300 most of these great centers had been abandoned It is widely believed that the "ancient ones" were some of the ancestors of present-day Pueblo people.

Sometime during the era of the Anasazi, a number of stone and adobe villages sprang up in the Santa Fe area. The largest of these, called Ogapoge or Kuapoge ("dancing ground of the sun"), once occupied part of Santa Fe. Scores of other small settlements, including the beginnings of present-day Taos Pueblo and other pueblos north of Santa Fe, were built along the Rio Grande.

Ogapoge and other settlements around Santa Fe were abandoned around 1425, during the worst drought in a thousand years. Others remained and continued to flourish, including Pecos Pueblo to the southeast and the present-day pueblos of Tesuque, Pojoaque, Nambe, San Ildefonso, Santa Clara, San Juan, Jemez, Picuris and Taos to the north. When the first Spaniards arrived in New Mexico, the Pueblo Indians (*pueblo* is Spanish for "village") were well established in some 150 adobe villages, large and small, scattered along the Rio Grande and its tributaries.

Before the arrival of the Spanish, the Pueblos lived a life of ceremony and the seasonal cycles of hunting and planting. They cultivated corn, beans and squash and gathered greens, berries, fruits and seeds. They hunted myriad species of wild game, from prairie dogs, rabbits and turkeys to deer, elk and antelope. They made clay pottery; wove baskets and mats from corn, cattail and yucca leaves; and fashioned blankets from feathers and animal hides.

Ancient rock art near Galisteo.

Courtesy Museum of New Mexico

Although they traveled exclusively on foot, they not only maintained close ties with each other, but also had trade links with the Indians on the plains, the Pacific Coast and in Mexico.

The ancient Pueblos, like their modern counterparts, spoke a number of different languages. They continually honored the Great Spirit and the forces of nature. Under ground they built circular chambers, called *kivas,* adaptations of their ancestral pithouses, that served as centers for prayer and teaching. They developed elaborate ceremonial dances that expressed their sense of oneness with nature. With the exception of raids from neighboring Plains tribes, their lives were generally tranquil until the arrival of the Spaniards from Mexico.

THE SPANISH INFLUENCE

One of the first Spaniards to come to New Mexico was Fray Marcos de Niza, a Franciscan friar who arrived in 1539 after hearing fabulous accounts of the Seven Cities of Cibola, supposedly made of gold. De Niza never visited these cities himself, but he embellished the stories he heard. His own overblown reports of riches spurred a massive expedition in 1540, in which Francisco Vasquez de Coronado rode north from Mexico City with 300 soldiers. Cibola turned out to be nothing more than the little pueblo of Zuni, which Coronado and his men conquered and subjugated. Other pueblos to the north were similarly invaded; yet neither Coronado nor those who followed him could find any gold. Thereafter, Spain turned its focus toward colonization.

The first official colonizer of the area was Juan de Oñate. In 1598, with 129 soldier-colonists and their families, 10 Franciscan friars and thousands of cattle, sheep, horses and mules, he set out to establish the first permanent Spanish settlement in New Mexico. Many of the horses escaped, eventually providing the Plains Indians and the rest of North America with a new form of transportation.

Oñate chose a spot across the Rio Grande from San Juan Pueblo, about 25 miles north of present-day Santa Fe. The settlement, called San Gabriel, was beset with problems from the beginning. Some settlers were apparently still under the illusion that they would find easy riches. Others balked at the hard labor and difficult living conditions, still others at the difficulty of converting the Indians to Catholicism. By 1600 almost half of the settlers had given up and gone back to Mexico. A few years later, referring to the fantastic stories of riches and abundance in the area, the viceroy of New Spain wrote to the king from Mexico City, "I cannot help but inform your majesty that this conquest is becoming a fairy tale. . . . If those who write the reports imagine that they are believed by those who read them, they are greatly mistaken. Less substance is being revealed every day."

Many Spaniards thought the most reasonable alternative was to leave New Mexico altogether. However, after long debate, they decided to stay, partly to maintain their claim to the huge territory west of the Mississippi but primarily because the friars were so reluctant to abandon the Indians to paganism. A new governor, Pedro de Peralta, was appointed and sent to New Mexico to found a permanent settlement. He chose a spot south of San Gabriel that offered more water and better protection. The result was La Villa de Santa Fe — The City of Holy Faith. (In 1823 St. Francis became its patron saint; hence its current name, The Royal City of the Holy Faith of Saint Francis of Assisi.) In 1610, a decade before the arrival of the Pilgrims at Plymouth Rock, the settlers laid out their new plaza and began building the Palace of the Governors, today the oldest continuously occupied public building in the United States. That same year supplies began moving northward to Santa Fe along the newly opened Camino Real ("Royal Road") from Chihuahua, Mexico.

Over the years the settler–soldiers built adobe houses and dug a network of *acequias*, or irrigation ditches, to divert water from the Santa Fe River. They cultivated fields of beans, squash, corn and wheat with hand-held plows and wooden hoes. Accompanied by Franciscan friars they ranged far and wide, subjugating the pueblos, building churches and trying to convert the Indians to Catholicism. By 1625, the Spaniards had built some 50 churches in the Rio Grande Valley, with forced Indian labor. More than half of the original pueblos had disappeared.

One that continued to thrive was Taos Pueblo, about 70 miles north of Santa Fe. (*Taos* is the Spanish version of a Tiwa phrase meaning "place of the red willows.") The first Spanish settlers moved there with Fray Pedro de Miranda in 1617. They settled near Taos Pueblo, even moving within its walls during the 1760s for protection against the Comanches.

The Indians constantly complained about Spanish encroachment. All through the Rio Grande Valley, Pueblo spiritual and political leaders were routinely abused, while others were forced to build churches, work in the fields and weave garments for export to Mexico. Conflicts between Spanish civil and religious authorities fueled the discontent. Over a 75-year period the Indians attempted a number of revolts, most of them stemming from attempts to outlaw their religious ceremonies. None were successful. Rebellions at Taos and Jemez Pueblos in the 1630s resulted in the deaths of several priests and were met with even more repression from the Spanish. While some governors allowed the Indians to continue their dances, most supported the Franciscans in their attempts to stamp out all remnants of Pueblo ceremony.

One of the most brutal of these attempts came in 1675, when Governor Juan Francisco de Trevino charged 47 Pueblo religious leaders with sorcery and witchcraft and sentenced them to death or slavery. One San Juan leader named Popé, who was frequently flogged and abused because of his religious influence, secretly vowed revenge. For several years he hid at Taos Pueblo, quietly plotting and sending out runners to orchestrate a revolt of all the pueblos.

The revolt took place on August 10, 1680. At the break of day, Indians in pueblos from Taos in the north to Acoma in the south to Hopi in the west, suddenly turned on the Spaniards killing men, women, children and priests and setting the mission churches ablaze. In Santa Fe about 1,000 settlers holed up in the Palace of the Governors. But when Governor Otermín learned of the widespread devastation, he and the others loaded their belongings onto mules and wagons and quickly abandoned Santa Fe on August 21.

The refugees eventually made their way to El Paso del Norte, the site of present-day Juarez, Mexico, where they lived in exile for the next 12 years. Meanwhile, the Indians took over the Palace of the Governors at Santa Fe, and, in spite of several attempts at reconquest, they lived largely unhindered by the Spaniards until 1692.

The Spaniards left deep and indelible marks on Pueblo society and even on the rebels themselves. After 70 years, Catholicism was almost as alive as Pueblo ceremonialism, and most of the Indians spoke Spanish as well as their native languages. Moreover, like their Spanish predecessors, Popé and other Indian leaders now ruled with an iron hand, demanding tributes and trying to stamp out forcibly all remnants of Spanish influence. Crop failures and attacks by the Apaches and Navajos eroded the Pueblo resolve, and by the time the new territorial governor returned in September 1692, the Indians seemed ready to submit once more.

That governor was Don Diego de Vargas, a man as bold and fearless as he was vain and arrogant. With only 40 soldiers, he confronted the fortified pueblo that had once been the Palace of the Governors. To allay the Indians' fears, he entered the palace completely unarmed. Reassured that they would be pardoned and protected from marauding Plains Indians, the Pueblos agreed to Spanish rule.

Spanish Colonial document signed by Don Diego de Vargas, 1696.

Courtesy Museum of New Mexico

Unfortunately, Vargas' reconquest was only briefly bloodless. When he returned the following December with more soldiers and colonists, he was met with defiance and hostility. After many days of suffering in the cold and snow, the Spaniards stormed the palace, killing 81 Indians in the process. In subsequent years Vargas met similar resistance; once his soldiers even rode north to raid Taos Pueblo after it refused to supply the starving settlers with grain. Only in 1696, after a number of bloody battles, another Taos revolt and the deaths of many Pueblo leaders, did the new governor finally succeed in establishing a new Spanish reign. Today Vargas is much revered in Santa Fe; however, it is often forgotten that he was eventually imprisoned by the very people he so gallantly led. Longing to return to his native Spain, he loathed Santa Fe as "last on earth and remote beyond compare."

With the exception of repeated Comanche raids on Taos, the 1700s were relatively peaceful, a time of festivity, drama and art. In the fall of 1712, the colonists celebrated the first annual Fiesta de Santa Fe, a holiday commemorating Vargas' "bloodless" reconquest of New Mexico and his return of La Conquistadora, the small statue of the Virgin Mary that the colonists believed protected them when they fled Santa Fe. Frequent dances, musicals and comedies celebrated the Spanish heritage. Silversmithing, goldsmithing, woodworking and weaving flourished among the Spaniards while the Pueblos supplied the colonists with cookware and crockery of all kinds.

Bob Nugent; Courtesy Museum of New Mexico

Detail of reredos, *or carved altar screen.*

Meanwhile, as the *acequias* flowed, farms and orchards around Santa Fe and Taos sprouted fields of wheat, corn, beans and a variety of fruits and vegetables. Gambling and smoking were popular among men and women, and cock fights were frequently held on the plazas in the afternoons. By the time of the American Revolution (which some wealthy Santa Feans helped finance), more than 100 colonial families were living in the Santa Fe area. Horses, cattle and sheep, first brought into the New World by the Spaniards, had proliferated and annual fairs at Pecos and Taos provided major trade opportunities between the Spanish, the Pueblos and the Plains Indians.

After the reconquest the Indians were no longer treated as slaves, and church and kiva coexisted side by side. By mid-century Franciscan friars, frustrated over their failure to stamp out native ceremonies after eight generations, were replaced by secular priests. The new priests seemed satisfied as long as the Indians professed to be Catholic. Some of the Indians still worked as indentured servants, and many were abused. On the other hand, fundamental changes took place after the reconquest that contributed to lasting respect and cooperation between Hispanics and Pueblos. One, they often banded together to fight their common enemies, usually the raiding Plains tribes. (On one occasion, the Villasur Expedition of 1720, Spaniards and Pueblos fought side-by-side against French and Pawnees who were encroaching on their eastern territory.) Two, the Pueblos incorporated Catholicism and certain

Segesser hide-painting depicting Spaniards (wearing broad-brimmed hats) and Pueblo Indians (with hair tied behind) fighting French and Pawnees in present-day Nebraska, 1720.

Courtesy Museum of New Mexico

Hispanic ceremonies (the Matachines dances, for example) into their own native traditions. More fundamental still, they intermarried; today the great majority of Pueblo people are of mixed blood, and many have Hispanic surnames.

ARRIVAL OF THE ANGLOS

Though the Spanish government forbade foreigners inside New Mexico, a few mountain men and explorers sneaked into the Santa Fe–Taos area in the early 1800s. One of these was Zebulon Pike, who was arrested by the Spaniards in 1807 on a mission to explore the area west of the Louisiana Purchase. As Pike was escorted into Santa Fe under armed guard, he made the following observations of the capital city:

Its appearance from a distance, struck my mind with the same effect as a fleet of the flat bottomed boats, which are seen in the spring and fall seasons, descending the Ohio River. There are two churches, the magnificence of whose steeples form a striking contrast to the miserable appearance of the houses.

After his release from prison in Chihuahua, Pike published his journals, which attracted more American adventurers to the area .

Gradually, especially during the Napoleonic Wars, Spain loosened its grip on its colonies and Mexico drifted farther away from the king. In 1821 Mexican independence was celebrated in Santa Fe with "universal carousing and revelry," according to American observer Thomas James. The great event brought many more Anglos, as mountain men filtered in from the Rockies to hunt and trap around Taos, and New Mexico was finally opened up to foreign trade.

That same year trader William Becknell drove a heavy-laden wagon over Raton Pass, making Santa Fe the western terminus of the Santa Fe Trail from Independence, Missouri, some 800 miles to the east. Now an unstoppable stream of Americans began rushing into and through the area. Stretching across the prairies like great billowing armadas, covered wagons initially took almost a month to get to Santa Fe. They carted tremendous amounts of merchandise — including textiles, tools, shoes, flour, whiskey, hardware, medicines, musical instruments, ammunition and even heavy machinery. Some merchants sold their goods in Santa Fe or Taos; others pushed on to Mexico over the Camino Real.

One of the most famous of those who stayed was Indian fighter and federal agent Kit Carson, who once observed, "No man who has seen the women, heard the bells, or smelled the piñon smoke of Taos will ever be able to leave." True to his word, Carson lived in Taos for 42 years, and many merchants, traders and mountain men followed suit.

During the 1820s the increasing number of Americans in New Mexico and Texas became a major threat to the Mexican government. Mexico itself was

Banquet at Fort Marcy
Headquarters Building, Santa
Fe, 1887.

Courtesy Museum of New Mexico

struggling with severe instability at this time, and it both neglected and over-taxed its northern colony. Colonial anger over these policies came to a head in 1837 when a group of northern New Mexicans formed a mob, decapitating Governor Albino Perez and killing 17 of his officers. The rebellion was put down by former governor Manuel Armijo, who was returned to office.

Armijo served New Mexico well, often bending the law to meet the real needs of the people. However, it soon became obvious that the United States was eyeing the area for westward expansion. In 1846, President James K. Polk declared war on Mexico and sent a contingent of 1,600 soldiers along with General Stephen Watts Kearny to take over Santa Fe and all of New Mexico. The takeover was bloodless. The few Spanish who resisted were put in jail, and Taos merchant Charles Bent was illegally appointed the new governor.

Bent's tenure was short. In January of the following year a large group of irate Taoseños, including enraged Hispanics and Indians fearful of losing their land, broke into Bent's house, killed and scalped him and then went looking for other Anglos. As the revolt spread, a contingent of U.S. troops under Colonel Sterling Price rode from Santa Fe to Taos, where the rebels had taken cover in the mission church at the west end of the pueblo. The soldiers destroyed the church with cannonballs, and the rebels were hanged after a brief trial. Today Bent's house is a museum (see *Culture*, page 91), and the remains of the mission church still stand as a grim reminder of the violence that undergirds today's multicultural New Mexico.

Mexico reluctantly signed the treaty of Guadalupe Hidalgo with the United States, giving up its claim to New Mexico, Texas, Arizona and California in 1848. Two years later, New Mexico officially became a United States territory, inspiring an even bigger rush of soldiers, traders and pioneers from the east.

From the outset the Americans had troubles with marauding Apaches and Navajos, but the Hispanics and Pueblos received even more constant abuse from the Anglos themselves. Racism and discrimination ran rampant, and wealth and property were systematically stolen with the help of slick lawyers.

The Glorieta Battlefield in June, 1880.

Ben Wittick; Courtesy School of American Research, Museum of New Mexico

The American government reneged on its promise to give the Pueblos full citizenship; instead, through forced education of Indian children and other measures, it greatly suppressed Pueblo religion and culture. Though New Mexico became the nation's 47th state in 1912, Indians were not recognized as U.S. citizens until 1924 and were not allowed to vote until 1948.

One of the men who resisted such actions and who fought vigorously for the rights of poor Hispanics in particular was Father Antonio José Martinez, head of the parish at Taos during the 1830–'50s. Martinez not only openly opposed the mandatory church tithe but fought Anglo land takeovers and championed Hispanic folk traditions. In these and other activities Martinez defied the authority of Bishop Jean Baptiste Lamy (subject of Willa Cather's novel *Death Comes for the Archbishop*). Though he was excommunicated in 1857, he continued to lead his people spiritually and politically until his death 10 years later. Lamy, though no champion of the poor, made major contributions to education and architecture, overseeing the construction of such lasting landmarks as Santa Fe's Romanesque Cathedral of St. Francis and the nearby Gothic-style Loretto Chapel.

During the Civil War Santa Fe fell briefly into the hands of Confederate troops when General Henry H. Sibley marched into New Mexico from Texas on March 10, 1862. Two weeks later Sibley was defeated at the Battle of Glorieta Pass, about 20 miles east of Santa Fe. After the Civil War railroads took the place of the Santa Fe Trail, reaching Santa Fe and Taos around 1880. Over the next several decades the iron horse brought hordes of farmers, gold diggers, outlaws, businessmen, health seekers and tourists to the land of enchantment.

Between 1880 and the turn of the century, the Anglo population of New Mexico quadrupled from fewer than 10,000 to almost 40,000. One of the first Anglos to popularize the area's attractions was Governor Lew Wallace, who in 1878 finished his famous novel *Ben Hur* while occupying the Palace of the

Governors. "What perfection of air and sunlight!" Wallace wrote to his wife after arriving in Santa Fe. "And what a landscape I discovered to show you when you come — a picture to make the fame of an artist, could he only paint it on canvas as it is."

The man usually given credit for igniting the art boom itself was Joseph Henry Sharp, who in 1883 spent the summer painting in Taos. He was followed by Bert Phillips, Ernest Blumenschein and Irving Couse, and a few years later these four founded the Taos Society of Artists. By the 1890s Anglo artists were displaying their works at the Palace of the Governors, a part of which was dedicated as the Museum of Fine Arts in 1917. Other artists and writers quickly filtered into the Santa Fe–Taos area. During the 1920s the Santa Fe Art Colony was founded by Will Shuster and four others who became known to some as *Los Cinco Pintores* ("the five painters") and to others as "the five nuts in adobe huts." Soon the area also boasted the likes of Mabel Dodge Luhan, Georgia O'Keeffe, Willa Cather, Mary Austin and D.H. Lawrence. Lawrence spent only a few seasons in Taos but was deeply moved, especially by pueblo life. Among his posthumous papers is the following passage:

You can feel it, the atmosphere of it, around the pueblos. Not, of course, when the place is crowded with sight-seers and motor-cars. But go to Taos pueblo on some brilliant snowy morning and see the white figure on the roof: or come riding through at dusk on some windy evening, when the black skirts of the silent women blow around the wide boots, and you will feel the old, old root of human consciousness still reaching down to depths we know nothing of.

Other events during the '20s and '30s contributed to Santa Fe's reputation as a center for the arts. Dr. Edgar Lee Hewitt, director of the Museum of New Mexico, and other Anglos, organized the first Indian Market in 1922. Three years later Mary Austin and others founded the Spanish Colonial Arts Society to encourage a revival of Hispanic folk art. In 1926 Will Shuster created Zozobra, an effigy of "Old Man Gloom" that each year since has been set ablaze to touch off the annual Fiesta de Santa Fe. At the same time Indian potters, such as Maria Martinez of San Ildefonso, began to achieve popularity. The Santa Fe Concert Series was founded in 1936, followed by the opening of the Wheelwright Museum of the American Indian. It was also during the '30s that the dedicated Dorothy Dunn began nurturing a new generation of artistic talent at the Santa Fe Indian School.

World War II brought more changes to the area. One of the most profound was the 1943 purchase of the Los Alamos Ranch School for Boys and its conversion into Los Alamos National Laboratory, birthplace of the atomic bomb. Since the war the labs have been a focal point for defense research, from hydrogen bombs to Star Wars technology. A lesser known fact is that during the war there was a Japanese detention camp in Santa Fe. Surrounded by

Santa Fe's annual Indian Market draws thousands from all over the country.

Murrae Haynes

barbed wire and located in the Casa Solana area, the camp imprisoned more than 4,500 Japanese-American men from the East and West Coasts who, by virtue of their origins, were considered to be "dangerous enemy aliens."

Yet the greatest waves of lasting change washed in after the war, when Santa Fe and Taos were discovered by various groups of outsiders. As artists and tourists continued to arrive, the first galleries began to sprout in downtown Santa Fe. During the latter half of the 1950s, the newly opened Taos Ski Valley spurred tourism in the area, as did the Santa Fe Opera and the Museum of International Folk Art.

At the same time, Santa Fe–Taos became known as a spiritual power center, attracting individuals and groups that have promoted everything from Oriental philosophies to American Indian and New Age thought. During the '60s and '70s Indians and Hispanic farmers accommodated thousands of hippies and experimenters in alternative living. And today both Santa Fe and Taos have large alternative healing communities offering everything from massage and acupuncture to herbology, ayurveda and past-life regression.

Since the war, the population of Santa Fe has nearly tripled, from about 20,000 to more than 54,000, and there is no end of growth in sight. Though Taos still remains a town of 4,000, its population swells markedly during the ski and summer tourist seasons, and more people come back to stay every year. In recent years this boom has been stimulated by an aggressive nationwide promotion that has produced countless magazine articles expounding the virtues of the land, the arts, and the varied people and their high level of cultural integrity. Yet along with this promotion has come a wave of development that has filled the hills with condos and housing complexes and glutted the streets with cars, gas stations and convenience stores. Today, while tourists marvel over the astounding mix of history, culture and art that comes alive in these two bustling centers, longtime locals mourn the passing of small-town feelings and quiet traditions.

Whatever the future holds for the Santa Fe–Taos area, it will be shaped by a combination of factors, including the national economy, the availability of water and the will of the people. If present trends are any indication, though, it will continue not only as a fascinating and fun-filled tourist center but as an ongoing stage for the interactions of the many diverse cultures that have shared in the area's rich and turbulent past.

CHAPTER TWO
Getting Here, Getting Around
TRANSPORTATION

Courtesy Museum of New Mexico

New Mexico stagecoach, ca. 1895.

For the traveler today, the rugged desert and mountain terrain of the Santa Fe–Taos region is a visual delight. But for the traveler of yesterday, it was an obstacle that took tremendous effort to overcome.

The first travelers in the area, of course, were Indians who traveled on foot with their worldly belongings strapped to their backs — and to the backs of the dogs that came with them. That's about as sophisticated as transportation got until the 16th century, when the Spanish appeared on the scene with horses, mules, burros and oxen. Still the area remained remote and isolated. For the next 200 years the only link to the outside world, aside from some minor trading with Indians to the east, was through the Camino Real, the trade route connecting Santa Fe to the Mexican town of Chihuahua.

Santa Fe's orientation began to shift from the south to the east in the early 1820s when the Mexican government abandoned the long-standing Spanish policy of excluding foreign traders. This resulted in the opening of the Santa Fe Trail. New Mexico's economy really began to boom following the American takeover in 1846, and the growth created a need for better and faster transportation. Wagon and pack trains were replaced to some extent by stagecoach lines, and mail service was taken over by the Pony Express. In the mid-1850s, the U.S. Army tried camel trains. At first they met with great success because the animals were faster and hardier than mules; but the fine, sharp gravel of the New Mexico desert proved too rough for the camels, lacerating their tender hooves and crippling them.

Transportation took a quantum leap forward in the 1870s and '80s with the coming of the railroad. The first train rolled into Las Vegas, 60 miles east of Santa Fe, on April 4, 1879. A year later the line was extended to Albuquerque, bypassing Santa Fe because of its mountainous location. This had an enormous long-term impact with Albuquerque quickly surpassing Santa Fe as a center of economic activity and growth. Santa Fe was not left completely in the lurch. A spur line off the Albuquerque–Las Vegas track was built in the early 1880s, and the Denver and Rio Grande line reached the city from the north by 1885. Unprecedented development followed, including a gold rush in the small towns immediately southwest of Santa Fe.

The railroad remained supreme well into the 20th century. (The state didn't even begin to build highways until 1919.) Consequently, the artists and writers who flocked to the area in the 1920s had a very hard time getting around. They could take the train right into Santa Fe, but a trip to Taos was an arduous, all-day motorcar journey along a bumpy — and in places barely navigable — dirt road.

Eventually, of course, highways were built, and trains faded from the scene. The Denver & Rio Grande Western line, also known as the Chile Line, was shut down in 1941, and the spur line from the southeast that first brought railroad traffic into Santa Fe eventually stopped carrying passengers altogether (although it remains a freight line). In the 1940s a small airport was built in Santa Fe, and later an even smaller one in Taos. But the major air center was, and is, Albuquerque, 60 miles from Santa Fe.

PRESENT POSSIBILITIES

Santa Fe and Taos are beautiful auto destinations — which is a good thing, because neither town is directly accessible by train or by major commercial airliners. The nearest train station is in the hamlet of Lamy, 25 miles southeast of Santa Fe. A shuttle bus service coordinates its runs with the arrival of trains, so this is one relatively easy way to reach Santa Fe without a car. Another is Greyhound, which provides bus service to Santa Fe from almost anywhere in the country. (A local bus line or a local shuttle service can take you from Santa Fe up to Taos). A third way is to fly directly into Santa Fe's modest airport, either by private plane or via Mesa Airlines, a small commercial carrier that flies from Denver and Albuquerque. (Mesa discontinued service to Taos in spring 1991 due to a lack of passengers.) The majority of visitors, however, simply drive from home or fly into Albuquerque and rent a car. By whatever means you arrive, once you're here it's nice to have a car, since towns tend to be many miles apart. Also, driving northern New Mexico's back roads, through centuries-old Hispanic villages, Indian pueblos, and magnificent desert and mountain scenery, is an experience you're not likely to forget.

For your convenience, a host of details about Santa Fe–Taos transportation follows.

GETTING TO SANTA FE AND TAOS

BY CAR

From Albuquerque: The quickest route to Santa Fe is I-25 north (65 miles). A more scenic route is I-40 east to Cedar Crest, then north along N.M. 14, known as the "Turquoise Trail" because it meanders through several old mining villages; Golden, the site of the first gold rush west of the Mississippi; Madrid, a coal town turned arts-and-crafts center; and Cerrillos, a once-bustling mining camp that is now a sleepy town with plenty of Old West character. Whichever way you go, if you're used to fog or smog at home, you'll be struck by the crystal-clear air and the expansive views.

The most direct way to get to Taos from Santa Fe is to take U.S. 84/285 north to Española, then N.M. 68 up the Rio Grande, a 70-mile drive. This is scenic all the way, but the last part, in which the road winds its way underneath the vertical walls of the Rio Grande Gorge and emerges on the expansive Taos Plateau, is particularly magnificent. Also a beautiful drive, but more time-consuming, is the High Road to Taos, which winds its way along the Sangre de Cristo range, passing through Hispanic villages, including Truchas, the setting for Robert Redford's film, *The Milagro Beanfield War*. Don't miss the church in the village of Las Trampas, a masterpiece of Spanish colonial architecture built in 1763. To follow this route, take N.M. 76 east out of Española to Peñasco, go east for a few miles on N.M. 75, then north on N.M. 518. This highway eventually hooks up with N.M. 68, the main route to Taos, a few miles south of the town. An alternate High Road route is to take N.M. 503 east from Pojoaque, connecting with N.M. 76 in Chimayó. Taos is 70 miles from Santa Fe and 135 miles from Albuquerque.

From Los Angeles: This is a two-day drive at minimum. Flagstaff is a good halfway point. The quickest and easiest route is to take I-15 northeast to Barstow, then I-40 east all the way to Albuquerque, where you'll take I-25 north to Santa Fe. Distance to Santa Fe: 850 miles.

From Dallas: Another long haul. Take I-20 west through Fort Worth, then go northwest on U.S. 84 through Lubbock, Clovis and Fort Sumner to Santa Rosa, where you'll take I-40 to Clines Corners. Then go north on U.S. 285 to El Dorado and south on I-25 to Santa Fe. Distance: 718 miles.

From Phoenix: Take I-17 to Flagstaff, then I-40 east to Albuquerque and I-25 north to Santa Fe. Distance, 525 miles.

From Tucson: Take I-10 east to Las Cruces, then I-25 north up the Rio Grande Valley to Santa Fe. Distance: 636 miles.

From Denver: A beautiful drive along Colorado's rugged Front Range. It's simple, too. Just go south on I-25, and after 386 miles you'll be in Santa Fe.

From Salt Lake City: There is no direct route from Salt Lake to Santa Fe. One option is to take I-15 south to I-70, then I-70 east through the heart of the Rockies to Denver, then I-25 south to Santa Fe for a journey of 879 miles. A more scenic and shorter route, but also more complicated, is to cut through the southeastern corner of Utah (magnificent canyons) and the southwestern edge of Colorado (equally magnificent mountains) before entering northern New Mexico. Or drive a little farther south into northeastern Arizona and see the Navajo and Hopi Indian reservations. There are any number of interesting ways to go; your best bet is to consult a map.

From Las Vegas: Take U.S. 95 to Hoover Dam, U.S. 93 to I-40, I-40 east to Albuquerque and I-25 north to Santa Fe. Distance: 625 Miles.

BY BUS

Greyhound-Trailways serves Santa Fe and Taos from outside the state. To get to Taos by bus, you must first stop in Santa Fe, no matter where you're coming from. So the information presented below is for service to Santa Fe unless otherwise specified. (For bus service between Santa Fe and Taos, see "Getting Around Santa Fe and Taos" later in this chapter.)

From Albuquerque (1.5 hours to Santa Fe, 2.75 hours to Taos): *Greyhound-Trailways* (247-3495; 300 2nd St. S.W.) runs three buses daily to Santa Fe. The 1991 one-way fare was $11, round-trip $21. The *Shuttlejack* (982-4311) leaves every two hours from the Albuquerque International Airport for Santa Fe. Drop-off spots in Santa Fe are the Inn at Loretto and the Hilton, both only a few blocks from the downtown plaza. The 1991 one-way fare was $20 for

Shuttlejack at Santa Fe's Inn at Loretto.

Murrae Haynes

adults. *Faust's Transportation Service* (758-3410) provides two buses a day to the major hotels in Taos from the Albuquerque airport. The cost of a one-way ticket in 1991 was $25. Two buses a day, operated by *Pride of Taos* (758-8340), make the run between the Albuquerque airport and Taos. In 1991 a one-way ticket cost $25.

From Los Angeles (20 hours): *Greyhound-Trailways* (213-629-8443) has four buses departing daily for Santa Fe from the downtown station at 208 E. 6th St. The 1991 one-way fare was $74, round-trip $137.

From Dallas (19 hours): *Greyhound-Trailways* (214-655-7082) runs four buses daily to Santa Fe from its station at 205 S. Lamar. The 1991 one-way fare was $92, round-trip $159.

From Phoenix (12 hours): Three *Greyhound-Trailways* buses (602-271-7429) leave daily for Santa Fe from the station at 525 E. Washington St. The 1991 one-way fare was $102, round-trip $195.

From Tucson (13 hours): *Greyhound-Trailways* (602-792-3475) provides three buses daily to Santa Fe from its station at 2 S. 4th Ave. In 1991 the one-way fare was $111, round-trip $209.

From El Paso (8 hours): *Greyhound-Trailways* (915-532-2365) has three buses leaving for Santa Fe every day from its station at 111 San Francisco St. A one-way ticket in 1991 cost $54, round-trip $104.

From Denver (9 hours): *Greyhound-Trailways* (303-292-0652) runs four buses daily to Santa Fe from its station at 1055 19th St. One-way ticket prices in 1991 were $67, round-trip $104.

From Salt Lake City (20 hours): Three *Greyhound-Trailways* buses (801-355-9579) leave daily for Santa Fe from the station at 160 W. S. Temple. One-way tickets in 1991 cost $127, round-trip $209.

From Las Vegas (16 hours): *Greyhound-Trailways* (702-384-9561) runs two buses a day to Santa Fe from its station at 200 South Main St. In 1991 one-way tickets cost $111, round-trip $209.

BY TRAIN

Getting to Santa Fe and Taos by train can be a fun and relaxing way to begin your visit. The train station servicing the area is in the village of Lamy, 25 miles southeast of Santa Fe. The *Lamy Shuttle* (982-8829) times its runs to meet the two trains — one eastbound and one westbound — that pass through Lamy daily. The 1991 cost was $12 for adults, $6 for children between the ages of six and 12. It's a good idea to call the shuttle service a day ahead to reserve a spot as the van holds just 15 people. Another way to get into town is to call a cab. **Capital City Cab Co.** (989-8888 or 982-9990) is the lone taxi service in Santa Fe. The 1991 fare from Lamy was $24.

Santa Fe cannot be reached by passenger train from either Dallas or Denver, but you _can_ take the train from Los Angeles, Chicago and New York.

From Los Angeles: Amtrak (1-800-872-7245) has a train leaving downtown L.A. each morning and arriving in Lamy the following afternoon. This has become a popular way for Southern Californians to travel to Santa Fe, so you'll want to make reservations early. 1991 round-trip rates ranged from $96 to $152. Call the toll-free number for further information on train travel from L.A. as well as from Chicago and New York.

From Chicago: Amtrak also runs a daily train from Chicago that takes approximately 24 hours to reach Lamy. The 1991 round-trip fare was $189.

From New York: The train ride from New York takes two days. The 1991 round-trip fare was $269.

BY PLANE

If you're like most people, you'll get to Santa Fe and Taos by flying into the Albuquerque airport. As you disembark and head for the baggage claim area, take note of the Southwestern decor, the pastel colors, the outstanding regional artwork on the walls, the huge cast-metal sculpture of a soaring Indian clutching an eagle's tail. The airport commissioned works by 93 major New Mexico artists, including 30 Native Americans. If you have doubts about New Mexico's reputation as a land apart, they'll begin to evaporate in this airport. Thanks to a multi-million-dollar renovation and expansion done in the late 1980s, it's one of the most attractive in the country.

You could bypass Albuquerque altogether and fly directly into Santa Fe or Taos, both of which have their own small airports. Currently, one option is to charter a prop plane from your home base. Expensive, but if you've got the money, why not splurge? Another alternative is to fly in on **Mesa Airlines** (1-800-637-2247, 473-4118), the only commercial carrier serving Santa Fe (there is no commercial service to Taos). The vast majority of Mesa's flights are in New Mexico, but Mesa does fly out of Denver. The 1991 fare was $152 one way and $304 round trip. Mesa also has three flights daily from Albuquerque to Santa Fe. The flight takes a mere 25 minutes. The 1991 fare was $42 for adults and $32 for children under 12.

Note: In 1991 a controversy was brewing in Taos over the proposed construction of an 8,500-foot runway to accommodate jet airliners. Depending on the outcome, this could soon expand travel options even further.

SANTA FE-TAOS ACCESS

The chart below will tell you how long a drive it is from the following cities to Santa Fe. Times do not include stops.

CITY	TIME	MILES
Albuquerque	1 hr.	59
Amarillo	6 ½ hrs.	348
Cheyenne	9 hrs.	481
Dallas	13 hrs.	718
Denver	7 hrs.	385
El Paso	6 hrs.	330
Flagstaff	7 hrs.	375
Houston	17 hrs.	959
Las Vegas, Nev.	12 hrs.	625
Los Angeles	15 hrs.	850
Oklahoma City	10 hrs.	607
Phoenix	10 hrs.	525
Reno	21 ¼ hrs.	1078
Salt Lake City	13 ½ hrs.	680
San Antonio	16 hrs.	952
Wichita	13 hrs.	754

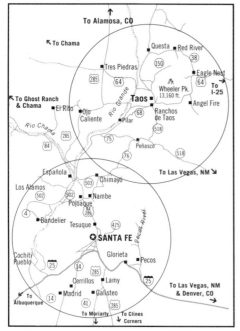

Taos is 70 miles north of Santa Fe, about a 1 ½-hour drive in good weather. The two circles on this map indicate points within a 30-mile radius of Santa Fe and Taos. These circles delineate the areas referred to in the text as "Near Santa Fe" and "Near Taos." All points within the circles are less than an hour's drive from either center.

GETTING AROUND SANTA FE AND TAOS

Given the relatively long distances between towns in the Santa Fe–Taos region, the best way to see the area is by car. Neither Santa Fe nor Taos has public transportation systems (Santa Fe city government hoped to have seven city buses running by the spring of 1992). However, there are other options.

BY BUS

Greyhound-Trailways runs two buses from Santa Fe to Taos daily, and two from Taos to Santa Fe. For current departure times, call 758-1144 (Taos) or 471-0008 (Santa Fe). The 1991 ticket price was $11 one way and $20 round trip. The Greyhound station in Santa Fe is located at 858 St. Michael's Drive, three miles from the city center. For transportation to and from the station, your best bet is to call a cab (see the section on taxis in this chapter). In 1991 the fare from the plaza to the station was $5. The Greyhound station in Taos is also located some distance from the city center — at the corner of Paseo del Pueblo Sur and Paseo de Cañon, two miles south of the plaza. Here again you'll probably want to catch a cab into town. The 1991 cab fare from the station to the plaza was $6.

Ski and Opera Specials

For skiers who would prefer not to have to deal with icy roads after a hard day on the slopes, there's hotel-to-slopes transportation available in Santa Fe and Taos. The *Shuttlejack* (982-4311) will pick you up at any of the major downtown hotels early in the morning, ferry you up to the Santa Fe Ski Basin in time to catch first powder and bring you back into town after the lifts have closed for $10 (1991 rate). The *Pride of Taos* (758-8340) does four runs up to the Taos Ski Valley and four runs back into town for the same 1991 rate. It will pick you up and drop you off at virtually any hotel or motel in Taos. Just call ahead of time.

Opera-goers can have their transportation needs taken care of as well. *Custom Tours by Clarice* (988-7179) will shuttle you out to the Santa Fe Opera, 10 miles north of town, for $15 (1991 round-trip price). The same operation provides shuttle service to the Santa Fe Chamber Music Festival, at St. Francis Auditorium a block west of the plaza, for the same price. To go to either event in style, try their "White Glove Champagne Shuttle," which will pick you up two hours prior to an opera or chamber performance, wine and dine you at a spectacular outdoor setting and whisk you to your seat just in time for the show. Seating is very limited, so make reservations well in advance. 1991 prices ranged from $60-$100 per person.

Faust's Transportation (758-3410) operates two buses daily from Santa Fe to Taos, and two daily from Taos to Santa Fe. They'll pick you up or drop you off at almost any motel or hotel in Taos. The pick-up and drop-off spot in Santa Fe is the Inn at Loretto, two blocks south of the plaza. The 1991 rates were $20 one way, $35 round trip. The 1991 rates were identical for Pride of Taos (758-8340), which also provides bus service twice daily between Santa Fe and Taos. They'll go right to your hotel door in Taos, but their only "station" in Santa Fe is the Hilton Hotel, three blocks west of the plaza.

BY PLANE

The quickest way between Santa Fe and Taos, of course, is by air. It's also a great way to get a sense for the lay of the land. The following charter airplane operations offer direct flights as well as sightseeing tours.

Santa Fe Aviation (based in Santa Fe)	471-6533
Capital Aviation (based in Santa Fe)	471-2525
Mountain Air Service (based in Taos)	758-9382

The average 1991 one-way cost for a single-engine plane (pilot plus three passengers) between Santa Fe and Taos was $210. The average one-way cost for a twin-engine plane (pilot plus five) was $400. The rates for sightseeing tours ranged from $50 an hour to as much as $215 an hour, depending on the size of the plane and the number of passengers.

BY TAXI OR LIMOUSINE

Want to be ferried around the Land of Enchantment in a full-service limousine, replete with wet bar, television and VCR? Or maybe you just need a good old-fashioned taxi to get you from point A to point B as quickly as possible. Here are some options (In the list below, (L) indicates limousine, (T) indicates taxi).

Capital City Cab has new vans.

Wendy Walsh

Santa Fe

Capital City Cab Co.	989-8888 (T)
Dream Limousine	982-5466 (L)
Elegante	473-1115 (L)
Limotion	982-5466 (L)

Taos

Faust's Transportation Service	758-3410 (T)
Taos Limousine Service	758-3524 (L)

BY RENTED CAR

Perhaps the simplest thing to do if you arrive by air is to rent a car at the Albuquerque airport. Virtually all the major car rental agencies are based there:

Avis	800-331-1212
Budget	800-527-0700
Dollar	800-800-4000
Hertz	800-654-3131
National	800-328-4567

Once you're in Santa Fe or Taos, you can also rent a car from one of the following companies:

Santa Fe

Avis (982-4361; 311 Old Santa Fe Trail at the Desert Inn, two blocks south of the plaza.)
Budget (984-8028; 1946 Cerrillos Rd.)
Hertz (982-1844; 100 Sandoval St. at the Hilton, three blocks west of the plaza.)
Thrifty (984-1961; 1718 Cerrillos Rd.)

Taos

Rich Ford (758-9501; at the Taos Airport, 10 miles north of town.)
Hertz (758-1668; at the Sagebrush Inn, on N.M. 68, four miles south of the plaza.)
Taos Motors (758-2286; on N.M. 68, three miles south of the plaza.)

Most of the rental cars come equipped with air conditioning for summer weather and all-terrain tires for icy conditions in wintertime. Virtually all of the agencies listed above also have a limited number of four-wheel-drive trucks or jeeps for bumpy dirt roads. Finally, ski racks can be requested, usually at a small additional cost.

BY BICYCLE

Northern New Mexico, with its abundant open space and miles of dirt roads, is prime mountain biking territory. Renting road bikes is next to impossible — the local bike shops simply don't do it. But mountain bikes can be rented at the following outlets, providing you have a credit card to leave as a deposit. 1991 prices varied widely — from $5 an hour to $125 a week.

Santa Fe

Downtown Bike Shop	983-2255
Gardenswartz Sport	473-3636

Taos

Taos Mountain Outfitters	758-9292
Native Sons Adventures	758-9342

For further information on biking in the Santa Fe–Taos area, see "Bicycling" in the recreation chapter.

ON FOOT

Perhaps the best way to see Santa Fe and Taos is on foot. Both towns are relatively compact, so it's easy to get around. Both are also congested and suffer from chronic parking shortages, particularly during the busy summer season. So by all means walk, if you can; you'll enjoy yourself more. Good walking maps can be found at the **Santa Fe Chamber of Commerce** (983-7317; 333 Montezuma Ave.), five blocks south of the plaza, or the **Taos County Chamber of Commerce** (758-3873; 229 Paseo del Pueblo Sur), two blocks south of the plaza. There are also hundreds of miles of superb hiking trails in the Santa Fe National Forest outside Santa Fe and in the Carson National Forest outside Taos. (For further information on walking, see "Hiking and Climbing" in *Recreation,* Chapter Six, "Tour Companies" in *Information,* Chapter Eight, or consult Elaine Pinkerton's book, *Santa Fe on Foot.*

NEIGHBORS ALL AROUND

Near the Santa Fe–Taos area are 10 Indian pueblos (see "Pueblos" in *Culture*), three ancient Indian sites and at least a score of old Hispanic villages, all in a marvelous desert-mountain setting that offers numerous recreational opportunities. Listed below are some of the things to do and places to see in the area.

NEAR SANTA FE

Santa Fe is flanked by two mountain ranges, the Sangre de Cristo to the east and the Jemez to the west. Both offer hiking, cross-country skiing, down-

Two Suggested Strolls

Santa Fe

For a 30-45 minute walking tour of Santa Fe, we suggest starting on the plaza, perhaps right at the base of the Civil War monument that stands in the middle of the old square. Take time to look at the blend of the old and the new, the Spanish and Territorial architecture that coexists with the gleaming art galleries and boutiques. Then head east for a block, stopping at Sena Plaza on Palace Ave., a hidden courtyard filled with shops. Turn south on Cathedral Pl., past tree-filled Cathedral Park, and pay a visit to magnificent Saint Francis Cathedral. Then go west on San Francisco St., back toward the plaza again, and peek in at La Fonda, a historic hotel at the end of the Old Santa Fe Trail. Stroll south along this famous commerce route and you'll soon come to lovely Loretto Chapel with its marvelous spiral staircase. Continue southward, across the Santa Fe River, until you come to San Miguel Mission, the oldest church in America. Nearby stands the oldest house in the country. The scene here is a little commercial, but these two structures, both of which date from the early 1600s, are worth seeing anyway. Continue southward for about another block and you'll come to the state capitol building, also known as the Roundhouse (see *Culture,* Chapter Four). A major renovation of the Roundhouse is scheduled to be completed by 1992.

Taos

For a similarly pleasant tour in Taos, start out at the Kit Carson Museum, half a block north of the plaza. The museum gives a nice sense of the region's history. Then walk toward the plaza and, just before you get there, turn north on N.M. 68, Taos' main street. A short stroll away is the historic Taos Inn, a popular gathering place for Taoseños. After you've poked your head in and maybe sat down to enjoy a cool drink or a warm fire, cross N.M. 68 (be careful, it's busy!) and amble down Bent St. It's filled with art galleries and all sorts of interesting shops. Then make your way to the plaza by any one of several routes and go straight to Hotel La Fonda where you can see artwork by D.H. Lawrence, including some erotic paintings that cost $3 to view. From the plaza go west one short block, turn south on Placitas Rd., and follow it until you come to Ledoux St., where you'll want to turn west again. Here is the former home of Ernest Blumenschein (see also *Culture,* page 91), one of the founding members of the Taos art colony. A beautiful example of Southwestern architecture, it looks just like it did in Blumenschein's day, and his private art collection is open for public viewing.

hill skiing (at Santa Fe Ski Basin or the Pajarito ski area near Los Alamos), fishing, car camping and backcountry camping — all within less than an hour's drive. If the region's Indian heritage is of more interest, there are a number of Indian pueblos to visit, as well as three major Indian ruins: Pecos National Monument (30 miles east of Santa Fe), Bandelier National Monument (45 miles west of Santa Fe) and Puye Cliffs (45 miles northwest of Santa Fe). For a taste of the rich cultural traditions of rural Hispanic New Mexico, you can do no better than to visit the old village of Chimayó (25 miles north of Santa Fe), known for its historic church and its tradition of fine Spanish weaving. And if it's the Old West you've got a hankering for, check out the old mining towns of Cerrillos and Madrid (20 to 25 miles southwest of Santa Fe).

NEAR TAOS

Taos is surrounded by natural and human-made marvels. Ojo Caliente hot springs, ancient bathing spot of Indians, is some 30 miles to the west. About 30 miles due south of Taos is Las Trampas Church, which dates from the early 1800s, and Picuris Pueblo, the only pueblo in the mountains (the rest are in the Rio Grande Valley or on the Taos Plateau). Less than an hour's drive north from Taos you'll find the Taos and Red River ski areas. Deep in the Sangre de Cristo Mountains, 30 miles to the east, shimmers Eagle Nest Lake, a prime fishing and boating spot, as well as Angel Fire Ski Resort. To the west of Taos the Rio Grande cuts the dramatic gash in the Taos Plateau known as the Rio Grande Gorge, a playground for boating and fishing enthusiasts.

OUTSIDE THE AREA

A little outside the area, about 30 miles west of Ojo Caliente on N.M. 84, sits the Hispanic village of Abiquiu, where artist Georgia O'Keeffe lived. You'll see why when you get a look at the landscape with its spectacularly colored cliffs and mesas. A few miles up the road you'll come to spacious Abiquiu Lake and the Ghost Ranch Museum, home of modern denizens of the desert. Speaking of landscapes, the nearby Chama, recently designated a Wild and Scenic River, flows through some of the most gorgeous desert scenery on the planet. Farther north, you can take a trip on the Cumbres and Toltec scenic railroad, an old-fashioned, smoke-belching clunker that runs between Chama and Antonito in southern Colorado. Snaking back and forth along the border through the San Juan Mountains, it's a wonderful way to see spectacular mountain scenery from the comfort of a railroad car. Beyond the Sangre de Cristos to the east, at the edge of the Great Plains, stands historic Cimarron, one of the major way stations along the Santa Fe Trail. A few hours' drive out-side the area to the west and north will take you to Chaco Canyon and Mesa Verde, two of the most spectacular Anasazi sites.

CHAPTER THREE

The Keys to Your Room
LODGING

Courtesy Museum of New Mexico

The old Exchange Hotel on E. San Francisco St., ca. 1866. Sketch by Theodore R. Davis.

There was a time when the only roadside lodge in northern New Mexico was at the end of the Santa Fe Trail, on the site now occupied by *La Fonda Hotel*. In the late 19th century the railroad brought more visitors, and the number of lodging establishments increased accordingly. The lodging boom didn't really get going until the motorcar appeared in the 1920s and '30s. Many of Santa Fe's and Taos' oldest hotels date from that era. The *San Geronimo Lodge* (1925), in rural Taos, was and is the site of local fiestas and annual balls. *The Taos Inn* (1936) is a gathering place for Taoseños of all stripes. Santa Fe's De Vargas Hotel (1924), now called the *Hotel St. Francis,* was a popular hangout for state and local politicians.

These were about the only historic lodgings Santa Fe and Taos had to offer. Then came an explosion of bed and breakfast inns (B&Bs) in the 1980s, many of them restored adobe and Victorian residences 100 to 200 years old, and in some cases even older. The *Preston House*, on Santa Fe's east side, dates from 1886 and is possibly the only Queen Anne Victorian in the world with a Spanish tin roof. Nearby is *La Posada*, a hotel and *casita* complex that includes the Staab House, a 19th-century Victorian house reputed to have a ghost roaming its corridors. The *Whistling Waters* bed and breakfast inn in Taos, a sprawling adobe structure, is so old no one knows when it was first built.

In addition to the B&Bs and the old-time hotels, the area includes a large number of roadside motels built in the 1940s and '50s. The bulk of them do not offer luxurious accommodations, but they do provide a sense of nostalgia, not to mention reasonable rates. Finally, there are the newer motels and hotels; some owned by chains, others by local developers. One, the *Hotel Santa Fe*, is principally owned by the Picuris Pueblo of northern New Mexico.

One thing is certain: there are plenty of accommodations in the area. In this chapter we present nearly 100 different lodging establishments in Santa Fe, Taos and surrounding communities. This is not an exhaustive list, but it does cover the spectrum, from low-budget to high-budget options. Historical significance, architecture, friendliness, convenience and, of course, that intangible quality called atmosphere are some of the criteria we used in our evaluations..

SANTA FE–TAOS LODGING NOTES

Rates

Rate increases generally occur in the spring, after the ski season and before the summer rush. In Santa Fe most lodging establishments have summer and winter rates, summer being more expensive because it's the high season. Taos gets a bigger ski crowd than Santa Fe, and its high season is not as well defined; consequently, many Taos lodges have one set of rates that applies throughout the year. The off-season rates in both Santa Fe and Taos are usually 20-30 percent lower than those during the high season. Price codes in this chapter are based on a per-room rate, double occupancy, during the high season.

Inexpensive	Up to $50
Moderate	$50 to $80
Expensive	$80 to $120
Very Expensive	Over $120

These rates exclude required room taxes or service charges which may be added to your bill.

Minimum Stay

Most of the higher-priced lodgings in Santa Fe and Taos, including B&Bs, require a minimum stay of two or three nights on high-season weekends and busy holidays. During such times your best bet for a single night's stay is a motel. The minimum stay requirement is carried to an extreme at Taos Ski Valley, where many lodges reserve rooms during the ski season only to guests who plan on buying seven-day ski packages.

Deposit/Cancellation

To reserve a room in Santa Fe and Taos, you generally must make a deposit to cover the first night, although more is sometimes required — particularly if you're going to be staying for several nights. In the event that you must cancel a reservation, you'll usually get your deposit back provided you cancel 10 days to two weeks prior to your arrival. Some establishments refund the deposit minus a 10-15 percent service fee; a few will refund only if your room gets rented and many do not give refunds at all for cancellations at peak times (such as Indian Market weekend and during the Christmas holiday). If you cancel only a few days before your expected arrival, you're most likely to lose your deposit, although sometimes it will be applied to a future stay. In high season the demand for lodging in Santa Fe and Taos often exceeds the supply, so plan well in advance — even months ahead for the most popular lodgings.

Other Options

For information on camping, from tents to RVs, see the section entitled "Camping" in the *Recreation* chapter. If you plan to camp with an RV, be sure to make reservations well in advance of your visit. If you plan on tent camping, most of the campgrounds in the national forests and state parks are available on a first-come, first-served basis, although a few can be reserved.

Information

For last-minute or emergency lodging arrangements in the Santa Fe and Taos area, here are some numbers to phone:

Santa Fe Central Reservations: 800-982-7669
Santa Fe Convention and Visitor Bureau: 984-6760
Taos Central Reservations: 758-9767, 800-821-2437
Taos Bed & Breakfast Association: 758-4747,
   800-876-7857
Taos Accommodations Unlimited: 758-8899,
   800-548-2146
Taos Enchanted Circle Reservations: 758-9767,
   800-827-6464
Taos Valley Resort Association: 776-2233,
   800-992-SNOW
Rio Grande Reservations: 800-678-7586

CONDOMINIUMS/SHORT-TERM RENTALS

Tired of the tourist scene? Want to live in Santa Fe and Taos like a native, in a real home or apartment, or at least in a condominium compound? You've got plenty to choose from. They're usually rented on a weekly or monthly basis, although some will rent for single nights. In the case of condominiums, you have the option to buy your own home-away-from-home in the Land of Enchantment. Rental prices vary widely. Weekly rates, for example, can run from several hundred to a few thousand dollars. Maid service is often (but not always) provided. Here is a partial list of condominium complexes and other short-term rental possibilities, as well as some property management firms that can mail you current listings in the Santa Fe and Taos areas.

Santa Fe

Casa Encantada	983-6506
Cielo Grande Condominiums	988-9891
Frontier Property Management	984-2192
Las Brisas Condominiums	982-5795
Las Casitas de Santa Fe	983-3523, 983-2832
Manzano House	983-2054
Pueblo Hermosa Condominiums	984-2590
Staab Street Vacation Rentals	983-4179
The Management Group	983-5775

Taos ("TSV" = Taos Ski Valley)

Adobe Home Rental	758-9749
Casa Otero	758-2492
Field's Cottages	758-9240
Kandahar Condominiums (TSV)	776-2226
Las Chamisas Compound	758-0192
Pescado del Cielo	758-7306
Powderhorn Condominiums (TSV)	776-2341
Ranchos Plaza Guest House	758-9737
Sierra del Sol Condominiums (TSV)	776-2981
Sonterra Condominiums	758-7989
Villacito Condos	776-8778

LODGING IN SANTA FE

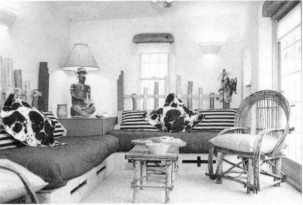

The Adobe Abode, a contemporary Southwestern B&B.

Courtesy the Adobe Abode

ADOBE ABODE
Owner: Pat Harbour.
983-3133.
202 Chapelle, Santa Fe, NM
  87501
4 blks. W. of plaza.
Price: Expensive.
Credit Cards: MC, V.

This small B&B is a wonderful jumble of architectural styles, antiques, cultural artifacts, knickknacks and works of art. It opened in March 1989, following a six-month renovation of the 68-year-old adobe. Pat Harbour, the owner, is a casual and friendly woman who lives on the premises and is a collector extraordinaire. Her finds include a hand-carved Philippine planter's chair, a 100-year-old French armoire, Balinese antique dolls, a shadow puppet from Java and 19th-century wooden ship moldings from Vermont. There are three units, two in the main house and a cozy *casita*, or guest house, converted from a one-car garage. The *casita* is predominantly Southwestern in style, but the other rooms are eclectic, combining New Mexican, Victorian and Art Deco furnishings and decor. None of the guest rooms is terribly spacious, but all are charming. This inn specializes in hearty breakfasts. It is located in a quiet residential area a few blocks from downtown.

ALAMO LODGE
Owner: Rose Ellen Guillen-
  Abeyta.
982-1841.
1842 Cerrillos Rd., Santa
  Fe, NM 87501.
Price: Inexpensive.
Credit Cards: All.
Handicap. Access: Limited.

This charming, family-owned roadside motel is 30 years old and none the worse for wear. It has a Mexican feel to it: red chile *ristras* decorate an attractive portico, hand-painted flowers arch over doorways, and dark brown *vigas* grace the ceilings of some of the rooms. There is no swimming pool, but there is cable TV.

ALEXANDER'S INN
Owner: Carolyn Lee.
986-1431.
529 E. Palace Ave., Santa
Fe, NM, 87501.
5 blks. E. of plaza.
Price: Expensive.
Credit Cards: MC, V.

In operation since 1988, this B&B is located in a wooded, residential area within easy walking distance of the plaza and Canyon Road. It was built of brick in 1903. Windows and skylights have been added to make it sunny, but it still has plenty of Victorian charm. If you like antiques, four-poster beds, stained glass and free-standing bathtubs, you'll love this place. The breakfast includes homemade muffins and granola, and an afternoon tea (also included in the room rate) offers cheese and cookies. There are five rooms, two with shared baths.

COTTONWOOD COURT
Owner: Sam Bhakta.
982-5571.
1742 Cerrillos Rd., Santa
Fe, NM 87501.
Price: Inexpensive.
Credit Cards: AE, MC, V.
Handicap. Access: Yes.

Here's an old, classic roadside motel with 15 rooms. It's a little shabby, but has two big advantages: it's cheap and near the east end of Cerrillos, not far from downtown.

EL FAROLITO
Owner: Gil Gonzales.
988-1631.
514 Galisteo St., Santa Fe,
NM 87501.
5 blks. S. of plaza.
Price: Very Expensive.
Credit Cards: MC, V.
Handicap. Access: Limited.

Opened during Christmas 1990, this B&B offers seven renovated adobe *casitas*, some with private courtyards, all with fireplaces. (Five more units were under construction in early 1991.) The owner, Gil Gonzales, is a local builder who has added a few unusual touches, like cedar ceilings and varnished plaster walls for a rough, antique look. It also includes the more typical features of Southwestern style: flagstone floors, Mexican hide chairs, *trasteros* (hand-carved, free-standing cabinets), Spanish style beds, exposed *vigas*, skylights, etc. The inn operates a van service, which provides transportation to most anywhere in the city. If you prefer to walk, the plaza can be reached on foot in 10 minutes. An enclosed hot tub adds a note of civilized luxury, as does an in-house massage therapist.

EL PARADERO
Owners: Thom Allen &
Ouida MacGregor.
988-1177.
220 W. Manhattan Ave.,
Santa Fe, NM 87501.
5 blks. S. of plaza.
Price: Expensive.
Credit Cards: None.

This family-owned and operated B&B has an informal air to it. The front part of the building was a Spanish farmhouse in the early 1800s. Later additions, both Territorial and Victorian, give the inn a rambling character. It's full of interesting nooks and crannies and includes several common areas. The rooms are charming, sunlit and accented with hand-woven textiles and folk art. Two suites in a nearby brick building are Victorian in design. The location, just off the Guadalupe St. shopping area and 10 minutes' walking distance from the plaza, is convenient but could be better from an aesthetic point of view. The inn is located between a parking lot and an office building. It is a testament to El Paradero's charm that these are only minor drawbacks. A major plus is the huge, delicious breakfast served every day.

The El Rey Inn is a motel classic.

Leslie Tallant

EL REY INN
Owner: Terrell White.
982-1931.
1862 Cerrillos Road, Santa Fe, NM 87501.
Price: Moderate.
Credit Cards: AE, DC, MC, V.
Handicap. Access: Limited.

This is easily the best motel in Santa Fe and possibly the city's best lodging bargain. When it was built in 1935 a few miles outside the city limits, it was surrounded by nothing but open space. Today it is a classic roadside motel, so well maintained it looks like it was built yesterday. Most of the 56 rooms are distinct in design and decor with flagstone floors, exposed *vigas*, Indian rugs, carved furniture and ornate tinware; nine include fireplaces. A large central courtyard is graced with a fountain and several large cottonwoods. Beautiful tile murals, inside and out, give the motel a Spanish flavor. A wing of passive-solar rooms overlooks a heated pool and an indoor hot tub sits nearby. The room rate includes Continental breakfast.

ELDORADO
Manager: Paul Margetson.
988-4455.
309 W. San Francisco St., Santa Fe, NM 87501.
2 blks. W. of plaza.
Price: Very Expensive.
Credit Cards: All.
Handicap. Access: Yes.

If any hotel in Santa Fe has an air of big city luxury, it's the Eldorado. Spacious and imposing, this member of the Clarion hotel chain has an underground parking lot, valet service, two restaurants, several retail shops, live music at night and the largest banquet halls in the city. It was built in the mid-'80s over the opposition of locals who felt it was simply too big. Indeed, the five-story hotel has a monolithic appearance that seems out of scale for Santa Fe. It also has a couple of oddities for a hotel its size: a postage-stamp-sized swimming pool and no lobby. The views from the top floor are magnificent.

The Eldorado Hotel in Santa Fe.

Leslie Tallant

GARRETT'S DESERT INN
Manager: Gene Garrett.
982-1851.
311 Old Santa Fe Trail,
    Santa Fe, NM 87501.
1.5 blks. S. of plaza.
Price: Moderate.
Credit Cards: AE, MC, V.
Handicap. Access: Yes.

Nothing fancy here. Just a standard motel that happens to have a central location — which is probably the reason the rooms are overpriced. Nonetheless, if you really want to be less than two blocks from the plaza, this is a relatively inexpensive way to do it. Many of the motels on Cerrillos Rd. provide similar accommodations at more reasonable rates.

Leslie Tallant

GRANT CORNER INN
Owners: Louise Stewart &
   Martin Walter.
983-6678.
122 Grant Ave., Santa Fe,
   NM 87501.
2.5 blks. W. of plaza.
Price: Expensive.
Credit Cards: MC, V.
Handicap. Access: Yes.

Grant Corner Inn does not look Southwestern, either inside or out. A graceful, recently-renovated Colonial manor house, it has a white picket fence in front, flower gardens and a gazebo. The interior features tieback curtains, wallpaper, old black-and-white family photographs, ceiling fans, brass and four-poster beds. It feels so much like New England that you half expect to see the Atlantic out the window. Breakfasts (not included in the room rates) are superb and include such exotic dishes as plum-cottage-cheese pancakes, green chile crepes and banana waffles (see *Restaurants*, Chapter Five). There is a *Grant Corner Inn Cookbook* worth taking home. The staff serves complimentary afternoon wine and cheese and leaves a piece of foil-wrapped chocolate on every bed. The 11 guest rooms are quaint, several of them rather small, four with shared baths. There are also two rooms in a nearby condominium. The plaza is only a minute away and the innkeepers, Louise and Pat, are especially warm and friendly hosts.

HIGH MESA INN
Manager: Carey C. Grigg.
473-2800.
3347 Cerrillos Rd., Santa
    Fe, NM 87501.
Price: Expensive.
Credit Cards: AE, D, DC,
    MC, V.
Handicap. Access: Yes.

The only surprise here is that the motel's restaurant serves Peruvian dishes. Otherwise this is a standard, if unusually large (211 rooms), Best Western motel done up in contemporary Southwestern decor. With an indoor pool, hot tub, exercise room, sports bar, and spacious banquet and convention facilities, it has all you could want — except atmosphere.

HILTON OF SANTA FE
Manager: Don Jackson.
988-2811.
100 Sandoval St., Santa Fe,
    NM 87501
2 blks. W. of plaza.
Price: Very Expensive.
Credit Cards: AE, MC, V.
Handicap. Access: Yes.

Southwestern decor cannot hide the fact that this is one of the chain's less remarkable hotels. It has all the standards: swimming pool, bar, restaurant, live music at night but there's nothing distinctive or unusual about it. The downtown location is convenient, however, and a shuttle bus to and from the Albuquerque airport stops here several times a day.

HOTEL PLAZA REAL
Manager: John H. Fleming.
988-4900.
125 Washington Ave.,
    Santa Fe, NM 87501.
0.5 blks. N. of plaza.
Price: Very Expensive.
Credit Cards: AE, MC, V.
Handicap. Access: Yes.

Opened in the summer of 1990, this is among the more attractive Territorial-style hotels (red brick coping, white window frames) in Santa Fe. It certainly makes the most of the space available to it. Located on a long, narrow property a block from the plaza, the three-story structure manages to house 56 rooms, an attractive lobby and an intimate bar without seeming cramped. Most of the rooms look out onto a brick courtyard that lends a New Orleans-style stateliness to the hotel. However, the massive wooden beams, hand-carved *trasteros* and Indian pottery remind you that this is the Southwest, as do a number of fine landscape paintings. Nearly every room has a fireplace, a balcony or both. Delicate wrought-iron chandeliers and small iron light fixtures adorn the hallways.

HOTEL SANTA FE

Manager: James A. Reed.
982-1200.
P.O. Box 15820, Santa Fe,
NM 87506.
1501 Paseo de Peralta at
Cerrillos Rd.
Price: Very Expensive.
Credit Cards: All.
Handicap. Access: Yes.

This three-story hotel at the southern entrance to the downtown area is distinctive. Opened in 1991, it is one of Santa Fe's newest lodging establishments. Its terraced, pueblo-style architecture — with numerous setbacks, balconies, and varied window sizes and shapes — gives the facade a pleasingly varied appearance. Most notably, the hotel is the result of a partnership between the Picuris Pueblo of northern New Mexico and a group of Santa Fe developers, the first such joint venture in the country to be located off reservation lands.

The hotel's 131 rooms are attractively furnished in contemporary Southwestern style and equipped with conveniences like direct-dial telephones, remote-control cable television and individually-controlled heating and air conditioning. The lobby, turquoise-carpeted with wooden beams and columns, serves as a dining room during the daily breakfast buffet and as a lounge with drinks and hors d'oeuvres in the afternoons and evenings. Laundry facilities are available and there is a free shuttle service to the plaza (10 minutes away on foot). There is a massage therapist on the premises.

The Hotel St. Francis retains its Roaring '20s charm.

Leslie Tallant

HOTEL ST. FRANCIS

Manager: Michaleen
Sawka.
983-5700.
210 Don Gaspar Ave.,
Santa Fe, NM 87501.
1.5 blocks S. of plaza.

Between the world wars, the De Vargas Hotel was one of Santa Fe's grand hotels, a popular gathering place for local politicians. Its glory had all but vanished by the early 1980s, when a group of local investors decided to restore its old romantic grace. After a $6 million renovation, it reopened in 1987 with a new name and a bright future.

Price: Expensive.
Credit Cards: AE, DC, MC, V.
Handicap. Access: Yes.

The renovation did not destroy the hotel's Roaring '20s charm. Art Deco lamps, potted plants and high-backed chairs adorn the most attractive hotel lobby in Santa Fe. The 83 rooms feature high ceilings, casement windows, brass and iron beds, porcelain pedestal sinks and period pieces of cherry and marble. A bar and a restaurant branch off from the lobby, where a daily afternoon tea is served.

Inn at Loretto decorated with farolitos.

Richard Twarog; courtesy Santa Fe Chamber of Commerce

THE INN AT LORETTO
Manager: James Bagby.
988-5531.
211 Old Santa Fe Trail, Santa Fe, NM 87501.
2 blks. S. of plaza.
Price: Very Expensive.
Credit Cards: AE, CB, DC, MC, V.
Handicap. Access: Yes.

Built in 1975 on the site of Loretto Academy, a girls' school founded in the 19th century, the Inn's terraced architecture is modeled after Taos Pueblo. It is brown stucco, of course, not real adobe, but the building is still an impressive sight, especially at Christmastime when it's decked out with hundreds of electric *farolitos*.

This is a good Best Western hotel. It includes a swimming pool, a bar with live entertainment, a restaurant and several retail businesses. The hallways are adorned with Indian-style murals and the rooms, while of standard design, are attractive. (Some of the Southwestern furnishings are made by local craftsmen.) Even so, the hotel has a generic feel to it.

INN OF THE ANASAZI
Manager: Alan Ireland.
988-3030.
113 Washington Ave., Santa
  Fe, NM 87501.
0.5 blks. N. of plaza.
Price: Very Expensive.
Credit Cards: All.
Handicap. Access: Limited.

Opened in the summer of 1991, this 59-room hotel is about as close to the plaza as you can get without actually being on it. Located half a block up Washington Ave., it is decorated in classic Pueblo Revival style, with *viga*-and-*latilla* ceilings throughout, stone floors and walls and a huge, two-story stone water-well. The artwork is local and reflects New Mexico's three major ethnic groups, as does the cuisine in the hotel's restaurant. For guests who like to stay physically fit, the staff will bring an exercise bike to your room or rent you a mountain bike for touring. For those more inclined toward mental workouts, the hotel maintains a small library stocked mostly with books on the Southwest. And if you like to splurge, an underground wine cellar with a capacity of 12 guests is available for dinner.

**INN OF THE ANIMAL
  TRACKS**
Owner: Daun Martin.
988-1546.
707 Paseo de Peralta, Santa
  Fe, NM 87501.
3.5 blocks E. of plaza.
Price: Expensive.
Credit Cards: AE, MC, V.
Handicap. Access: Yes.

Cozy and whimsical, this small inn has a distinctive personality. Each of its six rooms is named and decorated after an animal: "Sign of the Soaring Eagle," for example, is light and airy with six large windows (and lots of feathers on the walls); "Sign of the Gentle Deer" is tucked next to a hazelnut thicket, suggesting retreat. A central living room is filled with big pillows, soft chairs, a fireplace and what has to be the biggest teddy bear in Santa Fe. It's a perfect spot for reading or quiet talking. Breakfasts are sumptuous, with homemade breads, fresh fruit and a different egg dish every day. Afternoon tea offers a delicious array of goodies. Everything is cooked by the owner, Daun Martin. If you don't care for or are allergic to animals, this is not the place for you. Three cats and a huge but friendly Bouvier–Newfoundland mix named Barney roam the premises.

INN OF THE GOVERNORS
Manager: Charlotte Sliva.
982-4333.
234 Don Gaspar, Santa Fe,
  NM 87501.
2 blks. S. of plaza.
Price: Very Expensive.
Credit Cards: AE, DC, MC,
  V.
Handicap. Access: Yes.

Enclosed patios, carved *vigas* and deep red doors set this inn apart from standard motels. However, the Spanish Colonial accents go only so far and one guest room looks much like another. Those facing south on Alameda St., a popular cruising drag for teenagers, tend to be noisy on weekend nights.

INN ON THE ALAMEDA
Manager: Gil Martinez.
984-2121.
303 E. Alameda, Santa Fe,
   NM 87501.
3 blks. E. of plaza.
Price: Very Expensive.
Credit Cards: AE, DC, MC,
   V.
Handicap. Access: Yes.

Within easy walking distance of the plaza and Canyon Rd., this relatively new 42-room inn offers a tasteful mix of Southwestern style and modern convenience. Amenities include an outdoor whirlpool, a complimentary Continental breakfast, a full-service bar, a comfortable sitting room, a conference room and a secluded patio with outdoor fireplace. The rooms are attractively decorated along Southwestern lines. A few have fireplaces and private balconies.

INN ON THE PASEO
Innkeeper: Nancyellen
   Ruhe.
984-8200.
630 Paseo de Peralta, Santa
   Fe, NM 87501.
5 blks. N.E. of plaza.
Price: Moderate.
Credit Cards: MC, V.

Part of this inn, one of the newer B&Bs in Santa Fe, is a three-story A-frame, a rarity in this land of low-lying adobe. The other part is a recently-renovated brick home. One of the more luxurious rooms (there are 11 in all) is the honeymoon suite which has the third floor all to itself and a hot tub. Another has a wonderful brick fireplace and a classic French armoire. The inn is located next to a busy street, so it is not as quiet as it could be. The owners plan to add eight rooms in the next few years..

LA FONDA
Manager: Mickey Stewart.
982-5511.
100 E. San Francisco, Santa
   Fe, NM 87501.
On the plaza.
Price: Very Expensive.
Credit Cards: AE, DC, MC,
   V.
Handicap. Access: Yes.

For almost all of Santa Fe's nearly 400-year history, there has been an inn of some sort on the southeast corner of the plaza. Throughout most of the 19th century, the U.S. Hotel stood there and its location, at the end of the Santa Fe Trail, made it a destination for trappers, traders, merchants, soldiers, gamblers, politicians and others. Kit Carson and a brigade of Confederate soldiers stayed there, and Billy the Kid did a stint as a dishwasher. As you might expect, the hotel was not immune to frontier violence. In 1857, a man who couldn't pay his gambling debts was hung by a lynch mob in the hotel's back yard and a few years later a prominent judge was gunned down in the lobby.

By the 1920s, the old hotel, which had become a boarding house, was torn down. Within a few years a new hotel, La Fonda (*fonda* means "inn"), rose in its place. For a time it was operated by the Fred Harvey Company, a hotel chain that was an early promoter of Southwestern tourism. Wealthy tourists were treated to the spectacle of Indians dancing in the lobby and La Fonda was advertised as the gateway to Pueblo country.

Currently the hotel is locally-owned and the days when it was *the* hotel in Santa Fe are long gone. It remains, however, the only hotel on the plaza and

La Fonda is built around a central courtyard that serves as a restaurant.

Leslie Tallant

none of the others can match its storied past. The lobby, though a bit dark and musty, still has the feel of a crossroads; and the rooms exude old Spanish charm. Even if you don't stay here, pay a visit to the roof-top lounge for a marvelous view of the city. There's also a restaurant (see "La Plazuela" in *Restaurants)* in the enclosed, sky-lit courtyard, a swimming pool, hot tubs and a massage therapist on duty.

LA POSADA DE SANTA FE
Manager: Suhail Jundi.
986-0000.
330 E. Palace Ave., Santa Fe, NM 87501.
5 blks. E. of plaza.
Price: Very Expensive.
Credit Cards: AE, MC, V.
Handicap. Access: Yes.

A 19th-century mansion reputed to be haunted, a complex of Pueblo-style *casitas*, six acres covered with huge cottonwoods and fruit trees — these are just some of the hallmarks of this unusual inn. The central building is known as the Staab House, named after a 19th-century German immigrant, Abraham Staab. Staab made a fortune in the Santa Fe mercantile business and had the house built in the 1880s for his wife, Julia Shuster Staab. The three-story brick residence was a classic of its time, with a distinctive mansard roof, parquet floor and imported doors and windows. The top floor, which contained a ballroom, was destroyed by fire in the early part of the century; the rest of the building was plastered over in the 1930s with brown stucco to make it harmonize with the Spanish Pueblo Revival movement in architecture.(See *Culture*, Chapter Four.)

Interior of the Staab House at La Posada.

Leslie Tallant

Luckily, the original interior of the Staab House remains intact. On its main level is a restaurant and a Victorian lounge, a popular watering hole where you can rub elbows with Santa Feans (see "Staab House" in *Restaurants*). Upstairs are five turn-of-the-century rooms, including Room 256, where the ghost of Julia Staab is alleged to reside. The majority of guests stay in the *casitas*, where the decor is classically New Mexican: adobe *kiva*-style fireplaces, flagstone floors, archways, hand-painted tiles, stained-glass windows, Indian rugs, exposed *vigas* and skylights. La Posada has a good-sized swimming pool and a lovely courtyard for drinking and dining in nice weather.

PARK INN
Manager: Rand Levitt.
473-4281.
2900 Cerrillos Rd., Santa Fe, NM 87501.
Price: Inexpensive.
Credit Cards: AE, MC, V.
Handicap. Access: Yes.

This motel, once a Holiday Inn, has seen better times, but it has potential. The rooms (the preferred ones face the courtyard) are clean and spacious, and the swimming pool is Santa Fe's largest. Formerly called Del Camino Inn, the place has recently been spruced up with new carpets, drapes and furniture. There is no bar or restaurant, but a tenant who is renting the kitchen prepares pastries, juice and coffee for guests.

PECOS TRAIL INN
Manager: George Rodriguez.
982-1943.
2239 Old Pecos Trail, Santa Fe, NM 87505.
Price: Inexpensive.
Credit Cards: CB, DC, MC, V.
Handicap. Access: Limited.

This is the first motel you run across if you're coming into Santa Fe from the east. It is relatively inexpensive by Santa Fe standards, with a good-sized swimming pool and a passable restaurant. Unfortunately, it's a bit tacky and run-down, and, by spring 1991, a planned remodeling project had not gotten very far.

PICACHO PLAZA HOTEL

Manager: Sandra Esparza.
982-5591.
750 N. St. Francis Dr., Santa Fe, NM 87501.
Price: Very Expensive.
Credit Cards: AE, DC, MC, V.
Handicap. Access: Yes.

Located on a hillside on the north edge of town, this 167-room hotel has magnificent views of the city and the Sangre de Cristo range. It was a Sheraton hotel before the Village Resorts chain bought, renovated and reopened it in 1990 under its current name. It's nicer than it was, but it has a generic feel to it that even the spanking new Southwestern decor cannot hide. This wouldn't be so bad, except that it's pricey, too. On the up side, the pool area is pleasant, the Petroglyph bar is a nice place to have a drink and look at the lights of Santa Fe and the hotel's nightclub, which features flamenco dancers, is becoming a hot night spot.

PRESTON HOUSE

Owner: Signe Bergman.
982-3465.
106 Faithway Street, Santa Fe, NM 87501.
5 blks. E. of plaza.
Price: Expensive.
Credit Cards: AE, MC, V.

The Preston House may be the only Queen Anne Victorian in the world with a Spanish tin roof. But the juxtaposition is appropriate, for this B&B offers both Victorian and Spanish–Indian style accommodations. Six of the 15 rooms are located in the main house, built in 1886. (Past occupants include a notorious land speculator and a cure-all doctor.) Stained glass, heavy furniture, brass beds, frilly curtains, high ceilings and ornate woodwork abound. There are two lovely cottages in the back yard. The rest of the rooms, located in an adobe compound across the street, have a Southwestern flavor. A decanter of sherry and a bowl of fresh fruit await every occupant. You're even provided bathrobes. Other pluses include an in-house masseuse (advance notice required) and a splendid location on a cul-de-sac, five minutes from the plaza.

PUEBLO BONITO

Owners: Herb & Amy Behm.
984-8001.
138 W. Manhattan Ave., Santa Fe, NM 87501.
5 blks. S. of plaza.
Price: Expensive.
Credit Cards: MC, V.

Of all the B&Bs that popped up in Santa Fe in the 1980s, this one has perhaps the most charming and distinctive guest rooms. The look is rustic and colorful Southwestern, with wood floors, three-foot-thick adobe walls, small *kiva*-style fireplaces, Indian rugs, Mexican pottery and Spanish carvings of saints (*bultos*). The grounds are graced by private courtyards, narrow brick paths, adobe archways and huge shade trees. The only thing that keeps this place from being perfect is its location near a busy street. It deserves a quieter setting.

Private courtyards and thick adobe walls are characteristic of Pueblo Bonito.

Leslie Tallant

SANTA FE MOTEL
Managers: Chad &
   Gretchen Herd.
982-1039.
510 Cerrillos Road, Santa
   Fe, NM 87501.
5 blks. S. of plaza.
Price: Moderate.
Credit Cards: AE, MC, V.
Handicap. Access: Yes.

If you're looking for an attractive, affordable motel with a downtown location, this is the place. It's set just far enough off a busy road to have an air of seclusion. In addition to typical motel rooms, it includes seven or eight adobe *casitas* with patio entrances. There's even a two-bedroom adobe with fireplace across the street.

**SANTA FE YOUTH
   HOSTEL**
Owner: Preston Ellsworth.
988-1153.
1412 Cerrillos Rd.
Price: Inexpensive.
Credit Cards: None.
Handicap. Access: Yes.

For the most affordable lodging in Santa Fe (rooms cost between $9 and $12 a night in 1991), you can't beat the Santa Fe Youth Hostel. Like most hostels, men and women stay in separate, dorm-style rooms and the kitchen is available for a dollar a day. It's pretty spartan and there aren't many extras (no TV, no pinball, just a radio), but for little more than a song you've got a safe, warm place to stay.

**SILVER SADDLE
   MOTEL**
Manager: Penelope Aley.
471-7663.
2810 Cerrillos Road, Santa
   Fe, NM 87501.
Price: Inexpensive.
Credit Cards: MC, V.
Handicap. Access: Yes.

Clean and affordable, this motel has 26 rooms, six with kitchenettes. A Southwestern furniture outlet is located in the front.

STAGE COACH MOTOR INN
Owners: Bernard & Alicia
  Cawley.
471-0707.
3360 Cerrillos Road, Santa
  Fe, NM 87501.
Price: Inexpensive.
Credit Cards: D, MC, V.

As you might expect from the name, this motel has a Western flavor. On the upper end of inexpensive, it is still a little pricey for what you get — especially considering that it's a 15-minute drive from the city center.

TERRITORIAL INN
Owner: Lela McFerrin.
989-7737.
215 Washington Ave.,
  Santa Fe, NM 87501.
Price: Very Expensive.
Credit Cards: MC, V.
Handicap. Access: Yes.

The Territorial Inn is the last of the grand, turn-of-the-century homes that once stood on tree-lined Washington Ave., just north of the plaza. Built in the 1890s by a wealthy Philadelphian, the house incorporates some elements of Pueblo Revival style but remains essentially a fine example of Territorial architecture enhanced by a well-kept lawn, a rose garden and several large cottonwoods. Inside, heavy print curtains, Victorian antiques and ceiling fans — staples of the Territorial style — blend seamlessly with skylights, archways, enclosed patios and other hallmarks of the Pueblo motif. There are 10 rooms, three clustered round a main living area on the ground floor, one off to the side and the rest located up a curving, Spanish-style staircase. Eight have private baths and two have fireplaces. A Continental breakfast comes with the room, as does afternoon wine and cheese and brandy and cookies in the evening. The patio is a wonderful place sit in nice weather, and a gazebo-enclosed hot tub is relaxing at any time of the year. Here you're only two blocks from the plaza, so any number of restaurants and shops are within easy walking distance.

THUNDERBIRD INN
Manager: Giovanna
  Brandi-Gibbons.
983-4397.
1821 Cerrillos Road, Santa
  Fe, NM 87501.
Price: Inexpensive.
Credit Cards: AE, MC, V.

This is an old-fashioned roadside motel, the kind where you park right outside your room. It's been around a long time and looks a trifle run-down, but the rooms are clean, it has a pool and the price is right.

WARREN INN
Manager: Alice Gesek.
471-2033.
3357 Cerrillos Rd., Santa
  Fe, NM 87501.
Price: Inexpensive.
Credit Cards: All.

This is basically your standard motel, sterile but very affordable. It includes 138 rooms with kitchenettes, a swimming pool and free Continental breakfast with pastry, coffee, doughnut and juice.

WATER STREET INN
Owners: Al & Dolores
  Dietz.
984-1193.
427 W. Water St., Santa Fe,
  NM 87501.
5 blks. W. of plaza.
Price: Expensive.
Credit Cards: MC, V.
Handicap. Access: Yes.

This handsomely-restored adobe B&B evokes an air of romantic intimacy. It also has an excellent location on a quiet side street within strolling distance of downtown. The six rooms are spacious, with brick floors, beam ceilings and four-poster beds. Some have fireplaces and one has an antique wood-burning stove.

WIND HORSE INN
Owner: Irene Schleipman.
473-2877.
751-A Airport Rd., Santa
  Fe, NM 87501.
Price: Expensive.
Credit Cards: MC, V.

There's no other B&B in the country where you can look out the window and see an ornate Buddhist temple, or *stupa*. The inn's name, a rough translation of the Tibetan word for "breath," was chosen by owner Irene Schleipman because, as she says, "This is a place of peace and quiet." Indeed, there is a serene feeling to this inn, shaded by several tall cottonwoods and blessed by a picture-perfect view of the brilliantly-colored *stupa* next door. (Ask Schleipman to arrange a visit for you.) The five guest rooms are immaculate and decorated in Southwestern style, though they lack character. The inn's location, on the southern outskirts of Santa Fe about 10–15 minutes from the plaza (depending on traffic), is a plus if you want some distance from the hustle and bustle of downtown.

LODGING NEAR SANTA FE

THE BISHOP'S LODGE
Manager: Mark Weber.
983-6377.
P.O. Box, 2367, Santa Fe,
  NM 87504.
On Bishop's Lodge Rd., 5
  mi. N. of Santa Fe
Closed: Jan.-Mar.
Price: Very Expensive.
Credit Cards: None.

Bishop Jean Baptiste Lamy chose this magnificent spot in the foothills of the Sangre de Cristo range for his retirement home some 100 years ago. Back then it was known as Villa Pintoresca, a small ranch overlooking the Rio Grande Valley that had been planted with fruit trees by Franciscan priests in the early 17th century. Lamy added more fruit trees, as well as a private chapel and turned an old hillside adobe into his home. After he died, the property was briefly owned by publisher Joseph Pulitzer, who constructed two summer homes on the ranch. In 1918, James Thorpe, a Denver mining magnate, bought the property and turned it into a resort. His family continues to own it.

The lodge is activity- and family-oriented. Horseback riding, tennis, swimming, trap shooting and fishing are all available on its more than 1,000 acres. In the summer, a special program for kids age 4-12 provides a day of supervised play as well as puppet and magic shows. The rooms have plenty of

The Bishop's Lodge, former home of Archbishop Jean Baptiste Lamy.

Leslie Tallant

New Mexican flavor and the restaurant offers a very good Sunday brunch. Best of all, there's still an air of serenity here and Lamy's private chapel stands untouched.

THE GALISTEO INN
Owners: Joanna Kaufman & Wayne Aarniokoski.
982-1506.
P.O. Box 4, Galisteo, NM 87540.
On Rte. 41, 25 mi. S. of Santa Fe.
Price: Expensive.
Credit Cards: MC, V.
Handicap. Access: Yes.

The village of Galisteo, 30 minutes south of Santa Fe, was founded as a Spanish colonial outpost in 1614, following the massacre of hundreds of Indians whose home this was originally. Today it is a mecca for Anglo artists, writers, healers and the like. Its Spanish character remains predominant. No other place in northern New Mexico feels as timeless as Galisteo and few can match the expansive, windswept setting.

The Galisteo Inn, a restored 240-year-old adobe hacienda, is located in the heart of the village, on eight acres over which sway ancient and giant cottonwood trees. The grounds are gorgeous, but to walk into this luxurious inn with its polished wood floors, sparkling blue swimming pool and expensive restaurant is a little jarring, so funky and dusty is the village outside. Nonetheless, it's a wonderful place to stay. Dry sauna, bubbling whirlpool, soothing massage and exhilarating horseback rides leave one with few wants.

HACIENDA RANCHO DE CHIMAYÓ
Owner: Florence Jaramillo.
351-2222.
P.O. Box 11, Chimayó, NM 87522.
On Rte. 520, 25 mi. N. of Santa Fe.

This charming place is located in the heart of the ancient village of Chimayó, known for its historic church and its tradition of fine Spanish weaving. The inn was converted from a 19th-century rural hacienda in 1984. The plasterless, straw-streaked adobe walls are adorned with red chile *ristras* and the enclosed courtyard is bursting with fruit trees. Seven guest rooms, predominantly

Hacienda Rancho de Chimayó.

Murrae Haynes

Closed: Jan.
Price: Moderate.
Credit Cards: AE, MC, V.
Handicap. Access: Limited.

Spanish in appearance, feature dark, massive *vigas* and heavy curtains, hand-woven by a local artisan. Antiques, wallpaper and high ceilings give the rooms an almost American Colonial touch. Some rooms have private balconies and one has a fireplace. The hacienda is located directly across the street from the acclaimed Restaurante Rancho de Chimayó (see *Restaurants*, Chapter Five), also owned by Florence Jaramillo and her family.

LA POSADA DE CHIMAYÓ
Owner: Susan Farrington.
351-4605.
P.O. Box 463, Chimayó, NM 87522.
279 Cty. Rd. 101, near Rte. 76, 25 mi. N. of Santa Fe.
Price: Moderate.
Credit Cards: MC, V.

Hidden on a twisting dirt road in Chimayó, this place is a little-known gem. It has only two guest quarters, both in a solar-heated adobe nestled into a hillside of red dirt and green piñon. The style is traditional Southwestern rustic, with brick floors, Mexican hide chairs, hand-woven bedspreads, colorful tile work and rough-hewn *vigas* and paintings by local artists. Between the rooms is a tiny kitchen from which emerge hearty breakfasts every morning (the meal, included in the room rate, is brought to your door). A climb to the top of a nearby hill provides a spectacular view.

LA PUEBLA HOUSE
Owner: Elvira Bain.
753-3981.
Rte. 3, P.O. Box 172A,
  Española, NM 87532.
30 mi. N. of Santa Fe.
Price: Moderate.
Credit Cards: MC, V.

This B&B has an attractive rural location, on a dirt road in the village of La Puebla, outside Española. The front part of the inn has beautiful flagstone floors and a marvelous *latilla* ceiling of Ponderosa pine. But the rooms, located in a newer part of the building, are characterless, looking like they belong in a suburban home.

RANCHO ARRIBA
Owner: Curtiss Frank.
689-2374.
P.O. Box 338, Truchas, NM
  87578.
40 mi. N. of Santa Fe.
Price: Moderate.
Credit Cards: None.

You won't find a setting much more spectacular than this. Located on the Truchas plateau, above 8,000 feet, this hacienda-style adobe B&B is at the foot of the southern Rockies with spectacular views of the Rio Grande Valley. It's possible to see Sandia Peak, 100 miles to the south, and San Antonio Mountain, about the same distance to the north in Colorado. Closer to home, four miles east down a dirt road, is the Pecos Wilderness Area, a pristine land of spruce forest, alpine lakes and the towering, 13,000-foot Truchas Peaks. A mile to the west is the centuries-old Hispanic village of Truchas, one of the more picturesque of northern New Mexico's mountain communities.

Curtiss Frank, the owner, has lived in Truchas since the late '70s and has operated the inn since 1983. The four guest rooms are fairly small and none have private baths, but all are authentically decorated in Spanish colonial style. The inn, also a small working farm, is organized around a central courtyard big enough to qualify as a plaza. Breakfasts are served in a cozy common area with fireplace and *viga-and-latilla* ceilings. There is a porch that's perfect for viewing summer lightning storms. Frank knows the mountains well and can recommend hikes. In the winter he can sometimes be persuaded to take guests on horse-drawn sleigh rides.

RANCHO ENCANTADO
Owners: Betty & John
  Egan.
982-3537.
Rte. 4, P.O. Box 57-C, Santa
  Fe, NM 87501.
10 mi. N. of Santa Fe.
Price: Very Expensive.
Credit Cards: AE, DC, MC,
  V.
Handicap. Access: Limited.

This Southwestern-style ranch-inn has the Sangre de Cristo range directly behind it and the distant Jemez Mountains in front. The immediate environment is desert: red earth, green piñon pines and deep blue sky. Rancho Encantado faces west, and there is probably no better lodge in the Santa Fe area for viewing New Mexico's stunning sunsets. The expansive, enchanted setting has made the inn popular over the years with jet setters ranging from Princess Caroline to Robert Redford.

Sprawled over 168 acres, the inn offers horseback riding, tennis, archery and swimming — as

Rancho Encantado has hosted Robert Redford, Princess Caroline and the Dalai Lama.

Leslie Tallant

well as a fine restaurant and full-service bar. The rooms in the main building have an Old West flavor, but those in the *casitas* nearby are decorated in traditional New Mexican style, with *kiva* fireplaces, exposed *vigas*, brick floors, Indian rugs and hand-painted tiles. The resort recently expanded to include a cluster of nearby condominiums that have Southwestern accents but lack the intimacy and charm of the older rooms.

TRIANGLE INN
Owner: Peter Simmons.
455-3375.
P.O. Box 3235, Santa Fe, NM 87501.
U.S. 285, 10 mi. N. of Santa Fe.
Price: Expensive.
Credit Cards: MC, V.

Located on a triangular piece of property, this inn doesn't look like much from the outside. But the five adobe *casitas* clustered around an inner courtyard are charmingly rustic. They sleep from two to four people and come with fireplaces, wood-burning stoves, color TV, radio-casette players and refrigerators. Two have private courtyards. A Continental breakfast is included with the room price. There are a hot tub, exercise area and barbecue pit on the premises. There are splendid views of eroded red mesas against the blue Sangre de Cristo.

LODGING IN TAOS

ADOBE WALL MOTEL
Manager: Ted Mortsinger.
758-3972.
227 E. Kit Carson Rd., Taos, NM 87571.
3.5 blks. E. of plaza.
Price: Inexpensive.
Credit Cards: MC, V.
Handicap. Access: Yes.

An old-fashioned roadside motel, there are twenty clean, standard motel rooms surrounded by several tall cottonwoods. Five minutes' walking distance from the plaza.

BLUE DOOR
Owner: Patricia Allen.
758-8360.
P.O. Box 1168, Taos, NM
  87571.
La Morada Rd., off Rte.
  518.
Price: Moderate.
Credit Cards: MC, V.

This inn, part restored adobe farmhouse and part additions, is located in a rural area just south of Taos proper. Set in the midst of fruit trees, flower gardens, lawns and patios, it has a country-ish, family air about it. An inquisitive toddler named Nicholas roams the premises, as does an extremely amiable dog. Patricia Allen, the toddler's mother, owns and manages the inn, with some help from Nicholas' grandmother, who left Boston to join her daughter in 1991.

Breakfasts are special and may include green chile quiche and blueberry pancakes. There are two units located in the newer part of the house. They're nice, but don't compare to the central common area, a large Spanish-style living room of worn wood floors and massive, dark brown *vigas* that dates back to the turn of the century. A wonderful place to eat breakfast and an equally wonderful place to curl up with a book or a special friend.

THE BROOKS STREET INN
Owner: Susan Stevens.
758-1489.
P.O. Box 4954 / 119 Brooks
  St., Taos, NM 87571.
1 blk. E. of Rte. 68, 3.5
  blocks N.E. of plaza.
Price: Moderate.
Credit Cards: AE, MC, V.
Handicap. Access: Yes.

In 1988, *Country Inn's Bed and Breakfast Magazine* named this one of the 10 best in North America. Built in the '50s as a residence for a local artist, it is not a particularly remarkable structure. Nor is there anything unusual in its quiet, residential setting. Instead, the secret to its success is attention to detail: the bowl of freshly cut flowers and the decanter of sherry that await your arrival; the collection of Western and American Indian artifacts; the fine Southwestern art, weaving and local photography that adorn guest rooms and common area; the cozy reading alcove in the Aspen room; the beautifully carved screen in the Willow Room; the hand-painted antique bed in the Piñon Room; the two-person hammock out back. Add it up and you've got a first-rate place to stay. The fact that it's within easy walking distance of numerous art galleries and shops — and a short drive from Taos Pueblo — is just icing on the cake.

CASA BENAVIDES
Owners: Tom & Barbara
  McCarthy.
758-1772.
137 Kit Carson Rd., Taos,
  NM, 87571.
1 blk. E. of plaza.
Price: Very Expensive.
Credit Cards: AE, MC, V.
Handicap. Access: Limited.

Airy, light and colorful, this centrally-located B&B is bigger than it looks. In early 1991 it had 19 guest rooms, with two more under construction. They're spacious and modern with all the usual Southwestern accents: Navajo rugs, flagstone floors, ceiling fans, skylights, Indian pottery, *kiva* fireplaces. There are even a few surprises. For example, how many places where you've stayed have been decorated with authentic deerskin Indian drums and a real Indian tomahawk? Tom and

Barbara McCarthy, operators of the inn, are native Taoseños who have operated a number of different retail businesses in town. If you want to know where
the shopping bargains are, you can't do better than to consult them.

Burrell Brenneman; courtesy Casa de las Chimeneas

Casa de las Chimeneas, a hacienda-like B&B.

**CASA DE LAS CHIME-
NEAS**
Owner: Susan Vernon.
758-4777.
P.O. Box 5303 / 405 Cor-
doba Rd., Taos, NM
87571.
1 blk. E. of Rte. 68.
Price: Expensive.
Credit Cards: MC, V.
Handicap. Access: Yes.

Stately and serene, Casa de las Chimeneas is
screened from the surrounding residential
neighborhood by a high adobe wall that gives it
the feel of a place apart. Shaded by giant cottonwoods and willows, this hacienda-like inn offers
three guest rooms that look out onto a spacious
lawn and a brilliantly colored flower garden. Potted plants, hand-carved wooden columns, dark
brown , skylights, flagstone floors and regional
works of art make it an example of New Mexico
style at its most refined. Breakfast is different
every day but usually includes a fruit frappe, a fruit dish and a hot entree.
Cheese, crackers, salami, wine, juices and cake are served in the afternoon.

CASA EUROPA
Owners: Rudi & Marcia
Zwicker.
758-9798.
157 Upper Ranchitos Rd.,
Taos, NM 87571.
1.7 miles W. of Rte. 68.
Price: Expensive.
Credit Cards: MC, V.
Handicap. Access: Yes.

It's hard to say what's better at Casa Europa, the
inn (a 200-year-old restored adobe ranch house
that seamlessly blends European and Southwestern decor) or the delectable food. Maybe the best
thing about the place is Marcia and Rudi Zwicker,
the owners, whose qualifications as innkeepers
and food purveyors are impeccable. Rudi was
trained at the Grand Hotel in Nürnberg, Germany,
and the Zwickers ran the Greenbriar Restaurant in
Boulder, Colorado, for 20 years before moving to
New Mexico. Their culinary skill is evidenced by
a breakfast that may include fresh fruit salad, mushroom and asparagus
quiche and a superb homemade danish. For afternoon tea you may be presented with Raspberry Bavarian Cake or Black Forest Torte.

There are six guest rooms. The French Room has a marvelous 1860s' French brass bed, antique hand-hewn wood floors, a marble bath and a triangular blue mirror. The Spa Room has a full-sized whirlpool, while the Taos Mountain Room has a picture-perfect view of — you guessed it — Taos Mountain. There are 14 skylights throughout the inn, a graceful, curving staircase of whitewashed adobe, a crystal chandelier from France and a tin chandelier with electric candles from Mexico.

CASA FELIZ
Owners Noreen Perrin,
   Bonnie McManus, Harry
   Vedoe.
758-9790.
137 Bent St., Taos, NM
   87571.
1.5 blocks N.W. of plaza.
Price: Expensive.
Credit Cards: MC, V.
Handicap. Access: Limited.

Three of the guest rooms in this tiny B&B are clustered around an art gallery. The fourth is located in a next-door cottage. The decor, along with the art, is a little trendy, but it's colorful, playful and nicely done. A great location in the heart of Taos.

CASA DE MILAGROS
Owner: Helen Victor.
758-8001.
P.O. Box 2983 / 321 Kit
   Carson Rd., Taos, NM
   87571.
Rte. 64, 4 blocks E. of
   plaza.
Price: Expensive.
Credit Cards: MC, V.

Known by locals as "the old Ortiz house," this B&B has six guest rooms, a convenient location, an impressive collection of artifacts and artwork, an outdoor hot tub and probably the best homemade granola you'll find anywhere. Helen Victor, the owner and a photographer from New England, has a knack with Indian bread, coffee and blue corn pancakes. She sells the pancake mix, along with her photos, on the premises.

EL MONTE LODGE
Managers: George & Pat
   Schumacher.
758-3171.
317 Kit Carson Rd., Taos,
   NM 87571.
4 blks. E. of plaza.
Price: Moderate.
Credit Cards: All.
Handicap. Access: Yes.

This 1930s motel has a certain rustic charm. Its 13 rooms are located in *casitas* and its grounds are graced by cottonwoods. It is a bit pricey. The rooms, after all, are of standard motel design; you're paying for the location.

EL PUEBLO LODGE
Manager: Gretchen Martin.
758-8700.
P.O. Box 92 / 412 Paseo del
   Pueblo Norte, Taos, NM
   87571.

This motel dates from the early 1940s. It is a little run-down but the rooms are clean and some have fireplaces. An outdoor hot tub and pool are available for relaxation. If you want newer accommodations, there are condominiums on the premises.

4 blks. N. of plaza.
Price: Moderate.
Credit Cards: AE, MC, V.
Handicap. Access: Limited.

EL RINCON
Owners: Nina Meyers &
    Paul Castillo.
758-4874.
114 Kit Carson, Taos, NM
    87571.
0.5 blks. E. of plaza.
Price: Moderate.
Credit Cards: V, MC.
Handicap. Access: Yes.

The 12 guest rooms in this centrally-located inn are each dazzlingly different. The Los Angelitos room is decorated with a collection of angels from around the world. The Yellow Bird Deer Room is filled with authentic Indian beadwork, drums, Navajo rugs, Pueblo pottery, Sioux moccasins and kachinas nestled in *nichos*, nooks recessed into the walls. The Pioneer Room has a Franklin stove, a claw-foot tub, blacksmith's tools, a Winchester rifle hanging on a wall and a red-and-black-plaid buffalo hide coverlet on the bed. The Paisley Room (believe it or not) sports hand-carved teak woodwork, Afghani rugs, a Kuwaiti chest and a Balinese fertility goddess suspended over the queen-size bed.

Much of this amazing array comes from a trading post on the property. Five of the rooms have their own whirlpools and 10 have fireplaces. The guest rooms are located in three buildings: the two-story main building, the ground floor of which dates to the 1800s; an adobe compound with its own courtyard; and La Dona Luz, until 1984 one of the best and oldest restaurants in Taos.

HACIENDA DEL SOL
Owners: John & Marcine
    Landon.
758-0287.
P.O. Box 177 / 109 Mabel
    Dodge Ln., Taos, NM
    87571.
0.2 mi. E. of Rte. 64.
Price: Moderate.
Credit Cards: MC, V.

Shaded by giant cottonwoods, ponderosa pines, blue spruce and willows, this B&B abuts Taos Pueblo land and has an unobstructed view of Taos Mountain. Six guest rooms are located in the main house, a beautiful 180-year-old adobe that was part of art patroness Mabel Dodge Luhan's estate; a seventh is in a newly constructed adobe *casita*. Throughout the main building are brick and flagstone floors, pueblo-style archways, *viga*-and-*latilla* ceilings, *bancos* (adobe benches), *nichos* and stained-glass windows. The inn is also replete with modern luxuries. One room has a steam bath and the honeymoon suite has a double-size black jacuzzi on a mahogany platform with a skylight above it for stargazing. A bottle of champagne and flowers await the lucky occupants of this room.

HOTEL LA FONDA DE TAOS
Manager: Saki Karavas.
758-2211.

This atmospheric 1930s hotel is the only lodging establishment on the plaza. The lobby is lit by a stained-glass skylight, the walls are plastered with old newspaper clippings, paintings and Indian rugs. Off to the side is a room containing erotic

P.O. Box 1447, Taos, NM
  87571.
S. side of plaza.
Price: Moderate.
Credit Cards: AE, MC, V.

paintings by D.H. Lawrence (price of admission, $3). Twenty-four rooms are located upstairs, along red-carpeted corridors and behind turquoise doors. They are nothing fancy; a little cramped but they look like what they are: 1930s New Mexican hotel rooms. If you like authenticity and don't mind a little mustiness, this could be the place for you.

Art gallery at the Kachina Lodge.

Murrae Haynes

KACHINA LODGE
Manager: Betty Ditto.
758-2275.
N. Pueblo Rd., P.O. Box
  NN, Taos, NM 87571.
4 blks. N. of plaza.
Price: Expensive.
Credit Cards: AE, D, DC,
  MC, V.
Handicap. Access: Yes.

Just north of the city center, this Best Western is a classic, sprawling roadside motel straight out of the 1950s. (A recent renovation only enhanced its original character.) Don't miss the semicircular Kiva Coffee Shop, which is dominated by a bizarre, hand-carved totem pole. The 122 guest rooms look onto a spacious courtyard that has a broad lawn, tall pine trees and a large swimming pool. The Indian decor here is laid on so thick as to be exploitative and there are even Indian dances on summer nights. But that's how they did things 30 years ago. What saves this place — and what makes it — is that it evokes nostalgia without really trying, right down to the Naugahyde chairs in the Kachina Cabaret.

KOSHARI INN
Managers: Bill & Denise
  Lin.
758-7199.
P.O. Box 6612 / 910 E. Kit
  Carson Rd., Taos, NM
  87571.
1 mi. E. of plaza.
Price: Inexpensive.
Credit Cards: MC, V.
Handicap. Access: Yes.

A standard, affordable motel with 12 rooms, a swimming pool, barbecue pit and picnic facilities. The rooms are a little old-looking, but they are clean and feature typical Southwestern decor. One unusual touch: mountain bikes are available free of charge for those who wish to tour the countryside or transport themselves quickly and easily around Taos' often congested streets.

La Posada de Taos.

Murrae Haynes

LA POSADA DE TAOS
Owner: Sue Smoot.
758-8164.
P.O. Box 1118 / 309 Juanita
  Lane, Taos, NM 87571.
4.5 blks. W. of plaza.
Price: Moderate.
Credit Cards: No.
Handicap. Access: Yes.

Opened in 1984, this B&B — the first in Taos — has an air of seclusion, perhaps because it's located at the end of a quiet dirt road. Whatever it is, this is a very nice place to stay. The attractively landscaped inner courtyard has a wooden arbor as its centerpiece. The cozy common area has bookshelves and a *kiva*-style fireplace. French windows in the dining room open onto a patio, a garden and a superb view of dramatic Taos Mountain. And the guest rooms feature a distinctive mix of Southwestern, European, even Indonesian furnishings. The honeymoon suite has a skylight directly over the bed.

LAUGHING HORSE INN
Owner: Rosie Teo.
758-8350.
P.O. Box 4904, Taos, NM
  87571.
On Rte. 68, 1 mile N. of
  plaza.
Price: Inexpensive.
Credit Cards: MC, V.

You've never stayed *anywhere* like this. The inn describes itself as "a European-style hotel in a Southwestern setting," but that doesn't even come close. It's more like a blend of '60s funk, '90s technology and old, old Hispanic. Call it unorthodox — and a lot of fun.

Located right off Taos' main drag on the banks of the Rio Pueblo, this ramshackle, gaudily-painted adobe was at one time home to Spud Johnson, buddy of D.H. Lawrence and a quintessential Taos character during the 1920s. Here Spud published *The Laughing Horse Press*, a compendium of literary and satiric pieces, and entertained prominent artistic and literary figures.

The oldest part of the inn is a labyrinth of dark rooms, including a kitchen with a cracked mud floor. Attached to it is an enclosed passive solar wing filled with light. The 13 guest quarters vary in size, style and options. A spacious penthouse perched atop the main building sleeps seven, while many of the older rooms can barely handle two. Styles vary from classic New Mexican to modern A-frame to a room built onto a Chevy truck. Some rooms have fireplaces, one has its own sauna, another a waterbed, another a futon. Many rooms come with a VCR, color TV and/or audio casette player. The inn also has an extensive music and video library that you're free to use. Hearty breakfasts are available, although they're not included in the room rate. It also provides free use of 10-speed touring bikes. Finally, in the courtyard, a hot tub froths and foams under the New Mexico sky.

MABEL DODGE LUHAN
HOUSE
Manager: Rachel
  Chisholm.
758-9456.
P.O. Box 1529 / 242
  Morada Lane, Taos, NM
  87571.
1 mi. N. of U.S. 64.
Price: Expensive.
Credit Cards: MC, V.

Set on five acres at the edge of a vast, open tract of Indian land, this rambling, three-story, 22-room adobe hacienda is part of Taos history. It is one of only two B&Bs in the Taos area that are national and state historic sites. This is primarily because of Mabel Dodge Luhan, who arrived in New Mexico in 1918, when she was 39. She came at the urging of her husband, artist Maurice Sterne, who was in Taos to paint Indians. Sterne eventually left, but Mabel stayed, married a Taos Pueblo Indian named Tony Luhan, and bought and renovated this 200-year-old structure. It quickly came to be known as the Big House.

Throughout the '20s, '30s and '40s the Big House was visited by a procession of the brightest artistic and literary lights of the day and Mabel became known as a patron of the arts. D.H. Lawrence painted the windows of the second-story bathroom. A famous painting by Georgia O'Keeffe was inspired by a distant white cross that can still be seen from the east-facing windows. Carl

The Mabel Dodge Luhan House, a hub of Taos activity since the 1920s.

Murrae Haynes

Jung spoke at length about the collective unconscious on the outside patio. Other guests included Aldous Huxley and Willa Cather.

After Mabel died in 1962, the property was bought by actor-producer Dennis Hopper, who lived in it during the filming of *Easy Rider*. In 1977 a group of academics purchased the house and used it as a center for seminars, study groups and so forth. It became a B&B in the early '80s, although workshops are still held here, as are guided tours every Sunday, Monday and Friday (See *Culture*, Chapter Four).

If it sounds like peace and quiet are in short supply, keep in mind that it is indeed a very big house and that care is taken not to disturb guests. But there's no getting around the fact that the house is a hub of activity, as it always has been. That's why it's special. Besides history — and often, people — the house is filled with *viga*-and-*latilla* ceilings, arched Pueblo-style doorways, fireplaces and dark hardwood floors. Mabel's Bedroom Suite still contains her original bed; Tony's Bedroom opens out onto a sleeping porch; and the Solarium, accessible only by a steep, narrow staircase, is literally a room of glass (Mabel sunbathed in the nude here). There are nine rooms in the main house, a cottage for two and a newly-constructed guest house containing eight Southwestern-style rooms. Breakfast in the spacious dining room is on the house, but dinner (served seven nights a week) is extra.

OLD TAOS GUESTHOUSE
Owners: Tim & Leslie
  Reeves.
758-5448.
P.O. Box 6552 / 1028 Witt
  Rd., Taos, NM 87571
1.8 mi. E. of plaza.
Price: Moderate.
Credit Cards: MC, V.

Nestled in a grove of ponderosa pines, cotton-woods, willows and birches in a rural area just east of Taos, this 150-year-old, recently-renovated adobe hacienda has plenty of rural Spanish charm — not to mention wonderful views of the nearby Sangre de Cristo range and the Taos Plateau. Its six guest rooms look onto a lovely courtyard and the central living area (where breakfast is served) is classically Southwestern in design and decor. Innkeepers Tim and Leslie Reeves are outdoor enthusiasts and can discuss in detail what the Taos area has to offer in terms of downhill and cross-country skiing, hiking, mountain biking, whitewater rafting, even hot springs bathing.

THE RUBY SLIPPER
Owners: Diane Fichtelberg
  & Beth Goldman.
758-0613.
P.O. Box 2069 / 416 La
  Lomita, Taos, NM 87571.
2 mi. S.W. of plaza.
Price: Moderate.
Credit Cards: MC, V.
Handicap. Access: Limited.

The Ruby Slipper is named for the magical slippers that transported Dorothy from the Land of Oz back home to Kansas. The seven guest rooms are named after Oz characters. If you're getting the idea that this is a B&B with a bit of whimsy, you're on the right track. The rooms have some unusual touches, like an aqua-colored tile floor and a king-size waterbed. But the decor for the most part remains within the bounds of standard Southwestern: *kiva* fireplaces, Mexican tile bathrooms, handcrafted willow furniture. Nice, but it could have been more daring.

Nonetheless, this is a distinctive B&B in another sense. The innkeepers, Diane Fichtelberg and Beth Goldman, have made a special point of reaching out to the gay community, although non-gay guests are welcome as well. "It's the people that make the difference," says Diane. "We have an interesting mix here, both gay and non-gay, and we've found that when people meet in this kind of setting it's a great way to break down stereotypes and get to know each other as unique individuals."

SAGEBRUSH INN
Manager: Roger Mariani.
758-2254.
P.O. Box 557, Taos, NM
  87571.
Rte. 68, 3 mi. S. of plaza.
Price: Moderate.
Credit Cards: AE, DC, MC,
  V.
Handicap. Access: Limited.

The Sagebrush Inn is one of Taos' oldest hotels. Opened in 1929, it is also one of the town's hottest night spots, with live music, dancing and frequent appearances by singer and Taos resident Michael Martin Murphey. Built in Pueblo-Mission style, the inn is a sprawling structure with 81 rooms, two restaurants, a bar, a swimming pool, two whirlpools and two tennis courts. The decor is Indian and Spanish and includes a number of original paintings from Southwestern masters.

SAN GERONIMO LODGE
Manager: Craig Schumacher.
758-7117.
P.O. Box, 2491, Taos, NM 87571.
Witt Rd., 2 mi. E. of plaza.
Price: Moderate.
Credit Cards: All.

San Geronimo Lodge sits on 2.5 wooded acres near the juncture of the Taos Plateau with the Sangre de Cristo. It's the oldest resort hotel in Taos. Opened in 1925, the lodge includes a restored farmhouse that predates the 1800s, an outdoor swimming pool, a hot tub, a sauna and an art gallery. There are 18 rooms, six with fireplaces, all with private baths. The rooms in the older part of the inn are more rustic and interesting — a few actually have sloping floors.

SUN GOD LODGE
Manager: Joyce Ward.
758-3162.
P.O. Box 1713, Taos, NM 87571.
Rte. 68, 1 mi. S. of plaza.
Price: Inexpensive.
Credit Cards: AE, D, MC, V.
Handicap. Access: Yes.

A cute roadside motel done in pueblo style. The 33 rooms, organized around a parking lot and a grassy area with trees, are of standard motel design. Some have kitchenettes. An indoor hot tub awaits your weary body.

TAOS INN
Owner: Carolyn Haddock.
758-2233.
125 Paseo del Pueblo Norte, Taos, NM 87571.
0.5 blks. N. of plaza.
Price: Expensive.
Credit Cards: AE, DC, MC, V.
Handicap. Access: Yes.

If immersion in the colorful atmosphere of New Mexican arts, crafts and history is your cup of tea or tequila, you can't do better than to stay at the Taos Inn. Taos' answer to the Grand Hotel, the inn has National Landmark status and was thoroughly restored and modernized in the early 1980s. In the lobby you can meet all the social types Taos has to offer (a pleasantly motley crew); and branching off the lobby are the Adobe Bar and Doc Martin's Restaurant (see *Restaurants*, Chapter Five). Sometimes called "the community living room," the Taos Inn lobby is a people watcher's paradise. It serves as an art gallery with vibrantly colorful rugs displayed from the indoor balconies, as well as sophisticated graphic arts and even clothing on view.

The lobby was once an outdoor plaza with a well surrounded by distinguished 19th-century family residences. One of these was the home and office of Taos' first physician, Dr. T. Paul Martin. Many Taoseños were born and ministered to in what is nowadays the restaurant. Martin and his wife eventually bought the neighboring houses and converted them to apartments for local artists. The Taos Society of Artists was founded in the Martin's living room in 1915, and a Meet-the-Artist series is held at the hotel. The property has been an inn since 1935.

Each of the 40 guest rooms is graced with a distinct personality. Most rooms have *kiva* fireplaces (wood is supplied), Taos-style antique furniture, Mexican-

The lobby of the Taos Inn is also an art gallery.

Murrae Haynes

tile bathrooms, handwoven Indian bedspreads — plus cable TV! Squeaky, old-time wooden floorboards can be heard under the new wall-to-wall carpeting. Several rooms open onto a balcony overlooking the lobby, while several are adjacent tp a quiet courtyard in the rear (less historic) section of the inn. A swimming pool is open in warm weather and for weary skiers' bones and muscles, a whirlpool bubbles invitingly.

WHISTLING WATERS
Owner: Al & Jo Huston.
758-7798.
Talpa Rte., P.O. Box 9, Ranchos de Taos, NM 87557.
Ortiz Road, 0.5 mi. N. of Rte. 518.
Price: Moderate.
Credit Cards: None.

Like most adobe buildings in Taos, Whistling Waters is a sprawling structure of indeterminate age, parts of it probably more than 200 years old. The entry was once the residence of an herbalist who helped birth babies here. The dining room was a drive-up grocery store for horse-drawn wagons; the living room the grocery's storage area.

In 1986, when Al and Jo Huston bought this building just south of Taos, the roof was sagging and the walls were beginning to buckle. Today, after a wonderful restoration job, it is one of the most charming and affordable B&Bs in Taos. With its brick floors; *viga*-and-*latilla* ceilings; four-foot-thick adobe walls; low, arched doorways and sunny courtyards, the inn exudes Old World Spanish charm.

The water flowing through an ancient *acequia* out back gives Whistling Waters its name. But it's the owners themselves, transplants from Kansas, who seem to be whistling, so happy are they to be in Taos running a B&B. Their friendly informality, not to mention their substantial breakfasts, help make this a near perfect place to stay.

THE WILLOWS INN
Owner: Van de Kerckhove.
758-2558.
P.O. Box 4558, Taos, NM 87571.
Corner of Kit Carson and Dolan.
Price: Expensive.
Credit Cards: MC, V.
Handicap. Access: Limited.

Only a tiny green sign inlaid on a large adobe wall lets the passer-by know that there's a B&B here. Look behind that wall and you'll see a stately two-story adobe with spacious lawn and several tall, graceful willow trees. The former home of a well-known local painter, it has been a lodge since 1990. The innkeepers are European and they've imparted a dash of Old World sophistication. The five guest rooms blend Spanish, Mexican and Indian motifs. Breakfasts are hearty and different every day. The artwork throughout the inn is exquisite.

LODGING NEAR TAOS

THE ABOMINABLE SNOWMANSION
Managers: Phil & Penny Kirk.
776-8298.
P.O. Box 3271, Taos, NM 87571.
Rte. 150, halfway between Taos and Taos Ski Valley.
Price: Inexpensive.
Credit Cards: MC, V.
Handicap. Access: Limited.

Located in the old Hispanic village of Arroyo Seco, the Abominable Snowmansion wins, hands down, the contest for the most outrageously named ski lodge in the Taos area. It's also tops when it comes to friendly informality, fun and affordability. A member of American Youth Hostels, Inc., the Snowmansion is a hostel only during the off (non-ski) season. In the winter, it's a budget B&B, although hostel members get discounts.

The Snowmansion attracts mainly young people, although old-timers are more than welcome. The quarters are dormitory-style with bunk beds; sexes are segregated. The breakfasts, all you can eat, are straightforward: eggs, bacon, pancakes, etc. The common area, containing pinball machines, a pool table and a fireplace, is a social hub. In fact, meeting new people may be the best thing about this place. On a typical weekend night during the ski season, as many as 100 people bunk down here. The Snowmansion is run by Phil

and Penny Kirk, former professional ski racers and current outdoor enthusiasts. If you want in on things recreational in the Taos area, talk to these folks.

ALPINE LODGE
Owner: Ilse Woerndle.
754-2952.
P.O. Box 67, Red River, NM
   87558.
At the ski area.
Closed: End of ski season
   to mid-May.
Price: Inexpensive.
Credit Cards: AE, MC, V.
Handicap. Access: Yes.

This lodge is located on the banks of the Red River, within easy walking distance of the Red River ski area. It's been run by Ilse Woerndle, a native of Germany, and her family for over 30 years. Charmingly Bavarian, the cozy inn has 46 rooms, a restaurant, a bar with live music, and a ski rental shop.

AMIZETTE INN
Manager: Pat Walsh.
776-2451.
P.O. Box 756, Taos Ski
   Valley, NM 87525.
1.5 miles W. of Taos Ski
   Valley on Rte. 150.
Price: Moderate.
Credit Cards: AE, MC, V.

Nice setting, in a thick pine forest on the banks of the Rio Hondo. Though this inn lacks character, it's easily affordable and an indoor hot tub and dry sauna are available to soothe your weary bones after a hard day's skiing.

ARROWHEAD LODGE
Manager: Heinz Seifert.
754-2255.
P.O. Box 261, Red River,
   NM 87558.
Closed: End of ski season
   to Memorial Day.
Price: Moderate.
Credit Cards: D, MC, V.

This quiet, no-frills lodge sits on a side street off Red River's main drag, within easy reach of the ski area. There are 19 units, some with fireplaces, some with kitchenettes. In warm weather, a sun deck, barbecue pit and several picnic tables are available for guests' use.

AUSTING HAUS HOTEL
Owner: Paul Austing.
776-2649.
P.O. Box 8, Taos Ski Valley,
   NM 87525.
Rte. 150, 1.5 miles W. of
   Taos Ski Valley.
Price: Expensive.
Credit Cards: MC, V.
Handicap. Access: Limited.

Over 70,000 board feet of timber, with 3,000 interlocking joints, were used in the construction of this hotel, making it the largest timber frame building in the United States. An impressive feat, but this Alpine-style lodge is missing that intangible thing called character.

CASA RINCONADA
Owner: JoAnne Gladin de
   la Fuente.
579-4466.

Set in the ancient farming village of Rinconada, this reasonably-priced B&B borders a fruit orchard and is literally a stone's throw from the Rio Grande. There's just one unit, a small adobe

P.O. Box 10-A Star Rte.,
　Embudo, NM 87531.
Rte. 68, 20 mi. S. of Taos.
Price: Moderate.
Credit Cards: MC, V.

house painted pink, blue and yellow that can accommodate up to six people. It could be more tastefully furnished, but it has all you need: full kitchen, full bath, television, air conditioning, a wood-burning stove, even a small exercise room.

　　　The owner, a sculptor named JoAnne Gladin de la Fuente, lives next door. She won't cook for you, but she will provide you with the raw materials to cook your own breakfasts. She'll also provide a complimentary bottle of wine when you arrive. A lovely time to visit Casa Rinconada is in the spring when the apple, cherry, apricot and peach trees in the orchard are in full blossom. But harvest time in early fall is even better. The trees produce so much fruit that you're welcome to help yourself.

HONDO LODGE

Owner: Brooke Franzge.
776-2277.
P.O. Box 89, Taos Ski
　Valley, Taos, NM 87525.
Closed: Non-ski season.
Price: Expensive.
Credit Cards: AE, MC, V.

Hondo Lodge, in business since 1955, is the oldest hotel at the ski valley. It is also one of the few that doesn't offer a ski-week package plan. If you just want to stay at the valley for a night or two, this is probably the best place to go. It's located in the heart of the resort and has all you need: whirlpool and sauna, a cozy bar and a restaurant called The Loft that serves an extraordinary variety of cheese fondues. There are 25 rooms in the hotel, two more in a nearby apartment. They're not fancy, but they're functional and clean.

HOTEL EDELWEISS

Owners: Ilse & Bernard
　Mayer.
776-2301.
P.O. Box 675, Taos Ski
　Valley, Taos, NM 87525.
Price: Very Expensive.
Credit Cards: AE, MC, V.

One of the runs at the ski valley ends at Hotel Edelweiss' front door. It's hard to beat the cozy European atmosphere and impossible to get any closer to the slopes. The big stone fireplace in the lobby is a perfect place to warm up on a cold winter's morning before hitting the slopes. The hotel's restaurant, La Croissanterie, serves hearty soups and sandwiches, just the kind of fuel you need for afternoon skiing and a whirlpool, sauna and massage therapist await you at the end of the day. Hotel Edelweiss has no bar, so it's quieter here at night than at some of the other lodges in the valley.

HOTEL ST. BERNARD

Owner: Jean Mayer.
776-2251.
Taos Ski Valley, NM 87525.
Closed: Non-ski season.
Price: Very Expensive.
Credit Cards: AE.

Jean Mayer, owner of Hotel St. Bernard, is also technical director of the Taos Ski Valley Ski School. The only guests accepted at the hotel are those on the ski school's seven-day plan. The package includes three meals a day, including seven-course gourmet dinners prepared by French chefs. The hotel's 28 rooms are located in attractive A-frame units with sun decks at the bottom of the slopes. The ski season is usually booked by the end of August, so plan ahead.

THE INN AT ANGEL FIRE
Owners: Linda and Bill
   Shanhouse.
377-2504.
Drawer 578, Angel Fire,
   NM 87710.
Rte. 434, 30 mi. E. of Taos.
Price: Inexpensive.
Credit Cards: MC, V.
Handicap. Access: Yes.

One mile from the ski area, this 32-room inn has a cozy, country feel to it. There's a dry sauna here to relax in after a day's skiing and a video game room to keep the kids occupied. Ski packages, including lift tickets and meals, are available through the lodge.

INN AT OJO
Owners: Rob Dorival &
   K.C. Kennedy.
583-2428.
P.O. Box 215, Ojo Caliente,
   NM 87549.
U.S. 285, 35 mi. W. of Taos.
Closed: November.
Price Inexpensive.
Credit Cards: All.

A few years back, self-described travel addict Rob Dorival decided to settle down somewhere in northern New Mexico. He chose Ojo Caliente, an old Hispanic village known for its healing mineral springs. He bought a 1950s motel near the springs and converted it into the Inn at Ojo, part B&B, part youth hostel.

The nine guest rooms (three set aside for the hostel, six for the B&B) face a small courtyard of sycamore trees and look just like what they are: 30-year-old motel rooms. But they are clean, functional and, as Dorival puts it, "funky and friendly." Some units come with gas stoves and small refrigerators. Accompanying breakfasts are prepared at a tiny restaurant that specializes in gourmet natural foods. Off the restaurant is an equally tiny art gallery and bookshop.

The inn rents mountain bikes to guests and it can also arrange for horseback rides at a nearby stable. "We cater to people who love the outdoors," Dorival explains. "Not necessarily jocks, but people who go into nature for health and spiritual reasons."

THE LEGENDS HOTEL
Manager: Lynda Plante.
377-6401.
Drawer B, Angel Fire, NM
   87710.
At the ski area.
Price: Moderate.
Credit Cards: All.
Handicap. Access: Yes.

With 157 rooms, the Legends Hotel is by far the biggest lodging establishment in Angel Fire. The decor is contemporary Southwestern and the ski area right outside your window. The inn has two restaurants, a delicatessen, a lounge with a disc jockey and an indoor pool and hot tub.

MOORE REST INN
Manager: Owen Smith.
377-6813.
P.O. Box 138, Eagle Nest,
NM 87718.
N.M. 64, 30 mi. E. of Taos.
Price: Inexpensive.
Credit Cards: AE, D, MC,
V.
Handicap. Access: Yes.

This modest, 32-room motel on the shores of Eagle Nest Lake isn't fancy, but it is functional. A kitchen is available to guests, as is a recreation room with fireplace, video games and pinball machines. Owen Smith, the manager, has fishing tales to share and pointers for those who want to try their luck in the lake.

OJO CALIENTE
  MINERAL SPRINGS
Manager: Viron Huff.
583-2233.
P.O. Box 468, Ojo Caliente,
NM 87549.
U.S. 285, 35 mi. W. of Taos.
Price: Inexpensive.
Credit Cards: MC, V.

In the 1500s, Spanish explorer Cabeza de Vaca chanced upon these desert hot springs, a favorite bathing spot of local Indians, and described them as "wonderful waters bursting out of a mountain." (See "Spas and Hot Springs" in *Recreation*, Chapter Six.) Today they are the focus of this no-frills, 28-room resort located next door. It provides massage, herbal wraps and facials and has its own restaurant and gift shop. Owned by a longtime Ojo Caliente family, the resort is nothing fancy, but it's affordable and friendly. If you want luxury, all you have to do is get in the water.

THE PLUM TREE
Owner: Rich Thibodeaux.
758-4696
P.O. Box A-1, Pilar, NM
87531.
Rte. 68, 15 mi. S. of Taos.
Price: Inexpensive.
Credit Cards: MC, V.
Handicap. Access: Yes.

The Plum Tree is half youth hostel and half B&B. The hostel has a common kitchen, private rooms for couples, dorms for women and a bunkhouse for men. The B&B accommodations are spacious, rustic and a bit funky, but they offer wonderful views of the Rio Grande as it curls its way through the centuries-old village of Pilar. The inn offers workshops in painting and photography in the summer and a program of nature studies in the fall. If outdoor activities are your passion, you'll be happy here as whitewater rafting, hiking and cross-country skiing are all nearby. The Plum Tree is not the lap of luxury, but it's friendly, casual and affordable.

SALSA DEL SALTO
Owners: Dadou Mayer,
  Mary Hockett.
776-2422.
P.O. Box 453, El Prado, NM
87529.
Rte. 150, 8 mi. W. of Taos
  Ski Valley.
Price: Expensive.
Credit Cards: MC, V.

Salsa del Salto has the best of two worlds. Located at the point where the Sangre de Cristo rise dramatically from Taos Plateau, it offers easy access to the mountains and expansive views of the desert. The inn itself is light, airy and contemporary. Its six guest rooms are accented in Southwestern style, the central living and dining area is divided by a massive stone fireplace and green tennis courts and a sparkling blue pool beckon outside. Dadou Mayer, one of the owners, is an amateur ski racer and an accomplished chef — don't miss his eggs Benedict! — while his partner, Mary Hockett, is an experienced equestrian and a top-notch baker. This is the only lodge outside Taos Ski Valley that offers week-long ski packages. Rio Grande rafting packages are also available.

TAOS MOUNTAIN LODGE
Managers: Anne & Randel Waites.
776-2229.
P.O. Box 698, Taos Ski Valley, NM 87527
Rte. 150, 1 mi. W. of Taos Ski Valley.
Closed: End of ski season to mid-May.
Price: Moderate.
Credit Cards: AE, D, MC, V.
Handicap. Access: Yes.

This place is a pleasant surprise. Located on a south-facing mountainside, it has 10 rooms, including two split-level A-frame suites that can hold from four to six people. The suites are equipped with satellite television — a must in the mountains — and kitchenettes. All the rooms are done in tasteful, if typical, Southwestern decor. An indoor whirlpool is here to relieve your aches, and a small liquor and grocery store means you don't have to drive to satisfy the munchies. You can't get closer to the ski area proper without having to pay considerably more than you pay here.

THUNDERBIRD LODGE
Owners: Elisabeth & Tom Brownell.
776-2280.
P.O. Box 87, Taos Ski Valley, NM 87525
At the Ski Valley.
Closed: Non-ski season.
Price: Moderate.
Credit Cards: None.

The Thunderbird is in the heart of Taos Ski Valley, within easy walking distance of the slopes. Preference is given to guests on seven-day ski packages, which include unlimited use of all lifts, three meals a day and six ski lessons. The lodge will take guests not on the package, but they must stay a minimum of two nights.

The guest rooms are unremarkable, but the Thunderbird has a lot to offer: saunas and whirlpools, professional massage therapists, a fine restaurant specializing in European and Southwestern cuisine, a lively atmospheric bar with elk antlers and bearskins on the walls, a massive stone fireplace, live music seven nights a week; and regular wine and beer tasting. Like virtually all the lodging in the valley, the decor is supposed to be European alpine. If you've got any doubts, wall posters of the Swiss and Bavarian Alps will remove them.

CHAPTER FOUR
What to See, What to Do
CULTURE

Jesse L. Nusbaum; Courtesy Museum of New Mexico

Band concert under Palace of Governors portal, ca. 1915.

The renowned enchantment of the Santa Fe–Taos area has simple origins: the place is powerfully unlike any other in the world. Perhaps, nowhere else in this country can you enjoy such a distinctive blend of cultural traditions and opportunities. A vivid spectrum of art, crafts, music and architecture springs from the area's three primary cultures: Indian, Spanish and Anglo, and from their strong links to its compelling natural environment.

Culture in the Santa Fe–Taos area is more like a three-layer cake than the proverbial American melting pot: each layer is made with different ingredients and recipes. The Indian and Spanish traditions are especially rich and enduring. Native Americans were building impressive networks of roads and villages throughout the Southwest while Europe was still in the Dark Ages, and Santa Fe was founded by the Spanish more than a decade before the arrival of the Pilgrims at Plymouth Rock.

Many visitors are drawn to the art of the area's Indian and Hispanic peoples

72

— art that grows out of what Taos photographer Bill Davis calls "the mixture of the divine and the human in the landscape." The Pueblo Indians see no distinction between the physical and spiritual landscape. The land is home to the spirits, and the Pueblos read the earth as Europeans read their Bibles: mountains, rivers and mesas contain stories about historical events and how to survive on the land. Dancing, visiting shrines and creating pottery, jewelry and baskets are all acts guided by spirit.

Many Indian artists acknowledge spirit as the source of their talents. "Clay is very special," says Santa Clara potter Ray Tafoya. "It's giving us life. We can't use it out of disrespect." Artists typically operate within their own tribal tradition, building and adapting it to new needs and purposes to produce highly individualistic work.

For the Hispanics, by contrast, spirituality is not so much imbued in the land as it is an inseparable part of being. During their generations in New Mexico, isolated from their native homes, the land has been the mother who sustained them. In his environmental memoir *If Mountains Die*, Taos author John Nichols writes of "embracing this landscape not because it is picture-postcard beautiful, but because of the human legends and histories and personalities that transform the natural world into a living part of the complex social organism."

The art of the Hispanic people springs from an everyday life that is permeated with the Catholic faith. The statue of San Ysidro carried to the fields each spring to ensure a good planting, the *retablos* (paintings on wood slabs) of Our Lady of Guadalupe that are touched each morning with a whispered prayer are art that is both loved and used. Similarly, the murals of the Virgin that grace many adobe homes, the pageantry of the fiestas, the village parades on saints' days, and even the meticulously accessorized "low-rider" automobiles, are all forms of art in everyday life.

The Santa Fe–Taos area provides fertile ground for art that is rooted in northern Europe. In the early part of the 20th century, Santa Fe and Taos were home to a bevy of Eastern artists who established Southwestern "Sohos" of their day. You can admire their breathtaking landscape paintings in numerous area galleries (see "Traditional Art" under "Galleries" in *Shopping,* Chapter Seven). These painters — Josef Bakos, Nicolai Fechin, Ernest Blumenschein, Randall Davey and others — inspired generations of successors who continue to explore the landscape and the unusual clarity of light. Europe has also provided Santa Fe–Taos with world-class opera and chamber music, both of which thrive in the clear desert air.

An excellent place to begin your cultural exploration is at one of the fine museums described below. For Spanish folk art, start with the Millicent Rogers Museum in Taos and the Museum of International Folk Art in Santa Fe. The Museum of Indian Arts and Culture will introduce you to the amazing diversity of Pueblo Indian culture and art. The Museum of Fine Arts in Santa Fe and the Harwood Foundation Museum in Taos will open up the world of the early landscape painters for you.

If architecture is a passion, see the "Architecture" section, below, and explore further at the Southwest Room of the Santa Fe Public Library or the Harwood Library in Taos. Allow plenty of time for strolling and soaking in the region's adobe vernacular. Check with the chambers of commerce in each town for architecture tours. These are occasionally offered by local civic organizations.

History is at your fingertips at the Palace of the Governors Museum in Santa Fe and at several small private museums in Taos (see "Museums" in this chapter). The history of the Atomic Age unfolds in a presentation at Los Alamos National Laboratory. If you are interested in prehistory, drive out to Bandelier National Monument, Pecos National Historical Site or Chaco Culture National Historical Park. These ancient sites were bustling communities long before Columbus was born.

In addition, there are enough concerts, dance and theater performances and seasonal festivities to keep even the most vigorous traveler busy. Listing everything would be almost impossible, so be sure to glance at the entertainment sections of the local newspapers for each week's events.

ARCHITECTURE

Adobe architecture, as much as the landscape itself, gives New Mexico a distinctive identity. In a nation where more and more places look identical, the Santa Fe–Taos area still maintains its definition of itself. It's not that architecture here doesn't change — it certainly does — but the traditions have evolved during hundreds of years and reflect the contributions of three different cultures.

For a look at old adobe architecture, stroll around the Santa Fe Plaza, along E. De Vargas St. and up Canyon Rd. Or explore Taos Plaza and its side streets. The soft, rounded adobe structures appear to have grown out of the earth. Modern decorative flourishes notwithstanding, these buildings are the architectural descendants of mud-and-stick dwellings built thousands of years ago by the first Indian inhabitants of the Southwest.

As the centuries passed, the people adapted techniques and materials to suit their purposes. For example, mud walls were often built up a handful at a time, a technique called "puddling," or they were laid with "bricks" of mud cut from stream banks. Ruins, such as those at Chaco Canyon and Bandelier National Monument, reveal sophisticated use of sandstone and other rock for the construction of four- and five-story apartment-type buildings. The stone walls were mortared with mud.

When the first Spanish settlers arrived in the early 1600s, the Pueblo Indians quickly adopted their adobe brick-making techniques. Spanish knowledge of adobe construction and their use of the *horno* (OR-no), a beehive-shaped outdoor oven, was acquired from the Moors and derives originally from the Middle East and Mesopotamia.

*The Eldorado, an example of
modern Santa Fe style.*

Wendy Walsh

To get a feel for what an early adobe dwelling was like, visit the so-called "Oldest House in the U.S.A" at 215 E. De Vargas St. in Santa Fe. The city's first residents lived in similar houses. The cavelike interior features a corner fireplace of Spanish origin. The oldest parts of the walls are of puddled adobe. Contrast this with the modern, five-story Eldorado Hotel at 309 W. San Francisco St. to see how flexible the idea of mud construction can be. The Eldorado is a recent expression of the Santa Fe style or Spanish-Pueblo Revival style that has been in vogue since the 1920s. Like most of the newer buildings in Santa Fe, the Eldorado is not true adobe; it simply wears an adobe-style stucco facade.

In some ways, the transition from the "Oldest House" to the Eldorado has reflected a natural process of cultural and technological change. However, it also reflects a conscious effort by a small group of influential Santa Feans to save the city's architectural heritage from the forces of "progress."

Before the railroad arrived in 1880, the Spanish–Pueblo style of architecture prevailed. Most houses were square, one-story adobe structures built around a central patio. Protruding *vigas* formed the roofs, topped with rows of smaller poles and earth. The largest structures were adobe churches, built in the Spanish Mission style. This unique architecture became threatened with the advent of the railroad and the ensuing "Anglicization" of New Mexico. During the 19th century, visitors and settlers from the East often considered area dwellings "unsightly" and condemned the poverty and "backwardness" of the Hispanic residents. Responding to this bias, many natives as well as newcomers began to tear down the old and replace it with a hodgepodge of styles imported from the East Coast and Midwest.

These "progressive" Santa Feans were especially proud of their new state capitol. Dedicated in 1900, with a rotunda and an Ionic-columned portico, it was a fine example of the classical style then in vogue. This structure was completely redesigned in the 1950s to make it consistent with Spanish–Pueblo Revival style.

The movement to remake Santa Fe into an imitation of Midwestern and

Eastern cities would have succeeded had it not inspired a powerful counter-movement. A group of artists, archaeologists and others, alarmed by the loss of the city's architectural heritage, dedicated themselves to preserving older Spanish structures and to searching for a new regional building style. This group, led by archaeologist Edgar Lee Hewitt, staged an exhibition in 1912 to awaken interest in preserving the "Old Santa Fe" and to promote Santa Fe as the "unrivaled tourist center of the Southwest." It was this second goal that eventually won over the city's business community. People began to realize that tourism held potential, and that in order to attract tourists Santa Fe must preserve the qualities that made it unique.

Success did not come overnight. One of the key battles took place over the Palace of the Governors. Three years before the exhibition, "progressives" wanted to demolish this symbol of New Mexico's Hispanic past and erect a proper "American" courthouse. But in 1909, the "conservatives" — Hewitt and his group — persuaded the legislature to preserve the Palace as a histori-cal museum. In the restoration that followed, the building's Territorial-style *portal* and brick coping were replaced with a a Spanish–Pueblo *portal* and *vigas*. These renovations evoked the building's early history and helped estab-lish the newly-emerging "Santa Fe style."

The Museum of Fine Arts across from the Palace, designed by Isaac Hamil-ton Rapp, was another milestone. Building the structure of brick rather than adobe, Rapp nevertheless incorporated many elements of Hispanic Mission churches in the museum design. Though the Museum of Fine Arts was built in 1916-17, its evocative design makes it appear far older. Part of the museum, the St. Francis Auditorium, is reminiscent of a Spanish Mission church. Throughout the museum, careful attention was paid to traditional decorative techniques such as hand-carved and painted lintels and beams.

Two commercial buildings designed by Rapp to boost the Santa Fe style can still be seen: the Gross, Kelly & Co. Almacen, a warehouse near the railroad tracks on Guadalupe St. and La Fonda Hotel on the plaza. The warehouse, though in poor condition, clearly displays its Spanish-style towers, *portal*, *vigas* and *canales*. La Fonda was built in 1920 to Rapp's design and enlarged by architect John Gaw Meem in 1929.

As a result of the success of the Museum and Palace renovation, the city adopted the Santa Fe style for more than half of the construction of that era. This style, which eventually came to be called Spanish–Pueblo Revival, was carried on after Hewitt's death by enthusiasts like Meem and writer Oliver La Farge. Meem, who had sought New Mexico's climate as a cure for tuberculo-sis, stayed in Santa Fe to become the most eloquent architect of Santa Fe style. Memorable among his dozens of buildings is the Cristo Rey Church at the beginning of Upper Canyon Road. (See "Historic Buildings and Sites" in this chapter.) This massive structure, built in 1940 with 150,000 adobe bricks, bespeaks the architect's love for New Mexico's early Mission churches that he worked tirelessly to preserve.

The look of Santa Fe's central plaza also owes much to Meem, who remod-

Museum of Fine Arts, an early example of Santa Fe style.

Murrae Haynes

eled several Victorian commercial buildings, including the Woolworth, the Franklin store, the Renehan building, the old Masonic Lodge and both the original and present buildings of the First National Bank. He also designed the *portals* that run along three sides of the plaza.

In 1957, after six years of study, the city council adopted the Historic Zoning Ordinance and established Santa Fe's Historic District, which roughly encompasses the downtown area and Canyon Road. The ordinance gave the official stamp to two architectural styles: Spanish–Pueblo Revival and Territorial. The first, a modern version of the Santa Fe style, is characterized by massive walls, rounded parapets and hand-hewn woodwork. Territorial is recognized by brick coping atop adobe walls, milled woodwork and decorative pediments on doors and windows. A number of fine Victorian buildings from New Mexico's territorial days still survive in Santa Fe (for example, the First Ward School at 400 Canyon Rd., now a gallery); however, that style was deemed politically incorrect in 1957 and remains so today.

Anglicization came somewhat later to Taos, which lost many of its original buildings to "progress" in the 1920s and '30s. In 1984, the Taos Town Council approved an Historic Design Review ordinance that included many elements borrowed from Santa Fe's ordinance. The Historic District includes the plaza and several clusters of buildings within Taos' three-square-miles.

Though Spanish–Pueblo Revival style borrows some important features from Pueblo architecture (such as rounded contours, large blank surfaces and stepped-back levels), the philosophy and purposes of the two styles are quite different. To understand this difference, visit the older sections of some of the pueblos, particularly Taos Pueblo (see page 123). To the Pueblo Indians, "home" is much more than the building where one eats and sleeps. It begins at the center point of the pueblo and extends outward to encompass the fields beyond the village, the river, the foothills — even the mountains where the secret shrines lie. If an adobe wall cracks and threatens to destroy a house, the owner may decide to allow the house to "go back to the earth" and build a

*One of the older sections of
Taos Pueblo.*

Mark Nohl/New Mexico Magazine

new one. The event is not a disaster, only part of nature's process. Although Anglos may wonder at the starkness of Pueblo homes, it simply reflects their traditional function.

This is beautifully expressed by Santa Clara Pueblo native and architectural consultant Rina Swentzell. Reflecting on the old Pueblo world, she writes, "Landscaping, or the beautification of outdoor spaces, was a foreign concept. The natural environment was primary and the human structures were made to fit into the hills and around boulders or trees. In that setting, planting pretty flowers that need watering was ridiculous. Decoration for decoration's sake was unnecessary." In the Pueblo world, she concludes, "All of life, including walls, rocks and people, were part of an exquisite, flowing unity." This flowing unity, at the roots of New Mexico's architectural inheritance, continues to give it vitality in all its multicultural manifestations.

CINEMA

Santa Fe

CINEMATHEQUE

Besides producing a full range of arts programs, the Center for Contemporary Arts of Santa Fe (CCA) offers carefully selected foreign and U.S. art films, including recent films not screened elsewhere in the state. It also offers foreign and U.S. oldies. Ethnographic films and video art presentations by independent artists are popular with local audiences. Each March, CCA sponsors the Film Expo, a cinema festival that features world or U.S. premieres of new independent films. To get on the mailing list, call or write *CCA,* P.O. Box

148, Santa Fe, N.M. 87504, 982-1338. *CCA* is located at 291 E. Barcelona Rd., south of downtown between Old Pecos Trail and Don Gaspar.

JEAN COCTEAU

This former art film house screens mostly commercial first-run films. It's worth a visit for its intimate atmosphere and cozy coffee house. You can buy popcorn and soda and head straight into the small theater, or you can linger at a table for two by the fireplace and eat fresh cake or pastries. *Jean Cocteau*: 988-2711; 418 Montezuma, Santa Fe, NM 87501.

Murrae Haynes

FOOTSTEPS ACROSS NEW MEXICO

This multimedia production features slides, a relief map, music and narrative in a 30-minute summary of New Mexico's history. The large relief map portrays the movements of history-makers across the state and is a good introduction for first-time visitors and children. Shows are continuous, beginning at 9:30 a.m., seven days a week. $3.50 adults, $2.50 children 6 to 16. At the *Inn at Loretto*: 982-9297; 211 Old Santa Fe Trail, Santa Fe, N.M. 87501.

COMMERCIAL MOVIE HOUSES

Santa Fe's commercial movie houses include *Cinema 6* (471-6066) in the Villa Linda Mall at Rodeo and Cerrillos Rds.; the *Movies Twin* (988-2775) in De Vargas Mall, St. Francis Dr. and Paseo de Peralta; the *Lensic* (982-0301) at 211 W. San Francisco St.; the *Grand Illusion* (471-8935) at St. Michael's Dr. and Llano St.; and the *Yucca Drive-In* (471-1000) on Cerrillos Rd. near Rodeo Rd.

Taos

The *High Society Cinema* (758-9715), across from the Quality Inn on N.M. 68 and the *Plaza Theater* (758-9715) on Taos Plaza show first-run commercial releases. The *Taos Community Auditorium*, on Paseo del Pueblo Norte, about a half-block north of the plaza, screens films on Sunday and Wednesday evenings. Offerings are eclectic, from occasional first-runs to current foreign films and classics.

DANCE

Santa Fe

MARIA BENITEZ SPANISH DANCE COMPANY

Flamenco, a fiery Spanish dance, developed centuries ago in Andalusia, when Moorish, Byzantine and Hebraic influences meshed with Christian. Few who have seen Maria Benitez perform this highly stylized yet passionate dance can forget her powerful, concentrated energy. Benitez' group, the largest Spanish dance touring company in the country, performs each summer in Santa Fe at the Picacho Plaza Hotel (982-5591; 750 N. St. Francis Dr., Santa Fe, NM 87501). Write the hotel or call the box office (982-1237) for a schedule.

THE CENTER FOR CONTEMPORARY ARTS (CCA)

The *CCA* is Santa Fe's venue for cutting-edge dance performers and performance arts. Performance artist Pat Oleszko, who uses inflatable sculptures in her act, and the Joe Goode Performance Group, a San Francisco-based dance/theater ensemble, appeared there early in 1991. Call or write *CCA* for a schedule: 982-1338; P.O. Box 148, Santa Fe, N.M. 87504.

NEW MEXICO DANCE COALITION

Each May this Santa Fe-based coalition presents its Choreographers' Showcase at the Center for Contemporary Arts. Work is non-juried and ranges across the full spectrum of dance styles. For more information, write *NMDC*, P.O. Box 9142, Santa Fe, N.M. 87504.

SONYA BEZUBKA AND COMPANY

This modern dance company stages one fall and one spring production annually in the Santa Fe. The five-woman group performs physically demanding work and often collaborates with other area artists, from composers to blacksmiths. For more information, call 986-0100.

PRINCE STATE BALLET

This dance school, founded by Endelesia Prince, stages several performances annually. A favorite each December is *The Nutcracker*, which features guest artists from Washington, D.C. A spring performance presents the talents of Prince Ballet students. A summer program is also held. For more information, call 471-7035, or write *Prince State Ballet*, 1121 Calle La Resolana, Santa Fe, N.M. 87501.

SANTA FE DANCE FOUNDATION

This facility offers year-round classes and summer workshops taught by a professional faculty in ballet, modern, creative movement and jazz. Each spring the foundation stages an original production of *Alice in Wonderland*

Maria Benitez performing.

Lois Greenfield

with students and guest artists. For more information, call 983-5591 or write **SFDF**, 1504 Cerrillos Road, Santa Fe, N.M. 87501.

GALLERIES

Most galleries in the Santa Fe–Taos area are retail establishments (for listings, see *Shopping*). However, there are a handful of exhibition spaces that present art in an educational context.

Santa Fe

One of these is the ***Center for Contemporary Arts*** (982-1338; 291 E. Barcelona Rd., Santa Fe, NM 87501), whose mission is to promote the work that reflects our times and world culture. For example, the 1990 exhibition, *Playing With Fire*, featured six important New Mexico artists exploring nuclear issues. In 1988, the CCA installed an ambitious outdoor environmental sculpture project, James Turrell's *Skyspace*, which can be seen by appointment.

If you lean toward art that makes you think, trek over to ***TENGAM***, (983-1588; 403 Canyon Rd., Santa Fe, NM 87501) to see sculptor Tony Price's "atomic art." Dozens of sculptures with names like *Nuclear Hunter*, *Begging for Plutonium* and *The Last SALT Talks* are installed in both indoor and outdoor spaces. Price has garnered international attention with these heavy metal messengers, created from scraps gleaned at Los Alamos National Laboratory.

Several other educational Santa Fe galleries are well worth a visit. The *Governor's Gallery* in the Roundhouse (827-3000; State Capitol) presents changing exhibits by New Mexico artists. The *Fine Arts Gallery of the Southwest* at the College of Santa Fe (473-6555; 1600 St. Michael's Dr.) mounts exhibitions on various contemporary themes. *St. John's College Art Gallery* (982-3691; 1160 Camino Cruz Blanca) presents several exhibitions during the school year.

Near Santa Fe

THE FULLER LODGE ART CENTER (662-9331; 2132 Central, Los Alamos, NM 87544) emphasizes the work of northern New Mexican artists and craftspeople. The lodge, once the dining and recreation hall for Los Alamos Ranch School, was taken over for the Manhattan Project during World War II. An impressive log building, designed by John Gaw Meem (see "Architecture," in this chapter), it is now a National Historic Landmark.

Taos

THE STABLES ART CENTER (758-2036; 133 Paseo del Pueblo Norte, Taos, NM 87571) is the principal exhibitor of contemporary art in Taos. Located in the hacienda of Arthur Manby, one of the most eccentric characters in the town's history, the center offers a broad range of work by nationally- and regionally-recognized artists. Among recent exhibitions: *Taos Impressionists, Hispanic Folk Art* and *Non-Representational Art of Taos*.

HISTORIC BUILDINGS AND SITES

CANYON ROAD

One of Santa Fe's most colorful streets, Canyon Road, was originally an Indian trail to Pecos Pueblo (see "Pecos National Historical Site," page 90). In the 1920s, it was adopted by Anglo artists from the East Coast, but current property values are so high that few artists can afford to live there. The narrow, winding street now houses galleries, boutiques and fine restaurants.

A stroll along Canyon Road is a must. Enter off Paseo de Peralta, just south of Alameda about six blocks southeast of the plaza. Watch for traffic, but take time to look at the adobe structures, constructed in typical Spanish Colonial style with walls that begin at the edge of the street. Their plain exteriors can fool you; a compound may surround a lovely patio or garden. These historic buildings are not open to the public but can be enjoyed from the street.

Take note of 18th-century *El Zaguan* (545 Canyon Rd.), now an apartment complex owned by the Historic Santa Fe Foundation. The garden was originally planted by famed archaeologist Adolph Bandelier, who once lived there. The Spanish word *zaguan* refers to the long covered porch.

The *Olive Rush Studio* (630 Canyon Rd.) was the residence of one of the city's first Anglo artists. She bequeathed her property to the Santa Fe Society of Friends (Quakers), who use it as their meeting place.

The *Borrego House* (724 Canyon Rd.) is now a restaurant. Some sections of the house were built in 1753, and additions in the Territorial style were made in the 19th century when it belonged to the Borrego family.

Santa Fe

CRISTO REY CHURCH
983-8528.
1107 Cristo Rey, Santa Fe, NM 87501.
At intersection of Canyon Rd. and Camino Cabra.
Season: All year, 7–7 daily.
Call ahead to arrange tours.
Fee: None.

An outstanding example of Spanish Colonial Mission architecture (see "Architecture" in this chapter), Cristo Rey Church was designed by Santa Fe architect John Gaw Meem and built to commemorate the 400th anniversary of Coronado's arrival in the Southwest. One of the largest modern adobe structures in existence, it is constructed with bricks made from the earth on which it stands.

Murrae Haynes

The church contains a magnificent stone *reredo*, or altar screen, carved by craftsmen from Mexico in 1760, using stone quarried in the *Jacona* region north of Santa Fe. The *reredo* was originally installed in La Castrense, a military chapel on the plaza, and later placed in a parish church. Archbishop John Baptiste Lamy, who authorized the construction of St. Francis Cathedral at the site of the parish church in 1869, had the *reredo* concealed behind a wall. In 1940 it was placed here. It depicts God the Father, Our Lady of Valvanera, Santiago, St. Joseph, St. John Nepomuk, St. Ignatius Loyola, St. Francis of Solano and Our Lady of Light.

CROSS OF THE MARTYRS WALKWAY
Enter on Paseo de Peralta, between Otero St. and Hillside Ave.
Always open.

Though only a five-minute walk from the plaza, this historic walkway is not well known. It boasts the best view in town. A brick walkway winds up a small hill and plaques posted along the way summarize highlights of Santa Fe's prehistory and history. At the top, you can gaze across the entire city and beyond, to the Sandia and Manzano mountains 60 miles south, the Jemez

40 miles west, and the Sangre de Cristo to the northeast. The white metal cross at the summit is a memorial to the 21 Franciscan monks killed in the Pueblo Revolt of 1680.

LORETTO CHAPEL
988-5531.
211 Old Santa Fe Trail,
  Santa Fe, NM 87501.
Season: All year, 9–5 daily
  except Christmas.
Fee (1991): 50 cents;
  children under 12 free.
Gift shop.

Loretto Chapel was built at the same time as St. Francis Cathedral (see below) for the Sisters of Loretto, the first nuns to come to New Mexico. They established Loretto Academy, a school for young women, in 1853. The Chapel of Our Lady of Light, as it was called then, was begun in 1873 and was designed along the same lines as *Sainte Chappelle* in Paris. Stone came from the same quarry as that for St. Francis Cathedral and the same French architects and French and Italian stonemasons worked on the two structures. It was completed in 1878.

The first Gothic structure west of the Mississippi River, the chapel has another claim to fame. The architects were a father and son named Mouly.

Miraculous Staircase, Loretto Chapel.

Murrae Haynes

The son was killed before the chapel was completed and he left no plans for the stairway to the choir loft. Indeed, there wasn't enough space left for a conventional staircase. The story goes that the sisters prayed for help to St. Joseph, patron saint of carpenters. In due time, an unknown carpenter arrived who built an amazing circular staircase — a structure lacking both nails and visible means of support. He departed without leaving his name or asking for pay. You can view this "Miraculous Staircase," as well as the beautiful religious carvings that grace the chapel walls. You can also listen to a seven-minute informational tape. Loretto Chapel is now owned by the Inn at Loretto and operated as a private museum.

OLDEST HOUSE IN THE U.S.A.
983-3883.
215 E. De Vargas St., Santa Fe, NM 87501.
Season: Mon.–Sat., 9–4; closed mid-Jan.–mid-March.Fee: None; donations accepted.
Gift shop.

Though the exact age of this structure is not firmly established, there is little doubt that it's one of the oldest buildings in the city. This simple adobe, which you enter through the adjacent gift shop, is on one of the oldest streets in the country and in one of Santa Fe's oldest neighborhoods, *Barrio de Analco*, settled by Tlaxcalan Indian slaves brought by the Spanish from Mexico.

The lower walls are of puddled adobe, a technique used by Pueblo Indians before they learned adobe brick-making from the Spaniards. The corner fireplace was added during the Spanish era. According to the operators, tree-ring dating indicates that a large part of the house is contemporary with the neighboring San Miguel Church next door. The house has seen a colorful succession of residents: Indians, Franciscan friars, treasure hunters, traders — some say even a pair of witches!

PALACE OF THE GOVERNORS

(See "Museums" in this chapter.)

THE PLAZA
Center of town.
Always open.

Four hundred years of history speak from the Santa Fe Plaza. It is, quite literally, Santa Fe's "place of emergence," not unlike the *sipapu*, or sacred place of emergence, that each pueblo hon-

Santa Fe Plaza.

Wendy Walsh

ors in its own plaza. Originally the plaza was a rectangle, laid out according to plans specified by Spain's King Philip II in 1610. For much of its history, it was not landscaped. As the center of a Spanish colonial city, it consisted mainly of packed earth. Though it has been dusty, it has never been dull. Countless celebrations, both religious and secular, have been held here. This is the spot where Hispanic residents used to conduct Saturday night promenades, complete with strolling musicians.

Today cruising "low-riders" and teen-age "plaza rats" keep the plaza hopping on pleasant summer evenings. The music still rings out — especially during the city's free concerts held several times a week during the summer. Hardly anyone would think of holding a demonstration or vigil anywhere but the plaza and it is still the best people-watching spot in the city.

RANDALL DAVEY AUDUBON CENTER
983-4609.
P.O. Box 9314, Santa Fe, NM 87504.
At end of Upper Canyon Rd.
Season: Year-round, 9–5
Fee: None; donation requested.
Gift shop.

Wendy Walsh

One of the few historic homes in Santa Fe open to the public, the Randall Davey Center houses a state office as well as an environmental education center and wildlife refuge for the *National Audubon Society*. Set on 135 acres at the mouth of the Santa Fe River Canyon, the home of musician and artist Randall Davey is listed in national, state and city registers of historical and cultural buildings. The area was given to Manuel Trujillo as part of a Spanish land grant in 1731. In 1847 the first sawmill in the territory was built there to provide planks for the U.S. Army's Fort Marcy in Santa Fe. What is now the house was the original mill; the *acequia* behind it served as irrigation ditch and millrace. The house features massive, beamed ceilings and 16-inch-thick stone walls covered by plaster.

Randall Davey studied with New York artist Robert Henri and moved to Santa Fe in 1920. His innovative works are exhibited throughout the house and the adjacent studio. The center's wildlife area offers a good introduction to the flora and fauna of northern New Mexico. Trails wind through natural vegetation of piñon, juniper and ponderosa pine. A large meadow is thick with native grasses and plants of the Great Basin Desert and Rocky Mountains. The area is rich in bird life (more than 100 species have been observed), as well as mammals such as black bear, mountain lion, bobcat, coyote, raccoon and mule deer. The center offers an extensive schedule of bird walks, natural history workshops and school programs.

SAN MIGUEL CHAPEL
983-3974.
401 Old Santa Fe Trail,
  Santa Fe, NM 87501.
Season: Daily, year round.
  Mass Sun. 5 p.m.
Fee: None; donation
  requested.
Gift shop.

The oldest church in the United States, San Miguel is estimated to have been built around 1625. It seems likely that the original walls and adobe altar were built by Tlaxcalan Indians brought from Mexico by the Spaniards. These Indians lived in the *Barrio de Analco* and worshiped here.

During the Pueblo Revolt of 1680 (see *History,* Chapter One), Indian attackers burned the roof. The Spaniards returned in 1692, but they were too busy subjugating the Indians to devote full attention to restoration, which was not completed until 1710. Early in the 19th century, the church was remodeled and an unconventional three-tiered tower added. The steeple toppled in 1872, and rain and wind necessitated constant repairs. The present tower and stone support buttresses were added in 1887. In 1955 the interior was restored to its Spanish Colonial appearance.

The chapel contains several magnificent oil paintings believed to date back to 1710. Colonial buffalo hide paintings of the Crucifixion and of St. John the Baptist hang on the walls. Displays show pottery shards and other findings from archaeological digs that indicate Indian occupation of the site from around A.D. 1300. The chapel is owned and administered by the Christian Brothers.

**SANTUARIO DE
  GUADALUPE**
988-2027.
100 Guadalupe St., Santa
  Fe, NM 87501.
Season: Year-round, closed
  weekends Nov.–Apr.
Fee: Donation requested.
Gift shop.

The Santuario is a Santa Fe landmark and a performing arts center. It was built by Franciscan missionaries around 1796, with adobe walls three to five feet thick. The oldest shrine in the United States, it is dedicated to the Queen of the Americas, Our Lady of Guadalupe, who revealed herself in a vision to Indian convert Juan Diego in Mexico in 1531. The impressive structure stands just above the Santa Fe River at the end of the Camino Real, which ran from Mexico City to Santa Fe. Across the altar hangs a breathtaking painting of Our Lady of Guadalupe, the work of Jose de Alzibar, one of Mexico's finest Colonial painters. The painting was commissioned for the Santuario in 1783 and was transported in four sections from Mexico City on mule-back.

The Santuario has survived several architectural metamorphoses: in the 1880s it even suffered a New England-style steeple! In 1976, it was restored to what is believed to be its original appearance. It is operated by the Guadalupe Historic Foundation.

**ST. FRANCIS
   CATHEDRAL**
982-5619.
131 Cathedral Pl., Santa Fe,
   NM 87501.
E. end of San Francisco St.
Season: Year-round.
   Masses daily at 6, 7, 7:45
   a.m., 5:15 p.m.; Sun 6, 8,
   10 a.m., noon, 7 p.m.

This is one of Santa Fe's most spectacular structures — and also one of its most incongruous. Built in French-Romanesque style, it was the inspiration of Frenchman Jean Baptiste Lamy, Santa Fe's first archbishop. Lamy was sent to Santa Fe in 1850, about 25 years after Saint Francis of Assisi was chosen the diocese's patron saint. The cornerstone of the cathedral was laid in 1869, and construction proceeded with stone quarried in an area south of Santa Fe. The village near the quarry was subsequently named after Lamy, and a statue of the archbishop stands in front of the cathedral.

St. Francis Cathedral was dedicated in 1886 but never fully completed. Its stained-glass windows, including the rose window in front and the lateral nave windows, were imported from France and installed in 1884. The nave windows depict the Apostles as well as the coats of arms of the archbishops who have served since Lamy. The bronze doors of the cathedral, installed for the rededication, contain 16 panels depicting scenes in the history of the Catholic Church in Santa Fe. Also worth seeing is the *reredo* carved for the 100th anniversary celebration in 1986. At the center of the *reredo* stands a humble wooden statue of St. Francis that came from Mexico City in the 1700s. The story is that Archbishop Lamy replaced it with statues he considered more attractive.

La Conquistadora Chapel, an adobe structure on the northeast side of the cathedral, was built to house a statue of the Virgin Mary brought to Santa Fe in 1626. Originally called the Lady of the Rosary, the statue was renamed Our

St. Francis Cathedral, dedicated in 1886.

Murrae Haynes

Lady of the Conquest in 1692, when the Spaniards reentered the city 12 years after the Pueblo Revolt. It is probably the oldest representation of the Virgin Mary in the United States. *La Conquistadora* leaves her chapel each June for a processional to commemorate Don Diego de Vargas' return to the city.

<u>Note</u>: Visitors not attending Mass may slip into the cathedral quietly at other times, taking care not to disturb those at prayer.

SENA PLAZA
125-137 E. Palace Ave.
Enter on Palace Ave., just
    E. of the plaza.
Always open.

A separate world that resonates with the flavor of Colonial Santa Fe, Sena Plaza is reached by an adobe passage from busy Palace Ave. In the 19th century, the most gracious homes were built as compounds, with rooms surrounding a central *placita*, or courtyard. In the 1860s, Major José D. Sena built just such a home a block from the downtown plaza and kept adding rooms as children were born. Sena Plaza now houses private shops and a restaurant. Here you can stroll around and imagine the old days as you listen to the fountain, watch the birds and enjoy the flowers. The patio garden, where you can order a drink or lunch from *La Casa Sena* (see *Restaurants*), remains one of downtown Santa Fe's most enjoyable spots for relaxing and socializing.

Near Santa Fe

**BANDELIER NATIONAL
    MONUMENT**
672-3861.
46 mi. W. of Santa Fe. Take
    U.S. 285 N. to Pojoaque,
    then W. on N.M. 502
    and S. on N.M. 4.
Season: Year-round. Visitor
    Center 8–4:30 daily
    except Christmas; ruins
    trails, dawn to dusk.
Fee (1991): $5 per car,
    buses $2 per passenger,
    campsites $6 per night;
    over 62, free.
No pets on trails.
Gift shop, snack bar.

This lush Shangri-La tucked in a deep canyon on the Pajarito (pa-ha-REE-toe) Plateau was home to the ancestors of several Pueblo tribes between A.D. 1100 and 1550. The residents irrigated their corn, beans and squash with water from Frijoles (free-HOLE-ace) Creek and made their homes from the plentiful volcanic rock. Today you can climb among their cliff dwellings and ceremonial *kivas*. The trail that loops through the main ruins of Frijoles Canyon takes about an hour. Agile visitors can climb ladders, as the residents once did, to enter Bandelier's restored dwellings — including a spectacular ceremonial cave with *kiva*.

Bandelier's 50 square miles are federally-designated wilderness, with 70 miles of maintained trails that go onto mesas, into volcanic canyons and through high-altitude pine forests. Those in good physical condition can take day hikes to more remote ruins. The Visitor Center and Frijoles Canyon ruins tend to be crowded, but solitude is yours if you're willing to walk a bit. (See also "Hiking and Climbing" in *Recreation*, Chapter Six.)

PECOS NATIONAL HISTORICAL SITE
757-6414.
25 mi. S.E. of Santa Fe, off I-25.
Season: Daily, year round, 8–5 except Christmas and New Year's; open Memorial Day–Labor Day, 8–6
Fee (1991): $1 per adult or $3 per car; over 62 and under 17 free.
Book store.

In 1540, before the Spaniards arrived, Pecos was a thriving Pueblo Indian village with apartment-like houses four and five stories high. The Pecos people traded with other Pueblo villages and with the Plains Indians to the east. Coronado's men visited in 1541 and by the early 1620s, the Franciscans arrived to build a mission and to convert the Indians to the Spanish way of life. The Franciscans enlisted the Indians in building a magnificent church, 150 feet from altar to entrance, with walls 22 feet thick in places. The foundations can be seen, but the church was destroyed in the Pueblo Revolt of 1680. A smaller church built atop the ruins in 1717 also lies in ruins.

What happened to the thriving village? Historians believe Pecos was decimated by European diseases and Comanche raids in the 17th century. The last residents left in 1838 to live with relatives at Jemez Pueblo, across the Rio Grande Valley. The mission and village were abandoned to future archaeologists. Today a 1.25-mile trail on gentle terrain takes you around the mission and pueblo ruins, including a ceremonial *kiva* in which you can hear recorded Indian chants.

SAN JOSE CHURCH
No phone.
In Las Trampas, on N.M. 76 about 40 mi. N.E. of Santa Fe.
Season: Summer. Daily, 8–5
Fee: None; donations accepted.

Built in Las Trampas between 1760 and 1780, this is frequently described as the most beautiful Spanish Colonial church in New Mexico. It is on the National Register of Historic Places. The village of Las Trampas was established in 1751 by 12 Santa Fe families led by Juan de Arguello, who had received a land grant from Governor Tomas Velez Capuchin. In the summer, the church is usually open from 8 a.m. to 5 p.m.; in the winter, you'll probably find it locked. Ask at one of the nearby gift shops for the person who keeps the key.

SANTUARIO DE CHIMAYÓ
No phone.
In Chimayó, about 25 mi. N.E. of Santa Fe on N.M. 76.
Season: Year-round. Daily in summer, 9–5; winter, 9–4; Mass weekdays 7 a.m., Sun. noon.
Fee: None; donations accepted.
Gift shop.

The site of this chapel is believed to be a healing place of the Pueblo Indians. For generations Hispanic villagers in these remote mountains have attested to the miraculous healing powers of the mud from a certain spot in the chapel floor. The church, built in 1816, was the private chapel of the Abeyta family. Pilgrims bring their prayers for healing to the Santuario all year long but on Good Friday it is the destination of a special pilgrimage, when thousands walk to Chimayó from all over the state to receive blessings. The twin-towered Santuario is also a favorite subject of artists.

Santuario de Chimayó is a major pilgrimage site.

Murrae Haynes

Taos

ERNEST L. BLUMENSCHEIN HOME
758-0505, 758-0330.
222 Ledoux St., just S. of Taos Plaza.
Season: Year round, 9–5; closed Christmas, Thanksgiving, New Year's.
Fee: Variable; senior and group rates available.

Ernest and Mary Greene Blumenschein were among the founders of the Taos art colony around 1915. Their home, a 1797 Spanish Colonial adobe, is open for tours and exhibits of area artists' work. The house appears much as it did in the Blumenscheins' day: original adobe plaster inside and out, traditional Taos furniture, European antiques and artwork from around the world.

GOVERNOR BENT HOUSE
758-2376.
117 Bent St., 1 blk. N. of Taos Plaza.
Season: Year-round. Daily in summer 9–5; winter 10–5
Fee (1991): Adults $1, 15 and under 50 cents, under 8 free.
Gift shop and gallery.

Charles Bent, a prominent Taos citizen, owned Santa Fe Trail wagon trains as well as trading posts in Taos and Santa Fe. However, the peculiar politics of New Mexico proved to be his undoing. Illegally appointed the first U.S. governor of the territory of New Mexico when the Americans invaded in 1846, he awoke on the morning of Jan. 19, 1847 to find an angry mob of Hispanics and Indians breaking down the doors. When Bent asked what they wanted, the response was: "We want your head, gringo." Bent's family was allowed to leave, but he was killed and scalped. The adobe house, which contains historic artifacts, is on the National Register of Historic Places. (See also *History*, Chapter One.)

Courtesy Ernest L. Blumenschein Home

Ernest L. Blumenschein in his studio, ca. 1920.

FECHIN INSTITUTE
758-1710.
227 Paseo del Pueblo
  Norte.
2 blks. N. of Taos Plaza on
  N. Pueblo Rd.
Season: Memorial Day
  weekend–mid–Oct.,
  Wed.–Sun 1–5:30 and by
  appointment.
Fee: None; $3 donation
  suggested.

This distinguished adobe home was designed by renowned artist Nicolai Fechin, an emigrant from Russia. Built in 1928, the house features hand-carved woodwork that blends Russian and Spanish folk art. Fechin's Oriental art collection is on permanent display and exhibitions of his work are mounted each fall. The home and studio are operated as a culture and education center, with tours available.

KIT CARSON HOME
758-0505, 758-4741.
113 E. Kit Carson Rd.
0.5 blk. E. of the plaza.
Season: Year-round.
  Summer 8–6; winter 9–5;
  closed Christmas,
  Thanksgiving, New
  Year's.
Fee: Variable; senior and
  group rates available.
Gift shop.

As the guide for Western explorer John Charles Fremont, Kit Carson was the consummate mountain man, scout and soldier. He was also a family man. In 1843 he married Josefa Jaramillo and in this 12-room adobe they set up housekeeping and raised a large family. Kit and Josefa both died in 1868, a month apart. Three rooms of the house are furnished as they might have been during the years the Carsons lived there. Other rooms are filled with exhibits on Taos' colorful frontier history.

Spanish Colonial exhibit at Martinez Hacienda.

Courtesy Martinez Hacienda

MARTINEZ HACIENDA
758-0505, 758-1000.
2 mi. S. of Taos Plaza on Rte. 240 (Ranchitos Rd.), or 4 mi. W. of Ranchos de Taos on Rte. 240.
Season: Year-round, 9–5 except Thanksgiving, Christmas, New Year's.
Fee: Variable; senior and group rates available.
Gift shop.

The home of a distinguished family during the 19th-century, this hacienda features thick adobe walls and a windowless exterior. Twenty-one rooms enclose two central *placitas*. This fortress-like building was designed to withstand Comanche and Apache raids. Livestock were driven through the gates and into the *placitas* when raiders threatened.

This is perhaps the only hacienda in the Southwest that has been restored to its original condition. Rooms are furnished in Colonial style, reflecting a time when goods were either made by local artisans or hauled by ox cart from Mexico City. Exhibits tell the story of trade on the Camino Real and of the Spanish Colonial culture of New Mexico. Demonstrations of contemporary and traditional crafts are presented on a regular basis.

Near Taos

In the magnificent fierce morning of New Mexico one sprang awake, a new part of the soul woke up suddenly, and the old world gave way to a new.

— D.H. Lawrence, "New Mexico"

D.H. LAWRENCE RANCH & MEMORIAL
776-2245.
Near San Cristobal, 15 mi. N. of Taos on N.M. 522.
Season: Year-round. In winter call ahead for road conditions.
Fee: None.

D.H. Lawrence, the British writer who waxed ecstatic over New Mexico's landscapes and light, lived in northern New Mexico off and on. He died in France in 1930, but his ashes are enshrined here on a ranch given to his wife, Frieda Lawrence, by Taos art patron Mabel Dodge Luhan. The ranch is now owned by the University of New Mexico and operated as a retreat for writers in residence. The shrine with Lawrence's ashes is open daily to the public from dawn to dusk. You may be moved or amused by the paens and panegyrics to D.H. that have been written by visitors in the shrine's guest book. Devotees from all over the world leave words of praise for Lawrence's erotically adventurous prose. Picnic tables are available and spectacular views of the Taos Valley are another reward for the drive.

SAN FRANCISCO DE ASIS CHURCH

758-2754.
Ranchos de Taos, about 4 mi. S. of Taos on N.M. 68.
Season: Year-round.
Mon–Sat. 9–4:30; Mass Sat. 7 p.m., Sun. 7 a.m., 9 a.m., 11:30 a.m.
Fee (1991): Large groups only, $1 per person.
Gift shop across the street.

This church was started sometime between 1776 and 1813 and was in use by the Franciscans in 1815. It is the most frequently painted and photographed church in the United States. Viewed from the west, its massive, windowless adobe walls change appearance hourly as the light changes, posing an irresistible challenge to artists. Visitors are often intrigued by artwork inside the building, including Henri Ault's *The Shadow of the Cross*. At the church office across the street, a slide show and lecture on the history of the building are presented several times a day.

Murrae Haynes

Entrance to San Francisco de Asis in Ranchos de Taos.

FORT BURGWIN RESEARCH CENTER

758-8322.
P.O. Box 314, Ranchos de Taos, NM. 87557.
About 8 mi. S.E. of Taos on N.M. 518.
Season: Mid–May to end of Sept.
Fee: Varies with class; rental space for conferences.

Set in a small valley on a tributary of the Rio Grande, Fort Burgwin was a U.S. cavalry fort in the 1850s. Now it is an archaeological research and training center for Southern Methodist University of Dallas, Texas. During the summer, Fort Burgwin offers cultural programs and a lecture series that emphasizes archaeology. Call or write for current listings.

Outside the Area

**CHACO CULTURE
NATIONAL
HISTORICAL PARK**
988-6716.
60 mi. S. of Bloomfield in
N.W. New Mexico, via
N.M. 44 and unpaved
N.M. 57. Other routes
possible.
Season: Year-round; daily
except Christmas, dawn
to dusk; visitor center
8–5, 6 p.m. Memorial
Day to Labor Day.
Fee (1991): $3 per carload;
campsites $5 per night;
no hookups, group
reservations only.

Chaco Canyon is to North America what the
Pyramids are to Egypt and what Machu Pic-
chu is to South America. Humans have inhabited
the area for 6,000 years or more. About A.D. 900 the
Anasazi culture began to flower, and Chaco
Canyon was its crowning achievement: six large
pueblos and as many as 75 smaller towns, all built
in a relatively short time. The largest, Pueblo Bonito, was a community of four-story masonry apartment buildings with solar orientation, hundreds of
rooms and dozens of *kivas*. The Chacoan people
farmed with an elaborate irrigation and terracing
system and created stunning pottery and
turquoise jewelry. They built an astonishing 400
miles of arrow-straight roads connecting the

*Intricate stonemasonry at
Chaco Canyon.*

Murrae Haynes

canyon with outlying settlements, and they even traded with Mexico. Then, sometime around A.D. 1200, this thriving culture suddenly disappeared. Archaeologists haven't yet come up with a totally satisfying theory as to why; prolonged drought seems the most likely answer.

The ruins were known to Spaniards and Indians at least as far back as 1840 and the first archaeological excavations were started in 1896. Today, you can spend a couple of days or more exploring the ruins along the Chaco Wash. There are even more ruins atop the mesas. Rangers are available for guided walks, and the Visitor Center offers a good introduction with films and displays. The ruins are in surprisingly good condition, so it is easy to imagine Chaco Canyon alive with the laughter of children and the sounds of men and women at work in the courtyards and fields.

Note: Routes to Chaco Canyon, other than the one listed, are possible from Santa Fe and Taos. Consult a good map before setting out and call the park to check on road conditions. Also, there's no lodging, gasoline or food at the park; the nearest town is 60 miles away. Staples are available on weekdays at trading posts on N.M. 44. To make the most of your visit, plan to camp at Chaco. But get there early; campsites tend to fill quickly on weekends and most days during the summer.

LIBRARIES

If you want to delve a little more into Southwestern lore, several libraries in Santa Fe and Taos can help you scratch the information itch.

Santa Fe

The Santa Fe Public Library (984-6780; 145 Washington Ave.) is notable for its attractive architecture and furnishings. The Southwest Room contains a moderately large collection of works on the Southwest.

The Museum of New Mexico research libraries, open to researchers, are part of each of the four Santa Fe museums. (Be sure to call ahead.) *The History Library*; (827-6470) at the Palace of the Governors houses more than 12,000 volumes on regional history, as well as a vast repository of original documents and maps. Its Photo Archive section (827-6472) contains more than 340,000 historical images; prints are available for purchase or rental. The *Museum of Fine Arts Library* (827-4453) contains about 5,000 volumes emphasizing New Mexican and Southwestern art. *The Museum of International Folk Art Library* (827-6350) has more than 10,000 volumes. The *Laboratory of Anthropology* (827-6344), next to the Museum of Indian Arts and Culture, contains volumes on Southwest anthropology and archaeology.

Taos

The Town of Taos operates the *Harwood Library* (758-3063; 238 Ledoux St.) in the same building as the *Harwood Foundation Museum* (see "Museums," below). The 30,000-volume collection is strong in Southwestern literature and history and includes a good collection of the works of D.H. Lawrence, whose former residence is north of Taos. (See "D.H. Lawrence Ranch and Memorial" page 93.)

MUSEUMS

The state of New Mexico operates four museum facilities in Santa Fe under the aegis of the *Museum of New Mexico*. A special admission ticket will get you into all four over a two-day period. If you see all four, you will have given yourself an exciting introduction to New Mexico arts, culture and history. The museums include the *Palace of the Governors* and the *Museum of Fine Arts*, both on the plaza, and the *Museum of Indian Arts and Culture* and the *Museum of International Folk Art*, both on Camino Lejo about a five-minute drive southeast of downtown.

Santa Fe

INSTITUTE OF AMERICAN INDIAN ARTS MUSEUM
988-6281.
Cathedral Pl., Santa Fe, NM 87501.
Across from St. Francis Cathedral.
Opening summer 1992.

Founded during the Kennedy administration, the Institute of American Indian Arts (IAIA) proved to be a highly successful experiment of the federal government in art education for Native Americans. Some of the best-known names in Indian art — Allan Houser, Fritz Scholder, the late T.C. Cannon and others — were teachers or students at the IAIA. Since the late 1980s the IAIA has been operating independently of the Bureau of Indian Affairs. Students from all tribes attend the two-year degree program. The IAIA also has the nation's largest collection of contemporary Native American art. In 1991, a building in downtown Santa Fe was being renovated to house the collection; its opening was planned to coincide with the Columbus Quincentenary in 1992.

Murrae Haynes

MUSEUM OF FINE ARTS
827-4455; 827-6463 for 24-
   hr. information.
P.O. Box 2087 / 107 W.
   Palace Ave., Santa Fe,
   NM 87501.
On the plaza.
Season: Year-round. Daily
   10–5 except
   Thanksgiving,
   Christmas, New year's
   and Mon. in Jan., Feb.
Fee (1991): $3.50 adults,
   under 16 free; 2-day
   state museum pass, $6.
Gift shop.

The Museum of Fine Arts, a unit of the Museum of New Mexico, anchors the northwest corner of the plaza with its 1917 Spanish–Pueblo building designed by Isaac Hamilton Rapp. The mission-style structure houses more than 8,000 works of art, including paintings, prints, drawings, photographs and sculptures. The collection emphasizes 20th-century Southwestern American art. Among its highlights are Georgia O'Keeffe's *Red Hills and Pedernal*, Marsden Hartley's *El Santo*, Robert Henri's *Dieguito, San Ildefonso Drummer*, Bert Phillips' *Musicians of the Baile*, Jesus Moroles' *Mountain Fountain*, Laura Gilpin's *O'Keeffe's Studio* and John Marin's *Ranchos Church*. The museum owns only six other O'Keeffe works, much to the surprise of many visitors. Unfortunately, the prices commanded by her works are well out of reach of the state museum's budget.

On permanent exhibition are works by early 20th-century New Mexico artists such as Jozef Bakos, Gustave Baumann, Gene Kloss and William Penhallow Henderson. Also look for changing shows of traditional and contemporary art. The *Alcove Show*, which changes several times a year, features exciting contemporary work by area artists.

**MUSEUM OF INDIAN
   ARTS AND CULTURE**
827-6344; 827-6463 for 24-
   hr. information.
710 Camino Lejo, Santa Fe,
   NM 87501.

The newest of the state museums brings together the past and present of Southwest Indian culture. It houses an extraordinary collection of more than 50,000 Native American arts and crafts gathered over 61 years by the adjacent *Laboratory of Anthropology* (827-6344). Included are baskets,

Season: Year-round. Daily 10–5 except Thanksgiving, Christmas, New Year's and Mon. in Jan., Feb.
Fee (1991): $3.50 adults, under 16 free; 2-day state museum pass, $6.
Gift shop.

pottery, textiles, jewelry, clothing and other items. Artifacts rotate on exhibit, emphasizing the Navajo, Apache and Pueblo peoples. Highlights include the first black-on-black pot fired by renowned San Ildefonso potter Maria Martinez, a bridle that belonged to the Apache warrior Cochise, a 151-foot-long hunting net made of human hair and fiber from A.D. 1100 and a ceremonial bead cache from Chaco Canyon.

The museum was created by the state legislature in 1977 and opened in 1987. Outstanding programs include "Living Traditions" and "Artist-in-Residence," in which artists demonstrate such crafts as pottery making and basket weaving.

MUSEUM OF INTERNATIONAL FOLK ART
827-6350; 827-6463 for 24-hr. information.
706 Camino Lejo, Santa Fe, NM 87501.
Season: Year-round. Daily 10–5 except Thanksgiving, Christmas, New Year's and Mon. in Jan., Feb.
Fee (1991): $3.50 adults, under 16 free; 2-day state museum pass, $6.
Gift shop.

You'll never see art like this unless you travel to six continents and 100 countries. This amazing collection of folk art — the world's largest — was founded in 1953 by Florence Dibell Bartlett. According to a museum publication, Bartlett believed that the art produced by craftspeople, not highbrow artists, would unite the different cultures of the world. Judge for yourself as you wander among traditional clothing and textiles, masks, toys, miniatures and items of everyday use. The collection numbers more than 125,000 pieces, including 106,000 from the Girard Foundation Collection, given to the Museum in 1976. About

A few of the 125,000 pieces at the Museum of International Folk Art.

Wendy Walsh

10,000 pieces from this collection are on permanent display in an exhibition created by Alexander Girard, a graphic artist.

Among highlights are Mexican masks and costumes, Turkish folk art and work produced by National Heritage Fellowship awardees. Children are delighted by the miniature Mexican village scenes consisting of colorful and imaginative clay figurines. Traveling exhibits and those curated by the museum staff are presented year round.

The Hispanic Heritage Wing, opened in 1989, must also be described in superlatives. With about 5,000 artifacts dating from the late 1600s to the present, it is the largest collection of Spanish Colonial and Hispanic folk art in the United States. It emphasizes work from northern New Mexico but includes works from the international Spanish Colonial Empire — including religious art, textiles, tin-work, utilitarian implements, gold and silver jewelry and furniture.

PALACE OF THE GOVERNORS
827-6483; 827-6463 for 24-hr. information.
914 Palace Ave., Santa Fe, NM 87501.
On the plaza.
Season: Year-round. Daily 10–5 except Thanksgiving, Christmas, New Year's and Mon. in Jan., Feb.
Fee (1991): $3.50 adults, under 16 free; 2-day state museum pass, $6.
Gift shop.

In 1610, 10 years before the Pilgrims landed, the Palace of the Governors was built by the settlers who established Santa Fe. The palace has served as a seat of government for Spain, Mexico, the Confederacy and the United States. Between 1680 and 1692, it was home to the Pueblo Indians, who remodeled and used it after driving the Spaniards out of New Mexico. It became a museum in 1911. (See also "Architecture" in this chapter.)

Today the Palace of the Governors houses the Museum of New Mexico's collection of more than 17,000 historical objects. The collection comprises artifacts from the Spanish Colonial period, the Mexican–American War, the American expansion along the Santa Fe Trail, the transition from Mexican to U.S. control and the 20th century. Permanent exhibits illustrate the state's cultural heritage and special exhibits focus on aspects of history such as traditional celebrations and the Civil War.

One of the first "exhibits" is the *Portal Program*, where Indian vendors sell hand-crafted jewelry and other items under the Palace *portal*. Since Native Americans have been trading in this spot for centuries, they are considered a "living historical exhibit." Only New Mexico Indians may sell here and all work must be certified that it is made by the vendor or his or her immediate family. If you're interested in authentic Indian work, this is a good place to make purchases.

Within the palace compound is the *Palace Press*, which produces limited editions of works related to the Southwest, using historic hand-operated printing and binding equipment.

Indians selling jewelry under the palace portal.

Murrae Haynes

SANTA FE CHILDREN'S MUSEUM
989-8359.
1050 Old Pecos Trail, Santa Fe, NM 87501.
Season: Year-round, Thur.–Sat. 10–5, Sun. noon–5 June 1–Labor Day, Wed. also.
Fee (1991): Adults $2, children $1.
Gift shop.

This child-friendly museum is a place where youngsters are *encouraged* to touch, move, create, make noise and play. It is filled with such hands-on exhibits as "Make and Take," a wooden "house" where children can create collages with recyclable foam, spools, rubber, etc. In other exhibits, children can experiment in the arts, humanities, science and technology. The museum also sponsors family programs, workshops, demonstrations and performances.

SCHOOL OF AMERICAN RESEARCH
982-3584.
P.O. Box 2188, Santa Fe, NM 87504.
660 Garcia St.
Season: Year-round; public tours Fri. 2–3:30, reservations required.
Fee: Variable. Call for information.

A nonprofit center for anthropological research, the School of American Research (SAR) has a 7,350-piece collection of historic Southwestern Native American art. Its strongest areas are Pueblo pottery, Navajo and Pueblo textiles and 20th-century Indian paintings. Volunteer docents give guided tours of the collection, but these must be arranged in advance. The SAR bookstore stocks a wide variety of books and other literature, most having to do with anthropology and culture. Inquire about schedules and fees.

**WHEELWRIGHT
MUSEUM OF THE
AMERICAN INDIAN**
982-4636.
P.O. Box 5153, Santa Fe,
  NM 87502 / 704 Camino
  Lejo.
Season: Year-round,
  Mon.–Sat. 10–5; Sun. 1–5
Fee: None; donations
  welcome.
Gift shop.

Mark Nohl/New Mexico Magazine

*Outdoor sculpture at the
Wheelwright Museum of the
American Indian.*

ere's a story only the West could produce: Mary Cabot Wheelwright, a wealthy New England heiress, scholar and world traveler, went by horseback to the Navajo Reservation in 1921, at age 40. There she met Hosteen Klah, a powerful Navajo singer and healer. He spoke no English and she spoke no Navajo but somehow they developed a rapport. She wanted to know about his religion and he revealed that he was ready to pass on some of his knowledge to people who could write it down. Both feared that the traditional Navajo way of life was about to be lost to "progress."

Mary Cabot Wheelwright and Hosteen Klah spent years in research together on the vast Navajo Reservation. In 1927 they founded the *Museum of Navajo Ceremonial Art* in Santa Fe to house all the sacred materials they had collected.

As it turned out, Navajo culture proved much more resilient than these two had predicted. Even today the Navajo ceremonial system remains very much alive. In acknowledgment of that fact, the museum returned much of the sacred material to the Navajo Nation in the 1970s and its name was changed to the Wheelwright Museum of the American Indian to express the institution's interest in all American Indian cultures.

The Wheelwright's collection is strong in Navajo weaving, including tapestries of sand-painting designs made by Hosteen Klah himself; Southwestern jewelry, basketry and pottery; cradleboards from throughout the United States; and contemporary Indian art. Among special exhibitions planned for 1991 and 1992 are an invitational jewelry show, a powwow exhibit, a sand-painting exhibit and a show about the history of Santa Fe's Indian Market.

Don't miss the *Case Trading Post*; it's much more than a gift shop. Modeled after New Mexican trading posts of the early 1900s, the Case offers quality items in a range of prices, from Navajo blankets and Hopi baskets to old pawn jewelry and Pueblo pottery. There's a good selection of books on Native Americans of the Southwest and tapes of Indian music.

Near Santa Fe

If you are a scientist . . . you believe that it is good to find out how the world works . . . to turn over to mankind at large the greatest possible power to control the world and to deal with it according to its lights and values.

— J. Robert Oppenheimer, Manhattan Project Director of Research.

BRADBURY SCIENCE MUSEUM
667-4444.
Diamond Dr., Los Alamos, NM 87545.
35 mi. N.W. of Santa Fe via U.S. 285 N. and N.M. 502 W.
Season: Year-round, Tues–Fri. 9–5; Sat.–Mon. 1–5 except on major national holidays.
Admission: Free.

Photographs and documents give a glimpse of the unfolding of "Project Y," the World War II code name for the laboratory at Los Alamos that developed the first atomic bomb. An impressive display of the National Laboratory's weapons research program includes an actual rack for underground nuclear testing and presents an overview of the U.S. nuclear arsenal. A model of an accelerator and exhibits on the latest research in solar, geothermal, laser and magnetic fusion energy can be seen. Hands-on exhibits include microscopes, lasers and computers.

Films from the laboratory, screened in a small theater, include features on computer graphics, geothermal energy, the history of the Manhattan Project and the creation of the first atomic bomb.

LOS ALAMOS HISTORICAL MUSEUM
662-6272.
1921 Juniper, Los Alamos, NM 87544.
35 mi. N.W. of Santa Fe via U.S. 285 N. and N.M. 502 W.
Season: Year-round, Mon.–Sat. 10–4; Sun. 1–4 p.m.
Admission: Free.
Book store.

This museum is housed in a log-and-stone building that was originally part of the Los Alamos Ranch School, a prep school taken over by the federal government for the Manhattan Project during World War II. The museum covers a million years starting with when the *Jemez* volcano blew its top and created the *Pajarito* Plateau. Exhibits include artifacts of the first known residents, farmers and hunters who lived here about A.D. 1100. Another exhibit, "Life in the Secret City," reveals life in Los Alamos during World War II, when it was closed to outsiders as scientists rushed to make the bomb.

On the museum grounds are the remains of a Tewa Indian settlement of the 1300s. For a small fee, the museum provides a 12-page booklet for a self-guided walking tour. Guided tours are available by prior arrangement. There's a book shop with more than 600 Southwest titles.

**OLD COAL MINE
  MUSEUM**
473-0743.
In Madrid, about 20 mi. S.
  of Santa Fe on N.M. 14,
  next to the Mine Shaft
  Tavern.
Season: Year-round. Daily
  9:30 a.m. to dusk,
  weather permitting.
Fee (1991): $2.50 adults, $1
  children 6–12; group
  rates.

The village of Madrid was a thriving coal mine town until 1956, when its main client, Los Alamos, switched fuel sources. Madrid quickly became a ghost town full of decaying wooden Victorian houses. About 10 years ago, artists and entrepreneurs began moving back. At this wonderful, funky museum you can see a fully-restored 1906 Baldwin steam engine, an antique truck, the original mine office, a 1910 blacksmith shop and even a real seam of coal. Little Bits, the museum manager, says you can do the self-guided tour (with map) in about 25 minutes.

**EL RANCHO DE LAS
  GOLONDRINAS**
471-2261.
About 17 mi. S. of Santa Fe
  off I-25, via Exit 271.
Season: Guided group
  tours Apr.–Oct.; self-
  guided tours June–Aug.,
  Wed.–Sun. 10–4.
Fee (1991): Festivals $5
  adults, $3 seniors and
  teens, $2 ages 5–12.
  General admission $3
  adults, $2 seniors and
  teens, $1 ages 5–12.
Gift shop.

El Rancho de las Golondrinas (The Ranch of the Swallows) has seen settlers, traders, bishops, Indian raiders and more in its nearly 300-year history. Miguel Vega y Coca bought the ranch as a royal purchase in 1710 and it became the last stop before Santa Fe on the Camino Real from Mexico City through Chihuahua. Caravans of traders, soldiers and settlers regularly made the six-month, 1,000-mile round trip. Wagons brought iron, glass, wines, paper, books and other luxuries to the remote colony, and returned with raw materials like hides, wool and textiles.

Visitors can see an 18th-century *placita* house (rooms surrounding a central open space), a defensive tower, a molasses mill, a threshing ground, water mills, a blacksmith shop, a wheelwright shop, a winery and vineyards, weaving rooms, outdoor ovens and more. Plan to spend about two hours strolling the extensive grounds and outbuildings. The scene is complete with burros, sheep, goats, chickens, geese and other farm animals.

Las Golondrinas celebrates Spring and Harvest festivals with costumed villagers portraying life in Spanish Colonial New Mexico. San Ysidro, the patron saint of farmers, is honored in the spring with a procession and Mass, and visitors may enjoy hot bread from the *hornos*. Music, dances and plays are part of the celebrations. These two festivals are usually held the first weekends in June and October.

Stringing chile ristras *at Rancho de las Golondrinas.*

Jack Parsons

Taos

HARWOOD FOUNDATION MUSEUM
758-3063.
238 Ledoux St., P.O. Box 766, Taos, NM 87571.
Season: Year-round. Mon.–Fri. noon–5, Sat. 10–4; closed Sun. and major holidays.
Fee: None.

The Harwood Foundation, New Mexico's second-oldest museum, is a treasury of Taos art. Founded in 1923, it contains paintings, drawings, prints, sculpture and photographs by the artists who made Taos famous. Works by Victor Higgins, Ernest Blumenschein, Andrew Dasburg, Patrocinio Barela, Earl Stroh, Joe Waldrum, Larry Bell and Fritz Scholder are included in the collection. There is also a collection of 19th-century *retablos*.

The museum is housed in a 19th-century adobe compound that was purchased by Burt and Elizabeth Harwood in 1916 and transformed into an outstanding example of Spanish–Pueblo architecture. It is listed on the National Register of Historic Places. Operated by the University of New Mexico (UNM) since 1935, the museum presents special exhibitions by Taos artists and selections from the UNM collections throughout the year.

MILLICENT ROGERS MUSEUM

758-2462.
P.O. Box A, Taos, NM 87571.
4 mi. N. of Taos off N.M. 522. Turn left on Museum Rd. before blinking light and follow museum signs.
Season: Year-round. Daily 9–5 except Easter, San Geronimo Day (Sept. 30), Thanksgiving, Christmas, New Year's.
Fee (1991): $3 adults, $1 ages 6–16, $2 seniors, $6 families.
Gift shop.

One of the finest private museums in New Mexico was founded in 1953 by relatives of Millicent Rogers, a model who moved to Taos in 1947. Her subsequent study of regional architecture, Indian and Spanish-Colonial art inspired an extensive collection of Native American jewelry, textiles, basketry, pottery and paintings. By the time she died in 1953, her collection had become one of the most respected in the Southwest. It forms the core of the display that has recently been expanded to include religious and secular artwork of Hispanic New Mexico. The museum holds one of the most important collections of pottery by famed San Ildefonso artist Maria Martinez and members of her family. One of the museum's rarest and most striking pieces is a buffalo kachina doll, circa 1875, from Zuni Pueblo. Exhibits here tend to be rich in detail and cultural context.

Near Taos

TALL PINES MUSEUM

754-2241.
P.O. Box 567, Red River, NM 87558.
1.5 mi. from Red River in Red River Canyon.
Season: Daily May–late fall, 1:30–5:30
Fee: Small admission charge.

Winifred Hamilton operates this private museum in a pioneer log cabin, one of the first in Red River. Exhibits include local antiques and mining gear. Ms. Hamilton writes about local history and gives personal tours of the museum.

Outside the Area

FLORENCE HAWLEY ELLIS MUSEUM OF ANTHROPOLOGY

685-4333.
Ghost Ranch Conference Center, Abiquiu, NM 87510.
On U.S. 84, 35 mi. N.W. of Espanola.
Season: Year-round. Tues.–Sat. 9–noon and 1–5; Sun. 1–5; closed Mon.
Fee: None.

Dr. Florence Hawley Ellis, museum curator, a pioneer anthropologist of the Southwest has conducted excavations and research in Chaco Canyon and elsewhere. The museum specializes in excavated materials from the Ghost Ranch Gallina digs. The little-studied Gallina culture of northern New Mexico comprised the people who left Mesa Verde, Chaco Canyon and the Four Corners area during a long drought around A.D. 1200. Other exhibits feature the Spaniards of the area, Pueblo Indian clothing and prehistoric pottery making.

At the adjacent *Ruth Hall Museum of Paleontology*, be sure to see the copy of the *Coelophysis* dinosaur skeleton. The original was found near Ghost Ranch, one of the five most productive dinosaur quarries in the world. This sharp-toothed, birdlike carnivore, extinct for some 200 million years, is the official state fossil.

GHOST RANCH LIVING MUSEUM
685-4312.
Abiquiu, NM 87512.
14 mi. N. of Abiquiu on U.S. 84.
Season: Year-round. Easter–Labor Day daily 9–5:30; winter Tues.–Sun. 8–4:30; closed Mon.
Fee: None; $2 donation suggested.

This small museum, undergoing renovation in 1991, is home to animals that have been injured and cannot return to the wild. Exhibits focus on native Southwest plants and animals such as bears, mountain lions, elk, bobcats, deer, eagles, snakes, foxes and raccoons.

MUSIC

William Kirschke conducting the Orchestra of Santa Fe.

Murrae Haynes

Santa Fe

ORCHESTRA OF SANTA FE
988-4640.
P.O. Box 2091, Santa Fe, NM 87504.
Season: Sept.–May.
Tickets (1991): Singles $6–$27, depending on day, seat location and concert.

This professional chamber orchestra performs from the baroque, classical and contemporary repertories at Santa Fe's ornate Lensic Theater. Highlights of the season are the annual Bach Festival in February, featuring an exhilarating "Bach Marathon," and the Christmas presentation of Handel's *Messiah*. Founded in 1974, the orchestra is conducted by William Kirschke. Many concerts feature special guests — in 1991, for example, Petr Rejto, Ida Levin and the Irving Berlin Orchestra.

**SANTA FE CHAMBER
	MUSIC FESTIVAL**
983-2075.
P.O. Box 853, Santa Fe, NM
	87504.
Season: July–Aug.
Tickets (1991): $5–$28,
	depending on concert.

With a roster of about 70 internationally acclaimed musicians and a grand concert hall (the Saint Francis Auditorium), the Santa Fe Chamber Music Festival has been racking up a record of exciting programs since 1973. Sheldon Rich and Alicia Schachter founded the festival that year, with Pablo Casals as its first honorary president. The festival's highly recognizable visual symbol (its annual Georgia O'Keeffe art poster) was initiated the first season.

Through its composer-in-residence program, the festival has brought to Santa Fe some of the foremost composers in the United States, among them Tobias Picker, William Schuman, Leon Kirchner and the late Aaron Copland. The Composers' Forums and Composers' Workshops give music lovers an opportunity to talk with the composers. In 1987, the festival launched another highly successful innovation: the Music of the Americas series, celebrating the musical cultures of North America and Latin America and culminating with the Columbus Quincentenary in 1992.

You can sit in on daytime rehearsals for free; check the information board outside St. Francis Auditorium. Festival concerts are broadcast over the WFMT Fine Arts Network.

SANTA FE OPERA
982-3855 (box office).
P.O. Box 2408, Santa Fe,
	NM 87504-2408.
Season: Late June–Aug.
Tickets (1991): Seats
	$14–$82; standing room
	$5.

When the Santa Fe Opera opened in 1957, it filled a musical void and gave the city international stature. In June 1988, *Connoisseur* called it "the premiere summer opera festival in the United States . . . a daring, pioneering enterprise."

Founder and general director, John Crosby, mounts an ambitious repertoire each season and doesn't shrink from taking chances on unknown or new operas. He's known for his devotion to Richard Strauss; by 1990 he had staged 13 of Strauss' 15 operas. Each season usually includes popular operas along with a world premiere — sometimes a hit, sometimes not — or a forgotten masterpiece. Crosby is known for his careful choice of talent. He manages with a shoestring budget ($6.8 million in 1991), partly by attracting rising stars who are happy to pass up big bucks in exchange for a working vacation in Santa Fe. Often such stars return to perform after they've gained international reputations.

The opera's elegant outdoor amphitheater, with a soaring curved roof, contributes to the mystique. Seven miles north of Santa Fe on U.S. 285, the hilltop theater commands a spectacular view of the Sangre de Cristo Mountains to the east and the Jemez to the west. The 1,773-seat facility is famous for its architectural design, excellent acoustics and views of the stage. (Curtain time is 9 p.m. Take along a warm coat; temperatures tend to plummet after dark.)

Murrae Haynes

The Santa Fe Opera Theater.

SANTA FE CONCERT ASSOCIATION
984-8759.
P.O. Box 4626, Santa Fe, NM 87502.
Season: Sept.–May.
Tickets: Prices vary with concert; season tickets available.

Since 1931, this organization has been bringing outstanding musicians from all over the world to perform from a repertoire of classical and modern concert music. The 1990-91 annual Distinguished Artists Series included pianists Garrick Johlsson and Jan Pytel-Zak and the Borodin Trio. The Santa Fe Concert Association sponsors "Youth Concerts" as well as mid-December holiday programs and a Christmas Eve special. Most performances take place at St. Francis Auditorium in the Museum of Fine Arts on the Plaza.

SANTA FE DESERT CHORALE
988-7505.
P.O. Box 2813, Santa Fe, NM 87504.
Season: Mid-June–Aug.; also Christmas concerts.
Tickets (1991): $12–$15; group rates available.

With its premiere season in 1983, the Desert Chorale became something of a musical phenomenon. One of fewer than 50 professional choruses in the United States, the chorale has been described by the *Albuquerque Journal* as a "definitive choral performing ensemble." Founder and music director Lawrence Bandfield auditions between 24 and 30 singers nationwide every year. Twentieth-century works form the backbone of the chorale's repertory; however, music from all periods is performed, particularly from the Renaissance and baroque periods.

The 1991 season included the world premiere of a composition by Lawrence Cave of the St. John's College faculty in Santa Fe. Previous world premieres have included Dominick Argento's *A Toccata of Galuppi's*, Brent Pierce's *El Pocito*, Steven Sametz's *O'Llama de Amor Viva* and Grace Williams' *The Call of the Sea*. Some performances have been aired on National Public Radio. Santa Fe concerts are performed at the acoustically impressive Santuario de Guadalupe, an ancient adobe church at 100 Guadalupe St.

SANTA FE SYMPHONY
983-3530 (information),
983-1414 (tickets).
P.O. Box 9692, Santa Fe,
NM 87504.
Season: Sept.–May.
Tickets (1991): Singles
$10–$30; season tickets
available.

The Santa Fe Symphony (SFS), a young and ambitious group founded in 1984, performs under the direction of Stewart Robertson. Robertson, who is music director and principal conductor of Glimmerglass Opera in New York, and the Inland Empire Symphony Orchestra in San Bernardino, California, has conducted widely in Europe.

SFS's season consists of six subscription concerts of classical and contemporary compositions. Performances are held at the Santa Fe Convention Center, locally known as the Sweeney Center, 201 W. Marcy St. Imaginative programming is a hallmark of SFS; the 1991 season included a children's program and a Festival of American Music.

SANTA FE SUMMER CONCERT SERIES
256-1777.
Big River Productions, P.O.
Box 8036, Albuquerque,
NM 87198.
Season: Summer only.
Tickets: Prices vary with
performer.

The Paolo Soleri Outdoor Amphitheater, on the Santa Fe Indian School campus, Cerrillos Rd., is Santa Fe's summer venue for big-name popular musicians. Past concerts have included stars like Frank Zappa, Kenny Loggins, Suzanne Vega, Bob Dylan, Shadowfax and Santana. For summer 1991, Big River Productions scheduled more than two dozen concerts and other events. The amphitheater, designed by architect Paolo Soleri, is plain in appearance and blends with the landscape. At night under the stars, it becomes a magical space where performers and audiences unite. Buy your tickets early; they tend to sell out quickly — and bring your umbrella, just in case.

SUMMERSCENE
989-8062.
P.O. Box 1808, Santa Fe,
NM 87504.
Season: Mid-June–Aug.,
Tues. and Thurs., noon
and 6 p.m.
Tickets: Free.

Every Tuesday and Thursday on the plaza, Summerscene sets the mood with casual entertainment. These popular concerts feature local, regional and national artists in more than 50 concerts each season. Bankers, secretaries, construction workers and tourists bring lunch or buy a Frito pie at Woolworth, and enjoy the free show. There's something for everyone, from light opera to rhythm and blues, jazz, Cajun, salsa, Tex-Mex, bluegrass and Spanish folk. Also offered are storytelling and lectures by eminent scholars.

OTHER MUSIC IN SANTA FE

Several smaller groups lend variety and flavor to the musical scene year-round: *Serenata of Santa Fe* is a chamber group of professionals who perform year round on the last Thursday of the month at the Episcopal Church of the Holy Faith (311 E. Palace Ave., 989-7988 or 989-9258). In the summer, Serenata plays on Sunday afternoons at Oscar Huber Memorial Ballpark in Madrid, 20 miles southwest of Santa Fe. The *Sangre de Cristo Chorale* (662-9717 evenings, P.O. Box 4462, Santa Fe, N.M. 87502) is an ensemble directed by Sheldon Kalberg that performs a repertory of classical, baroque, Renaissance and folk music. The *Santa Fe Women's Ensemble* (982-9385) comprises 12 semiprofessional singers. The schedule includes spring and fall concerts at St. Francis Auditorium and four traditional Christmas concerts at the Loretto Chapel.

Taos

JAZZ LEGENDS AT TAOS SKI VALLEY
776-2280.
Twining Tavern, Thunderbird Lodge, Taos Ski Valley, NM 87525.
Season: First wk. in Jan.
Tickets (1991): $12–$15; reservations a must.

Ski season is the "second season" for Taos, and the Jazz Legends series has become a highlight. World-famous musicians perform in an intimate lounge setting. The 1991 lineup included clarinetist Kenny Davern, bassist Milt Hinton, drummers Gus Johnson and Jake Hanna, pianists Eddie Higgins and Gerald Wiggins and saxophonists Eric Schneider and Scott Hamilton.

TAOS COMMUNITY AUDITORIUM
758-4677 (performances), 758-2052.
133 N. Pueblo Rd., Taos, NM 87571.
Season: Year round.
Tickets (1991): $2–$20; call for schedule.

Local and out-of-town musical and variety acts are featured here. Recently appearing were the Brigham Young University Chorus, the Chinese Golden Dragon Acrobats, a Spanish-language theater group and a Puerto Rican salsa group. Chamber music is performed in the summer (see "Taos School of Music," below). Call for a current schedule.

TAOS SCHOOL OF MUSIC
776-2388.
P.O. Box 1879, Taos, NM 87571.
Season: Mid-June–early Aug.
Tickets (1991): $2–$10.

Established in the 1960s, this chamber music academy draws talented youngsters from all over the country to study piano and stringed instruments. They study at Taos Ski Valley and perform weekly in Taos. The 1991 season featured classical and contemporary chamber music concerts, as well as special performances by the American String Quartet.

Milt Hinton performing at the Thunderbird Lodge.

Ken Gallard; Courtesy Taos County Chamber of Commerce

Near Taos

MUSIC FROM ANGEL FIRE
758-4667.
P.O. Box 1744, Taos, NM 87571.
Season: Mid-Aug.–Labor Day.
Tickets (1991): $12, available at Total Arts Gallery, 122-A Kit Carson Rd., Taos, NM 87571.

An enterprising group of Taos and Angel Fire business people bring in New York-area musicians for a short but sweet season of classical and chamber music performances in Taos and Angel Fire, a ski community on U.S. 64 east of Taos.

NIGHTLIFE

Santa Fe and Taos are towns that roll up their sidewalks at night. For five weeks or so in the summer, the Opera and the Chamber Music Festival enliven Santa Fe evenings. For Taos, there's the Taos School of Music and Music From Angel Fire in summer and the ski season festivities in winter. Neither town has been invaded by the fern-and-brass bar syndrome. Taprooms tend to have the stamp of local tastes, history and individuality. For current happenings, check the Friday "Pasatiempo" section of the *New Mexican* in Santa Fe, and the weekly *Taos News* in Taos.

Santa Fe

Club West (982-0099; 213 W. Alameda) offers the only year-round venue for national talent and local dance bands. It has a long bar and roomy dance space. The *Bull Ring* (983-3328; 414 Old Santa Fe Trail) is a favorite hangout that features local rock 'n' roll bands. During the annual January-February sessions of the state legislature, the daily bluster at the capitol spills over from lunch until late at the night. Look to *Vanessie of Santa Fe* (982-9966; 434 W. San Francisco St.) for a more reserved cocktail-piano atmosphere. The pianist is Doug Montgomery.

La Fonda's *La Fiesta Lounge* (982-5511; 100 E. San Francisco St.) is another favorite place for locals and would-be Santa Feans to meet. Entertainment ranges from small jazz groups to flamenco guitar. In contrast to La Fonda's dark, intimate space, the *Eldorado Court Lounge* (988-4455; 309 W. San Francisco St.) is a large atrium with a variety of live music and, unfortunately, Sonoran Desert decor that is out of place in Santa Fe. *El Farol* (983-9912; 808 Canyon Rd.), ensconced in an ancient adobe, is a Santa Fe institution. Cozy and dark, with local landscape murals, it's a place where folks let their hair down. Great *tapas*, local bands and occasional national groups but a tight dance space. (See also *Restaurants*.) At *La Casa Sena Cantina* (988-9232; 125 E.

Dancing at Club West.

Murrae Haynes

Palace Ave.), the staff are professional singers, belting out Broadway and movie musical tunes while toting your margaritas. (See also *Restaurants*.)

If you're just looking for camaraderie and conversation, popular spots range from the restrained Victorian elegance of *La Posada de Santa Fe*'s four-room bar (986-0000; 330 E. Palace Ave.) to the funk of *Evangelo's* (982-9014, 200 W. San Francisco St.), where ersatz Polynesian decor achieves a remarkable kind of grace, if not style. *The Dragon Room*, the bar next door to the famous Pink Adobe Restaurant (983-7712; 406 Old Santa Fe Trail), Robert Redford's hang-out when he's in town, features a collection of dragon figures and a glowing fireplace to soothe winter chills. In summer, the Dragon Room becomes the dragon patio. No entertainment except the patrons themselves. This can be said as well of the *Mine Shaft Tavern* in Madrid (473-0743, Main Street; you can't miss it). It's totally unpretentious and all that the name implies: a place where coal miners could, and actually did, feel at home.

A dozen or so restaurants in Santa Fe and environs boast convivial bars and fairly regular live entertainment, such as Spanish classical guitar, flamenco, mariachi trios, contemporary jazz, Latin rhythms, country and western, and big bands. The musicians are mostly local and form a small cadre of the talent-ed and dedicated — willing to forgo big-city bucks for the fun of living in Santa Fe. Here's a partial list: *The Atrium* (988-3870, 731 Canyon Rd.); *Comme Chez Vous* (984-0004, 116 W. San Francisco St., 3rd floor of Plaza Mercado); *Coyote Cafe* (983-1615, 132 W. Water St.); the *Inn at Loretto* (988-5531, 211 Old Santa Fe Trail); *Manana, the Bar*, at the Inn of the Governors (982-4333, Alameda and Don Gaspar); *Maria's* (983-7929, 555 W. Cordova Rd.); the *Legal Tender*, in Lamy just south of Santa Fe (982-8425); the *Ore House* (983-8687, on the Plaza); *Peppers Cantina* (984-2272, Old Pecos Trail about six miles south of downtown); the *Palace Restaurant* (982-9892, 142 W. Palace Ave.), on the site of Dona Tules' 1835 gambling saloon; and *Tiny's* (983-9817, on the corner of St. Francis and Cerrillos Rds. at Pen Road Shopping Center). (See *Restaurants*, Chapter Five, for further information.)

In Taos

A good spot to begin or end your evening in Taos is at the Taos Inn's *Adobe Bar* (758-2233; 125 Paseo del Pueblo Norte). The inn itself is a lovingly-restored historic landmark, and though the bar is compact, you can be served in the adjacent library, on the patio in summer, or up on one of the balconies overlooking the two-story lobby. There's live entertainment on Wednesdays and Sundays and you'll rub elbows with many Taoseños, from artists to labor-ers to business people. The *Holiday Inn* (758-4444; 1005 Paseo del Pueblo Sur) is reputed to have the happiest happy hour in town, 5–7 p.m. weekdays, with free hors d'oeuvres and live music. (See also *Lodging*, Chapter Three.)

The *Sagebrush Inn* (758-2254; three miles south of Taos on N.M. 64) is coun-try and western headquarters in Taos. You can dance the two-step to live music every night or just listen from the comfortable bar. Michael Martin

Murphey, a Taos cowboy singer and former Texan whom New Mexicans love, performs there several times a year. Also good scenes for dance bands are the *Cabaret at the Kachina Lodge* (758-9190; Paseo del Pueblo Norte) and *Far West Club* at the Hacienda Inn (758-8610; S. Santa Fe Rd.). The hottest local groups provide plenty of dance tunes, from country and western and rock 'n' roll to salsa. (See also *Lodging*, Chapter Three.) The *Ski Valley Junction* (776-1441; Ski Valley Rd. at the blinking light) has dance bands several nights a week.

On the Taos Plaza, *La Cocina* (758-2412) is a landmark and a kind of town living room with bar. Everyone from skiers to local families rubs shoulders here. On Saturdays and Sundays musicians perform country and western, traditional Spanish and flamenco. And then there's *La Cocina's* mural of famous Taoseños and visitors, from Georgia O'Keeffe to Jane Fonda. (See also *Restaurants*, Chapter Five.) If you just want to kick back instead of kicking up your heels, head for the *Chile Connection* (776-8787, Ski Valley Rd.), where there's a lounge, big-screen TV, restaurant, and, in summer, an outdoor patio.

PUEBLOS

A trip to one of New Mexico's 19 pueblos can be a thrilling experience. If you are open minded, you may find yourself questioning some of your cultural assumptions. Many visitors have an especially hard time getting over their assumptions about time. "What time does the dance start?" is the question visitors ask most often. There is no definite answer: the dance starts when the dancers are ready. On the other hand, visitors may be astonished to see that Indians have new cars and modern homes.

The reality of Pueblo life is far from the Hollywood-influenced stereotype. The Pueblo Indians have occupied their villages for centuries, providing them a kind of continuity that is unimaginable for most non-Indians. For most of their history they were self-sufficient, producing beautiful pottery and jewelry and living in harmony with their surroundings. But when the Spaniards arrived, and later the Anglos, the native population suffered disease, cultural violation and loss of land and livelihood.

Today, Native Americans are regaining self-sufficiency, having learned to use the political and economic systems to their advantage. The Pueblo villages are self-governing, sovereign entities with their own schools, clinics and police forces. The Pueblo people operate many thriving businesses and are enterprising entrepreneurs. Many speak English and Spanish, in addition to their native tongue. Their artwork is popular and in demand and they continue to nourish their spiritual roots in the ways handed down from generation to generation.

The best time to visit is on a feast day, the major public celebration at each pueblo. Ostensibly, feast days are named after particular saints; however, the tradition predates the arrival of the Spanish priests, who applied the names of saints to what were already holy days for the Pueblo people. A feast day is a day of thanksgiving, when relatives return and everyone gives thanks for the well-being of the people. Dancers spend many days preparing their clothing and practicing the steps. Families prepare quantities of food for visitors and the intoxicating smells of *posole*, chile and baking bread waft through the air.

Pueblo Indian girl in traditional costume during feast day celebration.

Richard Twarog; Courtesy Santa Fe Chamber of Commerce

Feast days usually start with a Mass at the Catholic church. A priest may lead a procession of dancers to the church, and the dances begin sometime after Mass. In spring, summer and early autumn, dances like the Blue Corn Dance, Butterfly Dance and Harvest Dance may be performed in observance of the planting and harvest. In winter, the hunting cycle is celebrated with Deer, Elk and Buffalo Dances. (See individual pueblo listings for dates of feast days.)

On Christmas Eve and Christmas Day, you may see the Matachines Dance at Taos, Picuris, San Juan, Santa Clara and San Ildefonso pueblos. Dancers clothed in beaded headdresses with scarves over their mouths move to 16th-century Spanish music played on guitars and violins. The origins of the Mat-achines dance are obscure, but it is probably rooted in Moorish customs.

A good time to see dances and buy art is the annual *Eight Northern Indian Pueblos Artist and Craftsman Show*, held in July at one of the pueblos near Santa Fe. More than 600 Indian artists from Maine to California exhibit their work in the largest Native American-owned and operated arts-and-crafts show in the country. Pueblo pottery and jewelry dominate, but there's a wide variety of beadwork, kachina dolls, sculpture, painting, weaving and other crafts. Mutton stew, fry bread, Indian tacos, pies and outdoor-oven-baked breads are sold at colorful booths. You may see Plains and Pueblo Indian dances. Photography permits can be purchased. For locations and dates, call 852-4265.

Pueblo Etiquette

Here are some things to keep in mind when visiting a pueblo:

• Inquire ahead of time about visitor hours. Remember that some pueblos are closed to outsiders on certain days for religious activities.

• Drive slowly.

• Never bring drugs or alcoholic beverages to a pueblo.

• *Stop at the visitor center or tribal office when you arrive. This is a requirement at all pueblos.* Some charge fees; others ask visitors to register.

• Do not walk into or on a *kiva* (circular ceremonial structures).

• Homes, *kivas* and cemeteries are not open to non-pueblo visitors. However, if you are invited to come into someone's home to eat, it is considered impolite to refuse. (It *is* considered polite to eat and leave promptly, so that others can come in and eat.) Some pueblos operate food concessions on feast days where non-Indians can sample pueblo cooking.

• Remember that dances are religious ceremonies, not performances. Conduct yourself as you would in a church. Revealing clothing, like shorts and halter tops, is not acceptable. Don't talk or obstruct the view of others during the dances, don't applaud afterward and don't approach the dancers or ask about the meaning of dances. The pueblo people prefer not to discuss their beliefs with outsiders.

• Observe each pueblo's regulations on use of cameras, tape recorders and drawing. Most pueblos forbid these activities during dances. (See pueblo listings for particulars.) If you want to photograph a pueblo resident, ask permission first and give a donation to the family.

Near Santa Fe

COCHITI PUEBLO
465-2244.
Tribal Office, P.O. Box 70, Cochiti, NM 87041.
Cochiti Pueblo exit from I-25 about 25 mi. S. of Santa Fe.
Language: Keresan.
Feast Day: July 14, San Buenaventura.
Fee: None; cameras not allowed.

Cochiti (CO-chi-tee) Pueblo remains rooted in its past while building a strong future. The church built in 1628 in honor of San Buenaventura still stands, remodeled and maintained. Not far away is *Cochiti Lake*, a recreational community built on land leased from the pueblo, which also operates Cochiti Lake services. Cochiti Lake has an 18-hole golf course, tennis courts, swimming pool, marina and shopping center. (See also "Swimming" and "Water Sports" in Chapter Six.)

Cochiti Pueblo is known for its magnificent drums and evocative clay storyteller figurines. The storyteller figures were created in 1964 by Cochiti potter Helen Cordero, who says she was inspired by her grandfather telling stories to children. Many Pueblo potters make the storytellers in human and animal forms, but Cochiti storytellers are the most highly prized. Cochiti drums, essential to the pueblo's ceremonies, are also coveted by collectors.

NAMBE PUEBLO
455-2036.
Rte. 1, Box 117-BB, Santa Fe, NM 87501.
Drive 15 mi. N. of Santa Fe on U.S. 285, 3 mi. E. on N.M. 503 to sign for Nambe Falls, then 2 mi. to pueblo entrance.
Language: Tewa.
Feast Day: Oct. 4, St. Francis.
Fees (1991): Sketching $15, still cameras $5, movie /video cameras $10.

A small pueblo set near the Sangre de Cristo Mountains in a piñon and juniper valley, Nambe (nam-BAY) retains a few original buildings, including the ruins of a mission. Many tribal members work at nearby Los Alamos National Laboratory, in Española or in Santa Fe. Beautiful Nambe Falls, one of the state's few waterfalls, is the setting for the annual Fourth of July Ceremonials. From April through October, *Nambe Falls Recreational Site* offers fishing, picnicking, camping, boating and sightseeing. Fees are charged for each activity.

POJOAQUE PUEBLO
455-2278.
Rte. 11, Box 71, Santa Fe, NM 87501.
15 mi. N. of Santa Fe on U.S. 285.
Language: Tewa.
Feast Day: Dec. 12, Our Lady of Guadalupe.
Fees: Contact Governor's Office before sketching or filming.

The 20 businesses that line U.S. 285 at Pojoaque evince such prosperity that one would not guess that Pojoaque (po-WAH-kee) is a pueblo that has pulled itself back from near extinction. Only mounds of earth remain of the original pueblo, and in the late 1800s the people themselves were almost wiped out by a smallpox epidemic.

In the 1930s, a new Pojoaque was founded, and a milestone was reached in 1983 when tribal members danced for the first time in more than 100 years. Now they celebrate Our Lady of Guadalupe Day as well as an annual Plaza Fiesta Day during the first week in August. The fiesta honors the tribe's commercial enterprises with food, dances, hot-air balloon rides, entertainment and a sidewalk bazaar.

Pojoaque is proud of its planned shopping center and mobile home park, but tradition remains important. The Tewa language is taught in classes at the library, along with pottery and jewelry making. Arts and crafts by Pojoaque members are sold at the official state tourist center operated by the pueblo.

SAN FELIPE PUEBLO
867-3381.
P.O. Box A, San Felipe Pueblo, NM 87001.
About 40 mi. S. of Santa Fe on I-25.
Language: Keresan.
Feast Day: May 1, San Felipe.
Fees (1991): $2 per carload; no cameras or sketching; cameras may be confiscated.

This small pueblo on the banks of the Rio Grande has a timeless feel, perhaps engendered by the ceaseless flow of water past its softly contoured adobe buildings. San Felipe is known for its beautiful Green Corn Dance on May 1, its Feast Day. Men, women and children participate in day-long dances under the spring sun. Dances are in the plaza, which has been worn three feet below the ground surface by countless feet. A traditional, conservative pueblo, San Felipe is reviving its artisans' longtime skills in beadwork and *heishi* (HEE-she) jewelry made of tiny, hand-carved shell beads.

SAN JUAN PUEBLO
852-4400.
P.O. Box 1099, San Juan, NM 87566.
Drive 1 mi. N. of Española on N.M. 68, turn left onto U.S. 70 at San Juan Pueblo sign; entrance is 1 mi. farther.
Language: Tewa.
Feast Day: June 24, San Juan.
Fees (1991): Still cameras $5, sketching and filming $10, tape recording not allowed; some events restricted.

In 1598, conquistador Don Juan de Oñate declared this prosperous and friendly pueblo the first capital of New Mexico. When Spanish demands for gold and slaves became too insistent, the San Juan people asked Oñate to take his capital somewhere else. (It ended up in Santa Fe.) A San Juan native named Popé organized the Pueblo Revolt in 1680. (See also *History*, Chapter One.) Now San Juan is the headquarters of the Eight Northern Indian Pueblo Council.

The largest and northernmost of the Tewa-speaking pueblos, San Juan has two central plazas with a Catholic church and ceremonial *kivas* side by side. It also runs the O'ke Oweenge Arts and Crafts Cooperative, a multipurpose complex where visitors can view and purchase the pueblo's distinctive red incised pottery. Artisans excel at jewelry, carving, weaving and other arts. They are consummate potters, producing a ware whose luster and geometric designs are coveted by collectors worldwide. Members of the cooperative give demonstrations.

Across the street from the crafts cooperative is the Tewa Indian Restaurant, where you can munch Indian fry bread, dried fruit pies, red and green chile stews, *posole*, teas and other treats. Open weekdays. The San Juan Pueblo Bingo is open Wednesday through Saturday starting at 5:30 p.m. and Sunday starting at noon. Fishing at the tribal lakes is open spring and summer; permits available on site.

SAN ILDEFONSO PUEBLO

455-2273, 455-3549.
Rte. 5, Box 315-A, Santa Fe, NM 87501.
Drive 15 mi. N. of Santa Fe on U.S. 285, turn left at N.M. 502, go 6 mi. to entrance on right.
Language: Tewa.
Feast Day: Jan. 23, San Ildefonso.
Fees (1991): $3 per carload most days; sketching and filming usually $15, still cameras usually $5. No cameras permitted at Feast Day dances.

San Ildefonso is world famous for its black-on-black pottery, a technique that was developed and refined by Maria Martinez and her husband, Julian, in the 1920s. Maria was also among the first Pueblo potters to sign her work. Her pots are prized by private collectors and museums and her descendants continue to create pottery that is both innovative and traditional. You can see a private collection of work by Maria and her family at the *Popovi Da Studio of Indian Arts* (455-3332; call ahead for hours of operation), which also sells pottery, paintings, jewelry, baskets, kachina dolls and books. Other artisans sell wares out of their studios. Inquire at the visitor and information center (455-3549).

San Ildefonso operates a museum (455-2273; closed weekends) with displays of local arts, embroidery, photography, pottery-making techniques and Pueblo history. A stocked fishing lake is open year round, and permits can be purchased at the lake.

SANTA CLARA PUEBLO

753-7326.
P.O. Box 580, Española, NM 87532.
From Española drive 1.3 mi. on N.M. 30, cross to W. side of Rio Grande and entrance on left.
Language: Tewa.
Feast Day: Aug. 12, Santa Clara.

Set in the wide Rio Grande Valley, with vistas of mountains on either side, Santa Clara is home to 2,600 tribal members who farm, work at jobs outside the pueblo and create stunning red and black polished pottery, sculpture and paintings. They are the descendants of the ancient Puye Cliff Dwellers, and their name for their Pueblo, *Kha P'o*, means "valley of the wild roses."

Santa Clara potters are noted for their intricately carved pottery (sgraffito), particularly the etched miniatures. Look for "Pottery for Sale" signs on houses: you will be invited to come in and meet the artist. Santa Clara also offers guided tours of the pueblo and its historical church. On a tour, you'll be allowed to photograph, see pottery demonstrations, buy native foods and perhaps see

Fees (1991): Sketching $15, still cameras $4, movie cameras $10. No cameras allowed at some events. Puye Cliff Dwellings self-guided tour $4 adults, $3 seniors and children.

a dance. Tours are offered weekdays only, with five days' advance notice. Inquire at the Tourism Office, or phone the number above.

Singing Water Pottery and Tours (753-9663; Joe Baca, Rt. 1, Box 472-C, Santa Clara Pueblo, Española, N.M. 87532) specializes in Santa Clara pottery, walking tours, Black Mesa Cultural River Floats, Puye Cliff Dwellings and pottery demonstrations.

Santa Clara operates the *Puye* (POO-yay) *Cliff Dwellings,* a National Landmark west of the pueblo. The original dwellings were hollowed out of cliffs made of volcanic tuff. Later, houses were built below the cliffs and atop the mesas. The site was abandoned around A.D. 1500. You can follow three trails to see the ruins. Stairways in the rock connect the cliff dwellings with the 740-room pueblo ruins and *kiva* above. The mesa top affords spectacular views of mountains and valley. Guided tours are available by prior arrangement with the Tourism Office. Before visiting Puye, inquire at the Tourism Office about road conditions.

Puye Ruins.

Murrae Haynes

Santa Clara Canyon Recreational Area, a rugged natural spot, is open to visitors for camping, picnicking and fishing. It's open April through October; inquire about fees at the Tourism Office.

SANTO DOMINGO PUEBLO

465-2214.
P.O. Box 99, Santo Domingo Pueblo, NM 87052.
About 34 mi. S. of Santa Fe on I-25.
Language: Keresan.
Feast Day: Aug. 4, Santo Domingo.
Fees: None; donations accepted. No cameras, sketching or recording allowed.

Perhaps the most conservative of the Rio Grande pueblos, Santo Domingo is home to a large number of highly creative and enterprising artists. Many have taken the traditional *heishi* and turquoise jewelry making techniques and translated them into beautiful contemporary designs. Others have revived the ancient Santo Domingo pottery tradition and produce superb designs that are blends of old and new. Santo Domingo jewelry is available from artists selling under the *portal* of the Palace of the Governors in Santa Fe and at shops at the pueblo.

The *August 4th Feast Day Corn Dance* is an unforgettable scene, with hundreds of dancers, singers and clowns participating in all-day ceremonies. Santo Domingo operates a *Tribal Cultural Center* that sponsors an annual arts and crafts fair on Labor Day weekend.

TESUQUE PUEBLO

983-2667.
Rte. 11, Box 1, Santa Fe, NM 87501.
9 mi. N. of Santa Fe on U.S. 285. Main village is 1 mi. W. of highway.
Language: Tewa.
Feast Day: Nov. 12, San Diego.
Fees (1991): Still cameras $5, film and video $15, sketching $12, painting $25.

Though close to Santa Fe, Tesuque is one of the most conservative of the pueblos. The site was occupied as far back as 1250; however, the original pueblo was at another location that was abandoned after the Pueblo Revolt of 1680. Tesuque Indians played a major part in the revolt. Two of its leaders, Catua and Omtua, secretly notified the other pueblos of the plan and were arrested when someone betrayed them to the Spaniards. (See also *History*, Chapter One.).

The present pueblo was established in 1694. Listed on the National Register of Historic Places, Tesuque has a large central plaza with a Catholic church. The tribe operates a bingo parlor (984-8414) on U.S. 285, an RV park and store (455-2661), a campground in the Sangre de Cristo Mountains (983-2667) and *Tesuque Natural Farm* (983-2667), where certified organic blue corn, chile and other vegetables are grown. Several artists' studios are open to the public, selling mostly traditional Tesuque clay figurines, micaceous and other pottery, beadwork, drums, weaving and carvings. Inquire at the Tribal Office.

Near Taos

PICURIS PUEBLO
587-2957.
P.O. Box 487, Peñasco, NM
  87553.
Drive 17 mi. N. from
  Española to junction
  with N.M. 75. Turn right
  and drive 13 mi. to
  Picuris.
Language: Tiwa.
Feast Day: Aug. 10, San
  Lorenzo.
Fees (1991): Sketching $10,
  still cameras $5,
  movie/video cameras
  $10.

The last pueblo to be discovered by the Spaniards in 1519, Picuris (pee-ku-REES) is nearly hidden in the Sangre de Cristo Mountains. It was settled in the 1200s and about 200 years later had grown into a multi-story adobe complex. Picuris was abandoned after the 1680 Pueblo Revolt and reestablished in the 1700s. It has never made a treaty with another government and retains its status as a sovereign nation and tribe.

The smallest of the pueblos, Picuris operates several facilities for visitors. The Picuris Tribal Enterprise is totally computerized, containing a restaurant, convenience store, smoke shop, fishing shop and museum. The *Hidden Valley Restaurant* (closed Tuesdays) features a native Picuris and American menu. At the museum, you can purchase unusual mica-flecked pottery and view artifacts from recent excavations. For a fee, you can also tour ruins, camp or fish for trout in two stocked lakes.

TAOS PUEBLO
758-8626, 758-9593.
P.O. Box 1846, Taos, NM
  87571.
2 mi. N. of Taos off N.M.
  68.
Language: Tiwa.
Feast Day: Sept. 29-30, San
  Geronimo.
Fees (1991): Admission fee.
  Sketching $15, still
  cameras $5,
  movie/video cameras
  $10, painting $35. No
  filming or sketching at
  dances.

There was an established civilization at Taos long before Europe emerged from the Dark Ages. The present pueblo of multi-storied adobe apartment buildings has been occupied since about A.D. 1450. Today, as then, the clear waters of the Rio Pueblo flow down from sacred Blue Lake high in the Sangre de Cristo Mountains and through the pueblo. Today, as then, the residents draw their water from the stream. To honor their traditions, they have chosen to live as their ancestors did without indoor plumbing or electricity. In less traditional parts of the pueblo, these conveniences are available.

Architecturally, Taos Pueblo is the most spectacular of the northern New Mexico pueblos (see *Architecture* in this chapter), and it has captured the imaginations of countless artists. However, the beauty of the pueblo is only an outward manifestation of its spiritual strength. Taos was the seat of the Pueblo Revolt of 1680, when the Spaniards were driven out of New Mexico. It also played an active role in the 1847 uprising of Hispanics and Indians against the U.S. government. (See also *History*, Chapter One.)

Taos Pueblo, with about 1,100 residents, is governed by a council of 50 men who are participants in the secret *kiva* religion. The economy is based on government services, tourism, arts and crafts, ranching and farming. *San Geroni-*

Taos Pueblo's three-tiered adobe buildings.

Mark Nohl/New Mexico Magazine

mo Feast Day is a highlight of the year, with a sunset dance on September 29, foot races, an arts and crafts fair, ritual pole climbing, traditional dances and, of course, food. During the festivities, the "Black Eyes," a religious society, perform humorous acts that nonetheless have spiritual significance for pueblo members.

Visitors are welcome at the *Taos Pueblo Powwow*, held the second weekend of July each year. Native Americans from many tribes join in this colorful and popular dance event. (The powwow is a Plains Indian tradition, but Taos has been influenced by contacts with Plains tribes who came to trade and raid.) Other dances open to the public (no cameras) are the *Turtle Dance*, January 1; *Buffalo or Deer Dance*, January 6; *Feast of Santa Cruz Corn Dance*, May 3; *San Antonio Corn Dance*, June 13; *San Juan Corn Dance*, June 24; *Deer Dance or Matachines*, Christmas Day.

Taos artists are noted for their mica-flecked pottery, tanned buckskin moccasins, silver jewelry and their wonderful drums, made of hides stretched over hollowed cottonwood logs. A dozen or more shops on the Pueblo Plaza sell these goods, along with *hornos*, breads fresh-baked in adobe ovens

SEASONAL EVENTS

(Unless noted, admission is not charged for the following events.)

Santa Fe

ALL SPECIES DAY

A pageant for all ages in which animals and plants have their outspoken but playful say about what we're doing to our environment. Usually held the Saturday before Earth Day in April, the focus is the *All Species Parade* in which kids dressed as antlered elk, stilt-legged storks, lumbering buffalo and papier-maché birds parade from the plaza to Fort Marcy Park. There the animals hold a "creature congress" in which they speak, squawk, howl and bay for the earth. There are many festivities including a plethora of dancers, displays, floats, sideshows and storytellers. Started by Santa Fean Chris Wells, All Species Day celebrated its 10th anniversary in 1991.

CHRISTMAS

Christmas in Santa Fe is a delight of the senses, a time when each culture celebrates its own traditions. The Palace of the Governors usually sponsors **Las Posadas,** a traditional Spanish reenactment of Joseph and Mary's search for shelter on the night Jesus was born. The plaza is the setting for the pageant, performed by an area church group, and a choir and audience members follow the Holy Couple around the plaza.

Many area musical ensembles conduct seasonal concerts in December. Consult the Santa Fe Convention and Visitor Bureau or local newspapers for schedules. Also, many area pueblos hold special dances around Christmas (see "Pueblos," above). On Christmas Eve, Santa Fe is alight with thousands of *farolitos*, glowing candles placed in paper bags. The scent of piñon bonfires, or *luminarias*, fills the air as hundreds of people take to the streets in the Canyon Road neighborhood to see the *farolitos*, sing carols and socialize.

EIGHT NORTHERN INDIAN PUEBLOS ARTIST AND CRAFTSMAN SHOW

This is a large exhibition and sale of handcrafted Indian artwork and crafts, held at one of the pueblos near Santa Fe. (See "Pueblos," above.)

FEAST DAY DANCES

Each pueblo has a special Feast Day celebration annually on its patron saint's day. (See "Pueblos," above.)

Santa Fe

INDIAN MARKET
983-5220.
320 Galisteo, Suite 660,
Santa Fe, NM 87501.
Time: First weekend after
third Thurs in Aug.
Location: Plaza and
vicinity.
Fee: None.

Indian Market is the biggest weekend of the year in Santa Fe, when more than 1,000 Native American artists exhibit and sell their work at outdoor booths on and around the plaza. Indian Market is the largest exhibition and sale of Indian art in the world. Begun more than 70 years ago as an effort to help Pueblo Indians revive their pottery- and jewelry-making traditions, it has been the springboard for countless successful artistic careers. All participants are carefully screened: they must be Native American and their work must be totally handmade.

Activity starts before dawn on Saturday with artists unloading work at their booths and eager collectors lining up to get first chance at a coveted pot or necklace when the market opens at 8 a.m. Irresistible smells of fry bread, coffee, mutton stew and Navajo tacos fill the air, and the plaza slowly fills with people dressed in their flashiest duds. Artists demonstrate skills like sand painting or basket weaving, and the drums sound for social dances in the courtyard of the Palace of the Governors. The array of artwork is mind-boggling: from pottery, jewelry, beadwork and weaving to basketry, paintings, drums and rattles. There's something for everyone, from a $3 corn necklace to a $5,000 Navajo rug.

LA FIESTA DE SANTA FE
988-7575.
P.O. Box 4516, Santa Fe, NM 87502.
Time: Weekend after Labor Day.
Location: Plaza and vicinity.

The oldest continuously-observed festival in the United States, La Fiesta is the quintessential celebration of New Mexico's Hispanic culture. The first Fiesta was held in September 1712, with processions, sermons, candle lighting, pomp and circumstance in commemoration of Don Diego de Vargas' return into Santa Fe in 1692, following the 1680 Pueblo Revolt. (See *History*, Chapter One.)

Fiesta preparations begin far in advance, with

Zozobra goes up in flames, beginning La Fiesta de Santa Fe.

Murrae Haynes

the selection of young women to serve as the Fiesta Queen and her Court, and of young men to serve as Don Diego de Vargas and his 17-member retinue. All participate in a reenactment of De Vargas' return. On the Friday after Labor Day, La Fiesta begins with the Pregon de la Fiesta and Mass at Rosario Chapel.

An extremely popular addition to La Fiesta is Zozobra, or "Old Man Gloom," a 40-foot-tall papier-maché puppet that stands in Fort Marcy Park on Friday night of La Fiesta. Zozobra was born in 1926, the brainchild of Will Shuster, one of Los Cinco Pintores who started the Santa Fe art colony. As fireworks flare and dancers gyrate wildly around him, Zozobra goes up in flames, symbolically burning away the year's troubles so that the celebrations can begin. The cheering crowd then heads for the plaza for food, music and dancing. Plaza festivities continue through the weekend.

RODEO DE SANTA FE
988-3044, 471-4300.
Rodeo Grounds, Rodeo Rd.
  near Richards Ave.
Season: Mid-July.
Fee: Admission charged;
  call for details.

(See *Recreation*, Chapter Six.)

**SANTA FE BANJO AND
FIDDLE CONTEST**
983-8315, 982-8548.
c/o Rte. 7, Box 115-BK,
  Santa Fe, NM 87505.
Season: Late Aug.
Location: Rodeo Grounds,
  Rodeo Rd. near Richards
  Ave.
Fee: Admission charged;
  write or call for details.

You can hear nearly every way there is to play a fiddle or pick a banjo during this festive weekend. Fiddle competitions include children's, bluegrass, Spanish and old-time. There are also mandolin, flat pick guitar and song writing competitions and workshops for a number of different instruments and playing styles. The weekend includes a jam session and performances by competition winners.

SPANISH MARKET
983-4038.
P.O. Box 1611, Santa Fe,
  NM 87504.
Season: Last weekend in
  July.
Location: On the Plaza.
Fee: None.

During the centuries when New Mexico was a Spanish colony, its isolation from Spain and Mexico fostered the growth of unique folk arts. Many helped serve the religious needs of the settlers. Today they have undergone a revival, and the work of New Mexican artisans is in great demand by collectors and museums.

At Spanish Market, which celebrates its 40th year in 1991, you can see the finest Hispanic artwork produced in the state today: *santos, colcha* embroidery, woolen weaving, straw applique, carved and painted furniture, tin work, forged iron, *reredos* and more. About 150 artists exhibit in booths around the plaza. The scene is rounded out with native New Mexican folk music groups, food booths and artist demonstrations.

CONTEMPORARY HISPANIC MARKET

c/o Edward Gonzales, 826-C Camino de Monte Rey, Santa Fe, NM 87501.
Season: Last weekend in July.
Location: On the Plaza.

Contemporary work by Hispanic artists, including jewelry, painting, furniture and crafts, is exhibited and sold at this show, which operates alongside the traditional Spanish Market. This juried exhibition marked its seventh year in 1991.

Taos

FIESTAS DE SANTIAGO Y SANTA ANA

758-3873, 1-800-732-8267.
P.O. Drawer I, Taos, NM 87571.
Season: Late July.
Location: On the Plaza.
Fee: None.

Taos' patron saints are honored in this traditional three-day festival that begins with a Friday night Mass and candlelight procession to the plaza. The weekend is filled with events such as a parade satirizing local history, crowning of a Fiesta Queen, an arts and crafts fair and food booths.

Eyeing a mountain man at the Old Taos Trade Fair.

Elaine Avery; Courtesy Martinez Hacienda

**MEET THE ARTIST
SERIES**
758-2233, 1-800-TAOS-
INN.
Taos Inn, 125 Paseo del
Pueblo Norte, Taos, NM
87571.
Season: Spring, fall.
Fee: None.

The historic Taos Inn created this semiannual event more than 15 years ago to give locals and visitors a chance to meet some of Taos' most accomplished artists. At informal get-togethers, artists discuss their work and present slide shows and demonstrations.

OLD TAOS TRADE FAIR
758-0505.
P.O. Drawer CCC, Taos,
NM 87571.
Season: Late Sept.
Location: Martinez
Hacienda, Ranchitos Rd.
Fees (1991): $3 adults, $2
children 6–15.

This two-day fair, which coincides with San Geronimo Day at Taos Pueblo (see "Pueblos," above), brings to life Spanish Colonial culture in the 1820s. Held at the Martinez Hacienda (see "Historic Sites," above), an authentically-restored fortress-like home of that era, the fair features traditional craft demonstrations, native foods, caravans, muzzle-loading rifle demonstrations and Hispanic and Indian music.

TAOS ARTS FESTIVAL
758-3873, 1-800-732-8267.
P.O. Drawer I, Taos, NM
87571.
Season: Late Sept.–early
Oct.
Fee: None.

A roundup of arts festivities, this chamber-sponsored event celebrates the rich history, culture and art of Taos County. Events include gallery open houses, Taos Indian art exhibit, a tour of Taos artists' homes, a crafts fair on the Plaza, a juried exhibition of contemporary art, films and performances.

**TAOS MOUNTAIN
BALLOON RALLY**

(See *Recreation,* Chapter Six.)

TAOS POETRY CIRCUS
758-0081.
P.O. Box 2615, Taos, NM
87571.
Season: Mid-June.
Location: Call or write.
Fee: Call or write.

The Taos Poetry Circus is a marathon week of poetry workshops and readings by both established and emerging poets. The big night is the World Heavyweight Championship Poetry Bout, conducted like — you guessed it — a boxing match. You have to be there to believe it. You'll see performance poetry at its best in this thrilling event, especially when poets like Andrei Codresceu, Victor Hernandez Cruz, Anne Waldman, Ed Sanders and Deborah Salazar are pitted against each other. The 1991 bout involved a challenge of champion Waldman by Ntazake Shonge. There is a strong Beat influence at the Circus, and never a dull moment.

The Bear

The bear is a dark continent
that walks upright
like a man.
It lives across the thawing river.
I have seen it
beyond the water,
beyond comfort. Last night
it left a mark at my door
that said winter
was a long and hungry night of sleep.
But I am not afraid; I have collected
other nights of fear
knowing what things walked
the edges of my sleep,

and I remember
the man who shot
a bear,
how it cried like he did
and in his own voice,
how he tracked that red song
into the forest's lean arms
to where the bear lay weeping
on fired earth, its black hands
covering its face from sky

where humans believe god lives
larger than death.

That man,
a madness remembered him.
It is a song in starved shadows
in nights of sleep.
It follows him.
Even the old rocks sing it.
It makes him want
to get down on his knees
and lay his own hands
across his face and turn away
from sky where god lives
larger than life.
Madness is its own country
desperate and ruined.
It is a collector of lives.
It's a man
afraid of what he's done
and what he lives by. Safe,
we are safe
from the bear, and we have each other,
we have each other to fear.

Linda Hogan is a Chickasaw poet and associate professor at the University of Colorado who participated in the 1990 Taos Poetry Circus.

TAOS PUEBLO POWWOW

(See Taos Pueblo, page 124.)

TAOS SPRING ARTS CELEBRATION
758-0516.
P.O. Box 1691, Taos, NM 87571.
Season: Late May–Mid-June.
Fee: None.

In its ninth year in 1991, this seasonal extravaganza comprises visual, literary and performing arts in Taos. It includes dozens of events, from gallery openings and ethnic entertainment to readings and in-depth exploration of special topics.

TAOS WOOL FESTIVAL
776-2925.
P.O. Box 2754, Taos, NM
  87571.
Season: Last weekend in
  Sept.
Location: Kit Carson
  Memorial State Park,
  downtown Taos.
Fee: None.

The Taos area has a long history of sheep grow-ing and weaving, and a new influx of weavers keeps the traditions strong. The festival is a kalei-doscope of locally produced wools, handspun yarns in myriad colors and handmade woolen clothing; there are also spinning and shearing competitions. Sheep are for sale, along with fresh-ly prepared lamb delicacies. A couple of llamas usually show up, much to the delight of onlookers.

YULETIDE IN TAOS
758-0516, 1-800-732-8267.
P.O. Drawer I, Taos, NM
  87571.
Season: Dec. 1–15.
Fee: None.

Imagine Taos Plaza edged in snow, with colored lights and *farolitos* gleaming. This pre-Christmas celebration incorporates Taos' Hispanic and Indi-an traditions in a series of community events: *farolito* tours, candlelight dinners, dance perfor-mances, ski area festivities, ethnic holiday foods, a crafts fair, a Christmas parade and tree lighting on the plaza.

THEATER

Santa Fe

**GREER GARSON
  THEATER**
473-6511.
College of Santa Fe, St.
  Michael's Dr., Santa Fe,
  NM 87501.
Season: Oct.–May.
Tickets (1991): Single
  $5–$11, season $17–$30.

The Drama Department of the College of Santa Fe, a private liberal arts institution, stages four plays each season in a beautiful theater named for the department's benefactor, former Hollywood star Greer Garson, who owns a ranch near Santa Fe. Each season usually includes a drama, a come-dy, a musical and a classic. These fine productions play to packed houses.

**NEW MEXICO
  REPERTORY
  THEATRE**
983-2382.
P.O. Box 9279, Santa Fe,
  NM 87504.
1050 Old Pecos Trail, 0.5
  mi. S. of downtown.
Season: Oct.–May.
Tickets (1991): Single
  $12.50–$25, season
  $68–$120.

Many dreams about creating a repertory the-ater have crashed and burned in the New Mexico desert. So far, the Rep has exhibited the most power to stay aloft. In its eighth season in 1991, it is New Mexico's only professional resident theater. Artistic director, Andrew Shea, has been described as a "theatrical wunderkind who has beaten the odds . . . for the moment." Shea is com-mitted to producing plays that address the con-cerns of New Mexicans across the cultural spec-trum. The Rep has staged dramas dealing with the American West and Hispanics, as well as broader

A recent presentation of
Othello *at the New Mexico
Rep.*

Murrae Haynes

contemporary issues. The Rep has earned kudos for its productions of Mark
Medoff's *Children of a Lesser God*; Eduardo Machado's *Once Removed*; Sam
Shepard's *Fool For Love* and David Mamet's *Glengarry Glenn Ross*.

For the decade of the 1990s, the Rep is mounting its "Millennium Project," a
retrospective of 20th-century American theater. *The Great Divide*, written in
1906, kicked off the project. By the year 2000, 10 masterpieces of American
drama will have been produced. Each season's repertory is also staged in
Albuquerque at the historic KiMo Theater.

**SANTA FE ACTORS'
THEATRE**
982-8309.
430 W. Manhattan, Santa
Fe, NM 87501.
In Gross-Kelly Almacen,
next to Tomasita's
Restaurant on
Guadalupe St. at
Manhattan.
Season: Year round.
Tickets (1991): $8–$12.

In its fourth season in 1991, the Actors' Theatre
lends an experimental dimension to theater in
the city. The theater's home is a 1900s
Spanish–Pueblo warehouse fitted with a 100-seat
modular performance space. Six plays each year
range from cutting-edge modern theater to illumi-
nating stagings of the classics; from Sam Shepard
to Euripides. One recent production was a post-
apocalyptic staging of *Hamlet*.

The Actors' Theatre also hosts avant-garde, big-
city theatrical groups. These productions are
almost always refreshing and unconventional. A
range of acting classes is available. Call or write
Actors' Theatre founder, Nicholas Anthony Ballas,
for details.

SANTA FE COMMUNITY THEATRE
988-4262.
P.O. Box 2084, Santa Fe, NM 87504.
142 E. De Vargas St.
Season: Year-round.
Tickets (1991): Single $5–$8, special performances $10–$15, season $32; student and senior discounts.

Founded in the 1920s, the Community Theatre is the oldest theater group in New Mexico. Its home is in an intimate adobe theater building in one of Santa Fe's oldest neighborhoods. Year-round productions are a mix of musical comedy, mainstream drama and avant-garde. The theater's annual "One-Act Series" (usually early February) has drawn national notice. A favorite each fall is the Fiesta Melodrama, staged the week of La Fiesta. (See "Seasonal Events," above.) One of the best-kept secrets that week is which prominent citizens will be skewered in this irreverent satire.

SHAKESPEARE IN THE PARK
986-8222.
P.O. Box 2188, Santa Fe, NM 87504.
St. John's College, Camino de Cruz Blanca, about 1.5 mi. E. of downtown.
Tickets: Free, acquire in advance. Call for distribution locations.

Shakespeare in the Park stages free professional productions of the Bard's work in an idyllic outdoor setting. One play is produced per summer, on Friday, Saturday and Sunday evenings. The fun begins at 6 p.m., with picnicking and live music. "Curtain time" is 7 p.m. Shakespeare in the Park is the creation of Steven Schwartz-Hartley, a founder of the New Mexico Repertory Theatre, and is supported by community contributions and grants.

Near Santa Fe

MINE SHAFT TAVERN MELODRAMA
473-0743.
Mine Shaft Tavern and Restaurant, Turquoise Trail, Hwy. 14, Madrid, NM 87010.
Season: Memorial Day–Labor Day weekend, Sat., Sun. and holidays. Call ahead to confirm schedule.
Tickets (1991): $8 adults, $6.50 seniors, $4 children.

Audience-interactive theatrics at their most extravagant. The Engine House Theater adjacent to the Mine Shaft Tavern brings back the glorious days of villainy and heroism. Will the villain get the deed to the ranch? Will the dashing hero rescue the damsel in distress? Take the scenic 40-minute drive to Madrid, south of Santa Fe, and find out. Cheer the hero, throw marshmallows at the villain and see a happy ending in a Western ghost-town setting. On Fridays (mid-December to mid-February), there is dinner theater at the tavern ($20 for adults with buffet, $8 for theater only).

Taos

Taos Community Auditorium (758-4677) hosts a number of theatrical productions. Out-of-town troupes performing there recently were Missoula Children's Theater and Seattle Mime Troupe. A local group stages productions too, including Shakespeare and a musical. Theater professionals from New York and the West Coast who live in Taos participate.

CHAPTER FIVE
Pleasing the Palate
RESTAURANTS & FOOD PURVEYORS

Courtesy Museum of New Mexico

Interior of a New Mexico restaurant, ca. 1900.

The Santa Fe–Taos area offers a striking variety of dining experiences. There are roughly 300 restaurants, producing New Mexican, American, Continental, French, Italian, Chinese, Japanese and East Indian cuisines; while enterprising purveyors proffer drinks, baked goods, candies and delicacies. The combination is enough to whet and satisfy the most far-ranging or ravenous appetite.

There are more than 200 restaurants in Santa Fe, alone. It was an interesting and exciting challenge to choose a representative sample for review, though impossible for a single person to carry out such a task. As a result, nearly a dozen people chose the restaurants and contributed to the reviews.

Our criteria included variety in price range and quality — from gourmet restaurants to corner barbecue stands. We avoided all but the most intriguing fast-food and chain restaurants. Most of our experiences were enjoyable, some were not. Fortunately, we're free to tell you the truth since we are in no way beholden to any of these establishments. We reviewed about 80 restaurants and 40 food purveyors in the Santa Fe–Taos area. We hope the results will help you to have dining experiences you will enjoy.

One thing you will find on your gastronomic travels in Santa Fe and Taos is a plethora of northern New Mexican restaurants. *Northern* New Mexican cooking is a particular mix of Spanish, Mexican, Pueblo Indian and other fare. It includes many foods you may already know, like burritos, enchiladas and tacos, as well as less familiar dishes like *flautas*, *sopaipillas* and *chicharrones*.

The most important single ingredient in New Mexican cuisine is *chile*. *Chile* should not be confused with *chili*, the familiar heavy tomato sauce. New Mexican chile sauces have little tomato. They're flavorful, spicy, sometimes hot

134

sauces made with a mix of chile peppers and spices and they're served with almost every meal. Chile can be red or green, hot or mild, and there's no telling from the color which is which. So when your waiter says, "Red or green?" don't be afraid to ask which is hotter. Better yet, say "Christmas," and you'll get a little of both.

Before you leap into the sea of restaurants, we suggest you peruse one of two restaurant charts in the Appendix. One chart lists restaurants according to cuisine, the other according to price. Remember: all the restaurants listed in this book are given a price code based on the approximate cost of a single meal including appetizer, entree and dessert but *not* including cocktails, wine, tax or tip.

Reviews are organized first by area, then alphabetically. Any restaurant outside the city limits of Santa Fe is listed under "Restaurants Near Santa Fe." Similarly, any establishment that is outside the town limits of Taos is listed under "Restaurants Near Taos."

Dining Price Code	Inexpensive	Up to $10
	Moderate	$10 - $20
	Expensive	$20 - $30
	Very Expensive	$30 or more

Credit Cards	AE - American Express
	CB - Carte Blanche
	D - Discover Card
	DC - Diner's Club
	MC - Master Card
	V - Visa

RESTAURANTS

Santa Fe

CLOUD CLIFF BAKERY & CAFE
983-6254.
1805 2nd St., Santa Fe, NM 87501.
Closed: Wednesdays.
Price: Inexpensive.
Cuisine: American, New Mexican.
Serving: B, L, SB.
Credit Cards: MC, V.
Reservations: None.
Handicap. Access: Yes.
Special Features:
   Vegetarian dishes.

Cloud Cliff is as much a "scene" (politically left, spiritually correct, artistically daring) as it is a fine bakery and restaurant. It's a great place to experience a part of Santa Fe not in the visitors' brochures and to enjoy some of the best baked goods in town.

Cloud Cliff is known for creative vegetarian dishes such as the Ploughman's Brunch, with two small loaves of bread, a selection of goat, Brie and other cheeses and a choice of fruit or salad; grilled *polenta* with *ancho* chiles, Jack cheese and two eggs. The menu also includes a Black Bean Chili Omelette and Whole Wheat Pancakes smothered in fresh blueberries. The coffee is strong and the portions are large.

Warning: service at Cloud Cliff is often inefficient and sometimes neglectful. The atmosphere and the quality of the food make up for this, but it's definitely *not* a place for those in a hurry.

COMO'S RISTORANTE ITALIANO
989-9549.
125 W. Water St., Santa Fe, NM 87501
Closed: Mondays.
Price: Expensive.
Cuisine: Italian, Continental.
Serving: L, D.
Credit Cards: MC, V.
Reservations: Recommended.
Handicap. Access: Yes.
Special Features: Patio dining; Accordion player nightly.

Imagine the arias of Puccini's *La Boheme* wafting through the air as you dine on exquisite *Lasagne Franchese* subtly laced with nutmeg in an atmosphere of unpretentious coziness.

Como's traditional favorites include baked lasagna, linguini and clam sauce. All shrimp dishes feature Gulf shrimp. Plain spaghetti, tossed with oil and garlic, is a treat, and Como's has the best pizza this side of Berkeley. Specialties are accompanied by a crisp salad and toasted garlic bread. Como's has good house wines, espresso, cappuccino and a wonderful, mint-tinged iced tea.

A menagerie of folk art carvings overlook the dining area at Coyote Cafe.

Murrae Haynes

COYOTE CAFE
983-1615.
132 W. Water St., Santa Fe, NM 87501.
Open daily.
Price: Very Expensive.
Cuisine: Modern Southwestern.
Serving: L, D.
Credit Cards: MC, V.

Mark Miller, Coyote Cafe's owner-chef, publishes cookbooks, pops up on national talk shows and spreads his nouvelle Southwestern dogma to all corners of the country. Walking into the Coyote without a reservation during the summer season is foolish. Make it a point to call far in advance.

The menu includes appetizers such as the Dungeness crab trio featuring a taco, enchilada and tostada made with fresh, sweet crab meat

Reservations: Strongly
  recommended.
Handicap. Access: Yes.
Special Features: Outdoor
  dining; Live entertain-
  ment.

served with three types of salsa. The Cowboy Rib Chop, served under a mountain of red-chile onion rings, should not be ordered rare. A serving of three crab cakes in a *poblano* chile pesto sauce is subtly spicy, lightly fried and served with freshly made shoestring potatoes. Be sure to try a Chimayó cocktail, a wonderful concoction made with apple juice, tequila and Cointreau.

Coyote Cafe's desserts, made in-house, emphasize fresh fruits and chocolates blended into complex, innovative creations. They are overwhelming. The staff is efficient and friendly.

DAVE'S NOT HERE
983-7060.
1115 Hickox St., Santa Fe,
  NM 87501.
Closed: Sun., Christmas
  through New Year's.
Price: Inexpensive.

A fellow named Dave ran a popular local restaurant called Dave's. When he left town, the new owners wanted to retain his goodwill yet be honest. The result is Dave's Not Here.

Dave's is situated in the unfashionable west side of town. It is a one-room restaurant, funky and

Dave's Not Here: far from the tourist path.

Murrae Haynes

Cuisine: New Mexican,
  Hamburgers.
Serving: L, D.
Credit Cards: None.
Reservations: None.
Handicap. Access: Lim-
  ited.
Special Features: Vegetar-
  ian dishes.

down-home, with simple wooden chairs and tables, posters on the walls and a fair amount of noise. The prices are low, the portions large and the food more than acceptable.

Appetizers are limited to traditional salsa and chips, nachos and guacamole. It's a good idea to stick to beer or soft drinks. Dave's features a mammoth nine-ounce burger or a manageable four-and-half-ounce burger accompanied by a mountain of dark, freshly made French fries. The rest of the menu is New Mexican fare. Homemade desserts run the gamut from brownies to pies.

DELHI PALACE
982-6680.
142 Lincoln Ave., Santa Fe,
  NM 87501.
Open daily.
Price: Moderate.
Cuisine: East Indian.
Serving: L, D.
Credit Cards: AE, MC, V.
Reservations: Recom-
  mended.
Handicap. Access: Lim-
  ited.
Special Features: Lunch
  buffet; Takeout.

East Indian food is a pleasant and welcome addition to Santa Fe cuisine. Below street level and away from the bustle, the Delhi Palace is a place apart, with delightfully exotic food. The only problem is where to start.

One good place is with the Delhi Palace Special Non-Vegetarian Dinner, featuring *Mulligatawny Soup*, a light and wonderful lentil soup with chicken, herbs and mild sauces; sizzling hot, lobster-red *Tandoori Chicken*, marinated in yogurt and mild spices and baked over red-hot mesquite coals; then a *Shish Kabob*, minced meat marinated with spices, seaweed, mint chutney and onion, and finally either lamb or chicken curry with a mountain of saffron-spiced rice. If you have room, try the *Naan*, a plate-sized piece of light Indian bread baked on charcoal or a tasty rice pudding.

E.K. MAS
989-7121.
319 Guadalupe St., Santa
  Fe, NM 87501.
Closed: Mon.-Tues. winter,
  open daily in summer.
Price: Expensive.
Cuisine: Fresh seafood,
  International.
Serving: L, D, SB.
Credit Cards: MC, V.
Reservations: Recom-
  mended for dinner.
Special Features: Outdoor
  dining; Vegetarian
  dishes; Special diets.

In a poll of Santa Fe chefs and restaurant owners E.K. Mas placed an impressive second as a favorite eating establishment. We think E.K. Mas is every bit the equal of number one.

Situated in a 130-year-old adobe, the restaurant is small and comfortable; the service informal and flawless. Owners Doug Mohr and Robert Goodfriend, who is also the chef, have instilled their sense of caring in their staff. The restaurant features an extensive wine list and a variety of daily specials, mostly fresh seafood, plus an excellent regular menu.

The appetizers include an exquisite smoked tuna, sliced almost paper-thin and served with capers and pickled onions. Among the entrees, grilled mahi mahi is tender and firm, served in garlic butter given a special bite with *chipotle* chile, and King salmon is sauteed in a lovingly blended sauce of pine nuts, leeks and champagne butter.

Desserts at E.K. Mas are made on the premises. A Chocolate Mousse Cake with Coffee *Anglaise* was profoundly chocolaty. The Raspberry Mazarin and Sweet-Potato Pecan Pie were more robust than subtle. A meal at E.K. Mas is a rare delight to savor and remember.

El Farol specializes in New Mexican appetizers, called tapas.

Murrae Haynes

EL FAROL
983-9912.
808 Canyon Rd., Santa Fe, NM 87501.
Open daily.
Price: Expensive.
Cuisine: International tapas.
Serving: D.
Credit Cards: CB, DC, MC, V.
Reservations: Recom-mended.
Special Features: Live entertainment; Takeout and delivery.

Nestled into a hillside on Canyon Road, El Farol ("the lantern") serves Spanish appetizers, *tapas*. It has a large, rustic bar that offers live entertainment nightly, ranging from jazz to blues and flamenco. The entrance is a small room that displays a selection of standard *tapas* and gives a brief description of each. There are several cozy adobe-style dining rooms.

Cold *tapas* and wine are served in the bar. The house white is a lovely a Torres Vina Sol from Spain. Hot *tapas* can include halibut served with lemon, *Pato Adobo*, a grilled breast of duck with spicy *mole* sauce and Pasta with Piñon and Man-chego Cheese, a glorified macaroni-and-cheese dish. The four-layer chocolate cake is attractive.

EL PRIMO PIZZA
988-2007.
234 N. Guadalupe, Santa
Fe, NM 87501.
Open daily.
Price: Inexpensive.
Cuisine: Chicago-style pizza.
Serving: D.
Credit Cards: None.
Reservations: Not required.
Handicap. Access: Yes.
Special Features: Takeout
and delivery.

It is possible to get excellent pizza at El Primo, but you must know how to do it. Knowledgeable Santa Feans call in their order and arrive about the time it comes out of the oven. Simply walking in off the street could result in a wait of an hour or more. The pizza is excellent, with thick, whole-wheat crust, tomato sauce bursting with flavor, tasty homemade sausage, and the green peppers, mushrooms, black olives and onions are plentiful. El Primo is primo.

El Primo: the pizza is good, but order ahead.

Murrae Haynes

FABIO'S
984-3080.
227 Don Gaspar Ave.,
Santa Fe, NM 87501.
Closed: Seasonal hours;
call first.
Price: Expensive.
Cuisine: Florentine.
Serving: L, D.
Credit Cards: MC, V.
Reservations: Recom-
mended.
Special Features: Patio
dining; Vegetarian
plates.

Fabio's offers "a touch of Florence in the heart of Santa Fe" with decor that is of old Santa Fe and Florence. Candlelight against whitewashed adobe walls, racks of fine wines and simple wooden tables create a homey and relaxing atmosphere. Hosts Pilar and Fabio Macchioni are attentive and gracious. The staff is quick and efficient. Specials include fresh salmon and pasta with clam sauce. The menu features *Pollo alla Diavola*, a Cornish game hen cooked under hot bricks; *pappa al pomodoro*, spicy tomato-based bread soup; and *Panzanella*, a combination of bread, tomato, basil, translucently-thin cucumber and red onion tossed in Fabio's excellent dressing. The wine list is eclectic and well-priced.

Among the desserts are a raspberry Linzer torte and a creamy chocolate espresso torte. What can we say? — Fabio's is fabulous!

423
982-1552.
423 W. San Francisco St.,
   Santa Fe, NM 87501.
Open daily.
Price: Moderate.
Cuisine: American.
Serving: L (summer), D, SB.
Credit Cards: AE, DC, MC,
   V.
Reservations: Not necessary.
Handicap. Access: Lim-
   ited.
Special Features: Fireplaces;
   Patio dining; Live enter-
   tainment.

4 23 presents a light and fresh approach to decor, design and delicacies. The atmosphere is cool, the bar features generous drinks with spicy *pepitas* and the staff is warm and efficient. You can either dine in the dim recesses or sit on the cozy, shady patio that is garnished with a slice of turquoise sky.

The short, carefully chosen menu contains entrees such as a superb braised lamb shank in wine sauce served with new potatoes and juli-enned vegetables or a generous serving of fresh shrimp and homemade fettuccini in a basil and garlic cream sauce. The food is attractive, delicious and beautifully served.

Desserts are heavenly at 423. The Chocolate Chocolate is Ghirardelli chocolate packed under a pouf of whipped cream, crowned with mint and a cookie. The rich, cinnamon-dusted bread pudding is sweetened with pure maple syrup, studded with plump raisins and topped with whipped cream.

GARFIELD GRILL
988-9562.
322 Garfield St., Santa Fe,
   NM 87501.
Closed: Sundays.
Price: Expensive.
Cuisine: American, Conti-
   nental, Cajun.
Serving: L, D.
Credit Cards: DC, MC, V.
Reservations: Recom-
   mended.
Special Features: Vegetar-
   ian plates; Live enter-
   tainment.

T he Garfield Grill has been in operation since 1990. Its owners, Philip and Mary Howell, are succeeding admirably in presenting a cool, quiet atmosphere reminiscent of a high-ceilinged draw-ing room in Louisiana, the couple's home state. Fresh flowers, quiet classical music, candlelight and a generous list of fine wines create an atmo-sphere that is rare in Santa Fe, especially during the tourist season.

Chef James Lamoureux, formerly of Coyote Cafe and Piñon Grill, has a flair for blending South-western with nouvelle cuisine. Don't let his French name fool you; he's really a good old boy from Washington State who won't hesitate to come out of the kitchen and ply you with the desserts he's created for the day. ("Give them the chocolate mousse, Melissa! Have some apricot-strawberry torte with raspberry sauce!")

Portions at the Garfield do not disappoint, and neither does the food. Six tasty appetizers offer everything from chilled marinated asparagus spears with walnut vinaigrette to a Southwestern pizza with cilantro pesto and *chori-zo*. Soups include a Southwestern salmon corn chowder and a chilled avocado with cucumber bisque. The lamb chops emerge from their papillote cocoons steamed in a generous dose of fresh herbs, sun-dried tomatoes, mushrooms and mustard sauce. The menu features tantalizing entrees of grilled duck breast, salmon, pork loin, New York steak and chicken.

GRANT CORNER INN
(See Lodging, page 39)
983-6678.
122 Grant Ave., Santa Fe,
   NM 87501.
Closed: Jan. 1 - Feb. 1.
Price: Inexpensive.
Cuisine: Continental,
   Southwest.
Serving: B, SB.
Credit Cards: MC, V.
Reservations: Recom-
   mended.
Handicap. Access: Yes.
Special Features: Fire-
   places; Outdoor dining;
   Private dining.

Let us sing praises to the delightful Grant Corner Inn, a Victorian haven in the middle of the desert. Located on the corner of Johnson and Grant Sts., this B&B is easy to spot; it is surrounded by an archetypal white picket fence.

The robin's-egg-blue rooms are filled with rabbits of all kinds: rabbit salt-and-pepper shakers, rabbit napkin holders, rabbit this and rabbit that. Service is quick and pleasant (the owner will even scoop up your empty juice glass) and the low-key bustle is soothing.

Breakfast begins with a delicious, fresh fruit frappe, maybe a creamy apple/banana, accompanied by a selection of muffins and breads. Entrees, for example, tamale pancakes topped with salsa and sour cream, or delicious peach blintzes, are served with unlimited coffee and a fine selection of teas. The menu is *prix fixe* and varies from day to day and the breakfasts are always intriguing and tasty.

GUADALUPE CAFE
982-9762
313 Guadalupe St., Santa
   Fe, NM 87501.
Closed: Sun. evening, all
   day Mon.
Price: Moderate.
Cuisine: Northern New
   Mexican
Serving: B, L, D.
Credit Cards: MC, V.
Reservations: Unnecessary.
Handicap. Access: Limited.
Special Features: Children's
   menu; private dining for
   large groups.

Murrae Haynes
The cozy Guadalupe Cafe.

Beloved by locals and user-friendly for tourists, the Guadalupe Cafe is the place to visit if you want fast service and generous-sized portions of traditional northern New Mexican food in a cozy environment.

A good start for a meal is the colorful and generous guacamole salad that includes freshly made blue and yellow corn chips and a steaming bowl of *chile con queso*. Entrees range from moderately priced burgers and pastas to charbroiled New York steak served with all the trimmings. We recommend the *chalupa* plate, two corn tortilla baskets lavished with chunks of chicken breast, guacamole, beans, sour cream, salsa and cheese. There are eight varieties of enchiladas, from traditional blue corn and cheese to scrumptious shrimp and sour cream. Remember to have the enchiladas served "Christmas" — with a splash of both red and green chile — Guadalupe's red is *mucho intenso* and tends to be on the grainy side. All New Mexican-style entrees come with traditional *sopaipillas*. A "*sopa*" filled with honey will help to offset the heat of the chile.

Desserts include homemade pecan pie with a flaky and tender crust and an adobe pie with coffee and vanilla ice cream on a chocolate cookie crust, flavored with Amaretto. Beware the chocolate mousse; it tastes like an ancient Jello mix.

JAPANESE KITCHEN
988-8893.
510 N. Guadalupe St.,
    Santa Fe, NM 87501.
Closed: Sundays.
Price: Expensive.
Cuisine: Japanese.
Serving: L, D.
Credit Cards: AE, CB, D,
    DC, MC, V.
Reservations: Recom-
    mended.
Handicap. Access: Lim-
    ited.
Special Features: Live
    entertainment; Vegetar-
    ian plates.

For the best "dinner-and-show" outside Las Vegas, try the Japanese Kitchen. The *teppan-yaki* table — a long, stainless steel grill bordered with a wooden bar — becomes a stage where the chef slices, dices, tosses and seasons as flames leap, utensils fly and the chef's hands move deftly and with dizzying speed.

Teppan-yaki entrees include a mix of fresh shrimp, chicken, steak and vegetables, in tandem or solo, served with a delicate ginger-spiked broth, an iceberg lettuce salad dressed with a thin soy sauce concoction and green tea. The accompanying mustard and ginger sauces add a bit of pizazz. An eye-popping dish is the Boat Dinner, a con-

A chef at Japanese Kitchen prepares for the "show."

Murrae Haynes

glomeration of teriyakis, yakatoris, sushi samples, egg rolls and fresh fruit arranged on an authentic Japanese *fune*. For desert, green tea ice cream wrapped in pound cake, dipped in tempura batter and deep fried is an experience no one should miss.

JOSIE'S CASA DE COMIDA
983-5311.
225 E. Marcy St., Santa Fe, NM 87501.
Closed: Sat. - Sun.
Price: Inexpensive.
Cuisine: Northern New Mexican, American.
Serving: L.
Credit Cards: None.
Reservations: None.
Handicap. Access: Yes.
Special Features: Fireplace; Children's Menu; Vegetarian dishes.

Every so often when an out-of-town food writer "discovers" Josie's Casa de Comida, a rave review is published and hungry hordes descend from Kansas City or Memphis to wait in line for a table. Anyone wanting to sample Josie's fare has to be ready to dine when owners Josie and Raymond Gallegos are ready to receive them. If you arrive between 11:30 and 2:30, be prepared to wait in line anywhere from 15 minutes to an hour. However, if you're patient, you'll discover a place cherished by locals and visitors alike.

At first glance Josie's appears to be a throwback to the '60s, but after a few minutes in one of its funky, sky-blue booths, focus will quickly shift to the food. Appetizers include steaming bowls of vegetable-laden, chunky chicken and rice or black bean soups. The menu offers full and half orders and some of the best red chile in town. Chicken enchiladas are made with shredded white and dark meat, two blue-corn tortillas and a liberal dousing of red or green chile (both medium hot).

Josie's offers a mind-boggling array of homemade desserts — everything from creamy-textured lemon soufflé to outrageously delicious fruit cobblers.

JULIAN'S
988-2355.
221 Shelby St., Santa Fe, NM 87501.
Closed: Thanksgiving.
Price: Very expensive.
Cuisine: Italian.
Serving: D.
Credit Cards: AE, CB, DC, MC, V.
Reservations: Recommended.
Handicap. Access: Limited.
Special Features: Fireplaces; Outdoor dining; Private dining room; Live entertainment.

For superb food in an elegant atmosphere, we recommend Julian's. In the main dining area, a free-standing, double-sided *kiva* fireplace throws a warm glow into a room of whitewashed adobe. Candlelight and fresh flowers contribute to a feeling of relaxed elegance.

The menu includes handmade pastas, fine seafoods, tender chicken and beef, fresh vegetables and exquisite sauces. Two delicious appetizers are *Piatto di Pesce Affumicato* (smoked seafood with horseradish sauce, red onions and capers) and *Ostriche al Genovese* (oysters baked with Parmesan cheese, pesto and seasoned bread crumbs). The salad is wonderful, with an assortment of fresh greens, including Belgian endive, *argula*, radicchio, red mustard and baby chicory.

The luxurious *Spaghetti con Vongole Bianco* includes eight good-sized clams with a generous portion of perfectly cooked pasta in a sauce of melted butter, olive oil, garlic and white wine. The delicate *Vitello Piccata al Limone* is scallops of veal sauteed with lemon, shallots, capers and white wine. The lemon tart is flavorful and not overly sweet. We recommend a fine Italian wine from Julian's extensive wine list, rather than their unremarkable house wines.

The staff at La Casa Sena sings Broadway musicals as you dine.

Murrae Haynes

LA CASA SENA
988-9232.
125 E. Palace Ave., Santa Fe, NM 87501.
Open daily.
Price: Expensive.
Cuisine: Southwestern, Continental.
Serving: L, D, SB.
Credit Cards: AE, D, DC, MC, V.
Reservations: Recommended for dining room.
Handicap. Access: Yes.
Special Features: Fireplace; Outdoor dining; Private dining; Nightly music in cantina.

La Casa Sena offers one of the most entertaining dining experiences in all of Santa Fe. Tucked into a far corner of the lovely Sena Plaza courtyard, the formal dining room features Continental fare and local specialties, but what's unique is the *cantina*. The staff will treat you to a medley of songs from Broadway shows as you dine in informal surroundings.

This would be a fun place to eat even if the food were merely passable, but it is usually outstanding. For example, there is an unusual chile *relleno* appetizer, consisting of an extremely hot, *unfried* chile pod with delicate *chiva* cheese. A side dish of "Wouldn't It Be Loverly" from *My Fair Lady* or "I Cain't Say No," from *Oklahoma* helps it go down.

The entrees are faultless. Red chile pasta with cream and ricotta is full of shrimp, scallops and fresh salmon. The tortilla-wrapped burger is large and perfectly grilled. Avocado cheesecake with piñon nut crust is superb, as is an operatic rendition of "Summertime." It is best to arrive a half hour before show time to get a good table, as reservations are not taken in the *cantina*.

LA CHOZA
982-0909.
905 Alarid St., Santa Fe,
  NM 87501.
Closed: Sundays, major
  holidays.
Price: Inexpensive.
Credit Cards: MC, V.
Cuisine: New Mexican.
Serving: L, D.
Reservations: None.
Handicap. Access: Yes.
Special Features: Fire-
  places; Outdoor dining;
  Vegetarian plates; Take-
  out.

Cheery Spanish decor, mellow music, friendly service and excellent food combine to make this place a perennial favorite. The staff creates an environment of unpressured intimacy, and the restaurant operates like a well-oiled machine.

All dinner entrees are served with hearty, home-made yellow-corn chips and tomato salsa — and all are the same low price. The eight selections include enchiladas, tacos, tostados, bean burritos, tamales and wonderful red or green chile. Most dishes are served with well-seasoned *posole*, pinto beans, lettuce, tomato and toasted French bread that absorbs some of the heat from the chile.

The dessert selection consists of four items: particularly interesting mocha cake, cheesecake, a hot fudge sundae and a red raspberry sundae.

Murrae Haynes

La Choza, a Santa Fe favorite.

LA PLAZUELA AT LA FONDA
982-5511.
100 E. San Francisco St.,
  Santa Fe, NM 87501.
Open daily.
Price: Moderate.
Credit Cards: AE, DC, MC,
  V.
Cuisine: New Mexican,
  American, Continental.
Serving: B, L, D.
Reservations: Recom-
  mended.
Handicap. Access: Yes.
Special Features: Live
  entertainment; Vegetar-
  ian plates.

La Fonda has been host to a variety of notable guests, including Kit Carson, Sheriff Pat Garrett, General Ulysses S. Grant and Senator John F. Kennedy. La Plazuela's large dining area is covered with a skylight. A mix of Spanish-style and old Mexican furnishings on a flagstone floor gives it a centuries-old feel. The atmosphere is enhanced by folk paintings, chile *ristras* and, often, a guitar player strumming soft, romantic music.

La Fonda has good food and gracious service. It has an extensive wine list and some of the best fishbowl-sized margaritas in town. The Tequila Lime Shrimp, fresh-grilled and perfectly seasoned with tangy lime butter and a robust tequila, is a good appetizer and the *Gazpacho Ojeda*, a zestful blend of fresh vegetables and spices, is a delicious cold soup.

La Plazuela provides a festive dining area beneath a second-story skylight.

Murrae Haynes

The Petit Filet, a "Chef's Specialtie," is some of the tenderest steak you've ever tasted. The steamed vegetable accompaniment is fresh and lightly seasoned. Northern New Mexican dishes include the La Fonda Enchiladas. With or without chicken, they're tasty, served with beans, *posole* and somewhat leathery *sopaipillas.*

Dessert at La Fonda, though not exceptional, is usually good, featuring a few steady favorites such as *flan*, cheesecake, lime pie and carrot cake, as well as daily specials.

LA TRAVIATA
984-1091.
95 W. Marcy St., Santa Fe,
    NM 87501.
Open daily.
Price: Moderate.
Cuisine: Italian.
Serving: L, D.
Credit Cards: MC, V.
Reservations: Recom-
    mended.
Handicap. Access: Lim-
    ited.
Special Features: Vegetar-
    ian plates.

At lunch hour, La Traviata is easily spotted — the line extends out the door. In spite of its small size (one cramped and often smoky room) it is a favorite lunch spot.

The delicately seasoned *Insalata Caprese* with fresh mozzarella is a great beginning. Entrees include a delicious *Pasta Al Forno* (baked pasta with a rich blend of bechamel, ricotta and Romano cheese and tomato) and a completely satisfying *Pesce del Giorno Alla Brace* (grilled fresh Pacific redfish topped with a salsa of tomato, basil, garlic and olive oil and served on a bed of polenta).

For dessert, try the Chocolate Hazelnut Tart flavored with orange or the *Cassata Alla Siciliana*, a frozen layer cake — interesting and not too sweet. Kenneth Calascione serves a great cup of *real* dark-roast Italian coffee, regular or decaf, as well as cappuccinos and espressos.

LITTLE ANITA'S

473-4505.
2811 Cerrillos Rd., Santa
Fe, NM 87501.
Closed: Thanksgiving,
Christmas.
Price: Inexpensive.
Cuisine: New Mexican,
Continental.
Serving: B, L, D.
Credit Cards: AE, MC, V.
Reservations: None.
Handicap. Access: Yes.
Special features: Children's
menu; Vegetarian
plates; Takeout.

Little Anita's is a welcome respite from the rush of traffic on Cerrillos Road. This a a good family restaurant with spacious booths. The staff, in black slacks and green aprons, bustle about serving steaming plates of enchiladas, *rellenos* and other fare.

Try the skillet *fajitas* or Little Anita's Pueblo Pie, a combination of chicken, corn, tomatoes, *chorizo*, onions, butter and seasonings in a cornmeal crust. One of the best deals in town has to be Little Anita's New Mexico Green Chile Stew — a delicious mix of potato chunks, chile, pork, onions and carrots in a hearty broth. For inexpensive family fare, it's hard to beat. Parents with small children can relax and let the kids make a mess.

MARIA YSABEL

Owner: Bell Mondragon.
986-1662.
409 W. Water St., Santa Fe,
NM 87501.
Closed: Thanksgiving,
Christmas, Easter.
Price: Moderate.
Cuisine: New Mexican.
Serving: L, D.
Credit Cards: MC, V.
Reservations: Recom-
mended.
Handicap. Access: Yes.
Special Features: No smok-
ing inside; Patio dining;
Children's menu; Vege-
tarian dishes.

Here's a little restaurant with a special claim to fame. Owner Bell Mondragon, who prepares the tasty cuisine, has cooked in front of television cameras for *Good Morning America*. Moreover, her colorful haven has been written up in the *New York Times*, the *Washington Post* and *The Very Best in Mexican Restaurants*.

A genial waiter will bring frosted mugs of beer, along with superb appetizers that are included with each entree. The *Chile con Queso* features a spicy chile sauce with a white cheese that you can shamelessly stretch with your fingers and wrap around homemade nacho chips. The *Gorditas de Chicharrones y Guacamole* are special — crispy, curled tortilla cups laden with refried beans, guacamole and sour cream topped with paprika.

Pollo Asado, two chicken breasts topped with sauteed mushrooms, is moist and beautifully seasoned; Shrimp Enchiladas, with a special white mushroom sauce, offers a subtle taste of the sea. Even the refried beans, which often add little more than bulk and blandness to New Mexican dishes, have a distinctly memorable taste.

Topping it off is Bell Mondragon's famous "Hot *Capirotada*" bread pudding — her one and only dessert — with a delectable blend of raspberry, cinnamon, caramelized sugar, sherry and white cheddar cheese. All in all, a memorable treat. Maria Ysabel also offers hearty, eight-course family dinners.

MARIA'S NEW MEXI-CAN KITCHEN

983-7929.
555 W. Cordova Rd., Santa
Fe, NM 87501.
Closed: Christmas,
Thanksgiving.
Price: Moderate.
Cuisine: Northern New
Mexican, Steaks.
Serving: L, D.
Credit Cards: AE, CB, DC,
MC, V.
Reservations: Recom-
mended.
Handicap. Access: Lim-
ited.
Special Features: Outdoor
dining; Private dining;
Live entertainment;
Takeout.

Ah-ha! So this is where the locals hang out! And who can blame them? After all, Maria's practically hands you a money-back guarantee on their Grand Gold Margaritas as you walk through the door. If these lemon (not lime!) masterpieces aren't the best you've ever tried, by the time you've finished your second drink you'll be too tipsy to care.

Maria's is the only restaurant in Santa Fe with a glass-enclosed tortilla factory smack in the main dining room. The women who pull flour and corn tortillas off hot griddles put on quite a show during lunch and dinner.

Santa Fe folks know a great deal when they see it, and Maria's is a year-round favorite even with the teetotaling crowd. Guacamole at Maria's is on a level all its own, and the expertly marinated, tender and spicy *carne adovada* and the sizzling, authentic chicken *fajitas* served in a forest of green peppers and onions are simply wonderful. Watch out for the devilishly hot, *jalapeño*-loaded *Pico de Gallo*, served as a side dish to the *fajitas*. The dessert *flan* is a huge, smooth custard so tall it threatens to topple over at each swipe of the spoon.

NATURAL CAFE

983-1411.
1494 Cerrillos Rd., Santa
Fe, NM 87501.
Closed: Mondays.
Price: Moderate.
Cuisine: Vegetarian and
natural.
Serving: L, D.
Credit Cards: MC, V.
Reservations: Recom-
mended.
Handicap. Access: Yes.
Special Features: Smoking
prohibited; Outdoor
dining.

Santa Fe has a few restaurants that cater to vegetarians. Among them, the Natural Cafe is a place people rely on for sophisticated natural cuisine and casual, efficient service. A few dishes on owner Lynn Walters' menu are prepared with free-range chicken and farm-reared fish. This is the only place in Santa Fe where both Szechuan chicken and grilled East Indian tempeh burgers are on the same menu.

The Natural's guacamole and tortillas are a great way to begin a meal. The soups are outstanding, each steaming cupful loaded with fresh ingredients. The Natural's Szechuan chicken features a rainbow of spicy-sweet chopped, sliced and slivered veggies. There's also the vegetarian's delight, *gado gado*, which includes an Indonesian peanut sauce ladled over a medley of vegetables, a mound of rice and several healthy chunks of grilled tofu.

Coffee at the Natural is strong, fresh, and served with real cream. The fresh desserts, an assortment of cakes, pies and cobblers, are worth a visit in their own right.

O.J. SARAH'S
984-1675.
106 N. Guadalupe St.,
    Santa Fe, NM 87501.
Open daily.
Price: Inexpensive.
Cuisine: New Mexican.
Serving: B, L.
Credit Cards: None.
Reservations: None.
Special Features: Vegetarian plates.

This sunlit restaurant at the corner of Guadalupe and San Francisco Sts. has been one of the city's most popular breakfast and brunch spots for years. The coffee is only so-so, but service is bustling and the food is great.

O.J.'s is famous for corned beef hash, eggs benedict, homemade granola and platters of fresh fruit. We recommend the O.J. Omelette, three fluffy eggs mixed with cheddar cheese, sour cream and tomatoes and topped with green chile. Breakfasts are normally served with hash-browns and choice of muffin or toast. You can substitute a chunk of flaky fruit coffee cake (say, peach pecan) or a giant cinnamon roll for the relatively dry and tasteless hash-browns and toast; there's no comparison! O.J.'s has outrageous and enormous pancakes — particularly their cottage cakes topped with raspberry sauce or their traditional blue corn pancakes with real maple syrup.

O.J. Sarah's, a popular brunch spot.

Murrae Haynes

For lunch, O.J.'s offers an eclectic mix of burgers, sandwiches, soups, salads and traditional Mexican foods. You can get a good cup of coffee — *if* you forego the bland regular brand and order the espresso or cafe au lait.

PEPPERS RESTAURANT & CANTINA

984-2272.
2239 Old Pecos Trail at
Pecos Trail Inn, Santa
Fe, NM 87505.
Closed: Sundays.
Price: Inexpensive.
Cuisine: Northern New
Mexican, American.
Serving: B, L, D.
Credit Cards: CB, DC, MC,
V.
Reservations: None.
Handicap. Access: Yes.
Special Features: Smoking
in bar only; Private
dining; Takeout.

Peppers Restaurant & Cantina is at the cross-roads of two Old West trails: the Santa Fe Trail and the historic Old Pecos Trail, an ancient Indian footpath that connected Pecos Pueblo to the pueblos north of Santa Fe. Peppers is a well-run restaurant that doesn't take itself too seriously. The walls are decorated with *saltillo* blankets and multicolored, carved parrots. A pleasant, efficient staff assures that the whole family will enjoy a hearty, inexpensive meal, while owner Rick Helmick paces the floor with water pitcher in hand to make sure that all goes well.

The menu includes a varied assortment of dishes, including burritos, burgers, sandwiches and Mexican plates. The homemade sangria and a salt-rimmed Margarita Grande are served in large, frosted glasses. Appetizers include an enormous serving of nachos, piled high with *jalapeños* and layered with mild cheddar cheese. The lemon herb chicken, a tender, grilled portion of skinless breast meat, is served with sauteed, mixed vegetables and black beans. Entrees include some of the softest sopaipillas we have ever eaten.

Desserts at Peppers include a frozen Margarita Pie (which actually does taste like a margarita) a flawless *flan*, served chilled in a caramel sauce, old-fashioned apple pie and Chocolate Raspberry Bash, an assortment of dark and white chocolate on a brownie shortbread crust topped with truffled cream cheese and raspberries.

PINK ADOBE

983-7712.
406 Old Santa Fe Trail,
Santa Fe, NM 87501.
Closed: Christmas, New
Year's, Easter, Thanks-giving.
Price: Very Expensive.
Cuisine: Continental, New
Mexican with Cajun
twist.
Serving: L (Mon.-Fri.), D.
Credit Cards: AE, DC, MC,
V.
Reservations: Recom-mended.
Handicap. Access: Yes.
Special Features: Smoking
in bar only; Fireplaces;
Patio dining.

One of the most venerable of all Santa Fe restaurants, the Pink Adobe (or the "Pink," as many locals call it) has been in business on the historic Old Santa Fe Trail since the end of World War II. The restaurant is in an adobe building with many small rooms, all with fireplaces and rough-hewn wooden chairs and tables — a bit too closely spaced for privacy. The bar, across a narrow alley from the restaurant, features a live tree growing through the roof, as well as unlimited fresh popcorn.

The menu at the Pink Adobe is little changed. There are four appetizers — escargot, French onion soup, shrimp *remoulade* or cold artichokes — and about 15 entrees including steak, chicken, shrimp, lamb, pork and various New Mexican dishes. The emphasis is on hearty fare rather than delicacy; the steaks are superior, sometimes even sublime. Desserts include such items as Fuzzy Pear Pie, a kind of cobbler served warm with lemony whipped cream; cheesecake topped with a layer of caramel, chocolate and pecan sauce; and an apple pie with cinnamon sauce that's known far and wide as the best in town.

Service at the Pink is quick and friendly and the staff will understand if you want to take home half of your enormous steak and eat it the next morning; most people do. One important note: smoking is not permitted in any of the dining rooms.

PRANZO ITALIAN GRILL
984-2645.
540 Montezuma, Sanbusco
    Center, Santa Fe, NM
    87502.
Closed: Christmas,
    Thanksgiving.
Price: Moderate.
Cuisine: Northern Italian.
Serving: L, D (Sunday only).
Credit Cards: AE, MC, V.
Reservations: Recom-
    mended.
Handicap. Access: Yes.
Special Features: Patio
    dining; Vegetarian
    plates; Takeout.

Pranzo Italian Grill opened a few years ago in the remodeled Sanbusco Market Center and has earned a reputation as one of Santa Fe's choice gathering spots. Unfortunately, both the service and the food tend to be inconsistent. A fifteen minute wait for a San Pellegrino served in the bar is not uncommon. Although Pranzo is known for its northern Italian cuisine, the pasta of the day might be an over-spiced seafood mix with flavors that are neither blended nor well-balanced.

We must admit the Pranzo appetizers are worthy of respect. Pranzo salads are almost always lovely and fresh, offered with a choice of three tangy dressings. The *Ravioli di Ricotta e Spinaci alla Crema de Salvia* — ravioli stuffed with fresh spinach and ricotta cheese, served with a fresh sage cream sauce and the *Fettuccine al Pollo* — grilled chicken, pine nuts, sundried tomatoes, olive oil, balsamic vinegar and white wine are outstanding.

Buttery toasted hazelnut pound cake topped with ice cream and warm chocolate sauce is a knockout. Pranzo offers espresso, a varied selection of moderate to expensive Italian and California wines. The bar serves late-night light meals.

Rosedale serves some of the freshest seafood in the Southwest.

Murrae Haynes

ROSEDALE
989-7411.
907 W. Alameda, Solana
Center, Santa Fe, NM
87501.
Closed: Sundays.
Price: Expensive.
Cuisine: Seafood.
Serving: L, D.
Credit cards: DC, V, MC.
Reservations: Recom-
mended.
Handicap. Access: Yes.
Special features: No smok-
ing; Takeout.

Fresh seafood in the desert Southwest? Not just fresh, but some of the most succulent fish and shellfish to be had in a noncoastal city anywhere.

The original Rosedale was founded in New York City in 1906. Alan Neuman, a grandson of the founder, brought his family's seafood expertise to Santa Fe in 1988. Today's Rosedale in Santa Fe has a triple personality: wholesale, retail and restaurant, specializing in fresh fish from the Pacific, Atlantic, Gulf and inland waters. At night, the retail store closes, the lights go down, linens appear on the tables and Rosedale becomes one of Santa Fe's best-kept secrets. Don't be fooled by the deli-like decor. The beige, concrete-block walls adorned with fish-identification charts and stand-up coolers are quickly forgotten once you dig into some of the freshest and most flavorful fish you've ever eaten. The service at Rosedale is courteous and professional. The staff knows how dishes are prepared and will make recommendations.

An excellent pan-fried oyster appetizer is served in an understated sauce of Cajun spices, white wine and butter. Three grilled jumbo sea scallops are blessed by a tequila-cilantro sauce. A mildly spiced gazpacho, remarkable for the quality of its December tomatoes and a salad with bleu cheese dressing are a fine prelude for the main course. Western wilder salmon will arrive perfectly cooked with a cold honey-mustard glaze. Rosedale's somewhat bland Mississippi catfish filet is a healthy and satisfying dish. The wine special, a Fetzer Fumé Blanc, is clean and flavorful and six tasty desserts round out the menu.

SAKURA
983-5353.
321 W. San Francisco St.,
Santa Fe, NM 87501.
Closed: Mondays, Christ-
mas, New Year's.
Price: Moderate.
Cuisine: Japanese.
Serving: L, D.
Credit Cards: AE, MC, V.
Reservations: Recom-
mended.
Special Features: Private
tatami rooms; Patio
dining; Vegetarian
plates.

Sakura is a fine Japanese restaurant in the heart of downtown Santa Fe. The service is efficient, the surroundings crisp and simple. One side of the restaurant contains spacious tables and a sushi bar. Sakura also has small *tatami* rooms where diners sit on mats on the floor and rest their feet comfortably in wells under the tables. Four or fewer can have a delicious and intimate gathering, Japanese style.

The food at Sakura is consistently good. Lunch is a better bargain than dinner, with virtually the same dishes available at slightly more than half the price. California rolls are a specialty, either as appetizers or accompanying the main course. Jumbo combination lunches come with clear or spicy miso soup, a lettuce salad and a variety of main dishes. Salmon teriyaki is a treat, but ask for it to be cooked briefly; sometimes it's overdone. Shrimp and vegetable tempura is made with fresh ingredients in a light, tasty batter.

**SAN FRANCISCO
   STREET BAR & GRILL**
982-2044.
114 W. San Francisco St.,
   Santa Fe, NM 87501.
Closed: Christmas, New
   Year's Thanksgiving.
Price: Moderate.
Cuisine: American.
Serving: L, D.
Credit Cards: MC, V.
Reservations: None.
Handicap. Access: Yes.
Special Features: Chil-
   dren's menu; Vegetarian
   plates; Takeout.

It was impossible to find a first-rate hamburger in downtown Santa Fe until the San Francisco Street Bar and Grill opened half a block from the plaza and successfully filled that void. The name is a misnomer — this is no dark, macho bar but a casual family restaurant.

A huge hamburger with fries or coleslaw tops the menu at lunch and dinner. The meat is rich and tasty, but if you like it rare, make sure you insist. The fries are made fresh and are superior to the coleslaw. The small menu includes a fish sandwich, a chicken dish and a grilled cheese with pesto sandwich, as well as two sausage plates and a daily special. For dessert, try Dutch apple pie.

The wine list at San Francisco Street is short, with all wine available by the glass as well as by the bottle. The service is professional and, for the footsore shopper, the location can't be beat.

SANTACAFE
984-1788.
231 Washington Ave.,
   Santa Fe, NM 87501.
Closed: Christmas, New
   Year's.
Price: Very expensive.
Cuisine: New American
   with Southwest and
   Asian flair.
Serving: L (Mon.-Fri.), D.
Credit Cards: MC, V.
Reservations: Recom-
   mended.
Handicap. Access: Yes.
Special Features: Fireplace;
   Patio dining.

Almost immediately after its opening in 1983, SantaCafe was hailed as one of the city's gourmet dining experiences. That reputation remains strong, and a quick glance at the menu suggests why. A typical appetizer consists of "seared ginger beef *carpaccios* with black bean *tapenade*, pearl onion, *asiago* shavings and tortilla strips." An entree might include "barbecued Italian sausage with sun-dried tomatoes, roasted shallots, *poblano* chiles, garlic and Maui onions served with polenta triangles and *pecorino* Romano." In other words, we're not talking corned beef hash!

This complex fare is served in quietly elegant surroundings: small rooms containing four or five tables; bare adobe walls unadorned by artwork; flickering fireplaces in winter and patio dining by candle and moonlight in the summer. In all seasons the service is calm and efficient, friendly and knowledgeable.

The menu at SantaCafe changes with the seasons. There are daily specials, which always include a pasta or a pizza. The grilled lime-lemon chicken topped with roasted red pepper puree is as fine and succulent a chicken dish as can be had. Locally-grown produce is used whenever possible. Breads are baked on the premises and served fresh-from-the-oven, the sourdough in particular being both moist and firm. The wine list is extensive, and Stephanie Morris' desserts are exquisite.

SANTA FE GOURMET

982-8738.
72 W. Marcy St., Santa Fe,
   NM 87501.
Closed: Sundays.
Price: Moderate.
Cuisine: Country French,
   California Nouveau.
Serving: B, L, D.
Credit Cards: MC, V.
Reservations: Recom-
   mended.
Handicap. Access: Yes.
Special Features: Vegetar-
   ian plates; Takeout and
   delivery.

Murrae Hynes

The Sushi bar at Shohko.

SHOHKO CAFE

983-7288.
321 Johnson St., Santa Fe,
   NM 87501.
Closed: Major holidays.
Price: Moderate.
Cuisine: Japanese.
Serving: L (Mon.-Fri.), D.
Credit Cards: AE, MC, V.
Handicap. Access: Yes.
Reservations: Recom-
   mended.
Special Features: Sushi bar;
   Private dining; Vegetar-
   ian plates; Takeout.

Wedged between commercial buildings a block from the plaza, Santa Fe Gourmet compensates for its lack of architectural amenities with innovative cuisine. Co-owners Paul Hunsicker and Carol Moberg decorate with fresh flowers, an innovative collection of contemporary folk art and cotton tablecloths. The service is gracious and the food is good. An appetizer of marinated grilled shrimp served over a bed of *jalapeño* salsa fresca and a basket of warm herbed French bread is a good beginning for the feast. Follow this with a more-than-satisfying baked salmon *en papillote*. Every drop of the homemade, three-cheese ravioli is an absolute pleasure and will elicit a panoply of grins.

Save room for the white chocolate *ganache* cake with pecan crust and fresh fruit *coulis*. It is as light and sinful a dessert as you can find. Coffee is fresh-brewed and served with a tiny pot of cream. The wine list, a mix of local, California and imported selections, is short and inexpensive. Lunch includes sandwiches, salads and vegetarian specialties.

Shohko Fukuda studied macrobiotic philosophy and cooking under the famous George Ohsawa. Diners can choose from an extensive sushi menu, a well-balanced Japanese dinner menu as well as familiar Chinese specials — all without MSG. Shohko offers a specially prepared macrobiotic dinner, Japanese curry, weekend Dim Sum luncheons and a wide assortment of appetizers, desserts, wine and beer.

At Shohko you're ushered promptly to your seat, your napkin is spread politely on your lap and tea is provided immediately. Sushi is beautifully prepared, arranged in delicate, fan-shaped displays that make a feast for the eyes as well as the stomach. Shohko is pricey compared to most Chinese and Japanese restaurants; however, the service, atmosphere and food selection make it worth the extra dollars.

STAAB HOUSE

986-0000.
330 E. Palace Ave., Santa Fe, NM 87501.
Open daily.
Price: Moderate.
Cuisine: New Mexican, American.
Serving: B, L, D, SB.
Credit Cards: AE, DC, MC, V.
Reservations: Recommended.
Handicap. Access: Yes.
Special Features: Fireplace; Private dining; Patio dining; Live entertainment.

Serving the public as well as guests at La Posada, the Staab House is one of the most elegant Santa Fe restaurants. It features rustic decor, with dark *vigas* and heavy furniture, classical music, a huge fireplace and enormous picture windows opening out to a bright patio.

The service at Staab House is a little unpredictable — attentive at times and neglectful at others. The food likewise gets mixed reviews — sometimes memorable, sometimes not. Lunch selections varies from broiled fresh seafood to chicken *fajitas*.

Staab House serves elegant dinners. One of the more inviting appetizers is baked *Montrachet* with roasted peppers and fresh fruit. A delicious, grilled *Scallops Encinada* is wrapped in bacon and basted in tequila, lime and butter. Staab House also offers an interesting and exotic selection of sherry and dessert wines. Desserts are delicious, thanks to the creativity of the pastry chef who makes them fresh daily.

STEPHANIE'S BONES

989-7427.
238 N. Guadalupe St., Santa Fe, NM 87501.
Open daily.
Price: Inexpensive.
Cuisine: Smokehouse barbecue.
Serving: L, D.
Credit Cards: MC, V.
Reservations: None.
Handicap. Access: Yes.
Special Features: Patio dining; Takeout; Gourmet catering.

Here's a cheery little barbecue joint, Santa Fe's newest, located on busy N. Guadalupe. Soul and soft rock fill the air, while locals socialize at small tables and booths.

Owner Stephanie Daniels has created a spot somewhere between sit-down and fast food. Service is almost instant, and the food is fantastic: savory, hickory smoked ribs, delicious chicken and hot links, outstanding beef brisket sandwiches and a secret, spunky barbecue sauce. Stephanie's homemade fruit cobbler is rich and brown sugary delicious. We have two small complaints: unwieldy plastic forks and spoons and moist towelettes in place of napkins.

SZECHWAN

983-1821; 983-1558.
1965 Cerrillos Rd., Santa
  Fe, NM 87501.
Open daily.
Price: Inexpensive.
Cuisine: Chinese.
Serving: L, D.
Credit Cards: MC, V.
Reservations: None.
Handicap. Access: Yes.
Special Features: Vegetar-
  ian dishes; Takeout.

Tucked away on commercial Cerrillos Rd., Szechwan looks like a generic Chinese restaurant, Anywhere, U.S.A. However, neither the food nor the efficiency and friendliness of the staff is disappointing.

Szechwan presents an array of beef, seafood, chicken, pork and vegetable dishes. The Shrimp with Hot Garlic Sauce is particularly good. There are numerous inexpensive lunch combination plates, each served with soup, fried rice, fried wonton and egg roll. Sunday afternoons you can eat in or order out. We don't recommend the buffet. All in all, Szechwan is a good place to go when the Chinese food craving hits.

TECOLOTE CAFE

988-1362.
1203 Cerrillos Rd., Santa
  Fe, NM 87501.
Closed: Mondays.
Price: Inexpensive.
Cuisine: Northern New
  Mexican, American.
Serving: B, L.
Credit Cards: AE, MC, V.
Reservations: None.
Handicap. Access: Limited.

This is one of the most popular breakfast spots in town — you may have to wait in line, but the wait is worth it. Owners Alice and Bill Jennison, who opened the Tecolote in 1980 (*Tecolote* means "owl"), have created a cheerful Santa Fe institution. The walls are loaded with owls, oils, watercolors, needlepoint canvases and woodcuts by local artists.

The warm banana-raisin whole wheat biscuits will command your full attention. The breakfast burrito is moist; firm eggs and well-cooked ham or sausage topped with green chile and melted cheddar are a marvel. There's so much goodness to choose from: Scrambled Eggs and Lox; *Atole* Piñon Hotcakes; Shirred Eggs *Tecolote* (two eggs baked on a bed of chicken livers sauteed with tomato and onion); thick, creamy soups; and a host of northern New Mexican specials served with tortillas.

TINY'S RESTAURANT & LOUNGE

983-9817.
Pen Rd. Shopping Ctr., St.
  Francis Dr. & Cerrillos
  Rd., Santa Fe, NM 87501.
Closed: Sundays.
Price: Moderate.
Cuisine: Northern New
  Mexican, American.

Tiny's is a comfortable northern New Mexican restaurant. It is the kind of place where local families, politicians pump hands and office workers throw birthday parties. The decor is unpretentious and the food is fresh and flavorful. In fact, Tiny's cuisine was knighted the "best in the city" in 1988 by *Connoisseur* magazine. Aside from New Mexican fare, the menu also includes popular American dishes like steaks, seafood, sandwiches and salads.

Each New Mexican entree is served with well seasoned pinto beans, Spanish rice and *posole*.

Serving: L, D.
Credit Cards: AE, DC,
   MC, V.
Reservations: Recom-
   mended.
Handicap. Access: Yes.
Special Features: Patio
   dining; Fireplace; Vege-
   tarian plates; Takeout.

Also, we can't say enough about Tiny's *sopaipillas*. They are piping hot, flaky and tender, served with sweetened butter on the side — a rare accomplishment, indeed.

The wine list offers about a dozen average wines. The lounge, a favorite of locals, has live entertainment on Friday and Saturday nights.

TOMASITA'S
983-5721.
500 S. Guadalupe St., Santa
   Fe, NM 87501.
Closed: Sundays.
Price: Inexpensive.
Cuisine: Northern New
   Mexican.
Serving: L, D.
Credit Cards: MC, V.
Reservations: None.
Handicap. Access: Yes.
Special Features: Outdoor
   dining; Private dining;
   Takeout.

Everybody loves Tomasita's. Good food, lots of parking, quick service and great Margaritas all served in a remodeled railyard warehouse with minimal frills. So many people love Tomasita's, in fact, that unless you have a reservation you'll probably end up waiting anywhere from 15 minutes to an hour to be seated. The dining room is crowded and noisy, and the staff tends to rush you, but if you're looking for affordable food, you may not be bothered by the boisterous crunch.

TORTILLA FLATS
471-8685.
3139 Cerrillos Rd., Santa
   Fe, NM 87501.
Closed: Thanksgiving,
   Christmas.
Price: Moderate.
Cuisine: New Mexican.
Serving: B, L, D.
Credit Cards: MC, V.
Reservations: None
Handicap. Access: Yes
Special Features: Vegetar-
   ian plates; Children's
   menu; Takeout.

When this unpretentious New Mexican restaurant opened in 1986 in the middle of Santa Fe's motel row, it looked like just another fast-food joint. Word of its fresh, innovative cuisine and friendly and helpful service quickly spread. The restaurant has twice added new wings, more than doubling its seating capacity.

The quality has kept up with the popularity. In addition to the standard enchiladas and such, Tortilla Flats offers extras that few of its competitors attempt. Black beans are offered as an alternative to the normal pinto beans; a delicious vegetable mix called *calavacitos* — a blend of corn, squash and melted jack cheese — accompanies most dinner selections; and a mainstay of the menu is exquisite *quesadillas* — lightly grilled tortillas stuffed with your choice of chicken, beef or ham. Everything tastes fresh at Tortilla Flats and the portions, at prices in the $6 range for entrees, are immense. The dessert menu is simple — *flan*, chocolate cake and fruit pies — but it's unlikely there will be much room left for more than a morsel.

UPPER CRUST PIZZA
983-4140.
329 Old Santa Fe Trail,
 Santa Fe, NM 87501.
Closed: Christmas and
 Thanksgiving.
Price: Inexpensive.
Cuisine: Pizza, sandwiches.
Serving: L, D.
Credit Cards: None.
Reservations: None.
Handicap. Access: Limited.
Special Features: Free
 delivery; Patio dining;
 Takeout.

For tasty, relatively healthful pizza, Upper Crust is a good bet. Unless you want to sit on the sunny patio and watch the traffic on Old Santa Fe Trail, we suggest you eat it somewhere else. The restaurant is functional at best, junky at worst — a small, hang-loose place with wobbly formica tables where the draft beer is served in plastic cups and you try to cut a torpedo-sized sausage roll with a chintzy plastic knife and fork. For best results, order out or ask them to deliver.

Upper Crust offers a variety of traditional Italian or whole-wheat pizzas. The Veggie Supreme includes mushrooms, black olives, chile, bell peppers, onions, diced tomatoes and sesame seeds. There are good sandwiches and specialties such as Stromboli and Italian Calzone.

VICKIE LEE'S SOUTHERN BARBEQUE
986-0028.
1201 Cerrillos Rd. (at Alta
 Vista), Santa Fe, NM
 87501.
Closed: Christmas, New
 Year's.
Price: Inexpensive.
Cuisine: Southern barbe-
 cue.
Serving: L, D.
Credit Cards: None.
Reservations: None.
Handicap. Access: Yes.
Special Features: 100-inch
 video screen; Children's
 menu; Takeout.

In May 1990, Vickie Lee Williamson brought a taste of the Old South to Santa Fe from Louisiana — a red-hot barbecue pit where great quantities of beef, pork and chicken are smoked in oak and hickory ovens. Orders are placed at the bar with Vickie and patrons wait at one of the homey tables decked with red-and-white-checked tablecloths. While you're waiting for your sliced brisket or hot links, listen to Country Western tunes or watch the latest cable images on Vickie Lee's bigger-than-life, 100-inch video screen.

Cowboys, tourists and sports fans dig into a combination plate of barbecued beef, pork and chicken strips with a huge side of thick, deep-fried potatoes and seasoned pinto beans. The chicken is only slightly shy of luscious, although the other meats are a bit dry and dull and the rather thin barbecue sauces don't add much flavor. Vickie's highly-touted homemade Peanut Butter Chocolate Chip Cheesecake is likewise on the dry, dull side. On the other hand, the food is definitely hale and hearty, and there's plenty of it — maybe even more than you can eat. Add to this the atmosphere, complete with dart board, Confederate flags and Southern drawl and you've got a rebel outpost well worth visiting.

YIN YANG

986-9279.
418 Cerrillos Rd., Santa Fe,
NM 87501.
Closed: Christmas Day.
Price: Moderate.
Cuisine: Hunan, Cantonese.
Serving: L, D.
Credit Cards: MC, V.
Reservations: Recom-
mended for large parties.
Handicap. Access: Limited.

Until about 1980 there was no edible Chinese food in Santa Fe. Now there are half a dozen thriving Chinese restaurants. And Yin Yang, with its tasteful atmosphere, fine service and first-rate food, is among the best.

At lunch, Yin Yang offers a delicious and very inexpensive all-you-can-eat buffet that includes egg rolls, fried rice, beef and broccoli and sweet-and-sour pork. There are cold Chinese salads, a superb egg-drop soup and fresh fruit. Dishes from the regular menu are available for the same price.

At dinner, in addition to the usual Chinese dishes, Yin Yang offers a large selection of "chef's specialties," which offer exotic taste treats. There are two deserts to choose from: fried ice cream or plain ice cream. The wine and beer lists are short and adequate.

ZIA DINER

988-7008.
326 Guadalupe, Santa Fe,
NM 87501.
Closed: Major holidays.
Price: Moderate.
Cuisine: Modern Ameri-
can.
Serving: L, D.
Credit cards: AE, MC, V.
Reservations: Parties of 6
or more.
Handicap. Access: Yes.
Special Features: Smoking
in bar only; Outdoor
dining; Takeout.

The Zia is more than a diner. It has been a favorite with Santa Feans since its opening in 1986. To avoid a long wait, make reservations or plan to arrive early. Art deco design combined with a tri-level seating arrangement allow for an intimate yet cheery dining experience. Service is friendly and informed, and an open kitchen allows customers to view the Zia's well-organized operation.

The Zia knows how to please a variety of tastes without compromising quality. Connoisseurs of New Mexican cuisine will find the chicken enchiladas and black bean *flautas* rival any of Santa Fe's restaurants. Meat lovers will find everything from hamburgers to pork chops with green chile apple sauce. Vegetarians can enjoy fresh soups, salads, and a savory corn and *asiago* cheese pie or a pasta special. Even seafood lovers, far from shore, can choose between popular fish and chips and a daily seafood special.

The Zia justly boasts about its homemade pies and Black Midnight chocolate cake. The blackberry banana crumb is packed with fresh fruit and sweetened just enough to bring out the juicy blackberry flavor.

Murrae Haynes

Zia Diner: pleasing to eye and palate.

Near Santa Fe

ANGELINA'S
753-8543.
200 E. Oñate St., Española,
NM 87532.
Open daily.
Price: Inexpensive.
Cuisine: Northern New
Mexican.
Serving: B, L, D.
Credit Cards: MC, V.
Reservations: Large groups
only.
Handicap. Access: Yes.
Special Features: Vegetarian dishes; Takeout.

Angelina's in Española is proof that looks are deceiving. The run-down commercial building that houses this little jewel looks like it would be better suited as a tire store. Inside, it looks like the set for a Fellini film. The eight booths are "theme dining environments" constructed to look like anything from a hacienda *portal* to a frontier jail. Try the salsa and chips; Angelina's dipping sauce is a delight, as is the rolled cheese enchilada full of fresh, shredded cheese with a lovely homemade sauce. Among the sure-fire winners at Angelina's are the chile *rellenos*, the lovingly prepared lamb *fajitas* and the almost unbelievably tender *carne adovada*.

**ANTHONY'S AT THE
DELTA**
753-4511.
228 Oñate N.W., Española,
NM 87532.
1 blk. from City Hall.
Closed: Major holidays.
Price: Expensive.
Cuisine: Steak and seafood.
Serving: D.
Credit Cards: AE, DC, MC,
V.
Reservations: Recommended.
Handicap. Access: Yes.
Special Features: Fireplace;
Private dining;
Vegetarian plates.

Anthony's is an elegant enterprise that started as a neighborhood bar in 1949. Over the years it expanded to include a spacious, high-ceilinged restaurant, a flower market and a candy shop. Today the place is a Spanish Colonial haven, with plushly decorated rooms, handcrafted furniture, brilliant gardens and landscaped terraces. Ramon Rice's evocative paintings hang on the walls; a large *kiva* fireplace crackles with warmth; and winemeister Nick Hunsiker graciously offers you a glass from his impressive collection, even before you're seated. There is an attentive and thoughtful, although slow, staff.

The food gets mixed reviews. For instance, the Beef Bourgignon special is comprised of stringy beef chunks on a bed of delicious sauce-covered noodles, covered with a sauce so good it *almost* makes up for the canned peas hidden within. The Broiled Shrimp and Scallops are colorful and well-presented, but the shrimp is generally dry and overcooked. The same can be said for Anthony's desserts. The undersized Chocolate Mousse is often grainy and the under-cooked apple pie is sometimes too tart. On the other hand, Anthony's is such an enchanting place that you can forgive the failings and still have a pleasant dining experience.

Murrae Haynes

Anthony's at the Delta: gracious dining in a Spanish Colonial haven.

THE BLUE WINDOW
662-6305.
800 Trinity Dr., Suite H,
    Meri-Mac Mall, Los
    Alamos, NM 87544.
Closed: Sundays.
Price: Moderate.
Cuisine: International.
Serving: L, D.
Credit Cards: MC, V.
Reservations: Recom-
    mended.
Handicap. Access: Yes.
Special Features: Private
    dining; Children's
    menu; Takeout.

Although Los Alamos is not noted for its dining options, Chef Butch Wilder is attempting
to "make Santa Fe blue with envy" by developing
a sophisticated new menu and establishing a spe-
cial-evening-out place. He has had uneven success,
however, and favorites from The Blue Window's
"old" menu are still the best buy. Although the
new and more expensive dishes are in need of
work, the fresh spinach crepe, a standby from the
original menu, is light and flavorful, served in a
delicate cream sauce. The staff seems to have more
enthusiasm than experience.

The excellent desserts at the Blue Window are
offered in half portions — a fine idea. The delicious blackberry crepe is enormous and topped
with a scoop of real whipped cream.

CAFE DEL ARROYO
753-7890
P.O. Box 2053, Española,
    NM 87532. Arroyo Seco,
    2.5 miles south of
    Española on U.S. 285.
Closed: Mondays.
Price: Inexpensive.

Just south of Española, the Cafe del Arroyo has
been a popular local dining spot for more than
15 years. Though it has recently been spruced up
by its new owners, Eddie and Louella Williams, it
is still a basic vinyl tabletop and paper place-mat
kind of place, simple and functional.

Of course its main function is to feed you and it
does that well. The salsa and tortilla chips are salty

Cuisine: New Mexican,
  American.
Serving: B, L, D.
Credit Cards: MC, V.
Reservations: None.
Handicap. Access: Yes.

and warm from the oven. For a hearty del Arroyo sampler, try the combination plate (two delicious rolled meat and cheese enchiladas, a tamale and a taco with refried beans and Spanish rice). The chile *rellenos* tend to be on the oily side but are usually well cooked and have a snappy flavor. As for the homemade chile, either color is great, but caution: the red may set your face on fire.

Desserts at the del Arroyo are not particularly memorable. The drink menu includes domestic and imported beers and a small sampling of Blossom Hill and Almaden. Other fare includes inexpensive breakfast and lunch dishes (sandwiches, burgers, salads) and traditional American dinners. We recommend the New Mexican fare; it's what the del Arroyo does best.

EL NIDO
988-4340.
P.O. Box 488, Tesuque,
  NM 87574.
At junction of N.M. 590
  and 591, 5 mi. N. of
  Santa Fe.
Closed: Mondays.
Price: Expensive.
Cuisine: Steak and
  seafood.
Serving: D.
Credit cards: MC, V.
Reservations: Recom-
  mended.
Handicap. Access: Yes.
Special Features: Fireplaces.

Steak and seafood restaurants don't normally feature New Mexico charm, especially of the rural variety. An exception is El Nido in the quiet village of Tesuque. *El Nido* means "the nest," which is appropriate because the restaurant started out as a family home in the 1920s. It actually was a home for birds later on, when two elderly women raised canaries on the premises. Later it became a nest of a different kind, a brothel run by a madam named "Ma" Nelsen. In yet another incarnation the place was a rowdy dance hall that saw three fatal shootings.

Today El Nido remains colorful, with red chile *ristras* on white adobe walls, dark brown *vigas* across low ceilings, stacks of freshly cut piñon logs, large *kiva* fireplaces, and hand-painted scenes of birds and flowers. El Nido is known for its fresh seafood. Service is a team effort. Within two minutes of being seated, you're likely to be greeted by three different staff members — one to pour water, a second to ask about cocktails and a third to describe specials not listed on the menu.

The *Ceviche* is tangy, the Smoked Salmon and Capers, appealing. A cup of rich, sweet onion soup simmered with red wine makes a terrific beginning. The sirloin is perfectly prepared, tender and slightly smoky, and the steamed mussels are even better. Desserts, such as a rich, smooth chocolate mousse and a chocolate hazelnut torte, are good. The house wine, a California Chardonnay, is cloyingly sweet.

HOT SHOTS
662-2005.
2581 Trinity Dr., Los
   Alamos, NM 87544.
Open daily.
Price: Moderate.
Cuisine: Barbecue, sand-
   wiches, burgers.
Serving: L, D.
Credit Cards: MC, V.
Reservations: Groups of 6
   or more.
Handicap. Access: Yes.
Special Features: Chil-
   dren's menu; Patio
   dining; Takeout.

If the sudden urge for a plateful of juicy smoked pork ribs hits you, stop in at Hot Shots in Los Alamos and get down to some serious eating. The building that houses this roadside cafe has been through a number of reincarnations. There are some decidedly weird memorabilia nailed to the walls, including a six-foot sailfish wearing ear-muffs. But that's OK, because this finger-lickin' barbecue pit has found its stride under the guiding hand of owner Mike Smith.

Hot Shots' pork ribs plate is filled with eight juicy ribs. We've tried all three sauces — tradition-al, Cajun and Texas — and found little difference between them. Don't worry; no amount of sauce could cover up the delicate, mesquite-fired flavor of the ribs. A few may have been left on the grill a bit too long, but your fingers and face will be so slathered with sauce that you'll hardly notice. The brisket and grilled sausage are as good as the ribs. There's hardly a chunk of fat to be seen on any of these cuts. Mike Smith offers smoked chicken, smoked trout and a large selection of sandwiches with small portions of barbecue. For dessert we suggest the Texas Chocolate Funeral Pie, which is deadly indeed: light fudge on top, crushed pecans underneath and a moist, chocolate center.

Kids love it here. There are a couple of small rocking chairs and a toy oven to keep children entertained. Crayons and a coloring books are available to keep a child occupied while the grownups finish their desserts.

THE LEGAL TENDER
982-8425.
Lamy, NM 87540.
N. on I-25 to Exit 290, then
   S. on U.S. 285.
Closed: Mondays from
   Jan.-May; call ahead.
Price: Very Expensive.
Cuisine: American.
Serving: L, D, SB.
Credit cards: MC, V.
Reservations: Recom-
   mended.
Handicap. Access: Lim-
   ited.
Special Features: Historic
   building; Live music.

"This is the real Old West, where gunfighters, gamblers and beautiful ladies have dined, danced and dallied," declares the menu of the Legal Tender. To be sure, the past is alive in this Victorian saloon-turned-restaurant. Listed on the National Register of Historic Places, the two-story structure was built in 1881 as the Annex Saloon. Two years later a German immigrant bought and operated it as a general store. Later, under another owner, it reverted to a saloon. Then during the 1950s it was a can-can and vaudeville establish-ment known as the Pink Garter.

Linger at the hand-carved cherry bar that is said to have been visited by Billy the Kid, supposedly brought in chains by lawmen who recaptured him after his daring escape from the Lincoln County

Jail. Notice the steel engravings on the dining room walls, the railroad paintings and Thomas Moran chromo-lithographs hung in the balcony.

Food at The Legal Tender is good but not great. The steaks are best. Lunch specialties include the Legal Tender Burger and the Lamy Lamb Burger, *fajitas*, fettuccini Alfredo and broiled halibut, as well as an array of appetizers and salads. Entrees are served with fresh breads, soup or salad, potato or rice and a fresh vegetable. The wine list is well balanced and fairly priced. Service is gracious and attentive.

RANCHO DE CHIMAYÓ
351-4444.
P.O. Box 11, Chimayó, NM 87522.
Closed: January, Mondays Feb.-May and Sept.-Jan.
Price: Moderate.
Cuisine: Northern New Mexican.
Serving: L, D, SB.
Credit Cards: AE, MC, V.
Reservations: Recommended.
Handicap. Access: Yes.
Special Features: Fireplaces; Patio dining; Musicians in summer.

Restaurante Rancho de Chimayó is a beautiful remodeled ranch house that has been in the Jaramillo family since the 1880s. Restored and converted into a restaurant in 1965, it still has the definite feel and many of the trappings of northern New Mexico, including rustic wood floors, whitewashed adobe walls, hand-stripped *vigas* and a terraced patio. The Jaramillo family still runs the place, and the food is prepared from recipes that have been in the family for generations. The atmosphere is semi-elegant but relaxed. The staff bustles around in black slacks and burgundy bow-ties, and patrons in the intimate dining rooms and on the spacious patio wear anything from three-piece suits to jeans and sneakers.

The food is fairly good, the portions enormous and the service friendly and efficient. The nachos are particularly crisp. A huge, flaky *Sopaipilla Relleno*, though not exceptional, is stuffed to bursting with beef, beans and Spanish rice. The Chimayó chicken is usually moist and flavorful. If you're tempted to order *Burrito al Estilo Madril* (a huge plate of *carne adovada* wrapped in a flour tortilla), be forewarned: the pork is usually tender and tasty, but it's flame-thrower spicy, having been marinated in red-hot chile sauce for six hours. Once, when neither water nor beer could put out the fire started by this dish, our understanding waiter brought us a cool *Aguacate Relleno*, a half avocado filled with fresh jumbo shrimp on a bed of lettuce and tomato, at no extra charge.

Rancho de Chimayó serves three desserts, none particularly outstanding. We recommend the *flan*, a rich, creamy caramel custard with a pleasing tapioca consistency. The restaurant serves a small selection of house wines, brandies and liqueurs plus two good coffees.

ROADRUNNER CAFE
455-3012.
Pojoaque, N.M., 16 miles
	N. of Santa Fe on N.M.
	285.
Open daily.
Price: Inexpensive.
Cuisine: New Mexican,
	American.
Serving: B, L, D.
Credit Cards: MC, V.
Reservations: None.
Handicap. Access: Lim-
	ited.
Special Features: Chil-
	dren's menu.

A truck stop nestled in the scenic Pojoaque Valley, the Roadrunner is just what you'd expect:
inexpensive, loud and down-home. It offers
remarkably fresh and tasty dishes. Co-owner chef
Lorraine Montoya has decades of cooking under
her belt. A favorite for locals, truckers and state
troopers, the Roadrunner is a wear-your-dirty-ol'-
boots-and-jeans kind of place. The service is
prompt and friendly, and they keep that coffee
coming.

The menu offers hearty, served-anytime breakfasts, an assortment of burgers, sandwiches,
seafoods and steaks, and a variety of New Mexican specialties served with rice and beans. Don't
miss Lorraine's delicious whole-wheat *sopaipillas*.
For dessert, try one of her fresh fruit pies.

SAN MARCOS CAFE
471-9298.
N.M. 14, about 14 mi. S. of
	Santa Fe.
Open daily.
Price: Inexpensive.
Cuisine: Northern New
	Mexican.
Serving: B, L, D, SB.
Credit Cards: MC, V.
Reservations: Recom-
	mended on weekends.
Handicap. Access: Lim-
	ited.
Special Features: Wood-
	stove; Entertainment on
	weekends; Takeout.

A bout 100 feet down a dirt driveway off N.M.
14, a sign on the San Marcos Feed Store says
that 75-pound bales of alfalfa are available inside.
Surprisingly, neither this nor any other sign tells
you that some of the best food in the county is
served in the store's adjacent cafe.

The San Marcos is a down-home place, each of
its dozen tables equipped with a tin candle holder
and handmade ceramic sugar bowl. The crowd
here is an eclectic mix of ranch hands, prison
guards, artists and families. On a recent winter's
evening, a string trio sat next to a cranked-up
woodburning stove and serenaded diners with
folk melodies. Service was about as good as one
pregnant waitress running between a dozen tables
could make it. We liked her friendly manner and
followed her recommendations to a luscious meal.

The appetizers are a meal unto themselves — a
creamy, split-pea soup served with toasted garlic French bread and an open-
faced, blue corn tortilla *quesadilla* with mounds of melted cheese and a scoop
of sour cream. The blue corn enchiladas, served on an oven-hot metal plate,
were delicious. Another recommended dish is the green chile chicken stew,
full of flavorful, tender chicken and lots of onions, potatoes and green peppers. Desserts at San Marcos are an irresistible array of fresh pies, cinnamon
rolls, cakes and tarts.

TESUQUE VILLAGE MARKET

988-8848.
P.O. Box 231, Tesuque,
   NM 87574. At N.M. 591
   and Bishops Lodge Rd.
Closed: Christmas, New
   Year's.
Price: Inexpensive.
Cuisine: New Mexican,
   American.
Serving: B, L, D.
Credit Cards: MC, V.
Reservations: None.
Handicap. Access: Lim-
   ited.
Special Features: Patio
   dining; Takeout; Call-in
   picnic lunches.

Four years ago, Jerry Honnell decided to convert his neighborhood grocery into a combination restaurant-grocery-deli-and-gallery. The result is this popular community eatery. This strange little grocery has shelves stocked with canned goods and coolers stocked with beer. But look over there — an entire wall full of California and local wines. And there — a deli bar with an inviting assortment of cheeses, meats, cakes and breads! The narrow dining hall and "gallery" is complete with creaking wood floors, large fans spinning on the ceiling and regional color photos adorning the walls. The service is prompt and the dining hall is nonsmoking.

The menu is varied, as would be expected in a grocery store. Stop by for lunch, a late afternoon snack or dessert. They include a tangy smooth Lemon Mousse Pie and the three layer Chocolate Chanboard Cake.

Taos

APPLE TREE RESTAURANT

758-1900.
Taos Plaza, Taos, NM
   87571.
Open daily.
Price: Expensive.
Cuisine: New Mexican,
   Continental.
Serving: L, D, SB.
Credit Cards: AE, MC, V.
Reservations: Recom-
   mended.
Handicap. Access: Yes.
Special Features: Fire-
   places; Patio dining;
   Live entertainment.

As cozy a place as its name implies, the Apple Tree hums with the resonance of happy diners. Located just off the plaza, it is a "just right" dinner spot after a day of sightseeing or skiing — or the perfect lunch break following a morning of gallery hopping.

Apple Tree dinners are always special, featuring creative cooking and excellent service. A diner might select, as an appetizer, smoked red trout with sherried Dijon peppercorn sauce and an excellent local wine from the La Chiripada Vineyards. Entrees are imaginative; for instance, the Mango Chicken Enchiladas — two rolled enchiladas stuffed with chunks of spicy chicken breast, mango chutney and sour cream. Apple Tree provides a nice selection of steak, seafood and chicken dishes. The Chicken Normandy, a chicken breast with sauteed shallots, dried apricots and apples, covered with an original apple brandy cream sauce, is highly recommended. Desserts change nightly. We can almost guarantee that you will be pleased, whatever you order, from creamy *flan* to chocolate cake.

Dining on the patio at the elegant Apple Tree.

Murrae Haynes

CASA DE VALDEZ
758-8777.
Paseo del Pueblo Sur & Estes Rd., Taos, NM 87571.
Closed: Wednesdays.
Price: Moderate.
Cuisine: New Mexican, Barbecue.
Serving: L, D.
Credit Cards: AE, MC, V.
Reservations: Recommended.
Handicap. Access: Yes.
Special Features: Patio dining; Private dining.

A popular après-ski spot, Casa de Valdez is a chalet-style building with views of the Sangre de Cristo Mountains. It features traditional New Mexican cuisine, a mouth-watering selection of charbroiled steak and shrimp dishes, as well as beef, chicken and spareribs barbecued in a backyard pit. Owner Peter Valdez, who wants to pass on his hard-earned lessons about heart disease, serves organically raised poultry and the leanest cuts of aged beef. He cooks with cholesterol-free oil, natural white cheese (to avoid food coloring) and very little salt.

Service at Casa de Valdez is prompt and friendly, and the food is usually excellent. Dinner salads are prepared with the freshest of greens and topped with tasty homemade dressings. Homemade whole-wheat rolls arrive piping hot from the oven. A 12-ounce serving of spareribs from the pit, slow-cooked for 14 hours, was a little on the dry side but still delicious in a homemade barbecue sauce. Similarly, an eight-ounce rib-eye steak was tender and included rice pilaf with almond slivers and carrots, broccoli and cauliflower.

Our pecan pie was a sweet meal-end treat, but with its hard, institutional crust and extra-gooey consistency it was definitely not up to the standard of the rest of the meal. Casa de Valdez offers a narrow but fine selection of Napa Valley wines and a few fine French champagnes.

DOC MARTIN'S
758-1977.
125 Paseo del Pueblo
    Norte, Taos, NM 87571.
In the historic Taos Inn.
Open daily.
Price: Expensive.
Cuisine: Contemporary
    American.
Serving: B, L, D.
Credit Cards: AE, DC, MC,
    V.
Reservations: Recom-
    mended.
Handicap. Access: Yes.
Special Features:
    Fireplaces; Patio dining;
    private dining.

This adobe-style restaurant was, from the 1890s until the early 1940s, the home of local physician T.P. Martin. The restaurant is entered through the lobby of the Taos Inn which retains the flavor of a village gathering place. Doc Martin's staff is friendly and the food is far from folksy. The menu features many delights. One is continuous variety — the chef makes daily changes. He combines Continental cuisine with the best of local Southwestern cooking and ingredients.

For breakfast, tourists and locals alike can enjoy a stack of surprisingly light Blue Corn and Blueberry Hotcakes or a delicious but fiery Eggs with Venison *Chorizo*. The dinner menu features such delicacies as Steamed New Zealand Cockles with Pernod and Leeks and Grilled Lamb Satay. The satay is grilled to perfection, and its spicy cashew sauce is an interesting variation on the more common peanut version. The *Pollo Empanada de Piñon* (boned chicken breast breaded in ground pine nuts) is a highly successful entree accompanied by a lively Mexican green chile sauce. Dessert possibilities include standard tarts, tortes and ice cream.

The restaurant is famous for its 260-choice wine list, which *The Wine Spectator* has given an award of excellence four years in a row. The list, chosen by Andy Lynch and modified by John D'Arna, boasts wines from all over the globe. Prices range from the modest (with many bottles under $20) to outrageous; however, the Cruvinet allows many wines to be sampled by the glass.

DOUBLE A GRILL
758-1319.
332 Paseo del Pueblo Sur,
    Taos, NM 87571.
3 blks. S. of the plaza.
Closed: Wednesdays.
Price: Moderate.
Cuisine: American, New
    Mexican.
Serving: L, D.
Credit Cards: MC, V.
Reservations: 4 or more.
Handicap. Access: Limited.
Special Features: Vegetar-
    ian plates; Takeout.

The Double A is a schizophrenic kind of place that opened in August 1990. Outside, a glaring neon sign suggests a tavern. Inside, folded white napkins contrast with rustic knotty pine while rock music sometimes blares from the kitchen. Artwork on the walls varies from intriguing local landscapes to powerful masks and weaving. There's a global selection of wines, ranging from California to Spain.

The menu offers everything from soups, sirloin and Caesar salads to (not-so tasty) buffalo burgers. Most evenings the Double A is crowded with customers sampling the grill's daily specials: delectable-sounding dishes like pheasant stew, chicken and asparagus stir-fry, broiled quail with tarragon butter, roast duck breast with raspberry sauce — even salmon *fajitas*. For dessert, try the Double A's Bourbon Street Pecan Pie or Chocolate Chip Banana Cake.

EL PATIO DE TAOS
758-2121.
Address: Terasina Ln., on
    N.W. corner of plaza.
Open daily.
Price: Moderate.
Cuisine: American, Italian,
    New Mexican, Seafood.
Serving: L, D.
Credit Cards: AE, MC, V.
Reservations: Recom-
    mended.
Handicap. Access: Lim-
    ited.
Special Features: Fireplace;
    Guitarist on weekends;
    Vegetarian dishes.

This restaurant occupies the oldest building in town, which housed a Taos Pueblo trading post in the 17th century. The Spanish government used it for 200 years and New Mexico's first territorial governor maintained offices there. Today the small, romantic dining room is dominated by a central stone fountain. By day, light filters through a huge skylight; by night, candles soften white-washed walls.

El Patio is worth a visit for the environment alone, although the food is excellent. The menu includes a mix of pastas, seafoods and northern New Mexican specialties for lunch, with added dinner suggestions. A bowl of nicely seasoned green chile stew and excellent French bread is a good start for lunch. One entree, *Crepes de Fruits de Mer*, features two *crepes* in a delicate lobster sauce with generous chunks of salmon, shrimp and scallops. The other, chicken burritos are stuffed with lightly smoked chicken topped with a delicious chile sauce. A glass of Glen Ellen Chardonnay complements the *crepes* nicely. The daily dessert tray displays eight mouth-watering choices, including a rich, moist deep-chocolate cake and a cheesecake that is tasty but a bit dry.

**FLOYD'S RESTAURANT
& LOUNGE**
758-4142.
819 Paseo del Pueblo Sur,
    Taos, NM 87571.
Open daily.
Price: Inexpensive.
Cuisine: American, New
    Mexican.
Serving: B, L, D.
Credit Cards: None.
Reservations: None.
Handicap. Access: Yes.
Special Features: Takeout;
    Large group dining.

Floyd's is your basic small-town American restaurant: a bit dumpy, with a popular bar and lounge. The place serves burgers, steaks, sandwiches, enchiladas, burritos, banana splits, fruit pies, chocolate sundaes — fundamental fare that keeps the country going, and at prices most people can afford. The food, though not memorable, is down-home and plentiful, and the service is country friendly.

GARDEN RESTAURANT
758-9483.
P.O. Box 3317, Taos, NM
    87571.
N.W. corner of plaza.
Open daily.
Price: Moderate.
Cuisine: Continental.
Serving: B, L, D.

There are a number of restaurants packed into the Taos plaza, and the Garden is one of them. The name is a misnomer, however. For one thing, the funky cottage decor is accented with fake greenery. Although the menu indicates a specialty in healthful vegetarian fare, a visitor might find the Garden's salads wilted, its vegetables undercooked and the house wine decidedly weak. The

Credit Cards: AE, MC, V.
Handicap. Access: Limited.
Special Features: Chil-
dren's menu; Vegetarian
plates; Live entertain-
ment.

restaurant tends to be understaffed, leaving patrons tapping toes and fingers while they wait to be seated or served.

On the other hand, it can be a pleasant and inexpensive lunch stop for harried plaza shoppers. The Garden's wonderful pasta plates with their heavy French bread accompaniment can be recommended. Desserts, often overpriced, can be bland or delicious depending what is ordered and how long it's been sitting around. Try the double chocolate cake with hot fudge.

**GOLDEN DRAGON
CHINESE
RESTAURANT**
758-2611.
Camino del Pueblo Sur, S.
of plaza.
Open daily.
Price: Inexpensive.
Cuisine: Chinese.
Serving: L, D.
Credit Cards: AE, MC, V.
Reservations: None.
Handicap. Access: Limited.

Unfortunately, the Golden Dragon provides the *only* Chinese fare in Taos. It is a basic eating establishment decked out with Chinese lanterns, beer posters, a purple Buddha — even multicolored garbage-bag ties holding up the window shades. The menu offers the usual poultry, pork, beef and seafood dishes, an assortment of huge family dinners, plus an interesting and surprising variety of American, Japanese, Jamaican and Mexican beers. The Dragon puts together an all-you-can-eat buffet for about $5, that includes curried chicken, sweet-and-sour fish, egg rolls, won ton soup and fried rice. Get there early, though; the Dragon keeps the food neither hot nor fresh.

LA CIGALE
751-0500.
225 Paseo del Pueblo Sur,
Taos, NM 87571.
In Pueblo Alegre Mall
across from Smith's.
Closed: Tuesdays, 2 wks.
in April after ski season.
Price: Moderate.
Cuisine: French Bistro.
Serving: L, D, SB.
Credit Cards: AE, MC, V.
Reservations: Recom-
mended.
Handicap. Access: Limited.
Special Features: Vegetar-
ian plates; Takeout;
Live entertainment
on weekends.

At last — a *real* French restaurant in Taos! Owner Laurent Guerin studied cooking in his homeland and cooked at the Taos Ski Valley before opening this cheery, wonderful place in 1990. La Cigale ("the Cicada"), is about as close as you can get to Paris and stay in New Mexico. Cafe atmosphere, comfy tables, private booths, French posters, cold carafes, gracious service, the melodious voice of Jacqueline Francoise singing "C'est le Printemps" — even the recessed lighting in whitewashed adobe walls somehow seems French.

And the food — ah! Laurent likes to cook bistro style. His onion soup will take you right back to Paris. The *Coquilles St. Jacques* and poached salmon with lemon butter sauce will remind you just how light and delicate well-cooked fish can be. The luxurious pot of cheese fondue will sizzle and fume like white-hot lava as you dip your two-pronged fork in for another bite.

La Cigale's wine list is, naturally, French. Perusing the menu is an experience in French: *Assiette de Fromages* (cheese platter with Brie, goat cheese, Emmenthal and Port Salut); *Panier de Crevettes* (Breton artichoke stuffed with fresh shrimp salad and tossed with sour cream vinaigrette); *Creme Berlet*, a light custard with raspberry and caramel sauce.

La Cigale . . . *qu'est ce qu'on dit? C'est magnifique!*

LAMBERT'S OF TAOS
758-1009.
309 Paseo del Pueblo Sur,
    Taos, NM 87571.
Open daily.
Price: Expensive.
Cuisine: Contemporary
    American.
Serving: L, D, SB.
Credit Cards: AE, DC, MC,
    V.
Reservations: Recom-
    mended.
Handicap. Access: Lim-
    ited.
Special Features: Private
    dining; Outdoor dining;
    Takeout.

In 1989, after a 10-year stint as head chef of the historic Taos Inn, Zeke Lambert opened his own classy restaurant. Lambert's of Taos rates as a "must visit" for any serious epicurean. Once a rambling Victorian home, the restaurant has been remodeled into a comfortable arrangement of five elegant dining areas with plastered white walls and track lighting.

Lambert's cuisine, on the nouvelle side of classic American, changes every night. The menu offers seafood selections, roast quail, pepper-crusted lamb, pork tenderloin and steak, each with a different vegetable and pasta, beans or couscous. Lambert's wine list is loaded with pricey California selections.

A discerning diner might try the silver-dollar-sized slices of pink, lean Medallions of Pork Tenderloin accompanied by a flavorful mound of dill potatoes au gratin and a dozen lightly sauteed fresh English peas, the pods still intact. The moist salmon fillet served with a roasted shallot butter sauce on a bed of *linguini al dente* is among the best we've ever tasted. Desserts range from a pear tart with whipped cream to Chocolate Oblivion Truffle Torte with raspberry sauce.

MAINSTREET BAKERY
758-9610.
Guadalupe Plaza, Taos,
    NM 87571.
Open daily.
Price: Inexpensive.
Cuisine: Natural, Vegetar-
    ian.
Serving: B, L.
Credit Cards: None.
Reservations: None.
Handicap. Access: Yes.
Special Features: Patio
    dining; Live entertain-
    ment Sat.

The feel of the Mainstreet is retro-sixties. On any given morning you can see dreadlocked adolescents, long-haired hippies and gypsy-dressed earth mothers huddled around an endless cup of "politically-correct" Nicaraguan coffee. This is definitely the guilt-free alternative hangout of Taos.

Although Mainstreet has inexpensive lunches, the real draw is the generous breakfast menu. Try the Mainstreet Special (piquant hormone-free scrambled eggs, fresh spinach, green onion, mushrooms and cream cheese) or the Guadalupe Special (two fried eggs with cheddar and green chile on a bed of home fries). The menu offers tofu, omelettes, French toast, home-made granola and heavy-duty buckwheat pancakes.

The coffee at Mainstreet is fresh-ground. Alternatives to this wicked brew are provided in the form of Cafix, herbal teas or fresh-squeezed orange juice. Coffee beans and baked goods are available for take-out.

MICHAEL'S KITCHEN
758-4178.
Paseo del Pueblo Norte, Taos, NM 87571.
Open daily.
Price: Inexpensive.
Cuisine: Spanish, American.
Serving: B, L, D.
Credit Cards: MC, V.
Reservations: None.
Handicap. Access: Limited.
Special Features: Children's menu; Takeout.

Old plank floors, heavy pine tables, thick *viga* ceilings and an assortment of relics from deer heads to antique wood stoves set the tone for this rustic cafe. Michael's has a bunkhouse feel to it, with friendly service, good coffee and hearty fare — omelettes, waffles, pancakes, steaks, sandwiches, soups, salads, New Mexican dishes and baked goods.

The food is not only filling but delicious. You can order anything on the menu any time of the day. For breakfast wolf down the Viennese potato pancakes that represent country cooking at its best: potatoes, onions and eggs served with applesauce and sour cream. Try the enormous *Tortilla Renenada*, a remarkably delicate concoction of dried ham and lightly scrambled eggs with chives, wrapped in a flour tortilla smothered with green chile and a creamy cheese sauce. Michael's cinnamon rolls are wonderfully sweet and packed with raisins!

OGELVIE'S BAR & GRILLE
758-8866.
103-I E. Plaza, Taos, NM 87571.
Open daily.
Price: Moderate.
Cuisine: American, New Mexican.
Serving: L, D.
Credit Cards: AE, MC, V.
Reservations: Recommended.
Handicap. Access: Yes.
Special Features: Patio dining; Fireplaces; Live entertainment.

Lush greenery, skylights, rustic furniture and a patio overlooking the Taos Plaza make upbeat Ogelvie's a pleasant and popular place. The menu offers a little of everything: from nachos to buffalo wings; *calamari* saute to potato skins; and an array of soups, sandwiches, salads, pastas and New Mexican fare. The food is hearty and fairly good but, with the exception of its guacamole and salsa, nothing special. One gets the feeling that Ogelvie's tries to be all things to all people. It does many things but few things well. Also, it has no non-smoking section, which is a surprise and a disappointment.

Murrae Haynes

Ogelvie's offers rustic New Mexican charm.

PIZZA EMERGENCY
751-0911.
316 Paseo del Pueblo Sur,
Taos, NM 87571.
Open daily.
Price: Inexpensive.
Cuisine: New York Pizza.
Serving: L, D.
Credit Cards: AE, MC, V.
Reservations: None.
Handicap. Access: Limited.
Special Features: Free delivery.

"You gotta figure it's a real New York pizza when even the pizza box won't shuddup already." That's the way owner Mark Myers greets his delivery customers; his history is printed right on the box. When Myers decided to make pizza in Taos, he went to New York and ate pizzas all over town until he found what he considered the best. Then he said to the owner, Frank Gaudio, "Teach me to make that." Gaudio did, and the result is a delicious, crispy-bottomed pizza with imported Italian tomatoes and the most expensive pizza mozzarella on the market. Says Myers, "Hey, what's the fun of New York without the threat of going broke?"

Right on Taos' main street, Pizza Emergency features a pleasant decor, background music, pizza by the enormous slice and an assortment of wonderful toppings — from pepperoni, Canadian bacon and anchovies to pineapple, snow peas and artichoke hearts. There's a "pizza bar" where you can pile on whatever ingredients you like — and an "unlimited" pizza, with any number of toppings in any combination.

Near Taos

ANDY'S LA FIESTA
758-2813.
St. Francis Plaza, Ranchos
de Taos, NM 87557.
Closed: Mon.-Tues.
Price: Moderate.
Cuisine: Northern New
Mexican.
Serving: D.
Credit Cards: AE, MC, V.
Reservations: Recom-
mended.
Handicap. Access: Lim-
ited.
Special Features: Patio
dining.

South of Taos in the little village of Ranchos de Taos, the soaring adobe walls of the historic St. Francis of Assisi church have been standing since 1732. Across a tiny plaza from this church sits Andy's La Fiesta, crammed into the corner of an even older building that was once part of a Spanish fortress.

Andy's is a great place to stop and have a drink along with some well-prepared local delights. Andy and Angie Vigil have a reputation for making the best cocktails north of Santa Fe, including frothy margaritas. Andy himself is a gregarious fellow who thinks nothing of playing with his grandkids in the middle of the evening rush. Fortunately he's got an army of nephews and nieces running the place, so all the important things get done.

Aside from luscious, subtly spiced *chile con queso* and baskets of homemade tortilla chips, Andy's is noted for its *carne adovada*, a local specialty featuring large chunks of pork served in a bracing red chile sauce. The *carnitas* (sliced flank steak sauteed with green peppers and onions) are almost too much to eat. Andy's offers a short list of unremarkable wines. After your feast you may have little room for dessert, but we strongly recommend you try the *flan* anyway. It's an airy, creamy creation not to be missed!

BRETT HOUSE
776-8545.
P.O. Box 1686, Taos, NM
87571.
4 mi. N. of Taos at the
blinking light.
Closed: Mondays.
Price: Expensive.
Cuisine: Continental,
Nouveau American,
Southwestern.
Serving: L (July-Aug.), D.,
SB.
Credit Cards: AE, MC, V.
Reservations: Recom-
mended.
Handicap. Access: Limited.
Special Features: Fire-
places; Patio dining.

Brett House is the former home of Dorothy Brett, a legendary Taos artist whose father was a confidant of Queen Victoria. As a girl, Brett took dance classes at Windsor Castle and later went to parties with Winston Churchill. Her acquaintances and friends included Virginia Woolf, Bertrand Russell, Aldous Huxley and Georgia O'Keeffe. She first came to Taos with D.H. Lawrence and his wife, Frieda, intent on starting a utopian community. They founded the Flying Heart Ranch in the mountains north of Taos, on land given to them by Mabel Dodge Luhan in exchange for D.H.'s manuscript of *Sons and Lovers*. In 1943 Frieda Lawrence gave Brett a small piece of property away from the ranch, on which she built her home, the present-day Brett House. Painting and partying, she lived there until she died in August 1977, at the age of 93.

Brett House has been enlarged and spruced up, but it's got all of the old charm and none of the old squalor (Brett and her dogs were noted for leaving trails of bones lying around the house). It's a classic adobe, with homey and elegantly furnished rooms and breathtaking views of the Sangre de Cristo Mountains. The restaurant is intimate, with flickering fires, white tablecloths, pink carnations, quiet conversation and soft classical music. Its eagle-eyed staff graciously fulfill your every need. An extensive and reasonably-priced wine list is provided. Entrees such as chicken breast, roast duck, rack of lamb and poached salmon, are served with delicious sauces, all perfectly seasoned and meticulously arranged on the plate. Accompanying vegetables are firm and flavorful, often sculpted in colorful arrays.

A visitor might begin a memorable meal with light, fluffy rolls, New Mexico Crab *Beignets* with Mustard *Aioli* or impeccable corn chowder. Salads feature crisp romaine lettuce, fresh tomatoes, Greek olives and feta cheese. The entrees are memorable; for instance, Poached Salmon with Potato Scales (each potato slice placed with the care of a sushi chef) seasoned with cilantro pesto or Beef Tenderloin with Mushroom Sauce. Dessert choices include a Pecan Tart with Vanilla and Raspberry Sauce and the Chocolate Decadence, a cool and creamy cake.

If you're in Taos looking for a gourmet feast, don't miss the Brett House. Unfortunately there's no nonsmoking section, but the staff can usually find you a spot with fresh air if you ask.

The Brett House: spectacular views of the Sangre de Cristo Mountains.

Murrae Haynes

COYOTE CREEK CAFE
377-3550.
Mini Mart Plaza, Angel
 Fire, NM 87110.
Open daily.
Price: Inexpensive.
Cuisine: American,
 Continental.
Serving: L, D, SB.
Credit Cards: MC, V.
Reservations: Not
 necessary.
Handicap. Access: Limited.

This place, formerly called the Golden Nugget, offers a folksy flair along with inexpensive and eclectic fare. One local we know characterizes it as "a hole in the wall with world class food that keeps us all fat and happy." That food includes four or five homemade daily lunch and dinner specials that vary from vegetables Alfredo, blue corn enchiladas, the finest in European cuisine and killer pizzas. One of the Coyote's hottest sellers is Shrimp Brochette — eight spiced shrimp, wrapped in bacon and skewered, broiled and served on a bed of dark rye toast.

As for desserts, one night a baked Alaska will be offered, the next a German apple strudel or a Grand Marnier chocolate parfait. In other words, dining at the Coyote is almost always a surprise. One thing you do know: it'll be cheap and it'll be good.

EMBUDO STATION
852-4707.
P.O. Box 154, Embudo,
 NM 87531.
41 miles N. of Santa Fe, 25
 mi. S. of Taos on N.M. 68.
Closed: Mondays and
 Dec.-Jan.
Price: Moderate.
Cuisine: Barbecue, Smoke-
 house, New Mexican.
Serving: L, D.
Credit Cards: MC, V.
Handicap. Access: Yes.
Special Features: Patio
 dining; Brewery; Smoke-
 house; Rafting trips.

If you ever get caught around lunch or dinner time halfway between Taos and Santa Fe, don't miss a quick detour across the Rio Grande to Embudo Station. During the 1880s this little cluster of buildings was home to the narrow-gauge Chili Line railroad, which carted hides, wool and chiles out of the valley. Now it's home to a variety of delights, including patio dining under giant cottonwoods, home-brewed beer, local wines from La Chiripada Winery, and mouth-watering meats cooked long and lovingly in a stone smokehouse.

You can smell it when you walk in — whiffs of the barbecued and slow-smoked bacon, turkeys, hams and trout that have made Embudo Station famous since it first opened as a summer restaurant in 1983. Owner Preston Cox's oak-smoked delicacies have become so popular they're shipped all over the country. At Embudo you're tempted to start your meal with something unusual, like fried mushrooms and okra, or a Greek salad with black olives and feta cheese. Embudo also offers an assortment of delicious sandwiches, New Mexican dishes and outstanding desserts.

Brewmaster Steve Eskeback usually keeps several of his home-brewed beers on tap. If you want to work up your appetite, you can also visit Eskeback's beautiful stone brewery, the country smokehouse or the nearby Daniel Valdez art gallery. In season you can even take the Sunset Dinner Float, a two-hour raft trip that starts five miles north at Lover's Lane and ends up with dinner at Embudo.

THE FRENCH QUARTER
776-8319.
At Quail Ridge Inn, about
 .75 mi. E. of blinking
 light on N.M. 150.
Closed: 2 wks. in April
 after ski season, 2 wks.
 before Thanksgiving.
Price: Expensive.
Cuisine: Continental,
 Cajun, Creole.
Serving: B, D.
Credit Cards: AE, MC, V.
Reservations: Recom-
 mended.
Handicap. Access: Yes.
Special Features: Fire-
 places; Takeout.

The French Quarter is a spacious, richly decorated restaurant that's both outstanding and
disappointing. When we visited we sat down at
rick oak tables bathed in the romantic light of oil
lamps — but set with artificial white roses. We
were entranced by the temporary display of R.C.
Gorman lithos on the walls but disappointed that
a beautiful stone fireplace had no fire.

Likewise, service and food at the French Quarter
can be both excellent and poor. After we waited
long minutes to give our order while listening to
raucous laughter from the kitchen, our waiter
appeared, apologized and explained that the
maitre d' was a bit "spaced out." He more than
made up for the lapse, with a personal and attentive service we've rarely experienced. A bottle of
Guenoc Chardonnay (1988), one of the many fine
Napa Valley wines featured, was deep and pleas-
ing, but the bread was stale and served with papered pads of butter. Even the
lettuce in the dinner salads was a bit shabby and gritty.

Thank God for the entrees! The shrimp scampi sauteed in a combination of
butter, wine and garlic arrived beautifully arranged with an impressive Cajun
rice accompaniment. The fettuccini special was outstanding: perfectly cooked
fettuccini noodles swarming around big chunks of firm, flaky marlin, sword-
fish and catfish smothered in a rich, buttery wine sauce. The fresh snow peas
with red pepper garnish and equally tasty rosemary butter sauce added a
touch of heaven on the side.

Dessert was a return to the banal: lukewarm coffee and stale, hard-crusted
pies.

L. ROBERTO'S
758-4879.
1201 Paseo del Pueblo
 Norte, Taos, NM 87571.
Closed: Sat.-Sun.
Price: Inexpensive.
Cuisine: Burgers, New
 Mexican.
Serving: B, L.
Credit Cards: None.
Reservations: None.
Handicap. Access: Lim-
 ited.
Special Features: Patio
 Dining; Takeout.

From the highway just beyond the Taos town
limits, L. Roberto's (as opposed to "Roberto's,"
a restaurant on Kit Carson Rd.) appears to be
nothing more than a dumpy little shack with serving windows. And so it is — you can't really go
inside, and the few picnic tables offer little more
than basic shelter. On the other hand, for quick,
luscious burgers and Taos homestyle cooking, it's
certainly worth a stop. During breakfast and
lunchtime you can usually find cars and trucks
sidled up to the shack like cows to a water hole,
locals greeting one another and passing the time as
they order L. Roberto's tried-and-true breakfast
burritos, Navajo tacos, chile dogs, corn dogs and

such. Our recommendation: try the Hungry Bob, a hefty burger-and-fry combination featuring a large, fresh beef patty with all the trimmings, including green chile. Great views of the Sangre de Cristo from here, too.

**NORTHTOWN RESTAU-
RANT**
758-2374.
908 Paseo del Pueblo
   Norte, Taos, NM 87571.
Closed: Sat.-Sun.
Price: Inexpensive.
Cuisine: New Mexican,
   American.
Serving: B, L.
Credit Cards: None.
Reservations: None.
Handicap. Access: Limited.
Special Features: Catering.

Here's a popular little breakfast and lunch spot serving tasty, healthful fare just beyond the Taos town limits. Skiers on their way to Taos Ski Valley often stop for breakfast and down a stack of blueberry or pecan hotcakes. Northtown Restaurant serves blueberry or pumpkin muffins, zucchini and banana bread, rich apple coffee cake and a variety of hearty northern New Mexican lunches.

THE OUTBACK
758-3112.
P.O. Box 934, Taos, NM
   87571.
Behind the Video Casa, off
   Paseo del Pueblo Norte,
   about 2.5 mi. N. of the
   plaza.
Closed: Christmas.
Price: Inexpensive.
Cuisine: "Taos" Pizza.
Serving: L, D.
Credit Cards: MC, V.
Reservations: None.
Handicap. Access: Lim-
   ited.
Special Features: Takeout.

This funky little pizza joint slightly outside the Taos town limits is well named. Chances are, you wouldn't even be able to find it unless you were told exactly where it was. The only hint of it's location is an addendum on the Video Casa sign that says "Pizza." On our first visit, when we walked into the Video Casa and asked, "Where's the pizza?" we were told with a wry smile, "Out back!"

The Outback is one of the hippest pizza parlors around, complete with an old-fashioned gas pump in the corner, a bicycle strapped to the ceiling and a bunch of pleasant young folks happily making and serving pizzas, calzones and sandwiches — folks who love what they do and consider themselves part of an extended family.

The "family" was started by co-owner Dennis Robbins in 1990, when he decided to produce what he calls "Taos-style gourmet pizza" — featuring thin crusts and spicy, succulent ingredients. His trial-and-error approach has produced a pizza that's still evolving, he says. We found it a bit greasy and leathery, but regulars seem to crave it, and the place is often packed. In fact, Robbins says, people have told him Outback pizza has changed their lives.

THE STAKEOUT

758-2042.
P.O. Box 3317, Taos, NM
   87571.
On Stakeout Dr. off N.M.
   68, about 8 mi. S. of
   Taos.
Open daily.
Price: Expensive.
Cuisine: American.
Serving: D.
Credit Cards: AE, MC, V.
Reservations: Recom-
   mended.
Handicap. Access: Yes.
Special Features: Guitarist
   on weekends; Fireplace;
   Outdoor dining.

Located in a rambling adobe hacienda overlooking miles and miles of mountainous terrain, the Stakeout is a semiformal oasis in remote corner of dry scrubland. It offers spectacular views from a substantial new patio, huge picture windows, crackling wood stoves and fireplaces, a warm, wood-paneled bar and a selection of relatively inexpensive domestic, imported and dessert wines. But the food doesn't quite measure up.

As the name implies, this place offers steaks that are juicy executions of classic steakhouse fare, but with a paltry half-dozen overcooked mushroom slices, bland vegetable accompaniments, uninteresting salads and stale desserts. Be careful about what you order at the Stakeout. If you come for the view and a basic cut of beef, you'll probably enjoy yourself. Anything more and you'll probably leave disappointed.

FOOD PURVEYORS

A butcher shop on Water Street, Santa Fe, ca. 1900.

Courtesy Museum of New Mexico

Santa Fe and Taos have been agricultural communities and bastions of local produce and home cooking for the better part of 400 years. After the 1940s, however, emphasis shifted to mass production and few independent food purveyors survived. Nonetheless, you can still find local vendors selling seasonal fare, from fruits and vegetables to gallons of green chile. There are also a few old-time butchers, bakers and dairies. Since the area was "discovered," it has started to support a wide variety of specialty establishments, including ice cream and candy shops, delis, bakeries and gourmet markets. Here are some of the places and products, both old and new, that make the modern Santa Fe–Taos area such a gastronomic delight.

BAKERIES

Santa Fe

CLOUD CLIFF BAKERY & CAFE
Manager: Willem Malten. 983-6254.
1805 2nd St., Santa Fe, NM 87501.
Closed: Wednesdays.

Cloud Cliff is a major baking operation, supplying local grocers with bread, rolls, muffins and scones. A great place to get them is at Cloud Cliff itself. The cinnamon rolls are particularly mouth-watering. Cloud Cliff offers a wide variety of breads, including Aztec Amaranth, Crunchy Millet and Cinnamon Raisin. For all their tastiness, however, Cloud Cliff breads tend to be crumbly, a difficulty in sandwich construction.

FRENCH PASTRY SHOP
Owner: George Vadeyan. 983-6697.
100 E. San Francisco St., Santa Fe, NM 87501.
Closed: Christmas.
Cash and traveler's checks only.

George Vadeyan and his brother started the French Pastry Shop in 1972. Two years later they moved to their present location in La Fonda Hotel. The location, along with an array of delicious pastries and crepes, has made this little cafe a tourist mecca in the summertime, as well as a place many locals return to again and again. The reasons are obvious: croissants, raisin rolls, apple turnovers, Napoleons, strawberry tarts, eclairs, quiches, sandwiches, crepes, coffees, cappuccinos — you get the idea.

HAAGEN DAZS ICE CREAM SHOPPE
Manager: Marvin Martinez. 988-3858.
56 E. San Francisco St., Santa Fe, NM 87501.
Closed: Thanksgiving, Christmas.

You know about the ice cream (this shop offers 33 flavors), but do you know about the baked goodies? This Haagen-Dazs, with seven full-time bakers offers an astonishing variety; so much, in fact, that it's Santa Fe's biggest bakery. Stuffed chocolate croissants, cream cheese brownies, fruit pies, bearclaws, strudel, scones and herb baguettes are some of the many delectables offered. Sandwiches are served along with coffee, tea and a variety of espresso drinks. Located on the plaza, Haagen-Dazs is a gathering spot for locals and tourists alike. It's one of the best people-watching places in town.

PATIS CORBAE BAKERY & CAFE

Owner: Dee Blanco.
983-2422.
422 Old Santa Fe Trail,
    Santa Fe, NM 87501.
Closed: Thanksgiving,
    Christmas.

Lots of people enjoy summer breakfast and lunch on the sunny Patis CorBae patio. Many of them order one or more of 12 different kinds of croissants, including spinach feta, chile cheddar and whole-wheat with sun-dried tomatoes, ricotta cheese and almonds. Other homemade pastries include raspberry almond brownies and sugarless apple turnovers. Patis CorBae has a full range of espresso drinks and some of the best *latte* in town.

SWISS BAKERY & RESTAURANT

Owner: Marie-Jeanne
    Chaney.
988-3737.
320 Guadalupe St., Santa
    Fe, NM 87501.
Closed: September.

Here's a European-style bakery offering an array of pies, cakes, tortes, croissants and baguettes. The owner, Marie-Jeanne Chaney, came to Santa Fe from the French part of Switzerland in 1976, before most Santa Feans had ever seen a croissant. She produces crusty French breads and loves to visit with her customers. A restaurant on the premises serves breakfast, lunch and early dinner. Chaney is convinced McDonalds' breakfast croissant is a copy of her long-popular croissant stuffed with ham and eggs.

Taos

DAYLIGHT DONUTS

Owners: John & Jaxene
    Collier.
758-1156.
312 Paseo del Pueblo
    Norte, Taos, NM 87571.
Closed: Sundays,
    Christmas.

Here's a good stop for coffee and a bag of glazed doughnuts or bearclaws or sticky buns. The Daylight opens promptly at 4 a.m. and prides itself on doughnuts deep fried in soybean oil. It has an astounding array of Daylight Donut accessories, including coffee mugs, T-shirts, pop-sippers, caps and coloring books.

DORI'S BAKERY

Owner: Dori Vanilla.
758-9222.
402 Paseo del Pueblo
    Norte, Taos, NM 87571.
Open daily.

This cheery place started out as a tiny bakery in 1973, when owner Dori Vanilla began making cakes and cookies. Today it is a Taos institution with a reputation for tasty baked goods. Baclavas, cinnamon twists, blueberry muffins, almond croissants and other creations beg to be tasted and Dori's bagels are among the best in the state. She serves breakfast, lunch, espresso and dessert.

MAINSTREET BAKERY
Owners: Mike Griego,
  Nathan Garcia.
758-9610.
Guadalupe Plaza, Taos,
  NM 87571.
Open daily.

This local bakery is really one large kitchen-warehouse space with a cafe. Mainstreet produces 15 wholesome breads including chile-anadama and carrot poppyseed. All Mainstreet baked goods are sweetened with honey and use organic ingredients.

Co-owner Mike Griego and daughters show off some of the goodies at the Mainstreet Bakery.

Murrae Haynes

BOTTLERS OF SPECIAL DRINKS

Santa Fe

**BLUE SKY NATURAL
  BEVERAGE CO.**
Owner: Robert Black.
986-8777.
510 Don Gaspar Ave.,
  Santa Fe, NM 87501.
No retail sales on site.

Robert Black his wife and son began making fresh-squeezed orange and grapefruit juice in 1979, delivering their product to restaurants and markets by jeep. A few years later, Black expanded into the soda business. Today his "natural beverages" (no sugar, artificial colors, artificial flavors, caffeine or preservatives) are available in most area restaurants and grocery stores. They include Mandarin Lime, Lemon Lime, Cola, Grapefruit, Root Beer, Raspberry, Cherry, Vanilla Cream and three types of sparkling waters.

Murrae Haynes

SANTA FE SPRINGS
Owner: Harold Newman.
242-3494.
Natural Choices, 2101
  Commercial N.E., Albu-
  querque, NM 87102.
Closed: Sat.-Sun.

For centuries, Native Americans have enjoyed the healthful, natural spring water at Apache Canyon, a few miles east of Santa Fe. Natural Choices, Inc. in Albuquerque now bottles it and in addition to natural, sparkling spring water, Fiesta Orange, Mexican Lime or Wild Mountain Berry are available.

**SANTA FE BREWING
  COMPANY**
Owner: Mike Levis.
988-2340.
Flying M Ranch, Galisteo,
  NM 87540.
Closed: Sun.

It was the wine business that got Mike Levis thinking about the beer business. As part owner of a Phoenix-based wine bottle distributor, Levis knew of several New Mexico wineries but not a single brewery. In 1988 he decided to open one on his 65-acre ranch outside Galisteo. The brewery's best-known product is Santa Fe Pale Ale, available in bars, restaurants, liquor and grocery stores throughout New Mexico. The company makes five other beers that are available only at the brewery: Fiesta Ale, Porter, Wheat Beer, Barley Wine and Nut Brown Ale.

BUTCHERS

There are a number of small groceries and health-food markets in Santa Fe and Taos that offer specialty and custom-cut meats. The following are locations and short descriptions of some of the better ones.

Santa Fe

Johnny's Market (983-9231; 320 Tesuque Dr.) is one of the oldest and tiniest markets in town. If you're interested in old-fashioned, over-the-counter service with hearty, grain-fed Iowa beef, this is the place for you. *Kaune Food Town* (982-2629; 511 Old Santa Fe Trail) Kaune's offers a wide variety of meats, including natural beef and poultry, Colorado lamb and game meats such as venison, buffalo, rabbit and pheasant. You can get a variety of natural meats and poultry at Santa Fe's two health-food stores: *The Marketplace* (988-2729, 808 Early St.; 984-2852, 627 W. Alameda) and *Wild Oats* (983-5333; 1090 S. St. Francis Dr.).

Taos

Cid's Food Market (758-1148; 822 Paseo del Pueblo Norte) has a little butcher department worth a special mention. Here you'll find Coleman natural beef from Colorado; Pastores lamb, New Mexico's first certified organic lamb; and Shelton's grain-fed, hormone-free chicken. *Graham's Superette* (758-2924; 910 Paseo del Pueblo Norte) is a standard country grocery store. Owner Robert Graham oversees the only old-fashioned, full-service meat market in town. Here's a mind-boggling array of free-range fryers and turkeys; range-fed lamb, pork, beef and buffalo; and all the cuts you can imagine, from T-bones and top round to beef tongue and *burrinate* (lamb intestine). Graham will happily give you recipes and cooking tips.

CANDY AND ICE CREAM SHOPS

In addition to *Baskin-Robbins* (982-9031, 1841 Cerrillos Rd., Santa Fe; 758-0031, Calvary & Pueblo Rd., Taos) and *Haagen-Dazs Ice Cream Shoppe* (988-3858; 56 E. San Francisco St., Santa Fe), discussed under "Bakeries," above), Santa Fe and Taos have two other sweet-tooth centers worth mentioning.

THE CHOCOLATE MAVEN
Owner: Mandy Clark.
984-1980.
222 N. Guadalupe St.,
   Santa Fe, NM 87501.
Closed: Sundays.

For mouth-watering desserts you can't beat this place. Specialties include a staggeringly rich New Orleans fudge cake, a renowned fudge espresso brownie and a Southwest cake decorated with chocolate *vigas*, *corbels*, ladders and chile peppers. These and other concoctions can be specially ordered or obtained in local restaurants and markets. Additionally, a tea room on the premises is open from 8 a.m. to 5:30 p.m., six days a week.

Making candies at the Chocolate Maven.

Murrae Haynes

SEÑOR MURPHY CANDYMAKER
Owners: Susan & Michael Monahan.
983-9243.
131 E. Palace Ave., Santa Fe, NM 87501. Locations also at La Fonda and Villa Linda Mall.

Neil Murphy, whose ancestors sold candy in Dublin, Ireland, specializes in anything with piñon nuts — for example, piñon toffee, piñon fudge, and the piñon roll, a concoction with a fudge center dipped in caramel and rolled in piñon nuts. He makes spicy red and green chile jellies, outstanding condiments for meats or for hors d'oeuvres with cream cheese and crackers.

TAOS CANDY FACTORY
Owners: Michael & Anita Griego.
758-4000.
205 Camino de la Placita, Taos, NM 87571.
Behind plaza next to First State Bank.
Closed: Christmas.

Owner Anita Griego started making candies for friends and relatives when she was a child. Now she's the only candymaker in Taos, and a very good one. Go into her little shop and gawk at her sumptuous display of 35 candy varieties featuring piñon candies, truffles and Taos tortes. Check out the assortment of Fitzgerald ice cream flavors plus four of Anita's own rich, creamy delights, including mocha piñon fudge, a mix of coffee, fudge and pinenuts.

CATERERS

Santa Fe

ADOBO CATERING
Owner: Ron Messick.
989-7674.
1807 2nd St., Unit # 7,
    Santa Fe, NM 87501.
Closed: Sun., caters 7 days.

Adobo's owner Ron Messick catered for the Los Angeles Music Center; owner O'Brien worked for 14 years with Martha Stewart in Connecticut and New York. The staff pools its talents in Santa Fe to offer buffet tables with "unlimited" menus for most occasions and any cuisine, from Asian to New Mexican.

BECKER'S
    DELICATESSEN
Owner: Richard & Justine
    Becker.
988-2423.
403 N. Guadalupe St.,
    Santa Fe, NM 87501.
Closed: Sundays, major
    holidays.

Becker's will do anything from Southwestern dinner parties to country barbecues. Their presentations are well-balanced, colorful and created with attention to detail.

CELEBRATIONS
    RESTAURANT &
    CATERERS
Owner: Sylvia Johnson.
989-8904.
613 Canyon Rd., Santa Fe,
    NM 87501.

Celebrations serves breakfast and lunch to the public in a quaint old adobe restaurant on Canyon Rd. and rents out its restaurant for sit-down dinner parties (minimum 30 to maximum 75 people) at night. They'll do whatever cuisine you want, although northern New Mexican and Creole are their specialties.

WALTER BURKE
    CATERING
Owner: Walter Burke.
988-5001.
908 Don Juan St., Santa Fe,
    NM 87501.
Open daily.

Walter Burke's army of caterers have consistently proven themselves up to any catering job. They are the largest catering firm in town with 200 employees who have prepared just about every kind of cuisine imaginable.

Taos

APPLE TREE
    RESTAURANT
Owner: Ginny & Arthur
    Greeno.
758-1900.
123 Bent St., Taos, NM
    87571.
Open daily.

The Apple Tree caters a little bit of everything, with traditional New Mexican cuisine among its most popular offerings. Apple Tree prides itself on adaptability, fresh foods, local produce and desserts.

NORTHTOWN
RESTAURANT
Owners: Shelly Ratigan &
   Linda Vanzi.
758-2374.
908 Paseo del Pueblo
   Norte, Taos, NM 87571.
Closed: Sat.-Sun., cater
   daily.

Owner Shelly Ratigan thinks the main reasons for the Northtown Restaurant's catering success are quality, price and personal approach. Most folks who use their services are locals who have enjoyed the restaurant's homestyle cooking. Northtown does almost any kind of catering, from barbecues to gallery openings. As Ratigan says, "Let's not talk standard; let's talk what your guests are going to remember."

COFFEE SHOPS

There are so many good places to drink coffee in Santa Fe and Taos that it's difficult to list them all, much less do them justice, so we simply call your attention to a number of choice spots where you can find good, fresh coffee, tea, espresso and cappucino. The rest is up to you.

In _Santa Fe_, good coffee spots include the *Aztec Street Cafe* (983-9464, 317 Aztec St.), rather smoky with hip-beat-punk ambience; *Becker's Delicatessen* (988-2423; 403 Guadalupe St.) with tasty bagels and pastries; the *Bookroom*

Coffee and pastries bring a smile at the Galisteo News.

Murrae Haynes

(988-5323, 616 Canyon Rd.), sunny and peaceful with books, magazines and great Guatemalan cafe *lattes*; *Burnt Horses Bookstore and Cafe* (982-4799, 225 E. De Vargas), back of the Oldest House; *Cloud Cliff Bakery & Cafe* (983-6254, 1805 2nd St.); *Downtown Subscription* (983-3085; 376 Garcia St.), a courtyard nook crammed with newspapers and magazines, plus great pastries and coffees including a killer espresso; *Galisteo News* (984-1316, 201 Galisteo St.), another spot with a plethora of newspapers and magazines; *Haagen-Dazs* (988-3853, 56 E. San Francisco St. on the plaza) with rich, deep coffee and pastries; *La Traviata* (984-1091, 95 W. Marcy St.), a place to sip espresso, *Ohori's* (988-7026; 507 Old Santa Fe Trail), fresh-roasted beans and a different coffee every hour; *Patis CorBae* (983-2422; 422 Old Santa Fe Trail), bakery and cafe with the best cup of java and one of the best *lattes* in town; and **Pranzo** (988-3886; 500 Montezuma in the Sanbusco Center), with great espresso and pastries.

In **Taos** you'll find some good brews at **Taos Tea and Coffee** (758-4404; 124-F Bent St). This aromatic hole in the wall in the Dunn House complex becomes a pleasant wake-up spot most mornings as locals gather for a shot of coffee and some conversation before going to work. There's no place to sit down, but you can get your coffee by the cup or the pound, in flavors ranging from chocolate hazelnut to Sumatra. Other good coffee shops include the **Bent Street Deli & Cafe** (758-5787, off Bent St. in the Dunn House complex); **Dori's Bakery & Cafe** (758-9222, 402 Paseo del Pueblo Norte); and the **Mainstreet Bakery** (758-9610, Guadalupe Plaza).

A COOKING SCHOOL

THE SANTA FE SCHOOL OF COOKING
Owner: Susan Curtis.
983-4511.
116 W. San Francisco St., Santa Fe, NM 87501.
Closed: Easter, Christmas.
Classes several times weekly; call for reservations.

Interested in learning to cook Southwest gourmet food? Take a lesson from the Santa Fe School of Cooking. The school and food market, under the deft direction of Susan Curtis, are located on the second floor of the Plaza Mercado, a block from the plaza. There are beginning and intermediate classes in New Mexican cooking and more advanced classes in New Mexican and other cuisines ranging from Moroccan food to valentine candymaking. The class packs in 2 ½ hours' worth of technique, information, hints and farmer's wisdom.

At the end, the students eat all that delicious food for lunch and an invited guest can join in the meal for a fee. The enchiladas, *posole* and especially the *sopa* (bread pudding) made in the beginner's Traditional 1 cooking course are among the best and most memorable you'll eat in Santa Fe.

A DAIRY

RANCHO LAS LAGUNAS
Owners: Pablo Roybal Family.
455-2261.
RR-1, Box 92-A, Santa Fe, NM 87501.
20 mi. N. of Santa Fe via U.S. 285, N.M. 503 (2 mi.) and N.M. 113 (0.5 mi.)
Open daily.

For a trip to yesteryear, as well as a taste of deliciously fresh milk, drive out to Rancho Las Lagunas near Nambe Pueblo to see cows munching hay and a small pasteurizing and bottling plant. Most important, they sell fresh milk and cream in glass bottles. The farm has always been run on the honor system; patrons put their money in a slot. It maintains a family tradition of simplicity and trust.

By the time you see the sign on the other side of the cattle guard, you'll already see and probably smell the cows. Park by the corral, walk through the door past stainless steel washing and processing equipment to the cooler in the rear. There you'll find stacks of half-gallon bottles with color-coded caps: homogenized, pasteurized, low-fat, raw and cream. Take your pick to the front, check the price list on the wall and put your money in the slot. Next time you come, return the cleaned, empty bottle.

FARMER'S MARKETS

The most common farmer's markets in the Santa Fe–Taos area are along the highway — shacks or temporary stands strung with red chile *ristras* offering a variety of home-grown fruits, vegetables and piñon nuts. In season, the most abundant cluster of such spots can be found on N.M. 68 between Velarde and Dixon. From time to time families gather to sell their freshly harvested green chile in shopping centers. Keep in mind that not all the produce is locally grown. If in doubt, ask the vendor.

Between June and October, there are a number of excellent markets in the Santa Fe–Taos area. The largest is the *Santa Fe Farmer's Market* (983-4098, 983-9136; 500 Montezuma.) It is held on Tuesdays and Saturdays at the Sanbusco Market Center, a collection of specialty retail shops and restaurants housed in a century-old setting. You can get locally grown produce (much of it organic), as well as prepared foods such as salsas, jams and jellies — sometimes even apple cider and honey.

Three other regional markets affiliated with the Santa Fe Farmer's Market offer fresh local produce and specialty items between June and October. They include the *Taos Farmer's Market* (758-3800), which meets Saturday mornings near the county courthouse on Paseo del Pueblo Sur; the Española Farmer's Market (753-5340); and the *Los Alamos Farmer's Market* (662-2656), held Thursday mornings on Central Ave., just north of the county municipal building.

FAST FOODS

Fast-food spots are abundant in the Santa Fe–Taos area. Some are so ubiquitous and predictable as to need no mention, and they are equally easy to find. Others, particularly those unique to the area, are worth looking for.

In *Santa Fe* one of the best and most popular is the *Burrito Company* (982-4453; 111 Washington Ave.), less than a block from the plaza. Breakfast and lunch menus feature such favorites as fast burritos and chile dogs. Here you can get a respectable blue corn chicken enchilada for a song. They make and sell their own salsa and chile by the quart. It's a convenient local hangout, recommended for families and folks in a hurry.

While you're in the area, you might want to stop by *Woolworth* (982-1062; 58 E. San Francisco St.) — that's right, the little department store on the plaza — and pick up one of their Frito Pies. Woolworth is the originator of the justly-famous pie that consists of a fresh flour tortilla wrapped around a conglomeration of Texas red chile beans, grated cheese and, of course, Fritos.

If you're after a quick burger try **Blake's Lotaburger**, a chain that's popular for quick and easy family outings. Blake's is a New Mexico company that raises their own beef, and if you want a New Mexico chile cheeseburger, this is a good place to find one. In Santa Fe, there are two Lotaburgers on Cerrillos Rd., one on St. Michael's Dr., one on N. Guadalupe and one in Pojoaque, about 15 miles north of Santa Fe. Near Taos are Lotaburgers on S. Santa Fe Rd. and in El Prado, north of town.

At **Bert's Burger Bowl** (982-0215; 235 N. Guadalupe) in Santa Fe, the menu is written half in English and half in Spanish, reflecting the cuisine. The grease in these tasty burgers may close down your arteries, but the green chile will open them up again. **El Pollo Asado** on Cerrillos Rd. specializes in chicken dishes that are surprisingly tasty for the speed with which they're prepared.

GOURMET SHOPS

Santa Fe

BECKER'S DELICATESSEN
Owner: Richard & Justine Becker.
988-2423.
403 N. Guadalupe St., Santa Fe, NM 87501.
Closed: Sundays, major holidays.

Here's a deli where you can get just about anything, from an assortment of salads, sandwiches and pastries to sodas, cheeses and coffees. They're known for their fresh breads and bagels, piñon macaroons, cheesecake brownies and the best petite eclairs in town (not too sweet but plenty custardy). The adjoining restaurant serves excellent but somewhat overpriced breakfasts and lunches. The coffee is likewise expensive but strong.

Becker's Deli has some of the tastiest gourmet foods in town.

Murrae Haynes

KAUNE FOOD TOWN
Owner: Jim Downey.
982-2629.
511 Old Santa Fe Trail,
   Santa Fe, NM 87501.
Closed: Sundays, major
   holidays.

This funny little store is about 50 years old — ironically it is one of the younger stores in a chain started more than 80 years ago. It offers a dazzling array of gourmet foods, from imported prosciutto to exotic spices and high-end canned goods like hearts of palm and white asparagus. In addition, it has gourmet ice creams, fresh breads, jellies and teas as well as fresh meats.

Taos

**BENT STREET DELI &
   CAFE**
Owners: Tom Kennedy &
   Charlene DuLong.
758-5787.
120 Bent St., Taos, NM
   87571.
Closed: Sundays.

When this little deli opened, it was so deluged with customers that the owners had to close their doors on the first day. Since then they've learned how to deal with the throngs that come looking for a cup of coffee, warm Brie with apples and almonds, a jar of chile or chutney, a Bent St. Sub or a Shrimp Picatta dinner. Bent Street has comfy tables, pleasant music, picture windows facing a *placita*, lots of greenery poking out of wooden-animal planters — all in all a delightful spot.

HEALTH FOOD STORES

Santa Fe

THE MARKETPLACE
Owner: Dennis Burns.
988-2729, 984-2852, 438-
   9408.
808 Early St. / 627 W.
   Alameda / 1708 Llano
   St., Santa Fe, NM 87501;
   Wholesale warehouse at
   530 Guadalupe St.
Closed: Major holidays.

Santa Fe's locally-owned and operated Marketplace locations specialize in wholesome natural foods that are largely free of chemical preservatives, including organic produce (much from local vendors) and non-sugar products. They also feature a range of gourmet and deli items, chemical-free meat and fish and a wide variety of health and beauty aids. Not least, from the Marketplace point of view, proceeds from sales go back into the community.

Murrae Haynes

*The Marketplace: wholesome
natural foods.*

**WILD OATS
COMMUNITY
MARKET**
Manager: Steven Houpis
983-5333.
1090 St. Francis Dr., Santa
Fe, NM 87501.
Open Daily:

This airy, innovative market foundation has quality grains, meats and produce devoid of harmful chemicals. Seafood shelves are stocked with everything from Pacific Coast red snapper to bluenose bass from New Zealand flown in fresh daily. The bulk department features everything from grains and granolas to flours and seaweeds; more than a hundred kinds of herbs and spices; and even bulk oils, soaps and lotions. Full spectrum lighting and fresh flowers add a special touch to this market, as do the gracious and helpful personnel.

Wild Oats offers fresh breads, a full-service juice bar, a colorful salad bar and a deli. There is a responsible but festive air about the place, including such innovations as back rubs for tired shoppers and monthly food and education festivals. No ordinary market, this — a real shopping treat (albeit on the expensive side) and more than likely the shape of shopping to come.

Taos

AMIGOS FOOD CO-OP
Manager: Daniel Carmona
758-8493
326 Paseo del Pueblo Sur
Closed: Christmas & New
Years

Amigos Food Co-op strives to offer the best prices on all natural food staples, from grains and granolas to beans and teas. Eighty percent of Amigos' produce is organic. The most recent addition is a popular sit-down juice bar that serves juices, smoothies, sandwiches, salads, baked goods and deli items.

CID'S FOOD MARKET
Owners: Cid & Betty
Backer.
758-1148.
822 Paseo del Pueblo
Norte, Taos, NM 87571.
Closed: Sundays, major
holidays.

Since Cid's opened in 1986, owners Cid and Betty Backer have made it a point to purchase the freshest, purest food available. Cid's also offers a natural soaps, herbs, vitamins, non-animal-tested cosmetics and biodegradable cleansers. At the same time, it caters to the less fanatic with items such as Lindt chocolates and a selection of non-organic fruits and vegetables. Cid's has a first-rate meat department. It even offers rare seeds for far-west gardens, including such exotics as Tara-muhara Scarlet Runner Beans, Violet Queen Broccoli, and Cocozelle, an Italian straight summer squash.

POULTRY PRODUCTS

TAOS FARMS
Manager: Natalie Anderson.
758-0084.
P.O. Box 736, Taos, NM 87571.
N.M. 64, 7 miles S. of Taos Plaza.
Open daily.

Located just south of Taos in a collection of large Quonset huts, intrepid explorers are welcome to tour Taos Farms' egg production plant anytime from 12–4 p.m. Over 20,000 contented, non-hormone-fed chickens range freely producing eggs which are collected, hand graded, washed and packed in recyclable cartons. It's a great place to buy eggs at reduced prices, including CNDs ("cracked-and-dirties") that the folks at Taos Farms say are slightly imperfect but just fine. And if your garden needs fertilizing, have they got manure for you!

WINE AND LIQUOR STORES

Following are some convenient places to lift your spirits in Santa Fe and Taos. Most of them sell a wide selection of beers, wines and hard liquor — and many have employees who can make recommendations and help you find what you're looking for. Remember that sale of alcoholic beverages is illegal on Sunday.

Santa Fe

Andy's Liquorette 982-8271; 838 Agua Fria.
Barrel House 983-8571; 945 W. Alameda.
Cliff's Packaged Liquor Store 988-1790; 903 Old Pecos Trail.
El Toro Liquors 988-5222; 215 N. Guadalupe St.
Kaune's Grocery Co. 983-7378; 208 Washington Ave.
Lamplighter Liquors 471-8000; 2405 Cerrillos Rd.
Mr. Bottle 983-8961; Inn at Loretto, 211 Old Santa Fe Trail.
Owl Liquors 982-1751; 913 Hickox, Santa Fe.
Rodeo Plaza Liquors 473-2867; 2801 Rodeo Rd.
Santa Fe Trails Fine Wine 982-5302; 518 Old Santa Fe Trail.
The Winery 982-9463; 510 Montezuma. Ask wine buyer David Nolf about classes.

Near Santa Fe

Kokoman Fine Wines & Liquors 455-2219; Pojoaque, on U.S. 285, 15 mi. N. of Santa Fe.
Tesuque Village Market 988-8848; Tesuque, NM.

Taos

Del Norte Lounge 758-8904; S. Santa Fe Rd.
Don Quijote Lounge 758-1956; 408 Kit Carson Rd.
Wine Find, Inc. 758-WINE; Pueblo Alegre Mall.

Near Taos

Andy's La Fiesta Discount Liquors 758-9733; St. Francis Plaza, Ranchos de Taos.

El Prado Liquor Store 758-8254; El Prado, NM, 1 mi. N. of Taos on N.M. 3.

WINERIES

Thanks to a handful of adventurous vintners, New Mexico has experienced a wine-making renaissance over the last two decades. Grapevines were planted by missionaries in the late 1500s from cuttings brought from Spain. Wine-making flourished here for hundreds of years — all the way up to Prohibition. In the early '70s, after a hiatus of 50 years, commercial wine production began a comeback. There are now about a dozen wineries scattered throughout the state, a few of them located in the Santa Fe–Taos area.

Near Santa Fe

BALAGNA WINERY
Owner: John Balagna.
672-3678.
223 Rio Bravo Dr., Los Alamos, NM 87544.
In White Rock.
Open daily.

John Balagna first began making wine with his grandfather in Colorado. He came to Los Alamos in 1944 to work in the Los Alamos National Laboratory. When he retired in 1986, Balagna went into wine making full-time, and today makes a number of wines on his Pajarito Acres property. Among them are Celeste Blanco, a blend of Seyval and Muscat Canelli white grapes, a humorous blend called Dago Red ("I'm Italian," he laughs) to go with pastas and tacos, and a selection of conventional whites and reds from Chardonnay and Riesling to red Zinfandel and rosé. A congenial host, Balagna loves to give tours and to talk about wines and wine making.

SANTA FE VINEYARDS
Owner: Len Rosingana.
753-8100.
Rte. 1, Box 216, Española, NM 87532.
20 mi. N. of Santa Fe on U.S. 285.
Closed: Major holidays.

Len Rosingana learned to appreciate wine from his Italian grandparents in California. He restored the old Ruby Hill winery in the Livermore Valley and produced his own wine under the Stony Ridge label. He started Santa Fe Vineyards in 1982 in hopes that his wines would embody the spirit of northern New Mexico. To promote that image, he hired artist Amado Peña to design his evocative, colorful label. The first year Rosingana produced 200 cases of wine; today he's producing more than 5,000 cases a year, and his wines have repeatedly won top awards in state competitions.

Stop by for a tour. The smell of the place is enchanting, not to mention the Peña T-shirts and prints, green chiles, tortilla chips, pastas, pine nuts and wonderful, inexpensive wines. If your tastes are anything like ours, you'll particularly enjoy the 1989 Chardonnay, a delightfully fruity and spicy selection.

Santa Fe Vineyards specializes in inexpensive wines.

Murrae Haynes

Near Taos

LA CHIRIPADA WINERY
Owners: Mike & Patrick Johnson.
579-4457.
P.O. Box 191, Dixon, NM 87525.
About 3 mi. from N.M. 68 on N.M. 580.
Closed: Sun. & major holidays.

Sometime when you're shuttling between Santa Fe and Taos on N.M. 68, take a detour at the Dixon turnoff for a taste of heaven. Mike and Patrick Johnson started this little family vineyard in 1977 and began making wine in 1981. In spite of severe winter temperatures and a short growing season (at 6,100 feet, La Chiripada is the highest commercial vineyard in the United States), they successfully cultivate the heartiest grapes (two Pinot Noir hybrids, for example). Each year they crush 50 tons of fruit — a third from their own vineyards and two-thirds from those at lower elevations. The combined results, several of which have won bronze medal awards in the *Dallas Morning News* National Wine Competition, speak for themselves. Try the Primavera 1989, a crisp, lively blend of Vidal and Villard; the Vino Sonrojo 1989, an opalescent cocktail wine with a hint of wild strawberry; or the Special Reserve Riesling 1990, a Germanic styled wine with aromas of pear and pineapple. By the way, *La Chiripada* means "a stroke of luck." That's the way the Johnsons feel about their Dixon vineyards — and chances are you will too.

CHAPTER SIX
For the Fun of It
RECREATION

Courtesy Museum of New Mexico

Two campers in New Mexico, 1893.

With high mountain terrain, clear skies and several million acres of forest lands, the Santa Fe–Taos area offers a bountiful backdrop for year-round outdoor fun. Fishing, hunting, camping, golfing, boating, biking, horseback riding, running — every sport has its place and season. In the spring, rafters buck the rapids of the Rio Grande and balloonists float high over scenic hills. Summer hikers roam high back-country trails between 7,000 and 13,000 feet, while windsurfers sweep across the choppy waters of wide-open lakes. In the fall, hunters and fishermen take to rivers and hills with visions of lunker trout, kokanee salmon and trophy deer and elk. The winter mountains become a snowy wonderland, offering world-class skiing, cross-country trails and snowmobile highways. There are team and individual sports, too. Local parks abound with softball and soccer players, and fitness clubs include facilities for year-round racquetball, tennis, swimming, aerobics and yoga. For an overview of recreational sites in the area, see the map on page 301.

SPORTING GOODS STORES

Santa Fe

Alpine Sports 983-5155; 121 Sandoval.
Base Camp 982-9707; 121 W. San Francisco St.
Bradley Mountain Wear 982-8079; 107 E. Marcy St.
Buffalo Hunter 471-4411; 509 Airport Rd.
Champion Ski Works & Outdoor Recreation Rentals 989-7488; 1101 Cerrillos Rd.

Downtown Bike Shop 983-2255; 107 E. Marcy St.
Gardenswartz Sportz 473-3636; 2860 Cerrillos Rd.
Kellstedt Trading Company 983-7262; Agua Fria Box 134-A.
Oshman's Sporting Goods 988-4466, De Vargas Center Mall; 473-3555, Villa Linda Mall.
Santa Fe Windsurfing 986-1611; 905 St. Francis Dr.
Ski Tech Ski Rentals 983-5512; 905 S. St. Francis Dr.
Tom Tiano's Sport Center 473-1677; 1514 Rodeo Rd.
Water Sports 982-8085; 1301 Escalante.
Wilderness Exchange 986-1152; 513 W. Cordova Rd.

Near Santa Fe

L.M. Archery 753-3915; La Mesilla, Española.
Toby's Sports 753-6083; 823 Onate St., Española.
Sports Bag 662-2454; Los Alamos Community Ctr., Los Alamos.
Trail Bound Sports 662-3000; 771 Central Ave., Los Alamos.

Taos

Sierra Sports 758-2822; 207-A Paseo del Pueblo Sur.
Native Sons Adventures 758-9342; 813-A Paseo del Pueblo Sur.
Taos Mountain Outfitters 758-9292; 114 S. Plaza.

Near Taos

8000 Plus 377-3516; Centro Plaza, Angel Fire.
The Outpost 586-1289; Red River Hwy., Questa.
Sitzmark Sports 754-2525; Main and Malletta, Red River.
Valley Sports 377-2266; Hwy. 464, Angel Square, Angel Fire.
Williams Trading Post 754-2217; High Red River.

BALLOONING

For a bird's-eye view of the Santa Fe–Taos area, there's nothing better than to hop in a basket and cast your fate to the wind. In *Santa Fe*, the lone outfit running lighter-than-air trips is *Balloons Over Santa Fe* (471-2937; 1874-A Calle Quedo, Santa Fe, NM 87505). Pilot Sally Chapel offers individual and group rates, as well as special brunch flights from May through January. 1991 rates were $95 for a 30-minute flight and $150 for an hour-long trip with continental breakfast and champagne. Price includes transportation to and from your hotel and guests are welcome to help out with the launch.

In *Taos, Magic Mountain Balloons* books lighter-than-air trips at the Abominable Snowmansion (776-8298; P.O. Box 3271, Taos, NM 87571). Pilot Ron Stoney will be happy to take you wherever the wind blows, including sunrise flights over the scenic Taos Valley — or even "whitewater ballooning" directly over the foaming Rio Grande Gorge.

The Taos Mountain Balloon Rally attracts some 70 hot-air balloons each year.

Stuart Jones; Courtesy Taos County Chamber of Commerce

As for ballooning spectacles, during the last weekend in October, Taos hosts the **Taos Mountain Balloon Rally,** a sunrise flight of some 70 balloons near the Taos courthouse. You can walk onto the field and talk to the pilots as they inflate their colorful, whale-sized beasts of burden. With a little luck, you may even be able to hitch a ride. Unlike the Albuquerque festival, this invitation-only event is relaxed, noncompetitive fun. Local eateries supply food and drink, and in the evenings, celebrants enjoy country and western music at the Kachina Lodge. For information, contact the **Taos County Chamber of Commerce** (758-3873 or 800-732-TAOS; Paseo Del Pueblo Sur, Taos, NM 87571). There are also two Angel Fire balloon rallies — one in July and one during Winterfest in February. Call the **Angel Fire Chamber of Commerce** (1-800-446-8117 or 377-6353) for information.

BICYCLING

From smooth country highways to rugged mountain trails, you can't beat the Santa Fe–Taos area for ten-speed bicycle touring and mountain bike adventure. Biking is one of the best ways to see both towns. If your heart is set on touring, be sure to bring your own bike; currently, there are no 10-speed rentals in Santa Fe or Taos. If you are a mountain biker, remember: (1) mountain bikes are not allowed in wilderness areas; (2) be considerate of hikers and those on horseback; (3) trails are usually steeper and more difficult than forest roads; and (4) trail conditions change markedly with the weather. For a comprehensive listing of bike races throughout the state, call **TCR Associates** (266-9312).

Santa Fe Area

One of the best ways to start pedaling in Santa Fe is to get a *Santa Fe Bicycle Map* at the Public Works office at City Hall (984-6620; 200 Lincoln Ave., Santa

Fe, NM 87501) or at one of the bicycle dealers listed below. This map, compiled by the members of the **Sangre de Cristo Cycling Club** (Santa Fe Schwinn Cyclery, 471-3394; 720 St. Michael's Dr., Santa Fe, NM 87501) shows recreational and utilitarian routes in and around the city. The club also leads weekly bike tours. Other good publications are the *New Mexico Bicyclist's Guide*, compiled by the Highway Department, and *Santa Fe on Foot: Walking, Running and Bicycling Routes in the City Different*, by Elaine Pinkerton. These are available at most local bookstores and sports shops.

For a schedule of group rides in the Santa Fe area, call the **Touring Bike Hotline** at 986-1136. These weekend tours are among the best ways to get to know other bikers as well as the touring routes in the area — for example, the roads leading out to Galisteo, Bishop's Lodge, Lamy and La Cienega.

Local touring events include the **Santa Fe Century** (982-1282), a 25-, 50- and 100-mile noncompetitive tour from Santa Fe through Cerrillos, Madrid, Golden and Galisteo held the third Sunday in May; the **Santa Fe Hill Climb**, a competitive, autumn grind up to the Santa Fe Ski Basin; and the **Tour de Los Alamos**, a road race and criterium held on the the 4th of July weekend. All races are sanctioned by the U.S. Cycling Federation.

There are some great mountain biking trails minutes from downtown Santa Fe and plenty of places to rent the sturdy-framed, low-geared contraptions. (1991 rentals ranged anywhere from $15-$30 a day to $75-$150 a week.) Camino La Tierra leads to a number of easy trails on city-owned land. For aggressive riding, try the arroyo behind St. Johns College, the Chamiso Trail, Pacheco Canyon Road or any of the trails off the Aspen Vista parking lot near the top of the Ski Basin Road. If you have a day, pedal up the dirt road past Chupadero; it will take you all the way to Aspen Vista just below the Ski Basin. For other routes, call the **Santa Fe National Forest** at 988-6940.

Taos Area

The annual biking event in the Taos area is the **Enchanted Circle Century Bike Tour** (754-2366), a 100-mile, noncompetitive jaunt held the first Sunday after Labor day. Starting in Red River, more than 800 two-wheeler spin counterclockwise through Questa, Taos, Angel Fire and Eagle Nest, with a side trip west to the Rio Grande Gorge. The fee for this spectacular circuit through mountains, forests and valleys is around $20, and all are welcome. The course takes anywhere from four to eight hours, depending on whether you're touring or "truckin'." Angel Fire also hosts an annual bike tour the Memorial Day weekend (377-6353).

Mountain biking trails in the Carson National Forest off N.M. 64 will take you all the way to Angel Fire. A favorite route for families is Rio Chiquito, a long Forest Service road off N.M. 518 that connects with Garcia Park and includes beaver ponds and good picnicking. Picuris Peak, also with access off N.M. 518, is a good intermediate-to-expert route with a pretty steep grade and a great view. For more detailed recommendations, call or stop in at the **Carson National Forest** office (758-6200; 208 Cruz Alta Rd., Taos, NM 87571).

Murrae Haynes

Racers hang together in the early going of the Santa Fe Classic's opening hill climb.

For Taos area mountain bike racing, call **Native Sons Adventures** (758-9342). They sponsor a spirited competition each year around Father's Day. In September, Angel Fire hosts the **Chile Challenge Off-Road Bike Race** (377-6353), which is as hot a competition as the name suggests. Then there's the annual *Bump, Bolt & Bike Race* usually in April, in which racers ski Al's Run, sprint from the base of Al's, then bike downhill at the Taos Ski Valley. For this and other upcoming bike events, call the **Taos County Chamber of Commerce** (758-3873, 1-800-732-TAOS).

BICYCLE DEALERS

Santa Fe

Bradley Mountain Wear 982-8079; 107 E. Marcy.

Downtown Bike Shop 983-2255; 107 E. Marcy. Mountain bike rentals; giant directional wall map; topo maps; tips on where to go.

Gardenswartz Sportz 473-3636; 2860 Cerrillos Rd. Retail and mountain bike rentals; tips on where to go.

rob and charlie's 471-9119; 1632 St. Michael's Dr. Specialists in retail, parts and repair, with over 4,000 parts in stock; good biking info and BMX stud bikes for kids.

Santa Fe Schwinn Cyclery 471-3394; 720 St. Michael's Dr. Center for the Sangre de Cristo Cycling Club and a wealth of touring information.

Taos

Native Sons Adventures 758-9342, 1-800-753-7559; 813 Paseo Del Pueblo Sur. Mountain bike rentals.

Taos Mountain Outfitters 758-9292; 114 S. Plaza. Mountain bike retail and rentals.

Taos Sports Company 758-9831; 214 S. Santa Fe Rd. Retail mountain bikes; no rentals, but the best bike repair in town.

BOWLING

Want to spend a night downing pins? One of two good spots in Santa Fe and vicinity will probably suit your fancy. The largest is *BG's Kiva Lanes* (471-2110; 1352 Rufina Circle), with 32 lanes, food and cocktails, pro shop and video games. In White Rock, on the way to Los Alamos, you'll find the *White Rock Bowling Center* (672-3533; 111 Longview Drive, White Rock, NM 87544), with 12 lanes, video games, pool, lounge and snack bar.

CAMPING

Many first-time visitors are surprised and delighted to find a land of lush mountain wilderness, including scores of idyllic campsites. Public, vehicle-accessible sites in national forest and state park areas are usually open from May through October and available on a first-come, first-served basis. There are 25 campgrounds in the *Santa Fe National Forest*, 39 in the *Carson National Forest* and many more in *Bandelier National Monument* and nearby state parks, some with drinking water and some without. At some of the larger national forest campsites you should book reservations three months in advance by calling 1-800-283-CAMP. There are also back-country campsites for those on the trail, usually requiring overnight permits, plus a number of private camping areas that offer trailer hookups and tent sites with all the amenities. For maps and specifics on public areas, contact the government agencies listed under "Hiking and Climbing."

For information and reservations at private RV campgrounds, contact the following:

PRIVATE CAMPGROUNDS

Near Santa Fe

Apache Canyon KOA (982-1419; I-25 north of Santa Fe). Full hookups, pull-through sites, tent sites, groceries, laundry, bathrooms and rec room.

Los Campos Recreation Vehicle Park (473-1949; 3574 Cerrillos Rd., Santa Fe, NM 87501). The only full-service RV park in the city, with 100 full hookups, groceries, car rentals, swimming pool and sightseeing excursions.

Rancheros de Santa Fe Camping Park (983-3482; Rte. 3, Box 94, Santa Fe, NM 87505, on Old Las Vegas Highway). Wooded and open sites for tents, trailers and motor homes with pool, showers, restrooms, groceries, laundry and propane.

Santa Fe KOA (982-1419). Eight miles southeast of Santa Fe; exit 294 from I-25, then follow the signs. Includes full hookups, tent sites, showers, store, playground.

Tesuque Pueblo RV Campground (455-2661; Rte. 5, P.O. Box 360-H, Santa Fe, NM 87501). About 10 miles north of Santa Fe on N.M. 285 near Camel Rock. Includes 63 full hookups and pull-through sites, tent sites, security gate, laundry, phones, restrooms, and handicapped-accessible showers.

Near Taos

El Bordo Trailer Park (377-6617; Hwy. 434, Angel Fire, NM).

Golden Eagle RV Park (377-6188; Eagle Nest, NM).

Kit Carson Campground (1-800-732-TAOS) 22 full hookups, 15 tent sites.

Red River RV Park (754-6187; Box 777, Red River, NM 87558, on the corner of W. Main & High Cost Trail). Includes 28 full hookups by the river with cable TV, showers, bathrooms, laundry, rec room, plus a few tent sites.

Questa Lodge (586-0300; 0.25 miles off Hwy. 522, Questa, NM 87556).

River Ranch (754-2293; Lower Red River Canyon, Red River, NM 87558).

Roadrunner Campground Group (754-2286; P.O. Box 588, Red River, NM 87558; on Main Street.) Camping for 150 vehicles with 89 full hookups, laundry, showers, tennis court, restrooms, cable TV, playground, barbecue area, picnic tables, fire ring and tipis.

Silver Spur Lodge & RV Park (754-2378, 1-800-545-8372; P.O. Box 174, Red River, NM 87558).

Taos RV Park (758-1667 or 1-800-323-6009; P.O. Box 729, Ranchos de Taos, NM 87557). Includes 22 full hookups, 7 tent spots, rec room, showers, playground, horseshoe pit, phones, restrooms.

Valley RV Park (758-4469; Box 200, Ranchos de Taos, NM 87557, on Estes Rd.). Complete commercial campground including 35 full hookups, 75 water and electric hookups, 18 tent spots, playground, rec room, showers, phones, convenience store, laundromat.

Wagons West (1-800-732-TAOS) Offers 77 full hookups, 20 tent sites.

FITNESS CENTERS

Sometimes you don't need fishing, golf or a strenuous day on the slopes to feel good; you just need to work out. Whether it's weight training, aerobics, racquetball, stretching, swimming or yoga, there are plenty of gyms to suit your needs. Due to the growing fitness craze in the Santa Fe–Taos area, most of these places are churning with activity. Most of them employ fitness experts who are eager to help you with a program tailored to meet your needs. Membership rates vary between $30 and $85 a month, rates for non-members between $5 and $10 a day.

Santa Fe

Carl and Sandra's Conditioning Center (982-6760; 153-A Paseo de Peralta). Run by Olympic trainer Carl Miller and his wife, this gym specializes in individualized weight training, aerobics, nutrition, stress management and exercises for pregnant women.

Club at El Gancho (988-5000; Rte. 9, Box 52-A). A private club with membership and initiation fees, offering outdoor and indoor tennis, swimming, aerobics, squash, racquetball, yoga and Nautilus machines. Also has saunas, hot tubs and massage.

Club International (473-9807; 1931 Warner Ave.) Separate rooms specialize in Nautilus, free weights, cardiovascular exercise, aerobics and jazz, plus a lap pool, racquetball courts, treadmills, Stairmasters, Lifecycles, bicycles, uppercycles, whirlpool, individualized fitness programs, sauna and steam room.

Dimensions in Shape (986-8733; 450-A St. Michael's Dr.) Fitness experts lead classes in bench stepping, multilevel aerobics, children's fitness and individualized personal training.

Fitness Plus (473-7315; 2801 Rodeo Rd.) Specializes in muscle toning, aerobics, weight loss, massage and acupuncture.

Fort Marcy Complex (984-6725; Fort Marcy Park, Washington St.) The city's major sports complex, with gym, weight room, jogging course, racquetball courts, aerobic and workout room. Rates are $2 per visit or $25 per year. Nonmember and student rates also available.

Santa Fe Gold (988-2986; San Mateo at Pacheco). A hard-core weight training center. Specializes in free weights, sports massage, aerobics and fitness classes, prenatal and postpartum exercise and diet plans with nationally certified instructors.

Santa Fe Spa (984-8727; 786 N. St. Francis Dr., north of Picacho Plaza Hotel). Probably the fastest growing fitness spa in town. Includes indoor lap pool, racquetball courts, free weights, Universal and Nautilus equipment, Lifecycles, treadmills, Stairmasters, aerobics, dance and karate classes, sauna and steam rooms, whirlpool, massage, physical therapy and free child care.

Taos Area

Quail Ridge Inn (776-2211, ext. 190; P.O. Box 707, Taos, NM. 87571, on Ski Valley Rd.) Universal gym, Lifecycles, step machine, free weights, yoga, stretch and tone, squash, volleyball, racquetball, outdoor heated pool, hot tubs, sauna, six outdoor and two indoor tennis courts. 1991 non-guest rate was $10 a day, tennis courts $30 an hour.

Pumping cycles and iron at the Santa Fe Spa.

Murrae Haynes

Taos Spa & Court Club (758-1980; 111 Dona Ana Dr., across from the Sagebrush Inn). Includes racquetball, tennis, indoor and outdoor pools, aerobics, weight room with free weights and machines, hot tubs, sauna, steam rooms, child care and individualized instruction.

GOLF

Most people don't think of New Mexico as a golf haven, but whacking and tapping balls over manicured greens is popular in these parts. Local courses, varying between 6,000 and 8,600 feet in elevation, offer some of the highest fairways in the world, with terrain that ranges from brushy plains to rolling hills thick with conifers. Most clubs hold seasonal tourneys, with schedules available at the pro shops. 1991 greens fees ranged from $12 to $27.

GOLF AND COUNTRY CLUBS

Santa Fe

Santa Fe Country Club (471-0601; Airport Rd., P.O. Box 211, Santa Fe, NM 87504). This 18-hole, par 72 course, designed by one of the first PGA members more than 50 years ago, features a tree-shaded course close to town. Usually open March through November, it has four sets of tees with yardage totaling between 6,703 and 7,091 and a women's course measuring 5,955 yards. It includes a driving and chipping range and a practice putting green. 1991 greens fee was $22 weekdays, $25 weekends. Pro on duty is Joe Tiano.

Quail Run (986-2255; 3101 Old Pecos Trail, Santa Fe) is a private nine-hole course in Santa Fe, accessible by member invitation or reciprocity only. The pro on duty is Tom Velarde.

Putting Plus (Indoor-Outdoor Mini-Golf) (473-1333; 2731 Cerrillos Rd., Santa Fe, NM 87501. Year round mini-golf with game room, snacks and entertainment.

Near Santa Fe

The Cochiti Golf Course (465-2239; 5200 Cochiti Hwy., Cochiti, NM 87041) near Cochiti Lake, is rated number one in the state and among the top 25 public courses in the country. Set against a stunning backdrop of red-rock mesas and steep canyons, it features an 18-hole, par 72 course of 6,400 yards, a driving range, putting green, pro shop and restaurant. Pro on duty is Dave Kaesheimer. 1991 greens fee was $12.

Los Alamos Golf Course (662-8139; 4250 Diamond Drive, Los Alamos, NM 87544). This course is 18 holes, par 71, 6,500 yards; includes driving range, putting green, restaurant and bar. Pros on duty are Dennis McCloskey, Donny Torrez and Sam Zimmerly. 1991 greens fee was $12.

Near Taos

Angel Fire Golf Course (Legends Hotel, 1-800-633-7463). At 8,600 feet elevation, this is one of the highest and most wooded regulation courses in the world. Usually open from mid-May to mid-October, it's an 18-hole, par 72 course with driving range and putting greens, club and cart rentals, and a restaurant and bar. Pro instruction is offered by Chris Stewart. 1991 green fees were $25 weekdays, $27 weekends and holidays.

Red River Golf Course. This new course, higher than the course at Angel Fire, was under construction as we went to press and is slated to open sometime in 1992. For information, check with the Red River Chamber of Commerce (754-2366).

HIKING AND CLIMBING

Cradled by mountains containing two national forests and numerous wilderness areas and state parks, north central New Mexico offers more than three million acres of public forest land with hundreds of miles of lakeshore and mountain streams. Most of this land is truly wild and forested, inhabited by birds, deer, bear and mountain lion. There are more than a thousand miles of well-maintained trails that vary from a half-hour's guided nature walk to a two-week pack trip.

The primary recreation areas are the Santa Fe and Carson National Forests, which blanket most of the land on both sides of the Rio Grande. A few of the gems in these national forests are the 223,333-acre Pecos Wilderness east of Santa Fe with magnificent aspen and evergreen stands; the 5,200-acre Dome Wilderness in the volcanic Jemez Mountains to the west; the 41,132-acre San

Pedro Parks Wilderness with rolling, spruce-studded mountaintops and open meadows; rugged Wheeler Peak and lake-strewn Latir Peak Wilderness areas northeast of Taos.

A hike can become a climb, simply by leaving the trail and heading toward the peaks. Pros will be tempted by countless jagged peaks, rock faces and canyons that challenge feet, hands and head alike. If you're a hiker, for safety's sake stay on the trail. This is wild, confusing country and it's easy to get lost. Remember that in the summer months you'll need plenty of purified water (about two quarts per person per day). And whether you're hiking or climbing, make sure you have the proper information, equipment and experience. For maps, permits, guidebooks, advice and the latest conditions, any of the organizations listed below can help put you on the right trail.

NATIONAL FOREST OFFICES

Near Santa Fe

Santa Fe National Forest, Supervisor's Office (988-6940; 1220 St. Francis Dr., P.O. Box 1689, Santa Fe, NM 87504). Contact this office for general information, maps of the Santa Fe National Forest and detailed topo maps of Pecos and San Pedro Parks Wilderness areas. These maps include access and camping information and short descriptions of numerous hiking trails.

Coyote Ranger District (638-5526, 988-6999 in Santa Fe; Coyote, NM 87012). Handles San Pedro Parks Wilderness area.

Española Ranger District (988-6993, 753-7331; P.O. Box R, Española, NM 87532; Corner of Santa Clara St. and Los Alamos Hwy., Española).

Jemez Ranger District (988-6998, 829-3535; Jemez Springs, NM 87025, between Los Alamos and Jemez Springs on N.M. 4).

Pecos Ranger District (988-6996, 757-6121; P.O. Box 429, Pecos, NM 87552; Exit 299 Glorieta, Pecos, N.M. 50).

Near Taos

Carson National Forest, Supervisor's Office (758-6200; P.O. Box 558, 208 Cruz Alta Rd., Taos, NM 87571).

El Rito Ranger District (581-4554; P.O. Box 56, El Rito, NM 87530; At junction of N.M. 110 and N.M. 96).

Peñasco Ranger District (587-2255; P.O. Box 68, Peñasco, NM 87553).

Questa Ranger District (586-0520; P.O. Box 110, Questa, NM 87556; two miles east of Questa on N.M. 38). Handles 20,000-acre Latir Peaks Wilderness Area north of Red River.

Taos Ranger District (758-2911; P.O. Box 558, 302 Armory St., Taos, NM 87571). Handles Wheeler Peak Wilderness Area.

Tres Piedras Ranger District (758-8678; P.O. Box 728, Tres Piedras, NM 87577; one mile west of junction of U.S. 64 and N.M. 285).

NATIONAL MONUMENTS

Bandelier National Monument (672-3861; National Park Service, Los Alamos, NM 87544) includes nearly 50 square miles of mesa and canyon country with walking, hiking and overnight camping opportunities in the land of the Anasazi. Short trails in Frijoles Canyon lead through ancient ruins and cliff dwellings; longer trails lead south through canyons and west to the Dome Wilderness. Tsankawi, a smaller monument area off N.M. 4 near White Rock, offers several miles of trails and ruins.

Pecos National Monument (National Park Service, Drawer 11, Pecos, NM 87552) is two miles south of Pecos off N.M. 63. It includes a handicap-accessible, self-guided trail through ruins of the old Pecos Pueblo and a church. (For more information, see *Culture*, Chapter Four.)

STATE PARKS

New Mexico State Parks and Recreation (827-7465, 800-451-2541; P.O. Box 1147, Santa Fe, NM 87504).

Near Santa Fe

Hyde Memorial (983-7175; 12 miles northeast of Santa Fe via Ski Basin Rd.). 350 acres of mountains and streams with trails and camping and picnicking areas.

Santa Fe River (827-7465). Includes five narrow acres of greenery with a few picnic tables along Alameda St., a few blocks from the center of town.

Near Taos

Cimarron Canyon (377-6271; three miles east of Eagle Nest via U.S. 64). A 33,000-acre mountainous preserve with numerous trails, camping and picnicking areas.

Kit Carson Memorial (758-8234) in Taos. Offers short walks and a playground on 22 acres.

Rio Grande Gorge Park (758-4160; 16 miles southwest of Taos on N.M. 570). Includes shelter, barbecues, drinking water and campgrounds along the road by the river. Now under the jurisdiction of the Town of Taos.

Outside the Area

El Vado Lake (no telephone; 14 miles southwest of Tierra Amarilla via N.M. 112). Mostly water recreation but includes 1,720 mountainous acres with a variety of excellent hiking trails.

Heron Lake (588-7470; 11 miles west of Tierra Amarilla via U.S. 64 and N.M. 95). Offers 4,107 acres of mountainous terrain with trails, camping and picnicking and a variety of year-round sports.

ORGANIZATIONS AND GUIDEBOOKS

Santa Fe Area

For an excellent introduction to some of the fine trails in the Santa Fe–Taos area, we suggest you contact the **Santa Fe Sierra Club** (983-2703; 440 Cerrillos Rd., Santa Fe, NM 87501). During the spring and summer months they run two or three trips of varying difficulty every weekend, plus cross country ski tours about every other week in the winter. You need not be a member to join these hikes, but be sure to bring proper clothing and footwear and plenty of water. They have published a book entitled *Day Hikes in the Santa Fe Area*, detailing 37 short hikes, many of which can be made into overnight journeys. Another good hiking contact is the **Randall Davey Audubon Center** (983-4609).

For equipment, detailed maps and advice on Santa Fe area hiking and climbing, we suggest you contact **Base Camp** (982-9707; 121 W. San Francisco St.) or **Wilderness Exchange** (986-1152; 513 W. Cordova Rd.). The bookshelves of these two shops include some local best-sellers you might want to peruse. At the top of the list is the Sierra Club's *Day Hikes in the Santa Fe Area. A Trail Guide to the Geology of the Upper Pecos*, by Patrick K. Sutherland and Arthur Montgomery, is a collection of guided wilderness tours and probably the best hiking guide to the Pecos area. Two others are *Fifty Hikes in New Mexico* by Harry Evans and *A Guide to Bandelier National Monument* by Dorothy Hoard. You can also get topo maps of northern New Mexico at **Healy Matthews Stationers** (988-8991; 515 Cerrillos Rd., Santa Fe, NM 87501). The Santa Fe National Forest (988-6940) has produced a series of *Travel Management Maps*, old USGS topos updated with the latest forest service roads and trails.

Taos Area

One of the best wilderness contacts is **Taos Mountain Outfitters** (758-9292; 114 S. Plaza, Taos, NM 87571). In addition to routes and rentals, their salespeople are avid hikers and climbers. Their publication, *Taos Rock*, will steer you toward the best rock climbing in the area. A good contact for hikers is the **Moreno Valley Truckers** (377-6353; Box 261, Angel Fire, NM 87710), a small hiking group whose members take weekly treks into the wilderness. A third option is **Native Sons Adventures** (758-9342; 813-A Paseo del Pueblo Sur, Taos, NM 87571), which rents backcountry gear and offers a variety of wilderness treks. **Sipapu Lodge and Ski Area** (587-2240; Rte. Box 29, Vadito, NM 87579) offers hiking opportunities.

HORSEBACK RIDING

Packing through the Pecos Wilderness.

Mark Nohl/New Mexico Magazine

It's interesting to note that New Mexico was the first region of North America to benefit from the introduction of the horse. Brought in by the Spaniards from Mexico during the 1500s, this strong and versatile animal quickly proliferated and remained the most widespread means of transportation in North America for nearly 400 years. Horse travel is definitely alive and well. You can still get a whiff of the Old West as you saddle up and head on out, whether for a few turns around the corral, a picnic ride or a week-long pack trip. Following are some local outfitters. 1991 prices ranged from $15–$30 per hour, with special rates for longer trips. (See also "Hunting and Fishing.")

Near Santa Fe

Bishop's Lodge (983-6377; P.O. Box 2367, Santa Fe, NM 87504, Bishop's Lodge Rd.). Two-hour guided trail rides in the lodge's 1,000-acre grounds, starting at 9:30 a.m. and 2 p.m. except Sundays.

Camel Rock Ranch (986-0408; about 12 miles north of town on U.S. 285). Hay rides, cookouts and horseback rides across the Tesuque Indian Reservation. Longer trips available by arrangement.

Heels and Wheels Ranch (988-2196; RR Box 63, Santa Fe, NM 87501).

Galisteo Inn (982-1506; Box 4, Galisteo, NM 87540; 0.25 mile east of Hwy. 41 in Galisteo). Trail rides in Galisteo Basin. Limited to riders over 12.

Medicine Horse Ranch (983-5662, 984-8740; Rte. 22, Box 33-CF, Santa Fe, NM 87505; on U.S. 285 south on Los Caballos Estates between Eldorado and Lamy). Supervised trail rides on well-schooled ponies and horses in the Galisteo Basin.

Mountain Mama Packing & Riding Co. (986-1924; Rte. 3, Box 95, Santa Fe, NM 87505; Tesuque).

Rancho Encantado (982-3537; Rte. 4, Box 57-C, Santa Fe, NM, 87501). Trail rides for guests only.

Rocking S Ranch and Guest Lodge (438-7333; Rte. 2, Box 278, Santa Fe, NM 87505; eight miles south of Santa Fe off Hwy. 14). Trail rides, lessons, indoor and outdoor riding arena.

Santa Fe Stage Line (983-6565, 1-800-234-4675; on Hwy. 41 in Galisteo). Rentals by the half day, day or overnight.

Terrero General Stores and Riding Stables, Inc. (757-6193; P.O. Box 12, Terrero, NM 87573). Owners Huie and Sherry Ley run sightseeing and photography trips, as well as minimum four-day hunting, fishing and pack trips into the Pecos.

Taos Area

Bitter Creek Guest Ranch and Stables (754-2587; P.O. Box 310, Red River, NM 87558, 2 ½ miles north of Red River on Bitter Creek Rd). High country trail rides, photo and video trips, overnight pack trips.

Llano Bonito Ranch (587-2636; P.O. Box 99, Peñasco, NM 87553; off Hwy. 73 about five miles southeast of Peñasco). Hourly, half day, full day and extended pack trips, breakfast and supper rides.

Shadow Mountain Guest Ranch (758-7732; Taos Canyon, Rte. 64, Kit Carson Rd., six miles from Taos). Trail rides through alpine country; luncheon treks with llamas.

Sipapu Lodge & Ski Area (587-2240; Rte. Box 29, Vadito, NM 87579). Horseback riding and guided pack trips.

Taos Indian Horse Ranch (758-3212; P.O. Box 3019, Taos, NM 87571; on Miller Rd, Taos Pueblo). Horseback and sleigh rides, Indian storytellers and Taos Mountain music.

HORSERACING

When you get tired of riding, or want to see how the pros do it, go to the *Downs at Santa Fe* (471-3311; Rte. 14, Box 199-RT, Santa Fe, NM 87505; six miles west of Santa Fe off I-25 or Cerrillos Road). Each year the Downs entertains more than a quarter million fans with some of the state's best thoroughbred and quarterhorse races. The one-mile track allows for viewing and pari-mutuel betting on three levels: the Jockey Club with full food and beverage service; the Turf Club with indoor and outdoor seats; and modern grandstand box seats. The racing season, which runs from mid June through Labor Day, features numerous handicaps and derbies, including the renowned $150,000 Santa Fe Futurity for two-year-olds, the state's largest thoroughbred purse.

HUNTING AND FISHING

The Santa Fe–Taos area is a hunting and fishing paradise. Gun or bow hunters can bag not only deer, elk, squirrels, game birds and waterfowl, but also wild turkey, antelope, elk, bighorn sheep, javelina — even exotic species such as ibex and oryx. Lake fish include bass, perch, catfish and walleye. Five species of trout and kokanee salmon (introduced from the Pacific) abound in stocked lakes and streams.

Stringing a mess of trout at Nambe Lake.

Murrae Haynes

Be sure to get licenses and current rules and regulations from the **New Mexico Department of Game and Fish** (827-7911, 827-7882; Villagra Bldg., State Capitol, Santa Fe, NM 87503) or from a local sporting goods store. Keep in mind that there are fishing restrictions on some waters and that many license applications (with strict deadlines) are accepted by mail only.

Remember that hunting or fishing on private land is illegal. For information on hunting and fishing on Indian lands, see "Pueblos" in *Culture*, Chapter Four. You must have written permission and an official tribal document showing legal possession of any game or fish taken.

For information on conditions and places to go, talk to any local guide or outfitter. They can take you to prime fishing and hunting territory, both public and private. If you decide to use a guide, for your own protection check with the National Forest Service or the Bureau of Land Management to make sure the outfit has proper permits and insurance. Prices for guides and outfitters in 1991 ranged from $150–$200 a day to as much as $2,000–$3,500 for a five-day hunt.

GUIDES AND OUTFITTERS

Santa Fe

Buffalo Hunter (471-4411; 509 Airport Rd., Santa Fe). Guns, ammo, rods, reels, bows, black powder, scopes — the works. Full service hunting and fishing and referrals to guides and outfitters.

Gardenswartz Sportz (473-3636; 2860 Cerrillos Rd., Santa Fe). Manager Howard Edwards has everything in the hunting and fishing line except hand guns and archery equipment. Not only that, he has lived in the area since 1929 and he's been hunting and fishing here since he was six. Don't hesitate to ask him for advice and referrals.

High Desert Angler (988-7688; 435 S. Guadalupe St., Santa Fe, NM 87501). This is *the* fly-fishing center of Santa Fe, with instruction, guide service, rentals, equipment sales and expert, friendly advice from owners Mark and Jan Gruber.

Oshman's Sporting Goods (988-4466, De Vargas Center Mall). You'll find anything here from rifles and shotguns to spinning and fly rods with all the eggs, lures, flies, and accessories you'll ever need.

Near Santa Fe

Terrero General Stores and Riding Stables, Inc. (757-6193; P.O. Box 12, Terrero, NM 87573). Owner Huie Ley leads minimum four-day hunting and fishing trips into the wildest areas of the Sangre de Cristo. A native of Pecos, he's one of the best outfitter-guides anywhere.

Taos

Los Rios Anglers (758-2798; 226-B North Pueblo Rd., Taos, NM 87571). Owners Van Beacham and Jack Woolley are two of the best fly-fishing guides in the state. They run a complete fly-fishing shop offering gear, information and year-round pack and float trips — including mule trips into the Rio Grande Gorge and fishing on private lands.

Near Taos

Agua Fria Guide Service (377-3512; P.O. Box 844, Angel Fire, NM 87710). Owner Mike Bucks offers hunting, photo and fishing trips on public and private land in the Wheeler Peak area.

Bitter Creek Guest Ranch (754-2587; P.O. Box 310, Red River, NM 87558). Fully licensed outfitter and guide, featuring deer and elk hunts into the mountain area of Valle Vidal.

Deep Creek Wilderness (776-8423; P.O. Box 721, El Prado, NM 87529). This outfit is operated by Jesse Gonzales, whose ancestors have hunted and fished in the Taos area for generations. He offers hunting, fishing, horseback, camping and sightseeing trips in the Carson National Forest, Latir Lakes Wilderness and the Valle Vidal area, reputed to have one of the biggest elk herds in the country.

Eagle Nest Marina (377-6941; P.O. Box 66, Eagle Nest, NM 87718). Owner Mo Finley offers fishing equipment and trips for all seasons at Eagle Nest Lake, including cutthroat, rainbow and coho in the summer and ice fishing for kokanee with snowmobiles and sleds in the winter.

High Mountain Outfitters (377-2240; P.O. Box 244, Eagle Nest, NM 87718). Run by Pancho Trujillo, one of the best hunting guides in northern New Mexico. He specializes in big-game trophy hunts with gun and bow for elk, deer, antelope, sheep, bear, mountain lion and turkey, plus summer fishing and backpacking trips. All hunts include food, lodging, guides and transportation in the area.

Moreno Ranch East (377-6931; P.O. Box 27, Eagle Nest, NM 87718, seven miles north of Eagle Nest on Hwy. 38). This private, 20,000-acre ranch has been a family-owned operation for 40 years. Owners Albert and Deana Murphy run a high-class operation that includes elk hunts, private suites, gourmet meals, guide fees, licenses and permits in a single package. They run four private lakes stocked with trophy-sized (up to 10 pounds) rainbow and brown trout. Their plans for 1991 include an 18-hole regulation golf course!

Moreno Ranch West (377-6555). This is the sister operation to Moreno East, right across the highway — a similarly fancy setup owned by Bobby and Ginny Butler.

Rio Costilla Park (586-0542; P.O. Box 111, Costilla, NM 87524). Fishing and hunting trips on a 79,000-acre private reserve in the Latir Lakes area about 40 miles north of Taos. Trespass fee required for private hunting; call to arrange for guided trips.

Sipapu Lodge & Ski Area (587-2240; Rte. Box 29, Vadito, NM 87579).

PARKS IN TOWN

Wherever you are, it's nice to know you can find a quiet spot to relax — and that there are places where children can run free. The following is a list of parks in Santa Fe and Taos that offer open space and recreational opportunities for everyone. For maps and further information, contact the *Santa Fe Parks and Recreation Division* (473-7326; 1142 Siler Rd., Santa Fe, NM 87501) or the *Taos Parks and Recreation Department* (758-4160).

Santa Fe

Amelia White (Old Santa Fe Trail and Corrales Rd.). A small, natural park with pleasant sitting spots, walking paths and handicapped access.

Asbaugh (Cerrillos Rd. and San Jose Ave.). A long, narrow park next to the Santa Fe Indian Hospital with picnic tables, basketball and tennis courts, baseball and soccer fields, walking paths and handicapped access.

Cathedral (Palace Ave. and Cathedral Pl.). A quiet, fence-enclosed lunch spot a block east of the plaza.

Fort Marcy-Magers Field (Washington Ave. and Murales Rd., north of Paseo de Peralta). A major facility complete with picnic tables, restrooms, grills, tennis court, baseball field, indoor swimming pool, fitness room, gymnasium, playground, walking paths, parcourse and handicapped access.

Frank S. Ortiz (Camino de las Crucitas). A large neighborhood park with shelter, tennis courts, soccer field, walking paths, playground and handicapped access.

Gen. Franklin E. Miles (Siringo Rd. and Camino Carlos Rey). Many blocks of sports fields including restrooms, picnic tables, shelter, softball field, indoor swimming pool, paths, playground and handicapped access.

Larragoite (Agua Fria Rd. and Potencia St., near the Larragoite Elementary School). A neighborhood park offering picnic tables, tennis courts and softball field.

The Plaza. The city's oldest and most-used facility with benches and trees in the very heart of town.

Ragle (W. Zia Rd. and Yucca St.). Many acres near Santa Fe High School, offering picnic tables, grills, shelter, restrooms, athletic fields, pathways, playground and handicapped access.

Randall Davey Audubon Center (see *Culture*, Chapter Four, page 86).

Salvador Perez (Alta Vista and Letrado Sts.). A square block playground with picnic tables, restrooms, tennis courts, softball field, indoor swimming pool, horseshoe pit, racquetball, volleyball, fitness room, trails and handicapped access.

Santa Fe River (Alameda St.). Bordering the Santa Fe River, with picnic tables, handicapped access and a playground just off Guadalupe Street.

Villa Linda (Rodeo Rd. at Villa Linda Mall). Picnic tables, soccer field, playground and handicapped access.

Washington (Washington Ave. and S. Federal St.). A quiet, landscaped park with benches and big shade trees next to the post office and courthouse. A great picnic spot.

Taos

Fred Baca Memorial Park (758-4282; Camino del Media, just outside the town limits). A four-acre municipal park with picnic tables, restrooms, two tennis courts, basketball court, soccer field, volleyball court and playground.

Filemon Sanchez Park (758-8834; slightly outside the south side of town). Includes baseball diamonds and other recreation facilities.

Kit Carson Park (N. Pueblo Rd., a block from the plaza). A 20-acre park with bike and walking path, picnic tables, grills, playground, tennis court, basketball court, amphitheater and ice skating. Includes graves of Kit Carson and other Taoseños.

RACQUETBALL

Racquetball courts can be rented at many Santa Fe–Taos area fitness centers.

Murrae Haynes

For a quick, thorough workout that challenges legs, lungs and mind, few sports can equal racquetball. It has become a craze in the Santa Fe–Taos area, with new courts popping up in many fitness centers. You can rent a court in most centers. Call ahead for information about tournaments. The following are some popular court locations. (See also "Fitness Centers.")

Santa Fe

Club at El Gancho (988-5000; Rte. 9). Two courts.

Club International (473-9807; 1931 Warner Ave.). Six racquetball and handball courts.

Santa Fe Spa (984-8727; 786 St. Francis Dr.). Two courts.

Fort Marcy Complex (984-6725; Fort Marcy Park, Washington St.). Two courts.

Taos

Taos Spa and Court Club (758-1980; 111 Dona Ana Dr.).

Quail Ridge Inn (776-2211; P.O. Box 707, Taos, NM 87571).

RAFTING, CANOEING, KAYAKING

Northern New Mexico's wild and scenic waters provide some of the best whitewater thrills in the country, as indicated by the dozen or so rafting companies that do business in the area. If you want some placid paddling, try one of the lakes listed under "Water Sports." If you want a wilder experience, look into the possibilities of the Rio Grande or the scenic Chama. These rivers offer everything from quiet floats to lung-bursting whitewater adventure. (For information on sailing, water skiing and windsurfing, see "Water Sports.")

The best time for whitewater trips is late May through late July; however, stretches along the Rio Grande from Colorado to Cochiti Dam are negotiable all year. If you plan to float the Chama — particularly the Wild and Scenic run between El Vado Dam and Abiquiu Lake — apply in advance for a private boating permit. You can also float several stretches of the Pecos River between Cowles and Las Vegas.

For recorded information on river flows, call 758-8148. For maps and permit information, seasons and conditions, contact the **Bureau of Land Management** (758-8851; 224 Cruz Alta Rd., Taos, NM 87571). If you're serious about taking your own float trip, an indispensable publication is *New Mexico Whitewater: A Guide to River Trips*, published by the **New Mexico State Park Division of the Natural Resources Department** (141 E. De Vargas, P.O. Box 11471, Santa Fe, NM 87503) and available in most sport shops.

On Mother's Day weekend the little town of Pilar, situated about 20 miles south of Taos, hosts whitewater races. There's great viewing of this watery roller coaster from the highway between Pilar and Velarde.

Most commercial float companies provide half-day, full-day and overnight rafting trips on the Rio Grande and the Chama. The **Lower Rio Grande Gorge** is a relatively serene float. Two of the most popular whitewater stretches are the **Racecourse** and the **Taos Box** on the upper Rio Grande with foaming, Class IV waters that are bound to awaken your wild side. The Chama's Wild and Scenic waters offer beautiful overnight trips. If you want a mellow, two-day trip with little traffic, try Whitewater Canyon on the lower Rio Grande. Another outstanding overnighter is the placid La Junta stretch combined with the Taos Box for a raging finale the following day. 1991 prices varied between $37 for half-day trips to $180 for overnights with all equipment and meals provided. Three-day options are also available.

COMMERCIAL FLOAT TRIPS AND RENTALS

Santa Fe

Kellstedt Trading Company (471-7077; Rte. 6, Box 134-A, Santa Fe, NM 87501). The only outfit that rents kayaks and canoes as well as rafts. 1991

Don Laine; Courtesy Taos Chamber of Commerce

Rafting the Taos Box, the most exciting stretch of the Rio Grande Gorge.

rentals ran about $35 a day (less for an inflatable kayak), including all standard accessories.

Los Rios River Runners (776-8854, 800-338-6877; Santa Fe Detours, 100 E. San Francisco St., Santa Fe, NM 87501).

New Wave Rafting Company (984-1444, 455-2633; 107 Washington Ave.; in summer: Rte. 5, Box 302-A, Santa Fe, NM 87501). One of the largest and most popular rafting outfitters in the area.

Rio Bravo River Tours (988-1153, 1-800-451-0708; 1412 Cerrillos Rd., Santa Fe, NM 87501).

Rocky Mountain Tours (984-4914, 800-533-6980; 102 W. San Francisco St. 87501).

Santa Fe Rafting (988-4914; 710 Columbia St., Santa Fe, NM 87501).

Southwest Adventure Group (983-0876; 1-800-766-5443; Sanbusco Market Center, Santa Fe 87501).

Southwest Wilderness Center (983-7262 or 1-800-869-7238; P.O. Box 9380, Santa Fe, NM 87504). Located in Sanbusco Market Center off Guadalupe St.

Taos and Near Taos

Far Flung Adventures (758-2628, 800-359-4138; P.O. Box 707, El Prado, NM 87529).

Native Sons Adventures (758-9342, 800-753-7559; 813-A Paseo del Pueblo Sur, Taos, NM 87571).

Rio Grande River Tours (758-0762; Box 1-D, Pilar, Rte. Embudo, NM 87531).

RODEOS

Remember that the Santa Fe–Taos area has its roots in the Old West. No event emphasizes this more clearly than the rodeo, which hearkens back to the 19th Century when New Mexico was dominated by the cattle industry and its rough-and-tumble cowboys.

You can attend the *Rodeo de Santa Fe* around the middle of July. One of the most publicized stops in professional rodeo, it has some of the best riding and roping anywhere, with additional colorful Hispanic and Native American activities. Rodeo de Santa Fe has been providing thrills and spills for rodeo fans in the area for more than 40 years. This mid-sized, regional competition is sanctioned by the Professional Rodeo Cowboys' Association and offers a purse of more than $43,000. A downtown parade of riders kicks off the festivities.

Toward the end of July, visit the *Rodeo de Galisteo*, a smaller though no less exciting Wild West event. Toward the end of June you can take in the *Rodeo de Taos* (1-800-732-8267) at the Taos County Fairgrounds.

RUNNING

Out-of-town runners say the air is so fresh they have to work up to taking a full breath. This adjustment may have more to do with elevation than air content; even so, runners here enjoy an exceptional variety of terrain and unusually clean air. From mountain highways and trails to secluded city byways, there's no better place to develop your legs and lungs while enjoying unspoiled open spaces. Even in crowded downtown areas it's never far to the next quiet street. For a comprehensive listing of annual races throughout the state, call *TCR Management Associates* (266-9312) or the *New Mexico Athletics Congress* (255-0299; 118 Amherst N.E., Albuquerque, NM 87106).

Santa Fe

The Santa Fe Striders running club (983-2144; P.O. Box 1818, Santa Fe, NM 87504) starts warm-season fun runs from the plaza every Wednesday evening at around 6 p.m. (during daylight savings, around 5:30). The plaza is also the starting point for all major Santa Fe races, including the *Santa Fe Run-Around*, a nationally known 10-kilometer tour of the city held in early June, the five-kilometer *Women's Run* in early August and the *Old Santa Fe Trail Run*, a 5- and 10-kilometer race held during Fiesta week. There is a city-sponsored triathlon at Cochiti Lake the last weekend in July.

A few good running spots in Santa Fe include the east side, the banks of the Santa Fe River along Alameda Street, Old Santa Fe Trail and the St. Catherine's cross-country course. For information on these and other good routes, consult John Pollak of the *"Striders"* (983-2144) or *Santa Fe on Foot*, by Elaine

Racing up Canyon Road in the Santa Fe Run-Around.

Don Laine; Courtesy Taos Chamber of Commerce.

Pinkerton. For longer jaunts, try the Ski Basin Road and some of the routes listed under "Bicycling."

Taos

Each year Taos hosts one 10-km. race, one triathlon in the fall and a marathon in June. Since Taos has no organized running club, your best bet is to check for dates and times with the **Taos Chamber of Commerce** (758-3873, 800-732-8267; P.O. Drawer I, Taos, NM 87571). Other events in the area include the annual **Wheeler Peak Mountain Run** (754-2366), a half marathon usually held the last weekend in June and the **Bud Light/Angel Fire Mountain High Mini-Triathlon** 377-6353) in mid-September. The outskirts of Taos quickly lead to fairly flat, wide-open spaces, particularly toward the north, east and west.

SKIING

DOWNHILL SKIING

Santa Fe–Taos is a skier's paradise, boasting a half dozen areas with world-class slopes. And no wonder; many of the ski areas in these parts start at 9,000–10,000 feet and rise to 12,000 or more, making for vertical drops in excess of 2,500 feet, and there is up to 300 inches annual snowfall.

Although a few hardy souls began skiing at the Santa Fe Ski Basin shortly after World War II, the sport didn't really take off until 1955, when Ernie Blake began carving out the Taos Ski Valley. Other areas such as Red River, Angel Fire and Sipapu were developed during the 1960s. Since then, lifts, lodges, lounges, snowmaking and wild and groomed cross-country trails have appeared. Santa Fe–Taos has become a major resort area that draws skiers from all over the world.

Some of the beginner and intermediate runs will be open by late November, the remaining runs by the middle of December. Angel Fire, Red River, Santa Fe and Taos Ski Valley usually create a number of good trails by Thanksgiving. All areas are open daily from 9 a.m. to 4 p.m. with the exception of Pajarito Mountain near Los Alamos, which is open on Wednesdays, weekends and federal holidays only.

NEW MEXICO SKI INFORMATION

New Mexico Snophone (984-0606). Recordings 24 hours a day, updated daily at 1 P.M.

Ski New Mexico, Inc. (982-5300, 1-800-446-3898; P.O. Box 1104, Santa Fe, NM 87504).

Near Santa Fe

SANTA FE SKI BASIN
982-4429 (information),
  983-9155 (snow report),
  800-982-SNOW
  (reservations).
1210 Luisa St., Suite 10,
  Santa Fe, NM 87501.
15 miles N.E. of Santa Fe
  via N.M. 475 (Ski Basin
  Rd.)
Peak Elevation: 12,000 ft.
Vertical Drop: 1,650 ft.
Annual Snowfall: 250 in.
Snowmaking: 25% of area.

The Santa Fe Ski Basin was started in the 1930s when designer Graeme McGowen of Denver surveyed the land and suggested sheep and Indian trails as the basis for runs. The first ski area was developed at Hyde Park, when the Civilian Conservation Corps built a road and the stone lodge that today houses the Evergreen Inn. By 1947, two dogleg rope tows with Cadillac engines (which had to be warmed with blowtorches before they would start) pulled a few skiers to the top of a nearby hill. In the early '50s, the first chairlift was built at the present site — using Army Air Corps surplus seats from a B-24 bomber and a 50-year-old cable from a nearby mine.

Currently, four modern lifts take skiers to 12,000

Trails: 39 Downhill (20%
beginner; 40%
intermediate; 40%
advanced). No X-C.
Lifts: 4 Chairlifts (1 quad,
1 triple, 2 double); 2
rope tows.
Tickets (1990/91): Adults
$28, seniors and
children $17.
Ski School Pro: Ken
Odegaard.

feet, the second highest slope in the country. At the top of the juncture of Gayway and Parachute runs, you can take in 80,000 square miles of awe-inspiring views: mountainous terrain stretching into Colorado, as well as the magnificent, high desert country below. You'll find short lift lines and some of the best family skiing in the state, protected from high winds by tree coverage and the angle of the mountain.

Most runs are beginner and intermediate, but advanced stretches like Parachute and Wizard, not to mention Tequila Sunrise and Big Rocks with deep powder and ungroomed moguls in open groves of trees, provide challenges and thrills for the very best. Unlike many areas, Santa Fe Ski Basin encourages snowboarders, not only on the mountain, but with a recently-constructed half-pipe for acrobatics.

The ski school at the basin includes telemark and snowboard classes, and will take children as young as three. There's also the on-slope Totemoff Bar and Grill, La Casa Mall at the base of the mountain, a cafeteria, boutique and over 1,500 pairs of skis for rent.

The Santa Fe Ski Basin, 18 miles from downtown.

Don Strel; Courtesy Santa Fe Chamber of Commerce

PAJARITO MOUNTAIN
662-5725, 662-8105
(information); 662-
SNOW (snow report).
Los Alamos Ski Club, Inc.
P.O. Box 155, Los
Alamos, NM 87544.
7 miles W. of Los Alamos
via N.M. 502 and F.R. 1.
Peak Elevation: 10,441 ft.
Vertical Drop: 1,241 ft.
Annual Snowfall: 153 in.
Snowmaking: None.
Trails: 40 Downhill (25%
beginner, 35%
intermediate, 40%
advanced). No X-C.
Lifts: 4 Chairlifts (1 triple; 3
double) 1 rope tow.
Tickets (1990/91): Adults
$28, seniors and children
$17.
Ski School Pro: Jerry Byrd.

Pajarito was started in 1957 by a group of Los Alamos National Laboratory employees who wanted a convenient place to ski. The area is owned and operated by the Los Alamos Ski Club, whose members are mainly lab employees; however, it's open to the public.

Pajarito is geared toward the serious day skier with runs that are steeper, shorter and rougher than most areas and can be frustrating for beginners. Some experts consider these runs the most challenging in the state. "If you can ski bumps, you're in heaven," says one of our friends. "If you're a novice who gets stuck on a bumpy run or goes into the trees, it's just hell." There has been an effort to increase grooming in order to accommodate all levels of skiers.

There's no resort atmosphere at Pajarito — you will find neither bar nor lounge — but you will find a new three-story day lodge with ski rentals and a nice cafeteria. You also will find one of the rarest pluses of any ski area: no lift lines!

Near Taos

TAOS SKI VALLEY
776-2291 (information);
776-2916 (snow report);
800-992-SNOW, 992-
7669 (reservations).
P.O. Box 90, Taos Ski
Valley, NM 87525.
18 miles N.E. of Taos via
N.M. 64 and N.M. 150.
Peak Elevation: 11,819 ft.
Vertical Drop: 2,612 ft.
Annual Snowfall: 321 in.
Snowmaking: 35% of area.
Trails: 71 Downhill (24%
beginner, 25%
intermediate, 51%
advanced); No X-C.
Lifts: 8 Chairlifts (1 quad; 1
triple; 6 double); 2
surface lifts.
Tickets (1990/91): Adults
$32, children $17.
Ski School Pro: Henry
Hornberger.

Ski critics heap praise on this resort the way overnight clouds heap powder on its slopes. As *Ski Magazine* put it, "The secret of Taos Ski Valley is in the mixture. Take European style, Southwestern flavor, perfect snow and exquisite mountains and stir." This is not Aspen, with stretch limousines and outrageous fashions; just heavenly skiing, a laid-back cowboy- and cowgirl-atmosphere and a natural scene as inspiring as any in North America — and at a ski area as well run as any in the world.

Many people have helped to build Taos Ski Valley (TSV); none were more important than its indefatigable founder, Ernie Blake. Blake came to Santa Fe shortly after World War II. In 1949 he was general manager at the Santa Fe Ski Basin. He dreamed of his own resort and spent countless hours flying over the Sangre de Cristo Mountains, scouting for the perfect site. His ideal was based on the ski resorts of his native Switzerland. Blake located a valley, north of Taos and behind an old mining camp named Twining. TSV got an inauspi-

Taos Ski Valley's steep trails offer challenges for the best skiers.

Ken Gallard; Courtesy Taos County Chamber of Commerce

cious start as a ski resort, with unreliable investors and near inaccessibility; however, Blake persevered — and succeeded grandly.

The tradition at TSV is service, excellent engineering and design. From lift line management to trail marking to cafeteria food to ski school programming, the pattern is consistently high quality. Even with a record-breaking abundance of snow and people, the system works flawlessly. The parking problem is the exception that proves the rule. The valley is long and narrow, and so are the parking lots. We suggest you unload family, friends and equipment as close to the lifts as possible, sending the driver to the far reaches, or allow plenty of time and use the ski shuttle — it's pokey when traffic backs up.

To avoid crowds, try this: Arrive early, bear with the initial bottleneck at the quad chair, transfer to lift #7 or the newer #7-A; then, from the top, ski the upper half of the mountain until late morning or lunchtime. Use the trails on the perimeter of TSV — there will be plenty to keep you occupied.

Lowlanders will definitely feel the elevation here. Drink plenty of water (no alcohol) and take frequent rests. The views across the valley to neighboring Kachina Peak (12,481 feet) are worth a pause. Surrounded by Carson National Forest, TSV has the look of a wilderness setting. The skiing is challenging even for experts; however, there are intermediate and novice slopes that include a few from the very top. The combination of Honeysuckle, Winklereid and Rubezahl trails can bring even a first-day skier safely down from the peak.

If you're into pushing the envelope, you'll do no better than to bump and pump your way down such mogul-studded trails as the infamous Al's Run (under the #1 and #5 lifts) or the steep trails off the West Basin Ridge. Until about 1 p.m., if the snow is right, anyone with a partner may walk out to the top of the ridge to enjoy the precipitous views. Experts are allowed to take their skis (others may go in ski boots), and the ski patrol will not allow even experts to go it alone. Forget your vertigo and take a look.

Amenities are provided at the top of the mountain, at mid-station snack bars (Phoenix and Whistlestop) and in two lodges at the base. The rustic Tyrolean-looking Hotel St. Bernard is the oldest. In the early days, skiing was interrupted at lunch for everyone to come in for a family-style meal. Today the dining room and the cafeteria in the adjacent lodge provide food with gracious efficiency.

Jock Fleming, TSV's ski lift operations manager, told a tale of a quieter era when the Blake family had a large bell at the foot of the only lift. Late arrivals would ring the bell to call a staffer down the mountain to sell them tickets and rev up the lift for a ride. Those days are past; however, at TSV you'll ride chairlifts, period — and plenty of them.

Families are efficiently accommodated, with day care for tots ages six weeks and up, ski school for the kids, convenient lockers and storage baskets. A welcome addition is an active ski patrol that actually slows traffic down when necessary. No hot-dogging allowed here; the emphasis is on safe and sensible fun.

Right at TSV or within its alpine village, there are 1,300 pairs of rental skis, lodging for more than a thousand skiers, all manner of books and souvenirs in the Taos Bookshop, and frequent festive events, including the Ernie Blake Weekend in late March, with ski races, fireworks, parties and a torchlight parade.

Leave the limos to Aspen. From before Thanksgiving until early April, in a long and sunny season, a skier's dollar in America can't buy a better experience than at TSV.

ANGEL FIRE RESORT
1-800-446-8117 (information), 377-6401 (snow report), 800-633-7463 (reservations).
P.O. Drawer B, Angel Fire, NM 87710.
24 miles east of Taos via N.M. 64 and N.M. 434.
Peak Elevation: 10,608 ft.
Vertical Drop: 2,180 ft.

Texan Roy H. Lebus started Angel Fire in 1967, with little more than a dream and a handful of dedicated workers. Today Angel Fire is known as a family resort and a "cruiser's mountain," featuring a variety of long, well-groomed trails (the longest is 3.5 miles). It is tailored to beginning and intermediate skiers; however, it offers a number of outstanding expert runs, as evidenced by the fact that the 1982 World Cup Freestyle championships were held here. Widespread snowmaking guaran-

Avg. Snowfall: 140 in.
Snowmaking: 60% of area.
Trails: 55 Downhill (45%
   beginner; 40%
   intermediate; 15%
   advanced); No X-C.
Lifts: 6 Chairlifts (4
   double, 2 triple).
Tickets (1990/91): Adult
   $26, children $16.
Ski School Pro: Robin
   May.

tees 2,000 vertical feet of skiing even in the driest of years, and only in the very busiest of times does the lift line require more than a 10- or 15-minute wait.

The resort is family friendly, offering a ski week program for kids and reduced lift and lodging rates for about half the season, and one of the largest (3,000 beds), most affordable lodging bases in the state. During reduced-rate periods, it's possible for Dad and Mom and two kids under 12 to stay for little more than $100 a night. Angel Fire boasts more major (and offbeat) events than almost any other area — for example, the world shovel race championships, featuring the wild antics of riders careening down the mountain at over 60 miles an hour on scoop shovels; and speed ski races where contestants rocket across the finish line at 80 miles an hour. As one local enthusiast puts it, "In terms of per capita excitement, it's damn hard to find anything better."

RED RIVER SKI AREA
754-2382 (information,
   snow report), 800-331-
   SNOW (reservations).
P.O. Box 900, Red River,
   NM 87558.
37 miles N. of Taos via
   N.M. 522 and N.M. 38.
Peak Elevation: 10,350 ft.
Vertical Drop: 1,600 ft.
Avg. Snowfall: 190 in.
Snowmaking: 78% of area.
Trails: 42 Downhill (28%
   beginner, 46%
   intermediate, 26%
   advanced); No X-C.
Lifts: 5 Chairlifts (3 double,
   2 triple); 2 surface lifts.
Tickets (1990/91): Adults,
   $27, children $16.
Ski School Pro: Ron
   Pochran.

In the northern arc of the Enchanted Circle, there's another family-friendly ski area, with extensive snowmaking and numerous wide beginner and intermediate trails. Runs such as Kit Carson and Broadway allow plenty of room for everybody to fall down, while expert speedways like Cat Skinner and Landing Strip are enough to get anyone's adrenalin pumping. The area rents about 1,000 pairs of skis, with another 2,000 pairs available in Red River. It hosts on-slope bars and restaurants. Perhaps best of all, it's only a block from town.

Red River was started in 1961 by J.B. Veal, an Albuquerque physician. It features lots of family conveniences, not the least of which is its 4,200-bed lodging base only a block from the ski area; an annual winter Carnival with dogsled races and horsedrawn sleighs; and the annual New Mexico Cup in February, when amateur racers from around the state compete for ski equipment and "fastest man" and "fastest woman" in the state. There's also a Kinderski school for ages 4-10 and Buckaroo Child Care for ages six months to four years.

SIPAPU LODGE & SKI AREA
587-2240 (information, snow report).
Rte. Box 29, Vadito, NM 87579.
25 miles S.E. of Taos via N.M. 68 and N.M. 518.
Peak Elevation: 9,065 ft.
Vertical Drop: 865 ft.
Avg. Snowfall: 110 in.
Snowmaking: 5% of area.
Trails: 18 Downhill (20% novice, 55% intermediate, 30% advanced); No X-C.
Lifts: 3 Chairlifts (1 triple, 2 pomas).
Tickets (1990/91): Adults, $22, children $17.50.
Ski School Pro: Bruce Bissell.

S ipapu is a small, quiet, ski area with beginner and intermediate runs. The longest run, Beep-Beep, is about 1.5 miles from top to bottom. Generally, after a run, you can jump back on the lift without waiting. Folks at Sipapu think of their guests as family; the laid-back atmosphere helps everyone feel at home. The area includes a restaurant and a snack bar, about 750 pairs of rental skis, on-slope lodging for nearly 200 and another 375 beds nearby.

WHERE TO BUY AND RENT SKI EQUIPMENT

All the ski areas offer a good supply of on-slope rental equipment. You can also find ski rentals, sales and service at numerous shops in Santa Fe, Taos and other towns near the ski areas, including the following.

Santa Fe

Alpine Sports (983-5155; 121 Sandoval, Santa Fe). Downhill and cross-country sales.

Base Camp (982-9707; 121 W. San Francisco St.). Cross-country sales and rentals.

Bradley Mountain Wear (982-8079; 107 E. Marcy St.). Clothing only.

Gardenswartz Sportz (473-3636; 2860 Cerrillos Rd.). Downhill and cross-country sales, some rentals.

rob and charlie's (471-9119; 1632 St. Michael's Dr.). Snowboard rentals.

Ski Tech Rentals (983-5512; 905 S. St. Francis Dr.). Cross-country rentals.

Wilderness Exchange (986-1152; 513 W. Cordova Rd.). Sales and rentals.

Near Santa Fe

The Evergreen (984-8190; Hyde Park, Ski Basin Rd).

First Powder (982-0495; Hyde Park, Ski Basin Rd). Rental.

Sports Bag (662-2454; Los Alamos Community Center, Los Alamos).

Trail Bound Sports (662-3000; 771 Central Ave., Los Alamos).

Taos

Cottam's Ski Shops (758-8242; S. Santa Fe Rd.). Sales, rental and repair.

Olympic Ski Shop (758-0068; Paseo del Pueblo Norte next to Michael's Kitchen). Downhill and cross-country rental and repair.

Sierra Sports (758-2822; 207 Paseo del Pueblo Sur). Downhill and cross-country rentals.

Taos Mountain Outfitters (758-9292; South Plaza). Cross-country rentals only.

Terry Sports (758-8522, 758-8522; N. Pueblo Rd. next to the post office). Downhill and cross-country sales, rental and repair.

Near Taos

Alpine Ski Rentals & Lodging (377-2509; N.M. 434, Angel Fire). Rental and repair.

First Powder Ski Rental & Sale (776-8854; On Taos Ski Valley Rd. N.M. 150, 0.2 mi. from blinking light). Downhill and cross-country sales, rental and repair.

Forestwood Ski Shop (377-2377; Jackson Hole Rd., Angel Fire. Rental and repair.

Mickey's Ski Rental (377-2501; Main St., Eagle Nest). Rental and repair.

The Outpost (586-1289; Red River Hwy., Questa). Rental and repair.

Pioneer Ski Rentals (754-2232; P.O. Box 223, Red River). Downhill rental.

Ridge Runner Rentals (776-2876; Taos Ski Valley Rd. N.M. 150). Rental and repair.

River City Sports (754-2428; Main & Pioneer, Red River). Rental and repair.

Sitzmark Sports (754-2525; Main & Malletta, Red River). Downhill and cross-country rental and repair.

Skis to Boot (377-3235; Angel Fire). Rental and repair.

Valley Ski Rental (377-2286; Therma Dr., Eagle Nest). Rental and repair.

Valley Sports (377-2266; N.M. 464 in Angel Square, Angel Fire). Rental and repair.

Wild Bill's Ski Shop (754-2735; Main St., Red River). Rental and repair.

CROSS COUNTRY SKIING

If you want solitude and the sound of skis sliding quietly over backcountry trails, take a break from the lift lines and go Nordic. Almost anytime from December through March, you can find snow-covered trails lacing national forests and wilderness areas, as well as public and private trails in the area. For snow conditions and maps, contact the national forest offices listed below. You might want to consult one or more of the most popular books on the subject: *Ski Touring in Northern New Mexico*, by Sam Beard; *Skiing the Sun*, by Jim Burns and Cheryl Lemanski; and *Cross-Country Skiing in Northern New Mexico* by Kay Matthews.

Public Touring

Near Santa Fe

Excellent ski touring in the Santa Fe area is found in the *Santa Fe National Forest* (Santa Fe office at 988-6940; 1220 St. Francis Dr., Santa Fe). Some popular trails include those starting from Black Canyon Campground, about nine miles from town via the Ski Basin Rd.; Borrega and Aspen Vista Trails about 13 miles up the Ski Basin Rd.; and Windsor Trail off the Ski Basin parking lot. Area trails are administered by the *Pecos Ranger District* (757-6121).

In the *Los Alamos Ranger District* (776-5120), Peralta Canyon Rd. and Valle Grande are two good trails, as are Fenton Hill and Jemez Falls in the Jemez Springs Ranger District (829-3535). The *New Mexico Ski Touring Club* (821-0309; P.O. Box 8425, Albuquerque, NM 87198) maintains a number of groomed trails in the Jemez and nearby areas. They also organize ski tours weekly during the winter in the Santa Fe area.

Near Taos

The *Carson National Forest* has numerous public ski-touring trails, some located right next to the Taos, Red River and Sipapu ski areas. A popular trail in the *Camino Real Ranger District* (587-2255, 758-8268) is Amole Canyon off N.M. 518 near Sipapu. The national forest, in cooperation with the Taos Norski Club, maintains set tracks and signs along a three-mile loop closed to snowmobiles. Another popular snowmobile-free route off N.M. 518 is Picuris Lookout, with exceptional views. Capulin/La Sombra, about five miles east of Taos off N.M. 64, is a flat, 1.5-mile trail that's ideal for "skating."

Popular routes in the *Tres Piedras Ranger District* (758-8678) include Maquinita Canyon, Biscara Trail, Burned Mountain, and Forest Road 795. In the *Questa Ranger District* (586-0520 or 758-6200), try East Fork, Ditch Cabin, Long Canyon or Goose Creek.

Detailed guides for many of the trails listed are available at Carson National Forest offices. Remember that some trails are designated for skiers only, some for snowmobiles only and some are shared. Restrictions are posted, but be sure to check with the Forest Service for detailed information. Also get a copy of the Forest Service's *Winter Recreation Safety Guide*, which lists winter hazards and how to prepare for them. One of the most fun and memorable public ski touring events, is the *Tortoise and Hare Race Weekend* with classical and freestyle cross-country races for novices and experts alike. It is held at the *Red River Ski Area* (754-2366).

Private Touring, Tours and Instruction

Near Santa Fe

There are no private touring centers in the Santa Fe area; however, for instruction, tours and overnight packages, call Bill Neuwirth at *Tracks* (982-2586; P.O. Box 173, Santa Fe, NM 87504). La Fonda Hotel's *Detours* (983-7262

Cross country skiing near Taos.

Mark Nohl/New Mexico Magazine

or 1-800-DETOURS) will arrange half or full-day trips. **Southwest Wilderness Center** (983-7262 or 1-800-869-7238; P.O. Box 9380 Santa Fe, NM 87504) also offers Nordic ski programs with rentals, clinics and tours.

Near Taos

For cross-country ski instruction and tours in the Taos area, your best bet is to call **Miller's Crossing** (754-2374) in Red River. *The* place to go touring near Taos is the **Enchanted Forest Cross Country Ski Area** (754-2374; P.O. Box 521, Red River, NM 87558). It is east of Red River atop Bobcat Pass and offers 30 kilometers (18 miles) of groomed and ungroomed trails amid 600 forested acres. It's the only area in the state devoted to cross country skiing. The Enchanted Forest is prime ski terrain for classical, freestyle and telemark and there are instructors, patrols, warming huts and rentals. 1990-91 user's rates were $7 a day, rentals $9.50 a day.

The area hosts a number of ski events. In January there's the **Enchanted Forest Scramble,** a freestyle cross country match with five and 10-kilometer races. In March the **Just Desserts Eat and Ski** competition has participants ski to different sites, where they are presented with a wide variety of delicious goodies. On Easter Sunday skiers take part in the **Easter Egg Scramble,** a search for hollow eggs filled with candy and prize coupons.

SNOWMOBILING

There's a network of trails for snowmobilers through the Santa Fe and Carson National Forests. Many of these groomed mini-highways twist and turn through thick forests to high alpine meadows where speedsters can zoom across wide-open spaces to their hearts' content. Be sure to check with district Forest Service offices (listed under "Public Ski Touring" above) before you choose a trail. Remember to slow down and stay clear of skiers and snowshoers. For maximum safety and fun, choose a trail that's designated for snowmobilers only. Three of the best are Fourth of July Canyon, Old Red River Pass and Greenie Peak in the **Questa Ranger District** (586-0520) near Red River. A number of businesses in Red River provide safe, guided snowmobile tours, complete with mountaintop hot-dog cookouts. In January the **Angel Fire Ski Area** (1-800-446-8117) hosts the **Angel Fire Snowmobile Festival,** with races, free rides, buffet dinner and prizes presented by Yamaha and Budweiser.

SOCCER

Santa Fe

Soccer is one of the most popular participatory sports in Santa Fe. The **Northern New Mexico Soccer Association** has three leagues with 175 teams and 1,800 players. These include a children's league (call Debbie Shapiro, 982-4668); a competitive youth league (call Capital City Soccer Club — Mike Gray, 989-5507, ext. 39 or 988-3134); and an adult league, the Santa Fe Soccer Club (call Mike Maloney, 471-3004.).

Taos

In Taos call the **Town Parks and Recreation Department** (758-4160) for schedules of upcoming games and the annual kids' soccer camp, usually held in Kit Carson Park in August.

SOFTBALL

Santa Fe

Softball is a highly popular sport in Santa Fe, with about 200 teams batting leather at local fields from June through August. To get involved, call the **Santa Fe Softball League** (471-6902). There is a Santa Fe Mushball League (984-6871), a collection of coed teams that plays high-spirited games with a slightly larger, softer ball. If you want to watch some good amateur hardball, five youth baseball leagues, from Little League to Babe Ruth and American legion, are active in Santa Fe. Check with the park department for schedules.

SPAS AND HOT SPRINGS

Still bubbling and steaming in the aftermath of its geologically recent volcanic activity, northern New Mexico is dotted with natural hot springs. Private bath houses have been built at Ojo Caliente and Jemez Springs (outside the area), and numerous other outdoor hot springs can be found. There is a Japanese bathhouse offering everything you could want in a natural spring outside of Santa Fe.

Near Santa Fe

TEN THOUSAND WAVES
Japanese Health Spa.
988-1047, 982-9304.
Ski Basin Rd., Santa Fe,
  NM 87501.
Open daily.
Reservations: Strongly
  recommended.

Ten Thousand Waves can confidently claim to be the most beautiful and peaceful spa in the Santa Fe area. It provides a host of pleasures including private or public hot tubs. Several of the discreetly-screened mountainside tubs have lovely views through the pines. The public tub is a convivial place; private tubs provide the allure of romance or the challenge of solitary meditation. There are stunningly handsome locker rooms and showers with thoughtful attention to detail, in-

One of the private tubs at Ten Thousand Waves.

Murrae Haynes

cluding individual temperature controls. Kimonos and thongs, soap, shampoo, cedar lotion and hair dryers are provided. Massage therapy runs the gamut, from Swedish to Shiatsu. A well-stocked health-food bar and a cozy fireplace make lingering a pleasure.

Services are not cheap at Ten Thousand Waves, but the pleasures are priceless. Winter is a lovely season to visit; you may enjoy watching a blizzard from a bubbling tub as much as you would a starry summer's night. Memberships (families are welcome) are available.

Near Taos

OJO CALIENTE
  MINERAL SPRINGS
583-2233.
P.O. Box 468, Ojo Caliente,
  NM 87549.
S.W. of Taos on N.M. 285.
Closed: Thanksgiving,
  Christmas, Easter.
Reservations: Required.

This is the most popular spa in the area. It features natural hot waters containing therapeutic iron, arsenic and lithium. Indians used this site as a healing center for thousands of years. Currently, people enjoy moderately priced hot soaks, herbal wraps, massages and a quiet time at the adjacent inn (see *Lodging*, Chapter Three).

There are individual cubicles with 15-minute arsenic soaks and an enclosed outdoor grotto area with hot iron water. Full body massage is available; soaps and shampoos are provided.

SWIMMING

Opportunities for swimming abound in the Santa Fe–Taos area, from lakes and rivers to numerous fine municipal and private pools. Popular swimming lakes within the area include *Cochiti* (242-8302), *Abiquiu* (685-4371), *Heron* (827-7465), *El Vado* (827-7465), *Storrie* (827-7465) and *Eagle Nest* (377-2420). You can swim at *Rio Grande Park* (758-3873) and on other portions of the Rio Grande River, as well as in numerous mountain lakes accessible only by trail (see "Hiking and Climbing").

Santa Fe

In Santa Fe there are four indoor public pools and one outdoor pool available for a small fee for adults and free for children seven and under. For details on times, classes and activities, call the city swimming pools division (984-6758). For numbers and addresses of private pools, see "Fitness Centers" and individual entries in *Lodging*. Municipal pools include:

Salvador Perez Pool (984-6755; 601 Alta Vista).
Tino Griego Pool (473-7270; on Llano St.).
Bicentennial Pool (984-6773; on Alto St.). Open only in summer.
Fort Marcy Pool (984-6730; 490 Washington Ave.).

Taos

For swimming opportunities in Taos, there is one municipal pool (758-9171; 120 Civic Plaza) and one pool at the *Taos Spa & Court Club* (758-1980; 111 Dona Ana Dr.). Other pools are available in hotels and motels (see individual entries in *Lodging*).

TENNIS

With clean air and clear skies most of the year, courts in the Santa Fe–Taos area are usually popping except during the snowiest weeks of winter. Both towns have numerous private indoor courts that can be rented any time of the year.

Santa Fe

The City of Santa Fe has 27 public tennis courts and four major private tennis facilities, including indoor, outdoor and lighted courts. Public parks with tennis courts include Fort Marcy, Ortiz, Larragoite, Herb Martinez and Salvador Perez. For specifics and other locations, call the city recreation department (984-6864). The city offers two four-week instruction sessions in June and July, including a daily hour-long class with a final tournament. 1991 cost for the month plus the tourney was $25 for adults, $20 for kids.

Santa Fe-area clubs with tennis courts include the following:

Santa Fe Country Club (471-3378, 471-2626; off Airport Rd.).
Club at El Gancho (988-5000; Old Las Vegas Hwy.).
Bishop's Lodge (983-6377; Bishop's Lodge Rd.).
Sangre de Cristo Racquet Club (983-7978; 1755 Camino Corrales).

Taos

In Taos, the town *Parks and Recreation Department* (758-4160) maintains two tennis courts at Kit Carson Park and two at Fred Baca Park. There is a court at the *Taos Spa and Court Club* (758-1980; 111 Dona Ana Dr.). Taos also holds tennis camps for children aged 10 and over. *The Tennis Ranch* (776-2211; P.O. Box 707, Taos, NM 87571) has more than 100 guest rooms and tennis programs from Memorial day through October. It has two indoor courts, six outdoor courts, daily clinics, plus three USPTA-sanctioned tournaments a year. Indoor courts can be rented by non-guests for $30 an hour.

WATER SPORTS

New Mexico boasts more small boats per capita than almost any other state in the union. Some say it's because of the yearning for water in a state so high and dry. Others say it's the spirit of a land once covered by inland seas. But those who really know say it's simply because New Mexico has a lot of good boating. Canoeing, water skiing and fishing as well as boating activity can be found at the following lakes. (See also "Rafting, Canoeing, Kayaking.")

Near Santa Fe

Cochiti Lake (242-8302, 465-2300; Army Corps of Engineers, P.O. Box 1238, Peña Blanca, NM 87041). About half an hour southwest of Santa Fe off I-25, Cochiti is a "no-wake' lake with free public boat ramps, recreation center (465-2213) and rentals of canoes and paddleboats.

Nambe Reservoir, about 20 miles north of Santa Fe via U.S. 285 and N.M. 503 (take turnoff to Nambe Falls). For boating infomation contact Nambe Pueblo (455-2036; Rte. 1, Box 117-BB, Santa Fe, NM 87501).

Santa Cruz Reservoir, a small lake and recreation area near Española (988-6000; Bureau of Land Management, 120 S. Federal Pl., P.O. Box 1449, Santa Fe, NM 87504).

Near Taos

Eagle Nest Lake, east of Taos on the edge of the Enchanted Circle. Two shops there can give you information on boat rentals and activities: Eagle Nest Marina (377-6941; P.O. Box 66, Eagle Nest, NM 87718) and Lakeshore Marina (377-6966; Eagle Nest Lake, Eagle Nest, NM 87718).

Outside the Area

Abiquiu Lake (685-4371; Army Corps of Engineers). Northwest of Santa Fe on U.S. 84. The large, scenic reservoir behind Abiquiu Dam offers a little of everything, from canoeing and windsurfing to fishing and water skiing.

Heron and El Vado Lakes, near the town of Chama. Both are administered by the New Mexico State Parks and Recreation Division (827-7465), and both have boat ramps and camping facilities. Heron is a "no-wake" lake, especially popular for small sailboats and hobies. Water skiing is allowed at El Vado. For further information, contact the Stone House Lodge (588-7274; P.O. Box 22, Heron Lake Rd., Rutheron, NM 87563). Stone House rentals include 24-foot pontoon "party barges" with awnings and outboard engines, 18-foot "bath buggies" and 15-foot trollers.

Storrie Lake (827-7465) six miles north of Las Vegas via NM 518, one of the most popular windsurfing spots in the state.

For further information on water sports, call 545-2040. For more information on ramps, rentals and activities, contact the *New Mexico State Park and*

The winds on Chochiti Lake make for great windsurfing.

Murrae Haynes

Recreation Division (827-7465 or 1-800-451-2541). For new and used boats, motors, parts and accessories and a full-service shop, contact **High Country Marine** (471-4077; Race Track Frontage Rd., Rte. 14, Box 315-MC, Santa Fe, NM 87505).

WINDSURFING

Clear weather, strong breezes and easily accessible lakes combine to make windsurfing one of New Mexico's fastest growing sports. The most popular nearby lakes are **Cochiti** (242-8302) near Santa Fe, **Eagle Nest** (377-2420) near Taos, and **Storrie** (827-7465) and **Abiquiu** (685-4371) outside the area. Storrie, in particular, is a boardsailing mecca in the summer and hosts numerous regattas and family beach parties. The strongest winds tend to come up in the afternoon. Watch out for thunderstorms; they can blow in with the afternoon winds.

For details on windsurfing events, sales and rentals, contact the **Santa Fe Sailboard Fleet** (P.O. Box 15931, Santa Fe, NM 87506) or **Santa Fe Windsurfing** (986-1611; 905 S. St. Francis Dr., Santa Fe, NM 87501). In Taos contact the **Hotel St. Bernard** (776-2251; Eagle Nest Lake) or the **Taos County Chamber of Commerce** (758-3873).

YOGA

Yoga instructor Gail Ackerman and her associates teach classes in Iyengar yoga at the **White Iris Yoga Studio** (982-5399; 1351 Pacheco St., Santa Fe, NM 87501 on Monday, Wednesday, Thursday, and Friday mornings from 8:45–10 a.m., and Monday, Tuesday and Wednesday evenings from 5:30–7 p.m. For a full schedule of classes at the **Santa Fe Center for Yoga**, call 982-2216. (See also "Fitness Centers.")

CHAPTER SEVEN
Antique, Boutique and Untique
SHOPPING

Candelario's original curio store on San Francisco St., Santa Fe, ca. 1915.

T. Harmon Parkhurst; Courtesy Museum of New Mexico

Santa Fe and Taos are magnets for individualistic, creative people who love beautiful things and want to share them with others. Here is our list of the best and most interesting shopping that Santa Fe and Taos can provide. We chose from an amazing variety of possibilities — far more than any travel guide can present in detail. We focused primarily on the unique and the Southwestern, and we attempted to satisfy a wide variety of shopping goals, from the $10 Taos T-shirt to the $40,000 Navajo rug.

As you shop, keep in mind that generally, the closer you are to the main plazas, the higher the prices. Usually these higher prices reflect better quality, but not always. Be sure to ask the salesperson what materials were used to make the item you're considering, especially if it's in the craft field. Don't assume that everything in local shops is locally made. If you have a car and the time, drive out to some of the pueblos (see "Pueblos" in *Culture*, Chapter Four) to find handmade Native American pottery, jewelry and other crafts.

What is an "antique"? or a "collectible"? What are "antiquities"? Whole books have been written to settle this debate, but there's no final answer. Here, we provide a section on *Antiques* — dealers whose offerings are generally a mix of the sublime (expensive and worth it) and, sometimes, the ridiculous (inexpensive and rightly so). A few antiques dealers sell older art as well, such as paintings. Under *Galleries* we include a sampling of those offering both new and older arts and crafts. Thus, some things you might call "antique" could appear here as well. The *Galleries* section sorts it all out — fairly, we hope, but admittedly in a somewhat arbitrary way under these categories of art (and, in a few cases, antiquities): Contemporary Art, Hispanic Folk Art, Native American Art, Native American Antiquities, Photography, Traditional Art, and Studios to Visit. *Posters* get a section all their own, later in this chapter. Browse through our lists as you would through a gallery. You'll make a few discoveries.

A word about bargaining: Haggling over prices is not a widely accepted practice in New Mexico. In fact, some artisans may be turned off by it. Much time and work goes into the creation of a pot, a carving or a piece of jewelry, and Native American artists know the value of their work. However, if you have talked with the artist and feel he or she is receptive, a diplomatic discussion of price may sometimes be appropriate. Also remember that shop hours may vary according to the amount of traffic during a particular week. If you're making a special trip, it is always wise to call ahead.

ANTIQUES

Santa Fe

Arrowsmith's Relics of the Old West (989-7663; 402 Old Santa Fe Trail, next to the Pink Adobe Restaurant.) Immerse yourself in the myth of the Old West at this repository of cowboy and Indian paraphernalia: saddles, spurs, chaps and guns; Indian pottery, rugs, pawn jewelry and beadwork. Rex Arrowsmith is a longtime resident and expert on Indian arts. His son Mark enjoys talking with shoppers about Western lore.

The Bedroom (984-0207; 317 Guadalupe St.) is the place to find antique beds, table linens, vintage whites, quilts, and accessories. It also has lovely collectibles such as quilted bears, mirrors, dresser sets and antique household items. Proprietors Richard and Joan Yalman have made their cozy shop as comfortable as an old-fashioned bedroom and give a warm welcome to visitors. Their specialty is antique cast-iron beds, refinished to order.

Claiborne Gallery (982-8019; 558 Canyon Rd.) For 11 years, Omer Claiborne has been traveling the world in search of fine Spanish Colonial antiques for his Canyon Rd. shop. He is one of Santa Fe's most knowledgeable experts on this type of furniture and likes to share his stories with interested visitors as they peruse his intriguing collection from Mexico, Spain, Guatemala, the Philippines and South America.

Hansen Gallery (983-2336; 923 Paseo de Peralta.) is one of the most venerable antique galleries in Santa Fe. It is operated by Vic Hansen, who has amassed an eclectic collection of 17th- and 19th-century American, Oriental and European furniture, porcelain, pewter and silver. He also sells European and American paintings, both old and new, historic Indian pottery, antique scientific instruments, glassware and quilts.

Pegasus (982-3333; 1372 Cerrillos Rd.) specializes in collectibles of the Old West, from cowboy and Indian stuff to Mexican curios, vintage jewelry, dolls, toys and advertising items.

Scarlett's Antique Shop and Gallery (983-7092; 225 Canyon Rd.) The inventory is authentic early American antiques, no reproductions. For history buffs, there are railroad memorabilia, vintage jewelry and pre-1920 postcards.

Things Finer (983-5552; Inside La Fonda Hotel.) Displays a fascinating array of small treasures, featuring fine jewelry, antiques and silver. Be sure to look at their collection of rare Russian icons. They'll also do appraisals on items you bring in.

Taos

Dwellings Revisited (758-3377; 107 Bent St.) Step into New Mexico's history with these relics from the past, including time-worn furniture and architectural elements.

Hacienda de San Francisco (758-0477; No. 4 St. Francis Plaza, Ranchos de Taos.) The 18th-century Romero Hacienda has seven rooms full of Span-

Spanish Colonial antiques at Hacienda de San Francisco, Ranchos de Taos.

Courtesy Hacienda de San Francisco

ish–Colonial antiques from 17th- through 19th-century New Mexico, Mexico, Spain and Argentina. The collection includes silver, furniture, accessories, *santos* and more.

Old Taos (758-7353; 108 Teresina Lane, just off the plaza.) A wide-ranging collection, from Spanish Colonial furniture and cowboy and Indian items to folk art and fishing memorabilia.

The Taos Company (758-1141; The Dunn House, Bent St.) An interior design showroom specializing in Southwestern antique furniture and decorative accessories that range from the *de rigueur* cow skull to wrought-iron candelabra.

BOOKS

Here's a listing of local bookshops offering a wide variety of reading material. Keep in mind as you peruse them that most museums and many historic sites listed in *Culture* also have bookshops specializing in New Mexican material.

Santa Fe

The Ark (988-3709; 133 Romero, off Agua Fria west of downtown.) The quintessential New Age shop, the Ark has six rooms of books on mythology, self-help, world religions, magic, women's and men's issues, health and healing. Also Tarot cards, crystals, gemstones, jewelry, perfume, incense, tapes, gifts — even an aviary (the birds aren't for sale).

The Bookroom (988-5323; 616 Canyon Rd.) A tiny book and coffee shop with a carefully selected stock of new fiction, poetry, Southwestern works and more. Intimate atmosphere and a great staff.

Tiny but special.

Courtesy The Bookroom

Caxton Books and Music (982-8911; 216 W. San Francisco.) Specializes in travel books and maps, including topo, relief and Forest Service. They have a good selection of quality new work in hardback and paper.

Collected Works (988-4226; 208-B W. San Francisco St.) Lots of new fiction, poetry and Southwest material. Occasional readings are given by local poets.

Cornerstone Books, Etc. (473-0306; 1722 St. Michael's Dr., in St. Michael's Village near K-Mart.) Features Santa Fe's largest Bible selection, as well as Christian books, music, gifts, cards, tapes video rentals and an audio cassette lending library.

Enchanting Land (988-2718; De Vargas Center Mall, N. Guadalupe and Paseo de Peralta; 982-5546; 142 Lincoln #201.) Strictly for kids, Enchanting Land is chock full of quality books, games, music, educational toys and kits.

The Great Catsby (986-1794; 551 W. Cordova Rd.) A progressive bookstore and coffeehouse that focuses on works of interest to women — literary, political and more.

Horizons (983-1554; 328 Guadalupe St.) The physical world — for kids and adults — is the theme of Horizons. Books on natural history and science, maps and globes, atlases and outdoor guides. Also, many educational science items for children.

Los Llanos (982-9542; 500 Montezuma at Sanbusco Market Center.) More than 40,000 titles, specializing in Southwest works, travel, reference and cookbooks. They stock many fine hardcover art books and children's titles.

USED AND RARE

The following shops specialize in used and/or rare volumes: ***Blue Moon Books & Vintage Video*** (982-3035; 329 Garfield at Guadalupe.), metaphysical, psychology, philosophy, women's studies; ***Book Gallery*** (471-6889; Airport Rd. and Jemez.), 30 tons of used volumes; ***Books and More Books*** (983-5438; 1341 Cerrillos Rd.), literature, travel, general interest; ***Margolis & Moss***

Moby Dickens in Taos: a bright and sunny place for book browsing.

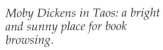

Murrae Haynes

(982-1028; 129 W. San Francisco St.), rare books, prints appraised, bought and sold; *Nicholas Potter* (983-5434; 203 E. Palace Ave.), used and rare hardbacks bought and sold; *Palace Avenue Books* (986-0536; 209 E. Palace Ave.) specializes in Southwest, broad range of other titles; *Parker Books of the West* (988-1076; 142 W. Palace Ave.) Western history and fiction, maps; *Reader's Harvest Books* (438-0574; 1610 St. Michael's Dr., St. Michael's Village West.), used and collectible, title search service; *Santa Fe Bookseller* (983-5278; 203 W. San Francisco St.) art books, Southwest, scholarly titles.

Taos

Brodsky Bookshop (758-9468; 218 Paseo del Pueblo Norte.) An intimate shop with a wide range of Western and Southwestern titles, particularly New Mexican authors; an interesting range of other titles.

Moby Dickens Bookshop (758-3050; 124-A Bent St.) A browser's heaven, with several rambling rooms and at least one friendly cat. Owner Willi Wood likes to regale visitors with tales about Taos. She has furnished the shop with irresistible chairs and window seats full of sunshine where you can relax and read a few pages of the book you're going to buy.

Taos Book Shop (758-3733; 122-D Kit Carson Rd., parking in rear.) Billing itself as the oldest bookstore in New Mexico, the Taos Book Shop offers a large inventory of fiction, nonfiction, poetry and metaphysical titles, out-of-print and Southwestern works. There is a room of children's books. They carry calendars, journals, posters, cards, and Spanish, Indian and New Age tapes. You can relax on the landscaped patio.

USED AND RARE

G. Robinson Old Prints & Maps (758-2278; Bent St.)
Ten Directions Books (758-2725; 228-C Paseo del Pueblo Norte.)

CLOTHING

Folks in Santa Fe and Taos don't cotton much to national clothing trends; for that reason they have been dubbed un-fashion-conscious. Actually, quite the opposite is true. They are individualists who are very much aware of style and either look for the unique or adapt the commonplace to their own personal tastes. For this reason, Santa Fe and Taos are bursting with boutiques that sell a dazzling array of one-of-a-kind designer styles, unusual imports, costumes and hand wovens. The following are some of the best.

CONTEMPORARY

Santa Fe

Bodhi Bazaar (982-3880; 500 Montezuma, Sanbusco Market Center.) Sophisticated international styles for men and women who like a casually elegant look.

Crazy Fox Boutique (984-2224; 227 Don Gaspar Ave. at Santa Fe Village.) The outlet for dresses by San Francisco designer Karen Alexander. Flowery prints, feminine but not delicate.

Spectrum Cottonwear (983-1331; 207 W. Water St.) Colorful, all-natural cotton in casual, up-to-date styles for women and girls. Here's where you can dress in Santa Fe style affordably and have lots of fun doing it.

Taos

Blue Fish (758-3520; 140 E. Kit Carson Rd.) Unique reversible designs in coats, dresses and ensembles for women and men. Unusual fabrics are dyed and block-printed by hand.

ETHNIC

Santa Fe

Origins (988-2323; 135 W. San Francisco St.) For sheer richness of designs and fabrics, nothing tops Origins. Styles range from borrowed ethnic to pure fantasy. Most are one-of-a-kind by Southwest designers, plus imports from Italy, France and other locales.

Spirit of the Earth (988-9558; 211 Old Santa Fe Trail, at the Inn at Loretto.) More Moroccan than New Mexican, these soft, flowing garments in drapeable fabrics are handmade and romantic as the desert moon. Accessories are abundant, from blanket coats and handmade jewelry to scarves and suedes.

Taos

Kathmandu Connection Asia Bazaar (758-0885; 109 Brooks St., opposite the Taos Post Office.) Clothing from India and Nepal — handwoven sweaters, coats, dresses, shirts, pants and accessories. Fifty percent of the store's profits go to support a preschool in Nepal.

From the Andes (758-0485; Taos Plaza, under Ogelvie's Restaurant.) The owner travels to South America to bring back handmade sweaters, skirts, dresses, vests, ponchos, hats, bags, hangings, dolls and more.

HANDWOVENS

Santa Fe

Handwoven Originals (982-4118; 211 Old Santa Fe Trail at the Inn at Loretto.) The elegant and the casual in coats, blouses and scarves by three Santa Fe designers.

Santa Fe Weaving Gallery (982-1737; 124-1/2 Galisteo.) Features one-of-a-kind and limited edition women's clothing by 28 designers. Clothing is either handwoven or constructed of hand-dyed fabrics and there are some astounding beadwork accessories.

Spider Woman Designs (984-0136; 225 Canyon Rd.) This weaving and design studio is a delight to visit. Highly original handwoven clothing and textiles displayed in a Southwestern setting.

LEATHER

Santa Fe

Char (988-5969; 104 Old Santa Fe Trail.) An exclusive boutique featuring exciting designs in very contemporary colors.

Desert Son (982-9499; 725 Canyon Rd.) Features custom leather work, beadwork, bags and hats. Well known for their belt selection.

Santa Fe Sheepskin Store (982-5233; 125 W. San Francisco.) A great selection of everything you'd ever want in sheepskin for men and women.

Tom Taylor (984-2231; in La Fonda Hotel, 108-110 E. San Francisco St.) Visiting celebs flock to Tom Taylor's for custom belts, buckles and boots — classic and updated Western styles.

Taos

Overland Sheepskin Co. (758-8820; N.M. 3 just north of Taos.) Shearling coats to see you through the coldest Taos winter, plus hats, slippers and much more. Overland has its own production facility near Taos, and you can see the wool producers grazing right outside the store.

Southwest Moccasin and Drum (758-9332, 1-800-447-3630; 803 Paseo del Pueblo Norte.) A dozen or more brands of moccasins, plain to fancy, plus Taos drums.

SOUTHWESTERN STYLES

Santa Fe

Cooper's Western Wear (982-3388; DeVargas Center Mall; 471-8775; Villa Linda Mall, at Rodeo and Cerrillos Rds.) Men's and women's apparel, including Western boots and hats, Australian outback dusters, jeans, shirts and more.

Montecristi Custom Hat Works (983-9598; 118 Galisteo.) If you're looking for a serious hat, pardner — a hat you'll love for the rest of your life — look at Montecristi.

Sanbusco Outfitters (988-1664; 550 Montezuma at Sanbusco Market Center.) The designers for Sanbusco Outfitters have adapted basic, down-to-earth Western and Native American clothing styles for men who don't necessarily want to get their clothes dirty. Elegant suede and denim clothing, leather accessories and headgear.

Santa Fe Fiesta Fashions (983-1632; 651 Cerrillos Rd.) Just Lindee, designer and manufacturer of Southwestern apparel, has a great selection of traditional Santa Fe Fiesta wear — off-shoulder blouses and broomstick skirts, all trimmed with miles of rickrack.

Santa Fe Pendleton (983-5855; 53 Old Santa Fe Trail.) The finest Southwestern apparel for men and women, with all the quality the name implies.

Taos

Eloise Contemporary Clothes (758-3230; E. Kit Carson Rd.) Original designs in Southwestern styles, including men's ribbon shirts and handwoven belts.

Martha of Taos (758-3102; 121 Paseo del Pueblo Norte.) Quintessential Santa Fe and Taos style clothing for women. Martha is an original. In business for 36 years in Taos, she does her own designs based on Spanish and Indian clothing.

Yukio's (758-2269; 226-C Paseo del Pueblo Norte, two blocks north of the plaza.) Reasonably priced, hand-painted and handmade clothing, Southwestern fabrics and silver jewelry.

SPORTS AND OUTDOOR WEAR

Santa Fe

Alpine Sports (983-5155; 121 Sandoval St.) Men's and women's ski wear, casual classic sportswear for women, tennis clothing, bathing suits, shorts and T-shirts, athletic shoes.

Base Camp (982-9707; 121 W. San Francisco St.) Bandanas to boots, everything for the hiker and camper.

Taos

Taos Mountain Outfitters (758-9292; 114 S. Plaza.) All kinds of wilderness wear, including brands such as North Face, Royal Robbins and Sierra Designs.

T-SHIRTS

For fun and affordable souvenirs, check out the original Southwestern T-shirt designs at the following shops.

Santa Fe

Plaza Shirt Co. (988-2757; 54 E. San Francisco St.)
Virginia Trading Post (983-6165; 82 E. San Francisco St.)
Santa Fe Mercantile Co. (982-5233; 125 W. San Francisco St.)

Taos

The I Love Taos Co. (758-8565; Taos Plaza.)
The Shirt Factory (758-9711; 231-C, S. Pueblo Rd.)
Taos T-Shirt Co. (758-1680; 111 N. Pueblo Rd.)

GALLERIES

Santa Fe has between 150 and 200 galleries and Taos about 85 — practically a lifetime supply of browsing for eclectic art lovers. We have included the "don't miss" galleries as well as a selection of those that are known among locals for consistent quality and integrity. Most Fridays during the tourist season there's a plethora of openings with food, drink, great art and great crowds. Check the Santa Fe *New Mexican*'s "Pasatiempo" section, a Friday publication, for times and places. The Gallery categories are: Contemporary Art, Hispanic Folk Art, Native American Art, Native American Antiquities, Photography, Traditional Art, and Studios to Visit. See also *Posters* in this chapter.

CONTEMPORARY ART

Here are some fine-arts galleries featuring recent paintings, sculpture and prints in both representational and abstract styles. Some carry Southwestern-inspired work; others are distinctly nonregional in their approach.

Santa Fe

Allene Lapides Gallery (984-0191; 225 Johnson St., off Grant Ave. north of the plaza.) Non-Southwestern. Lapides' stable of modern masters and contemporary emerging artists includes the renowned Ida Kohlmeyer.

Barbara Zusman Art and Antiques (984-1303; 233 Canyon Rd.) Fine art by Pamela Adger, Dobee Snowber, Ray Belcher and Jim Klukkert. Also many strange and wonderful things, such as an armadillo basket, a chair made entirely of horseshoes, exotic textiles, antique jewelry and folk art. This shop is not to be missed.

Elaine Horwitch (988-8997; 129 W. Palace Ave.) Elaine Horwitch started her career as an art dealer by selling prints from the back of her station wagon. Now she runs a multimillion-dollar business, with galleries in Scottsdale and Palm Springs as well as Santa Fe. Her artists produce attention-grab-

Pamela Adger's mixed media sculpture at Barbara Zusman.

Courtesy Barbara Zusman

bing work on Southwest themes and her exhibition openings are the best in town.

Hand Graphics Gallery and Atelier (988-1241; 418 Montezuma.) Exciting lithographs, etchings and monotypes by prominent New Mexico artists, including muralist Zara Kriegstein. The shop is also a printmaking atelier where artists can frequently be found at work.

LewAllen Fine Art (988-5387; 225 Galisteo.) Contemporary work by important emerging regional and nonregional artists like Luis Jimenez, Emmi Whitehorse and Tina Fuentes. Owner Arlene LewAllen and her assistant Geoff Gorman love to spend time with visitors as they check out the latest exhibit.

Linda Durham (988-1313; 400 Canyon Rd.) Though most of Durham's artists live and work in New Mexico, they paint in a nonregional, contemporary style — an ambitious collection that includes sculpture and photography. Durham and her staff enjoy talking about the artists and their work.

Shidoni Sculpture Gardens, Galleries and Bronze Foundry (988-8001, 800-333-0332; five miles north of Santa Fe on Bishop's Lodge Rd.) A must-visit on any trip to Santa Fe, Shidoni, in a lush river valley setting, is nationally known for its contemporary sculpture .

Taos

Bryan's Gallery (758-9407; 121-C North Plaza Art Center.) Contemporary work in a range of media, from oils to sculpture to jewelry. Two dozen or more artists, among them painters Miguel Martinez and Bill Rane, the latter a rising star in the international art world for his surrealistic mythological works.

New Directions Gallery (758-2771; 107-B North Plaza.) Contemporary work by Larry Bell, Agnes Chavez, Cliff Harmon, Linda Tasch and others.

Rod Goebel Gallery (758-2181; 117 Camino de la Placitas, just southwest of the plaza.) Original oils by this internationally-acclaimed Impressionist painter, including still lifes, landscapes, portraits and florals.

Tally Richards Gallery (758-2731; 2 Ledoux St.) One of Taos' first contemporary galleries, featuring landscapes by Donald Anderson and others.

HISPANIC FOLK ART

New Mexico's isolation from Spain meant self-sufficiency for the descendants of the early colonists. Working in the traditions of Spain and Mexico, New Mexican craftspeople created the things they needed for everyday life: furniture, clothing and religious objects. Today these creations are recognized as objects of a vibrant folk art legacy that is unique to the Southwest. The Spanish brought the first sheep to the New World, using their wool for clothing and rugs. New Mexican cottonwood and other woods were used to make *bultos* (three-dimensional carvings of saints), *retablos* (paintings of saints on wooden plaques) and *reredos* (carved altar screens for churches). Ordinary straw, in the hands of an artisan, was turned into delicate, appliqued designs on crosses and other objects. With the arrival of wagon trains from the East on the Santa Fe Trail, tin became available for working into elaborately incised and stamped candleholders, frames, boxes and other useful items.

Like the arts of the Pueblo Indians, the Hispanic folk arts declined when the railroad brought inexpensive manufactured household goods in the latter part of the 19th century. However, the interest of tourists, collectors and museums and the tenacity of the craftspeople themselves has led to a revival of all these arts. Following are some of the galleries that specialize in these unique artforms. (For more information, see "Museum of International Folk Art," page 99.)

Santa Fe

Davis Mather Folk Art Gallery (983-1660; 141 Lincoln Ave., a block north of the plaza.) One of the best collections of New Mexican animal woodcarvings and Mexican folk art. Owner Davis Mather delights in recounting how he discovered the work of Felipe Archuleta, who popularized the making of animal woodcarvings from native cottonwood beginning in the 1960s.

Montez Gallery (982-1828; Sena Plaza Courtyard, 125 E. Palace Ave., #33.) Masterpieces of New Mexican folk art by artisans such as Spanish Market award-winning *santero*, Charles Carrillo.

Santa Fe Store (982-2425; Inn at Loretto, 211 Old Santa Fe Trail.) A large collection of local and international folk art. Be sure to see the fanciful snake and fish carvings of Davila, whose work is also in the Museum of American Folk Art.

Badger, *by Felipe Archuleta,*
Davis Mather Folk Art Gallery.

Courtesy Davis Mather Folk Art Gallery.

Near Santa Fe

Centinela Traditional Arts (351-2180; on the High Road to Taos, Rte. 76, Box 4, Chimayó.) The Trujillo family makes stunning Rio Grande weavings using natural dyes and traditional designs.

Galeria Ortega (351-2288; on the High Road to Taos, next to Ortega's Weaving Shop, N.M. 520 at N.M. 76.) Hispanic folk art carvings in cedar, cottonwood and other woods, as well as straw inlay pieces and contemporary crafts.

Ortega's Weaving Shop (351-4215; on the High Road to Taos, see preceding entry.) Authentic wool blankets, rugs, coats, vests and purses made in the Chimayó weaving style by the descendants of Gabriel Ortega, an 18th-century Chimayó weaver.

Oviedo (351-2280; on the High Road to Taos, 1.2 miles east of junction of N.M. 520 and N.M. 76, by appointment 10 a.m.-7 p.m.) Members of the Oviedo family have been carvers since 1730. Award-winners at the annual Spanish Market, they create traditional wood and bronze sculptures.

Near Taos

Martinez Hacienda (see "Historic Buildings and Sites, page 93.) A variety of quality, locally-made New Mexican folk art pieces, from carvings to paintings and tinwork.

Millicent Rogers Museum (see "Museums," page 106.) *Santos, retablos,* tinwork, and Rio Grande and Chimayó weavings.

NATIVE AMERICAN ART

Santa Fe is a center for the sale of Native American art. Most Native American artisans from the Southwest make pottery and jewelry, but there are also many fine weavers, basket makers, carvers and painters — including a number who have achieved international stature.

Most potters tend to work within the context of their own pueblo's traditions, though they usually find room for innovation. Each pueblo's pottery has distinctive characteristics in design, shape and colors; but traditional pottery, no matter which pueblo it comes from, is all made by the same labor-intensive process. The clay is gathered and processed by hand; pots are shaped by the coil method, winding a long, thin roll of clay into the desired shape; paints and slips (a thin clay soup painted on the outer surface of the pot to smooth it) are made by hand from plant and mineral sources; and firing is done in an outdoor kiln. Thus, many hours and much skill are required to create even a small pot. The pueblos that are best-known for their fine pottery are San Ildefonso, Santa Clara, San Juan and Acoma, as well as the Hopi villages of northeastern Arizona.

If you want to purchase an authentic traditional pot, be sure to ask whether the pot in question is hand-made or slip-cast (commercially molded.) Some artists buy slip-cast pots and paint them. These are fine decorator items, but they will never appreciate in value. A well-made, hand-coiled pot will.

Jewelry-making is also an ancient art among the Pueblo Indians. They are known to have crafted fine turquoise and shell beads many centuries ago, and late in the 19th century they learned silversmithing. As with pottery, jewelry-making by traditional methods is a painstaking, time-consuming process and an artisan may apprentice for several years before he or she can make a living at the craft.

The Navajos are the acknowledged masters of silverwork, crafting the turquoise and silver jewelry and *concha* belts that epitomize the Southwest. The Hopi produce a unique kind of silverwork called overlay, characterized by angular geometric repeat patterns on rings, bracelets, necklaces, bolos, etc. The Zuni of west–central New Mexico produce the finest lapidary work, such as needlepoint and petitpoint, in which bits of turquoise are individually shaped and fitted precisely into silver settings. The Santo Domingo natives are the most skilled creators of *heishi,* or finely carved beads made of shell.

If you're buying from artists who sell under the *portal* at the Palace of the Governors on Santa Fe's plaza, it is good to know that this area is reserved *only* for New Mexican Indians and that all items must be made by hand by the seller or by members of his or her family. In shops, clerks should be able to provide information on who made an item and something of its tradition. Following are some shops and galleries that specialize in Native American art. If you have time, though, we suggest you visit the pueblos themselves (see "Pueblos" in *Culture,* Chapter Four.) There, you're not only likely to get the best prices, but artisans in numerous shops and galleries can give you first-hand information on their culture as well as their craft.

Santa Fe

Gallery 10 (983-9707; 225 Canyon Rd.) Houses the work of some of the most sought-after contemporary Native American artists, such as Hopi potter Al Qoyawayma and Hopi kachina doll carver Loren Phillips.

Glenn Green Galleries (988-4168; 50 E. San Francisco St. on the plaza.) Wander in and gaze in awe at the monumental sculptures of Apache artist Allan Houser, the grandfather of contemporary Native American sculpture.

Kachina House and Gallery (982-8415; 236 Delgado, off Canyon Rd.) Under the same owner since 1951, the Kachina House specializes in authentic (Hopi-made) kachina dolls, which represent spirits of the Hopi religion. Some non-Hopi artists also produce kachina dolls, but collectors and other experts do not consider these to be authentic.

Keshi — the Zuni Connection (989-8728; 227 Don Gaspar Ave., inside Santa Fe Village.) The best shop for authentic jewelry and carvings of the Zuni Indians. The Zuni are known for their fetishes, or stone carvings in the shapes of totem animals. Fetishes made by non-Zuni are not considered authentic.

Robert F. Nichols (982-2145; 419 Canyon Rd.) Fine Native American art, specializing in pottery.

Palace of the Governors Museum Shop (827-6474; entrance at Palace Ave. and Washington St.) All authentic, Indian-made items in all mediums. No state sales tax is charged here.

Shop of the Rainbow Man (982-8706; 107 E. Palace Ave.; 758-4101.) In business since 1945, Bob and Marianne Kapoun are authorities on the documentation and history of Indian trade blankets. The eight-room Santa Fe shop is

Zuni bear fetish.

Courtesy Keshi

Taos artist R.C. Gorman, at work

Don Laine; Courtesy Taos County Chamber of Commerce

stuffed with treasures, from Zuni fetishes to Hopi kachina dolls, pottery, jewelry and Navajo rugs.

Wind River Trading Co. (989-7062; 113 E. San Francisco St.) A range of prices in jewelry, pottery and kachina doll carvings. The staff is knowledgeable about the merchandise.

Taos

Don Fernando Curio and Giftshop (758-3791; on the plaza.) The oldest Indian arts shop on the plaza, Don Fernando's has storyteller figurines by Margaret Quintana of Cochiti, black-on-black pottery, folk art carvings by Navajo Johnson Antonio, jewelry and Taos Mox, a locally made moccasin.

Navajo Gallery (758-3250; 210 Ledoux St.) Renowned Navajo artist R.C. Gorman owns this shop, where you can find his oils, sculptures, drawings, acrylics, lithographs, silkscreens, tapestries, cast paper, etched glass and other works.

Silver and Sand Trading Co. (758-9698; North Plaza.) A collection of quality Hopi kachina dolls, Navajo sandpaintings, Pueblo pottery, Navajo rugs, sculpture, baskets old and new and jewelry from Hopi, Santo Domingo, Navajo and Zuni.

Taos Drums (758-3796; P.O. Box 1916, Taos, N.M. 87571. Call or write for information.) Internationally known, traditional Taos Indian drums are made by hand from hollowed-out logs and tanned hides.

NATIVE AMERICAN ANTIQUITIES

Many of the nation's foremost dealers in Native American antiquities are headquartered in Santa Fe. Here are a few of the places where you can find anything from cradleboards and deerhide clothing to ancient pots and hunting tools: *Morning Star Gallery* (982-8187; 513 Canyon Rd.), the largest gallery of its kind in the country; *Channing Dale Throckmorton* (984-2133; 53 Old Santa Fe Trail, upstairs on the plaza), periodically featuring fascinating speakers on Native American topics; *Dewey Galleries Limited* (982-8632; 74 E. San Francisco.) Not to be missed.

PHOTOGRAPHY

Santa Fe

Andrew Smith Gallery (984-1234; 76 E. San Francisco St.) Masterpieces of 19th- and 20th-century photographers of the West and the American Indian, among them Ansel Adams and Edward Curtis as well as classic landscapes by contemporary photographers like David M. Kennedy.

Scheinbaum and Russek (988-5116; 328 Guadalupe St., Ste. M.) Rare and contemporary photography, prints and limited edition portfolios. Among the artists are Ansel Adams, Manuel Alvarez Bravo, Henri Cartier-Bresson, Beaumont Newhall, Eliot Porter and Edward Weston.

TRADITIONAL ART

A number of American and European artists moved to Santa Fe and Taos in the early decades of the 20th century when both towns were largely Hispanic and Indian. Inspired by the spectacular landscape and light, they started landscape-painting movements that became known as the "Santa Fe School" and the "Taos School." By viewing these artists' work, you can share in their wonderment over the Land of Enchantment. As you might expect, their landscapes and portraits of local people are executed in a realistic style that remains highly popular throughout the region.

Santa Fe

Fenn Galleries (982-4631; 1075 Paseo de Peralta.) This rambling old adobe is full of the finest classic Western and American art of the 19th and 20th centuries. Among the artists: Joseph Henry Sharp, E. Irving Couse and Ernest Blumenschein of the Taos Society of Artists; Henriette Wyeth; and sculptors Glenna Goodacre and Doug Hyde. This is one of the city's most important galleries.

Gerald Peters Gallery (988-8961; 439 Camino del Monte Sol, off Canyon Rd.) One of Santa Fe's most prestigious galleries. Deals in classic Western and Taos School paintings, 19th- and 20th-century American painting and sculpture, Impressionist, European and modern American masters.

Owings Dewey Fine Art (982-6244; 74 E. San Francisco St.) 19th- and 20th-century American art, including Western, traditional and contemporary paintings, watercolors and original graphics.

Woodrow Wilson Fine Art (983-2444; 319 Read St.) In business since 1971, Woodrow Wilson (not related to the U.S. president) has a reputation as one of the most discerning dealers of traditional art in the city. Selections for both connoisseurs and beginning collectors include Early Taos and Santa Fe Schools, 19th- and 20th-century American and European art, original prints, historical photographs and regional contemporary work.

Wyeth Hurd Graphics (989-8380; 112-116 W. San Francisco St., level one of Plaza Mercado.) Four generations of this New England family of painters — including N.C. Wyeth, Henriette Wyeth Hurd, Andrew Wyeth and others — are represented here in affordable graphics and prints.

Zaplin-Lampert Gallery (982-6100; 651 Canyon Rd.) Located in a beautiful adobe building, Zaplin-Lampert specializes in 19th- and 20th-century paintings, watercolors, drawings and prints, mostly Southwestern. They carry art of the Taos School, as well as some museum-quality Native American antiquities.

Taos and Near Taos

Burke Armstrong Fine Art (758-9016; 121 North Plaza.) Traditional and Western oils, watercolors, sculpture, and original woodcuts by C.P. Fels.

E.S. Lawrence Gallery (758-8229; 132 E. Kit Carson Rd.) Mostly traditional paintings and sculpture of the West and Indian subjects, as well as watercolors, pastels, ceramics and photography.

The Shriver Gallery (758-4994; 401 Paseo del Pueblo Norte.) Traditional fine art with a Western emphasis, including a selection of paintings, drawings, etchings and bronze sculptures.

Stewart House Gallery and Inn (776-2913; Taos Ski Valley Rd., 0.5 miles north of the blinking light.) Traditional and Western art, including sculpture, oils, mixed media, watercolors, ceramics and jewelry by more than 20 artists.

Total Arts Gallery (758-4667; 122-A E. Kit Carson Rd.) Traditional to modern fine art, including sculpture, watercolors, mixed media, oils and graphics.

STUDIOS TO VISIT

Part of the fun of viewing art is meeting artists and learning about how they live and work. Following is a selection of artists' studios that receive visitors by appointment.

Near Santa Fe

Cloud Eagle Studios (455-2662; 800-288-4824; Nambe Pueblo, call for directions.) Cloud Eagle is a Nambe Pueblo stone carver and sculptor in bronze and mixed media. He and his apprentices create small- to large-scale works honoring the spiritual heritage of Pueblo Indians.

David Ross Studio and Gallery (988-4017; 132 W. Palace Ave.) David Ross creates folk-art animals as functional furniture. His library step-stools in the forms of dalmatians, cheetahs and other creatures are internationally known. He also decorates handmade wooden furniture in a light, almost impressionistic style.

Star Liana York (983-1647; Cuyamunge, north of Santa Fe, call for appointment and directions.) York works in bronze to bring to life the people of the

David Ross with his animal creations.

Courtesy David Ross Studio and Gallery

Old West, from Native Americans to cowboys and cowgirls. Colored patinas give a fresh, contemporary look to the bronze.

Veryl Goodnight (982-9310; next to Rancho Encantado, 10 miles north of Santa Fe on N.M. 590.) Sculptor Goodnight creates traditional bronzes of subjects like running horses and soaring eagles.

Taos

Aliah Sage Studio (758-9564; Ledoux St.) Sage, who has lived in Taos since 1977, creates large-scale murals and architectural installations, as well as more intimate 3-D constructions. Her materials are tile, wood and metal. Moveable parts encourage the viewer to create different compositions with the work.

IMPORTED GIFTS

If you're looking for something unforgettable (yet still affordable) for your friends back home, the following shops will delight and inspire you.

Santa Fe

Fourth World Cottage Industries (982-4388; 102 W. San Francisco St.) Imports from Central and South America in a range of prices. Textiles, women's and men's casual cotton and wool clothing, handwoven tapestries, pottery, jewelry, carvings, bags and backpacks of Guatemalan cotton.

Jackalope (471-8539; 2820 Cerrillos Rd., about five miles south of the plaza.) This is where Santa Fe shops. Affordable furniture, pottery, textiles and tinwork, mostly from Mexico. During summer and Christmas, Jackalope has several Mexican artists demonstrating their work. There is a good New Mexican restaurant at the store, as well as a greenhouse. Next door is *Jackalope Furniture* (471-5390) with Mexican imports. Downtown is *Jackalope Station* (989-7494; 231 Galisteo St.), a smaller store with selections from the main store.

Pachamama (983-4020; 125 E. Palace Ave.) Antique and traditional folk art from Latin America. Santos, jewelry, and an excellent selection of weavings, masks, musical instruments, baskets and *retablos*.

Worldly Possessions (983-6090; 330 Garfield St., a 10-minute walk south of the plaza.) A range of prices in imported clothing, linens, jewelry, beads, decorative accessories and toys. Watch for their frequently scheduled exhibitions of folk art from around the world.

An antique Ecuadoran angel at
Pachamama in Santa Fe.

Courtesy Pachamama

Near Taos

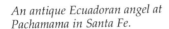

Coyote Pottery (758-3030; Ranchos de Taos, across from St. Francis Church on S. Santa Fe Rd.) Mexican pottery and other affordable gift items from Mexico, also New Mexico red chile *ristras*.

Follow Your Heart (758-4881, Bent St.; 776-8160, Taos Ski Valley in the New Resort Center.) Imported cuckoo clocks, candles, mukluks, sweaters, caps and hats, handmade dolls and other delights from around the world for skiers and shoppers.

FURNISHINGS AND RUGS

New Mexico's distinctive furniture originated with the Spanish settlers, who 400 years ago brought with them the ornately carved furniture of Old Spain. That furniture eventually wore out, of course, and not much came over the tortuous 2,000-mile trail from Mexico City to replace it. Using the native trees of New Mexico's forests, Hispanic craftsmen recreated those old styles and developed their own versions as well. Furniture-making still thrives today; and though the tools are more refined, the simple geometrics, rosettes, fans, spirals and other carved designs are as charming as ever. Listed below are a few of the area's better furniture craftsmen. Also included are importers of furniture, design elements and Oriental rugs.

Santa Fe

Artesanos Imports Co. (983-5563; 222 Galisteo, Santa Fe, NM 87501.) More than 150 styles of hand-painted Mexican tiles and ceramic murals for interior and exterior decoration. Write for a color catalog.

David's Spanish Furniture (438-3211; Rte. 14 La Cienega, Box 234, Santa Fe, NM 87506; call for directions.) David E. C'de Baca wins top awards at Santa Fe's annual Spanish Market for his traditional Spanish New Mexican furniture. His pieces are in the collections of the Millicent Rogers Museum in Taos and the Museum of International Folk Art in Santa Fe.

Dell Woodworks (471-3005; 1326 Rufina Circle, off Siler Rd.) Finely handcrafted furniture in native New Mexican styles; custom work available. Showroom/workshop is open to visitors.

Doolings of Santa Fe (471-5956; 525 Airport Rd., off Cerrillos Rd. about five miles south of the plaza.) Ten craftspeople at Doolings produce finely crafted and finished Southwestern country furniture.

L.D. Burke III (988-3100; 72 E. San Francisco St.) Something of a phenomenon among furniture makers, L.D. Burke is known internationally for his cowboy furniture. There's more of Texas than Spain in his creations, and a lot of humor. His furniture and unusual mirrors are shown at *Simply Santa Fe;*

L.D. Burke III with Gunfighter III Children's Horn Rack.

Courtesy L.D. Burke

Spider Woman Designs (984-0136; 225 Canyon Rd.); or his showroom at 1516 Pacheco St. Call for an appointment: 986-1866 or 983-8001.

Seret and Sons Rugs and Tapestries (988-9151; 149 E. Alameda; 983-5008; 224 Galisteo.) For 29 years, Seret has been importing from Afghanistan. Besides flat-weaves and decorative carpets, he has tables, armoires, doors, columns and custom-made furniture.

Southwest Spanish Craftsmen (982-1767, 800-777-1767; 328 S. Guadalupe St. at Guadalupe Station.) This company has been specializing in Spanish Colonial and Spanish Provincial styles for more than 50 years. It furnishes reproductions to museums and private clients nationwide. Catalog is $5; write SSC, P.O. Box 1805, Santa Fe, NM 87504.

Taos

Afghan Caravan (758-4161; 119-A Bent St.) Afghan imports, mostly rugs and antique clothing.

Lo Fino (758-0298; 201 Paseo del Pueblo Sur, one block south of the plaza.) Lo Fino starts with Spanish Colonial furniture but doesn't stop there. Ten designers create imaginative works inspired by New Mexico's heritage and spiced with folk-art humor.

Taos Country Furniture and Folk Art (758-4633; 534 Paseo del Pueblo Norte, about 1.25 miles north of the plaza.) Best-known for delightful painted folk-art furniture by local artists. Also traditional Southwestern and contemporary country pieces.

Several woodworking shops in the Taos area specialize in authentic hand-carved furniture in the Spanish Colonial tradition. Among them are *Fernandez de Taos Woodworks* (758-1700; 101-B Cantu Plaza.) and *Native Furniture of Taos by Greg Flores* (758-8010 or 758-9516; 134-C Bent St.).

JEWELRY

(See also "Native American Art.")

Santa Fe

Eldorado Gold (988-3177; Eldorado Hotel, 309 W. San Francisco St.) El Dorado was the "Gold Man" of Spanish legend. This store offers one-of-a-kind jewelry designs in gold and silver with precious and semiprecious stones. It also carries a great line of *concha* belts.

Jett (988-1414; 110 Old Santa Fe Trail.) A unique assortment of contemporary jewelry including titanium, mixed metals and lots of whimsy.

Judith Cameron of Santa Fe (988-1326; 1259 Cerro Gordo, off E. Palace Ave.) Ethnic-looking styles in earrings and necklaces made of handpainted leather, semiprecious stones, beads and other materials. Studio open to visitors.

Mahdani (986-0807; 135 W. Palace Ave.) Breathtaking gold and lapis jewelry. The lapis comes from the mountains of Afghanistan and is placed in settings of pure gold by master craftspeople.

Maya (989-7590; 108 Galisteo St.) A fun shop, with the biggest variety in imported and contemporary earrings in town. Hundreds of styles, a range of prices, and lots of surprises.

Nancy Brown Custom Jewelry (982-2993; La Fonda Hotel, 111 Old Santa Fe Trail.) Unusual designs in handcrafted work by local and regional artisans. Gold, silver, gemstones, turquoise in contemporary and ethnic styles.

Ross LewAllen (983-2657; 105 E. Palace Ave.) Ross LewAllen, when he isn't designing and making silver jewelry, roams the world in search of new/old motifs. His latest is Australian Aborigine designs and other Outback inspirations, such as "Kissing Croc" pendants and pins. Each piece is a story in itself.

Taos

Artwares (758-8850; on the plaza.) Taos' only contemporary jewelry shop. Rings, earrings and other pieces in silver and gold, as well as gemstones and turquoise. Artwares is known for its fetish necklace, a sleek, contemporary silver bear.

Emily Benoist Ruffin (758-1061; 119 Bent St.) Custom and limited-edition gold jewelry with gemstones, in contemporary styles. Appointment preferred.

KITCHENWARE

Santa Fe

Cook Works (988-7676; 316 Guadalupe.) Lots of lovely imported copper cookware, elegant gear for all kinds of gourmet cookery and gourmet coffees, spices and food.

La Mesa of Santa Fe (984-1688; 225 Canyon Rd.) A shop full of handcrafted dinnerware, pottery, glassware, linens and rugs, as well as hand-blown glass sculptures.

Nambe Mills Showroom (988-3574; 112 W. San Francisco St.) Nambe Ware is a secret metal alloy (no silver, lead or pewter) that shines like sterling silver yet can be used for cooking and retains heat or cold for hours. Nambe dishes, platters, trays, plates and bowls are cast at a foundry in Santa Fe. Nambe designs have been honored by the Museum of Modern Art.

Santa Fe Pottery (988-POTS; 323 S. Guadalupe St.) One of Santa Fe's favorite lines of handcrafted stoneware, lamps, tableware and accessories. Complete place settings in several evocative Southwestern designs.

Taos

Taos Cookery (758-5435; 113 Bent St.) Handmade pottery and unusual items for the kitchen and table.

POSTERS

Santa Fe

The Santa Fe Opera, Santa Fe Chamber Music Festival, Santa Fe Indian Market and Santa Fe Spanish Market all publish quality art posters each year that become collector's items. In particular, the Chamber Music Festival's Georgia O'Keeffe poster series remains very popular. A number of Southwestern artists and photographers also publish some of their work in poster form. The following poster shops are all in the plaza area:

Plaza Poster Gallery (989-8770; 54 E. San Francisco St.)

Posters of Santa Fe, (982-6645; 111 E. Palace Ave. and 983-9697; 644 Canyon Rd.).

Twenty-First Century Fox (983-2002; 217 W. Water St.).

White Hyacinth (983-2831; 137 W. San Francisco St.)

Taos

Festival Posters (758-4667; 122-A Kit Carson Rd.)

Final Touch Frame Shop (758-4360; Padre Lane, off Don Fernando west of Taos Plaza).

Frameworks (758-4572; 732-B S. Paseo del Pueblo Sur at Sleeping Boy Plaza).

Taos Framing Co. (758-0388; 314-B Paseo del Pueblo Norte at Mariposa Plaza.)

TEXTILES AND FIBER

Santa Fe

Quilts Ltd. (988-5888; 652 Canyon Rd.) Antique traditional, Southwestern and Plains Indian quilts and clothing made from quilted fabrics.

Quilts To Cover Your Fantasy (983-7370; 201 Galisteo St.) These craftspeople have a large selection of vibrant, original contemporary quilt designs that blend well with Southwestern decor. Also pillows, accessories and clothing in contemporary quilt patterns.

Wool tapestry by Rachel Brown.

Rick Mai; Courtesy Rio Grande
Weaver's Supply

Sew Natural (982-8389; 500 Montezuma at Sanbusco Market Center.) Natural fiber fabrics for sewing, including Liberty of London cottons, Guatemalan cottons and imported silks. Sew Natural has its own line of patterns for Southwestern clothing.

Textile Arts (983-9780; 1571 Upper Canyon Rd.) Mary Hunt Kahlenberg, a former curator at the Los Angeles County Museum of Art and author of works on Navajo and Indonesian textiles, is a dealer in museum-quality tapestries and textiles from around the world. For serious collectors.

Taos

Clay and Fiber Gallery (758-8093; 135 Paseo del Pueblo Norte, behind Stables Art Center.) Finely crafted fiberart pieces and clay sculptures by contemporary craft artists.

La Lana Wools (758-9631; 136 Paseo del Pueblo Norte, just north of the plaza.) An inspiring, quality selection of hand-spun and hand-dyed wools by Taos wool growers. Also machine-spun yarns from local sheep in natural colors, as well as original handwoven clothing and accessories.

Rio Grande Weaver's Supply (758-0433; 216-B Paseo del Pueblo Norte, Taos, N.M. 87571, just north of the plaza.) Hand-dyed yarns for apparel, rugs and tapestries; weaving and spinning equipment, including the Rio Grande Loom; books and videos; dyes. $1 for mail-order catalog and price list; write above address. Next door is their retail outlet and tapestry gallery, *Weaving Southwest*, which features contemporary and traditional tapestries in highly original designs.

Twining Weavers and Contemporary Crafts Ltd. (776-8367; downtown Arroyo Seco, nine miles north of Taos on Ski Valley Rd.) Southwestern contemporary handwoven rugs, placemats, table runners and fabric; custom designs in rugs, pillows and fabric; designer clothing by Sally Bachman; commercial and hand-dyed wool yarns.

CHAPTER EIGHT
Practical Matters
INFORMATION

Office interior of the Santa Fe
New Mexican *in early 1900s.*

Courtesy Museum of New Mexico

Here is a modest encyclopedia of useful information about the Santa Fe-Taos area. Our aim is to ease everyday life for locals and help ensure that vacation time goes smoothly for visitors. This chapter covers the following topics:

AMBULANCE, FIRE, POLICE

The general emergency number (fire, police, ambulance) for Santa Fe is **911**. Other emergency numbers for **Santa Fe** include the following:

Poison Control	1-800-432-6866
Rape Crisis	473-7818
Crisis Intervention (Esperanza)	473-5200

For **Taos,** the emergency numbers are as follows:

Fire	758-2201
Police	758-2216
Sheriff	758-3361
Ambulance	758-1911
Poison Control	1-800-432-6866

AREA CODE, ZIP CODES, CITY HALLS/ LOCAL GOVERNMENT

AREA CODE

The *Area Code* for all of New Mexico is 505.

CITY HALLS

Santa Fe, New Mexico's capital, is governed by an eight-member city council (the mayor breaks tie votes). It is also the county seat of Santa Fe County, which is headed by a five-member county commission. Taos is governed by a four-member town council (again, the mayor breaks tie votes). It is the county seat of Taos County, which is headed by a three-member county commission. The two other major cities in the region with sizeable local governments are Española and Los Alamos. In addition, there are eleven Indian pueblos in the area located on reservations. Politically and legally, each pueblo is a sovereign nation led by a tribal governor and a tribal ruling council. In addition, each has its own police force. For general information, call the following numbers or write to the city or county clerk, care of the city or county in question; or to the tourist information centers at the pueblos.

Town	Telephone	Zip Code
Cochiti Pueblo	465-2244	87041
Española	753-2377	87532
Los Alamos County	662-8010	87532
Nambe Pueblo	455-2036	87501
Picuris Pueblo	587-2519	87553
Pojoaque Pueblo	455-3460	87501
Rio Arriba County	753-2992	87532
San Felipe Pueblo	867-3381	87001
San Ildefonso Pueblo	455-3549	87501
San Juan Pueblo	852-4400	87532
Santa Clara Pueblo	753-7330	87532
Santa Fe	984-6500	87504
Santa Fe County	984-5080	87504
Santo Domingo Pueblo	465-2214	87052
Taos	758-4282	87571
Taos County	758-8836	87571
Taos Pueblo	758-8626	87571
Tesuque Pueblo	983-2667	87574

BANKS

Most banks in Santa Fe and Taos are linked electronically to nationwide automatic teller systems. So if you're visiting and need extra cash, you shouldn't have any problems. Here is a list of telephone numbers and addresses of some of these banks' main offices.

Santa Fe

The Bank of Santa Fe (984-0500; main office at 241 Washington Ave.) Linked to Money, Lynx, Cirrus and Pulse systems.

First Interstate Bank (982-3671; main office at 150 Washington Ave..) Linked to Cirrus, Lynx, and Bank Mate systems.

First National Bank of Santa Fe (984-7400; main office on the plaza.) Linked to Lynx, Banquick, Plus, Pulse, and Bank Mate systems.

Sunwest Bank (471-1234; main office at 1234 St. Michael's Dr..) Linked to Amigo, Plus, Lynx, Pulse, and Bank Mate systems.

Taos

Sentinel Bank of Taos (758-4201; main office at 512 Paseo del Pueblo Sur.) Linked to Cirrus, Lynx, and Pulse systems.

First State Bank of Taos (758-6600; main office at 120 S. Plaza.) Linked to Plus and Lynx systems.

Western Bank Taos (758-8100; main office at 723 Paseo del Pueblo Sur.) Linked to Cirrus, Lynx, Plus, Pulse, and Money Card systems.

BIBLIOGRAPHY

For the traveler who enjoys reading about a region as much as visiting it, we've put together a list of some of the many books that have been written on the Santa Fe–Taos area. *Books You Can Buy* lists books available at most Santa Fe and Taos bookshops, bookstores elsewhere or from the publishers. (For information on Santa Fe–Taos booksellers, see "Bookstores" in *Shopping*.) *Books You Can Borrow* lists books that are out of print or no longer for sale. The best sources for book borrowing are described under "Libraries" in *Culture*.

Books You Can Buy

AUTOBIOGRAPHIES, BIOGRAPHIES & REMINISCENCES

Chavez, Fray Angelico. *But Time and Chance: The Story of Padre Martinez of Taos 1793-1867*. Santa Fe: Sunstone Press, 1981. 171 pp., $11.95.

Church, Peggy Pond. *The House at Otowi Bridge: The Story of Edith Warner and Los Alamos*. Albuquerque: University of New Mexico Press, 1959. 149 pp., $9.95.

Dispenza, Joseph and Turner, Louise. *Will Shuster: A Santa Fe Legend*. Santa Fe: Museum of New Mexico Press, 1989. 134 pp., $19.95.

Horgan, Paul. *Lamy of Santa Fe*. New York: The Noonday Press, 1975. 523 pp., $17.95.

Luhan, Mabel Dodge. *Winter in Taos*. Taos: Las Palomas de Taos, 1935. 237 pp., $14.95.

Miller, Michael, ed. *A New Mexico Scrapbook: Memoirs de Nuevo Mexico; Twenty-Three New Mexicans Remember Growing Up*. Huntsville, AL: Honeysuckle Imprint, 1991. 161 pp., $18.

Ortega, Pedro Ribera. *Christmas in Old Santa Fe*. Santa Fe: Sunstone Press, 1973. 102 pp., index, $6.95.

Russell, Marian. *Memoirs of Marian Russell Along the Old Santa Fe Trail*. Albuquerque: University of New Mexico Press, 1954. 163 pp., index, illust, $10.95.

CULTURAL STUDIES

Bullock, Alice. *Living Legends of the Santa Fe Country*. Santa Fe: The Lightning Tree — Jene Lyons Publishers, 1978. 96 pp., illust., $7.95.

Edelman, Sandra A. *Summer People, Winter People: A Guide to the Pueblos in the Santa Fe Area*. Santa Fe: Sunstone Press, 1986. 32 pp., index, $4.95.

Gibson, Arrell Morgan. *The Santa Fe and Taos Colonies: Age of the Muses, 1900–1942*. Norman, OK: University of Oklahoma Press, 1983. 345 pp., index, illust., $13.95.

Pearce, T.M., ed. *New Mexico Place Names: A Geographic Dictionary*. Albuquerque: University of New Mexico Press, 1965. 187 pp., index, $8.95.

Simmons, Marc. *Witchcraft in the Southwest: Spanish and Indian Supernaturalism on the Rio Grande*. Lincoln, Neb.: University of Nebraska Press. 183 pp., $6.95.

Steele, Thomas J. *Santos and Saints: The Religious Folk Art of Hispanic New Mexico*. Santa Fe: Ancient City Press, 1974. 220 pp., index, $12.95.

Weigle, Marta and Fiore, Kyle. *Santa Fe and Taos: The Writer's Era 1916–'41*. Santa Fe: Ancient City Press, 1982. 229 pp., illust., index, $16.95.

LITERARY WORKS

Anaya, Rudolfo A. *Bless Me Ultima*. Berkeley, CA: Tonatiuh-Quinto Sol International, 1972. 247 pp., $11.95.

Bradford, Richard. *Red Sky at Morning*. New York: Harper & Row, 1968. 256 pp., $8.95.

Cather, Willa. *Death Comes for the Archbishop*. New York: Vintage, 1927. 297 pp., $8.95.

Crawford, Stanley. *Mayordomo: Chronicle of an Acequia in Northern New Mexico*. New York: Anchor Books Doubleday, 1988. 231 pp., $8.95.

Hillerman, Tony ed. *The Spell of New Mexico*. Albuquerque: University of New Mexico Press, 1976. 105 pp., $9.95.

Horgan, Paul. *The Centuries of Santa Fe*. Santa Fe: William Gannon Publishers, 1956. 363 pp., Index, $9.95.

La Farge, Oliver. *Laughing Boy*. Boston: Houghton Mifflin Co., 1929. 192 pp., $4.95.

Nichols, John. *The Milagro Beanfield War*. New York: Ballantine Books, 1974. 629 pp., $5.95.

Waters, Frank. *The Man Who Killed the Deer*. New York: Farrar Rinehart, 1942. 217 pp., $3.95.

LOCAL HISTORIES

Chauvenet, Beatrice. *Hewett and Friends: A Biography of Santa Fe's Vibrant Era*. Santa Fe: Museum of New Mexico Press, 1983. 248 pp., illust., index, $16.95.

Covey, Cyclone ed., trans. *Cabeza de Vaca's Adventures in the Unknown Interior of America*. Albuquerque: University of New Mexico Press, 1983. 160 pp., $9.95.

DeBuys, William. *Enchantment and Exploitation: The Life and Hard Times of a New Mexican Mountain Range*. Albuquerque: University of New Mexico Press, 1985. 394 pp., index, illust., $15.95.

Foote, Cheryl J. *Women of the New Mexico Frontier 1846–1912*. Niwot, CO: University Press of Colorado, 1990. 198 pp., index, $19.95.

Gregg, Josiah. *The Commerce of the Prairies*. Lincoln, NB: University of Nebraska Press, 1967. 343 pp, index, $9.95.

Horgan, Paul. *Great River: The Rio Grande in North American History*. Austin, TX: Texas Monthly Press, 1984. 1020 pp., index, $14.95.

Jenkins, Myra Ellen and Schroeder, Albert H. *A Brief History of New Mexico.* Albuquerque: University of New Mexico Press, 1974. 87 pp., index, illust., $8.95.

La Farge, Oliver. *Santa Fe: The Autobiography of a Southwest Town.* Norman, OK: University of Oklahoma Press, 1959. 436 pp., index, illust., $15.95.

Noble, David Grant, ed. *Santa Fe: History of an Ancient City.* Santa Fe: School of American Research Press, 1989. 155 pp., index, $16.95.

Simmons, Marc. *New Mexico: An Interpretive History.* Albuquerque: University of New Mexico Press, 1988. 207 pp., $10.95.

PHOTOGRAPHIC STUDIES

Brewer, Robert and McDowell, Steve. *The Persistence of Memory: New Mexico's Churches.* Santa Fe: Museum of New Mexico Press, 1991. 152 pp., $39.95.

Clark, William; and Klanner, Edward; and Parsons, Jack; and Plossu, Bernard. *Santa Fe: The City in Photographs.* Santa Fe: Fotowest Publishing, 1984. 72 pp., $14.95.

Morand, Sheila. *Santa Fe: Then and Now.* Santa Fe: Sunstone Press, 1984. 96 pp., index, $14.95.

Nichols, John and Davis, William. *If Mountains Die: A New Mexico Memoir.* New York: Alfred A. Knopf, 1987. 144 pp., $19.95.

Robin, Arthur H., Ferguson, William M., and Ferguson, Lisa. *Rock Art of Bandelier National Monument.* Albuquerque: University of New Mexico Press, 1989. 156 pp., index, $29.95.

Sherman, John. *Taos: A Pictorial History.* Santa Fe: William Gannon Publishers, 1990. 164 pp., $19.95.

RECREATION

Matthews, Kay. *Cross-Country Skiing in Northern New Mexico: An Introduction and Trail Guide.* Placitas, NM: Acequia Madre Press, 1986. 96 pp., maps, $7.95.

Pinkerton, Elaine. *Santa Fe on Foot: Walking, Running and Bicycling Routes in the City Different.* Santa Fe: Ocean Tree, 1986. 125 pp., illust., maps, $7.95.

Santa Fe Group of the Sierra Club. *Day Hikes in the Santa Fe Area.* 1990. 192 pp., index, $8.95.

Ungnade, Herbert E. *Guide to the New Mexico Mountains.* Albuquerque: University of New Mexico Press, 1988. 235 pp, index, $10.95.

TRAVEL

Chronic, Halka. *Roadside Geology of New Mexico.* Missoula, MT: Mountain Press Publishing Co., 1987. 255 pp., index, $11.95.

Fugate, Frances L. and Roberta B. *Roadside History of New Mexico.* Missoula, MT: Mountain Press Publishing Co., 1989. 483 pp., index, $15.95.

Smith, Toby. *Odyssey.* Albuquerque: University of New Mexico Press, 1987. 182 pp., $11.95.

Workers of the Writers' Program of the Work Projects Administration in the State of New Mexico. *The WPA Guide to 1930s New Mexico*. Tucson: The University of Arizona Press, 1940. 458 pp., index, $16.95.

Books You Can Borrow

Blacker, Irwin. *Taos*. Cleveland, OH: World Publishers, 1959. A fictional account of the 1680 Pueblo Revolt which drove the Spaniards out of New Mexico for 12 years. Current Spanish-Indian relations in New Mexico cannot be understood without knowing the historical reasons for the revolt.

Boyd, E. *Popular Arts of Spanish New Mexico*. Santa Fe: Museum of New Mexico Press, 1974. A photographic (color) study of the entire spectrum of Hispanic art in the Land of Enchantment.

Henderson, Alice Corbin. *Brothers of Light: The Penitentes of the Southwest*. N.Y.: Harcourt, Brace & Co., 1937. One of the best treatments of the Penitente phenomenon.

Kendall, George. *Narrative of the Texan-Santa Fe Expedition*. Albuquerque: University of New Mexico Press, 1844. Illust., maps. This is the history of the beginning of the conflict between Texas and New Mexico that is still evident today, mostly in attitudes.

Magoffin, Susan Shelby. *Down the Santa Fe Trail and Into New Mexico*. Yale University Press, 1926. Illust. The diary of the teenage bride of a Santa Fe trader who was a member of the first wagon train into New Mexico following the conquering United States Army in 1846.

Robertson, Edna. *Artists of the Caminos and Canyons: The Early Years*. Peregrine, 1976. A study of the turn-of-the-century artists in Santa Fe and Taos.

Ross, Calvin. *Sky Determines*. Albuquerque: University of New Mexico Press, 1948. A unique book covering New Mexico history, weather, art, landscape, etc.

Spivey, R. *Maria*. Flagstaff, AZ: Northland Press, 1979. About the famous San Ildefonso Pueblo potter.

Twitchell, Ralph E. *Old Santa Fe*. Santa Fe: New Mexican, 1925. A portrait of the city from its beginnings to the 20th century.

CLIMATE AND WEATHER REPORTS

CLIMATE

Santa Fe and Taos are blessed with a healthful, dynamic, high-desert climate. Throughout the year the air is dry, and at 7,000 feet (the approximate elevation of both cities) nights are always cool. There are 300 days of sunshine a year.

Sound wonderful? It is. But you'll enjoy it more if you take a few precautions. Bring suntan lotion no matter what time of year you visit. At this altitude, serious sunburns can develop after ten minutes' exposure. You'll also

Santa Fe's night sky lit up by an electrical storm.

Kitty Leaken

want to have chapstick and skin lotion. Be sure to take it easy when you first get here to give your body a chance to adjust to the altitude. To keep your energy up, eat foods that are high in carbohydrates, like pasta, rice and pancakes — and go easy on alcohol, tranquilizers and sleeping pills.

Santa Fe averages 14 inches of rain a year; Taos, 12. By way of contrast, Los Angeles, a relatively dry city, gets 9 inches of moisture annually, while drizzly Seattle receives 40 inches. Most of the rain comes in the summer, during brief, sometimes violent, afternoon thundershowers. If you visit during July and August you'll benefit from an umbrella.

The average snowfall in both Santa Fe and Taos is 35 inches. In the mountains, the snowfall increases dramatically. Approximately 200 inches of snow falls on the Santa Fe Ski Area every winter, while Taos Ski Valley is regularly buried under 320 inches of white stuff, making it one of the best ski resorts in North America.

Be sure to dress warmly in winter. Santa Fe's normal high in January is 40 degrees, the low 18; in Taos the January high is also 40, but the low is a chilly nine degrees.

In Santa Fe the mercury soars to 82 on a typical July day and drops to 55 at night; while in Taos, July daytime temperatures average 86 but plunge to 49 at night. For outdoor evening activities in the summer, like a night at the Santa Fe Opera or an after-dinner stroll around Taos Plaza, you'll want a sweater.

Temperatures are more moderate in spring and fall. Average Santa Fe temperatures in April are 59 during the day and 35 at night; in Taos April temperatures average 63 during the day and 28 at night. In a typical October, Santa Fe's temperatures average 61 by day and 38 by night; Taos 66 by day and 31 by night.

For current weather information in the Santa Fe area, call 473-2211. In Taos, call 758-8878.

DAY-CARE

Child-care options abound in Santa Fe but are less common in Taos. Services include nurseries and pre-schools, churches and private babysitting organizations. Here is a sampling of what's available.

Santa Fe

Bright Beginnings Child Development Centers (473-9525).
Eastside Preschool (983-8212).
Garcia Street Club Day Care-Preschool Center (983-9512).
Santa Fe Kid Connection (471-3100).

Taos

Leaping Lizards Preschool & Summer Camp (758-1311).
Trudy's Discovery House (758-1659).

GUIDED TOURS

There are a number of fun and informative sightseeing tours in the Santa Fe-Taos area. For something relatively brief and informal, a local cab driver can usually be persuaded to drive you around and impart colorful histories that only a cabbie might know. For more organized, detailed tours, consider the following:

Santa Fe

The Grayline (983-9491 or 983-6565), a bus and trolley service, provides a number of different sightseeing tours of Santa Fe and surrounding areas. A three-hour historical tour of the city is offered year round (open coach in summer, closed van in winter). The 1991 rate was $15 per person. A shorter tour of the city (1.25 hours) can be had by boarding *Grayline's Roadrunner* bus, an open coach that departs from the northwest corner of the plaza every hour during the summer. Gray Line also visits Bandelier National Monument (a half-day tour at $35 per person in 1991) and Puye Cliff Dwellings (another half-day tour at $38 per person in 1991).

If you want a leisurely walking tour of the downtown area, there are a number of options to choose from. One of the best is *Afoot in Santa Fe Walking Tours* (983-3701), led by longtime resident Charles Porter. In the winter, you must call Porter ahead of time to arrange a tour. But in summer he offers two tours a day, Monday through Saturday, and one on Sunday. Departure times are 9:30 a.m. and 1:30 p.m. (the Sunday tour is in the morning). Meet him at the southeast side of the parking lot at the Inn at Loretto, located at 211 Old Santa Fe Trail, a block southeast of the plaza. The tour lasts approximately 2.5

hours and is well worth the fee ($10 in 1991). Porter is knowledgeable on Santa Fe's history and culture, and can clue you in on shopping bargains.

Frank Montaño, a Santa Fe city councilor, will take you on *Historical Walking Tours of Santa Fe* (984-8235). The focus here is on the city's historic sites. Call Montaño for information on departure times and rates. Another first-rate walking tour of the downtown area is offered by *Waite Thompson*. Departure times, rates and length of tours are identical to Afoot in Santa Fe. Meet Thompson in the La Fonda Hotel lobby at the Santa Fe Detours desk. Reservations aren't necessary, but if you want further information call 983-6565.

Discover Santa Fe (982-4979), *Santa Fe Detours* (983-6565) and *RojoTours* (983-8333) provide customized expeditions not only of Santa Fe but of nearby Indian pueblos and other sites. *Pathways Customized Tours* (982-5382) provides a similar variety of excursions, including trips to the magnificent redrock country of Abiquiu, an hour north of Santa Fe, where Georgia O'Keeffe lived and painted. For an entertaining, knowledgeable tour guide, you can't do much better than Bruce Kaiper, a well-known writer and filmmaker. He'll take you virtually anywhere you want to go, including visits with the best Indian, Spanish and contemporary artists in their studios or homes. Call Kaiper at *Artifacts Customized Tours* (753-9762 or 455-2262) for more details. Another excellent tour guide is *Rain Parrish* (984-8236), a Native American, who will introduce you to the Indian pueblos, ancient Indian sites and contemporary Indian artists. If you have your own car and want your own guide, try *Chamisa Touring Service* (988-1343). They'll provide you with guides trained in Southwestern anthropology who'll take you to Indian dances, secluded Spanish villages and Old West ghost towns.

Speaking of ghosts, *Ghost Tours of Santa Fe* (983-0111) will take you to 14 places in and near the Santa Fe plaza that are reputed to be haunted. During the summer, 90-minute tours begin at 7:30 p.m. at the plaza's southeast corner (the 1991 rate was $10 for adults). In winter, dinner or desert parties with ghost stories told around a fire are available for groups of 10 or more.

Taos

The *Grayline* (983-9491) in Santa Fe makes round-trip scenic tours to Taos daily in the summer. Highlights include a ride on the High Road to Taos and a stop at Taos Pueblo. *Faust's Transportation* (758-3410 or 758-7359) offers a day-long tour of Santa Fe (the 1991 rate was $40 per person) that includes visits to historical sites and popular Canyon Rd., filled with shops and art galleries. Faust's also provides afternoon tours of Taos, with stops at museums, shops, Taos Pueblo and the Rio Grande Gorge Bridge (the 1991 ticket price was $20 for adults).

For a tour of Taos on foot, try *Charlotte Graebner's Taos Tours* (758-3861). Graebner is a 20-year resident with a wealth of information on history, art, folklore and shopping bargains. From June through September she offers tours every day except Sunday. The tour starts at the Kit Carson House Museum, located one block east of the plaza on Kit Carson Rd., at 10 a.m. The rest of the year apppointments must be made in advance, and tours are only given if the roads aren't too icy.

Perhaps the most thrilling way to see Taos' beautiful setting is from the air. *Horizon Air Service* (758-9501) offers scenic flights for $50 a person per hour (1991 rate).

HANDICAPPED SERVICES

Both Santa Fe and Taos have made serious efforts in recent years to improve access for the disabled. The Santa Fe city government has put together a free, 68-page booklet entitled *Access Santa Fe,* which identifies where handicapped parking spots are located and which establishments in town are handicapped-accessible. To obtain a copy, call 984-6568 or write the *City of Santa Fe, Community Services Division*, P.O. Box 909, Santa Fe, NM 87504-0909. Out-of-state handicapped visitors can obtain a temporary placard for handicapped parking by calling the *New Mexico Motor Vehicle Division* at 827-7601. *Capital City Cab Co.* (988-1211) offers disabled people a 45-percent discount on fares. No listing of handicapped parking spaces or of handicapped-accessible facilities is available in Taos. Your best bet for information is the *Taos County Planning Department* (751-2000).

HOSPITALS

Santa Fe

St. Vincent Hospital 983-3361; 455 St. Michael's Dr.

Española

Española Hospital 753-7111; 1010 Spruce St.

Los Alamos

Los Alamos Medical Center 662-4201; 3917 West Rd.

Taos

Holy Cross Hospital 758-8883; 630 Paseo del Pueblo Sur.

LATE NIGHT FOOD AND FUEL

If the munchies hit or your fuel gauge drops perilously low in the wee small hours, there are places you can go. Santa Fe in particular has an abundance of convenience stores, restaurants and gas stations that stay open 24 hours a day.

CONVENIENCE STORES

Allsup's 3000 Cerrillos Rd., Santa Fe.
Allsup's 2000 St. Michael's Dr., Santa Fe.
Allsup's 507 Paseo del Pueblo Norte, Taos.

GASOLINE STATIONS

Chevron Food Mart 3354 Cerrillos Rd., Santa Fe.
Cerrillos Self-Serve 1103 Cerrillos Rd., Santa Fe.
Stop 'n' Go St. Francis Dr. at Sawmill Rd., Santa Fe.
Allsup's 507 Paseo del Pueblo Norte, Taos.

RESTAURANTS

Carrows 1718 St. Michael's Dr., Santa Fe.
Denny's 3004 Cerrillos Rd., Santa Fe.
Dunkin' Donuts 1085 S. St. Francis Dr., Santa Fe.
The Kettle 4250 Cerrillos Rd., Santa Fe.

MEDIA: MAGAZINES AND NEWSPAPERS, RADIO AND TELEVISION STATIONS

MAGAZINES AND NEWSPAPERS

Adobe Press (758-6522; 1048 Paseo del Pueblo Sur, Taos). A weekly newspaper that offers international and local news and feature stories. Covers Taos and environs.

Albuquerque Journal (1-800-641-3451; 320 Galisteo St., Santa Fe). A statewide, daily morning newspaper that includes a "Journal North" section published Tuesday through Saturday and distributed in northern New Mexico.

Crosswinds (986-0105; 914 Baca St., Santa Fe). A progressive monthly newspaper with a focus on the environment, the arts, education and local politics.

New Mexico Magazine (827-0220; Joseph M. Montoya Building, 1100 St. Francis Dr., Santa Fe). A general-interest monthly published by state government, covering New Mexico culture, history and travel.

The New Mexican (983-3303; 202 E. Marcy St., Santa Fe). A general-interest daily distributed in northern New Mexico.

Sangre de Cristo Chronicle (377-2358; Drawer I, Angel Fire). A news weekly covering Taos, Angel Fire, Red River and Eagle Nest.

The Santa Fe Reporter (988-5541; P.O. Box 2306, Santa Fe). An award-winning weekly newspaper known for in-depth articles and eye-catching special supplements. Published each Wednesday and distributed free of charge throughout Santa Fe.

The Santa Fean Magazine (983-8914; 1440-A St. Francis Dr., Santa Fe). A monthly arts-oriented publication.

Santa Fe Sun (989-8381; 322 Montezuma, Santa Fe). A community-oriented monthly newspaper that focuses on New Age issues, grass-roots activism and local news and feature stories.

Taos Magazine (984-1773 or 758-4047; Box 1380, Taos). An arts magazine published eight times a year, in January, March, May, July, August, September and October.

Taos News (758-2241; 120 Camino De La Placita Taos). Taos' biggest weekly newspaper, covering local news and human interest. Comes out every Thursday.

RADIO STATIONS

KBAC-FM 98.1 (471-7110) Santa Fe; Alternative.

KBOM-FM 106.7 (982-0088) Santa Fe; Contemporary Spanish.

KDCE-AM 970 (753-2201) Española; Spanish.

KIVA-FM 105.1 (983-4487) Santa Fe; Rock.

KKIT-AM 1340 (758-2231) Taos; News, sports, weather, music.

KLSK-FM 104.1 (983-5878) Santa Fe; Classic rock.

KNYN-FM 105.9 (471-5696) Santa Fe; Country.

KTAO-FM 101.7 (758-1017) Taos; General.

KTRC-AM 1400 (982-2666) Santa Fe; General.

TELEVISION STATIONS

KCHF-TV Channel 11 (473-1111) Santa Fe; Religious.

KNMZ-TV Channel 2 (982-2422) Santa Fe; Old movies and sitcoms.

The major television stations are located in Albuquerque:

KGGM-TV Channel 13 (243-2285; CBS affiliate.

KNME-TV Channel 5 (242-5555); Public.

KOAT-TV Channel 7 (884-7777); ABC affiliate.

KOB-TV Channel 4 (243-4411); NBC affiliate.

REAL ESTATE

Skylights, adobe, brick floors, rough-hewn *viga* ceilings, intimate *kiva* fireplaces, expansive views — that's Santa Fe Style. If owning a home in the Land of Enchantment sounds like a dream come true, then you might be interested in a little housing information.

The housing market in Santa Fe and Taos continues to boom. Property values are on the rise again, after a brief leveling out in early 1991. For many who live here, the trend is alarming. Old-time Santa Feans and Taoseños are driven out of their communities because of escalating costs. This has caused some resentment against the growing number of wealthy "outsiders." However, most people here are naturally friendly. Every newcomer will be welcome, provided he or she is respectful of the area's peoples and traditions.

If you're shopping for real estate in the Santa Fe or Taos areas, you can get information in a variety of ways. To get a list of Realtors, consult the *Yellow Pages* or, contact the local chambers of commerce. The **Santa Fe Chamber of Commerce** (983-7317) is located at 333 Montezuma Ave., Santa Fe, NM 87501. The mailing address for the **Taos Chamber of Commerce** (758-3873) is P.O. Drawer 1, Taos, NM 87571. Both organizations will send lists of their Realtor members.

If you're thinking about buying property here, it is a good idea to familiarize yourself with local zoning laws, building permits, restrictive covenants and so forth. A good source of information is a small book called *Understanding Santa Fe Real Estate* by Karen Walker, available at most Santa Fe bookstores or from **Ancient City Press** (982-8195; 517 Alarid, 87501). For telephone numbers to city halls and county offices, see "Area Codes" in this chapter.

Another way of getting real estate information is to follow the market in the newspapers (see "Media" in this chapter) or various periodicals published by realty agencies. *Homes and Land of Santa Fe and Northern New Mexico* is a free monthly publication that provides up-to-date information on the housing market. It's distributed monthly at various shops around town. You can have a copy sent to you by calling 1-800-277-7800, or 982-2210; or by writing P.O. Box 5756, Santa Fe, NM 87502. Other home buyers' guides include the free monthlies, *The Real Estate Book* (473-5225, 1-800-841-3401; 2442 Cerrillos Rd., Suite 309, Santa Fe, NM 87501); *Home Santa Fe Style* (984-0111); and *Classic: The Magazine of Fine Homes from Santa Fe Properties* (982-4466; 1000 Paseo de Peralta, Santa Fe, NM 87501). There are no similar publications in Taos, except for brochures distributed by various real estate firms that you can get from the chamber of commerce.

RELIGIOUS SERVICES AND ORGANIZATIONS

With many distinct cultures and strong reputations as spiritual centers, Santa Fe and Taos have unusually active and diverse religious communities. They include the various Protestant sects, Spanish Catholicism and indigenous Native American religious practices, a healthy Tibetan Buddhist sect in Santa Fe, a group of Hindu Sikhs in Española, and a Moslem community in Abiquiu. The New Age movement, a mix of mysticism, psychology and alternative medicine, is also here in full force.

For information about church and synagogue services in Santa Fe, consult the Saturday edition of the *New Mexican*. In Taos, consult the *Taos News*, which comes out every Thursday. The Friday "Pasatiempo" section of the *New Mexican* lists dates and approximate times of sacred Indian dances at the pueblos (for more precise information, call the pueblos themselves — see "Local Government" at the beginning of this chapter or "Pueblos" in *Culture*, Chapter

Four). For a complete listing of mainstream religious organizations and their telephone numbers, see the Yellow Pages of the Santa Fe and Taos phone books.

Perhaps the most famous of the local New Age practitioners is Chris Griscom, who did past-life regressions for Shirley MacLaine and who runs the **Light Institute of Galisteo** (983-1975). Other practitioners run the gamut, from the mystical end of the movement with its channelers, crystal healers, astrologers and aura balancers to the medical end with its array of acupuncturists, massage therapists, herbalists, naturopaths, iridolgists and others. A variety of psychologists also employ orthodox and unorthodox techniques (Freudian, Jungian, Gestalt, Reiki and more) to help people live more balanced, harmonious, and productive lives.

For specific information on this eclectic, esoteric bunch, helpful publications include *Who's Who in the Healing Arts*, by Julie Von Erffa, a guide to healers in the Santa Fe area available in most Santa Fe and Taos bookstores; and *New Age Networking Journal*, a similar guide that can help you hook up with various New Age groups, healing ceremonies and such.

ROAD SERVICE

Here is a listing of some 24-hour emergency road services in the Santa Fe–Taos region.

Santa Fe

A-1 Towing (983-1616).
Jaffa's Towing Service (471-7036).

Taos

Cohn Brothers Wrecker Service (758-2053).

Española

Holmes Wrecker Service (753-3460).

Los Alamos

Knecht Automotive (662-9743).

SCHOOLS

PUBLIC SCHOOLS

Santa Fe

There are 18 elementary schools, three middle schools and two high schools in the Santa Fe Public Schools system. For further information, call the administrative offices of the **Santa Fe Public Schools District** (982-2631).

Taos

Six elementary schools, one middle school and one high school make up the **Taos Municipal Schools** system (758-5200).

PRIVATE AND PAROCHIAL SCHOOLS

Santa Fe

The Brunn School (983-8432).
Capital Christian School (982-2080).
Cristo Rey School (983-8411).
First Baptist Church (983-9141).
Little Earth School (988-1968).
Rio Grande School (983-1621).
Santa Fe Indian School (988-6921).
Santa Fe Preparatory School (982-1829).
Santa Fe Waldorf School (983-9727).
St. Anne School (982-3712).
St. Catherine Indian School (982-1889).
St. Francis Cathedral School (982-0331).
St. Michael's High School (983-7353).

Taos

San Francisco de Asis Catholic School (758-1236).
Sangre de Cristo School (758-4131).
Taos Christian Academy (758-3388).
Taos Valley School (758-4155, 758-4148).
Trudy's Discovery House (758-1659).
Vista Grande (758-9306).

COLLEGES

The College of Santa Fe (473-6011).
St. John's College (982-3691).
Santa Fe Community College (471-8200).

Glossary

Glossary

For the most part, Spanish pronunciation is phonetic. That is, it sounds the way it looks with a few exceptions: *ll* sounds like "yuh"; *j* sounds like "h"; *qu* sounds like "k," and *ñ* sounds like "ny." There are also a few tricky rules — for example, double *r*'s are trilled and *d* is often pronounced "th," but we'll leave these details for Spanish classes. Following, then, are reasonable pronunciations and short definitions for Spanish words (and a few other terms) that are commonly used in the Santa Fe-Taos area.

acequia (Ah-SEH-kee-ya) — irrigation ditch.

Anasazi (An-a-SAH-zee) — Navajo word meaning "ancient strangers," used to refer to the peoples who inhabited such places as Chaco Canyon, Mesa Verde and Bandelier National Monument from 900-1300 A.D.

arroyo (a-ROY-oh) — dry gully or streambed.

arroz (a-ROSS) — rice.

banco (BONK-oh) — adobe bench, usually an extension of an adobe wall.

bulto (BOOL-toh) — traditional Hispanic, three-dimensional carving of a saint.

burrito (Boo-REE-toh) — flour tortilla usually wrapped around a filling of beans, meat, cheese and sauce.

canales (ka-NAL-ess) — gutters, rainspouts.

cantina (kan-TEE-na) — saloon or barroom.

capirotada (ka-pi-ro-TA-da) — bread pudding.

carne (KAR-ne) — meat.

carne adovada (KAR-ne ah-do-VA-da) — meat chunks (usually pork) marinated in red chile sauce.

carne asada (KAR-ne ah-SA-da) — roast beef.

carreta (ka-RET-ah) — wagon.

casita (ka-SEE-ta) — cottage, one-room guest house.

chile, or *chili* (CHEE-leh) — sauce made from either red or green chile peppers that is used for seasoning most foods in northern New Mexico.

chile relleno (CHEE-leh re-YEH-no) — crisp, batter-fried green chile pepper stuffed with chicken and/or cheese.

chorizo (cho-REE-so) — spicy Mexican sausage.

con queso (cone KEH-so) — with cheese.

concha (KON-cha) — belt of inscribed silver plates originally made by the Navajo Indians.

corbel (Kor-BELL) — wooden beam support, usually ornately carved.

chimenea (Chee-me-NEH-ya) — chimney.

curandera (Coor-an-DEH-ra) — female Hispanic healer who uses a combination of herbal and other folk remedies.

empanada (em-pa-NAH-da) — fried pie stuffed with seasoned, chopped meat and vegetables or fruit, then sealed and deep fried. In northern New Mexico often filled with piñon nuts, currants, spices and wine.

enchilada (en-chi-LA-da) — flour tortilla filled with cheese, chicken or meat and covered with red or green chile.

fajitas (fa-HEE-tas)— small strips of highly seasoned, charbroiled meat eaten in a rolled tortilla with guacamole and sour cream.

farolito (far-oh-LEE-toh) — paper bag containing a glowing candle, often displayed in rows around Christmastime to symbolize the arrival of the Christ Child.

flan (flan) — caramel custard covered with burnt-sugar syrup, a traditional northern New Mexican dessert.

fry bread (not "fried bread") — *sopaipillas* made by the Pueblo Indians.

guacamole (gwok-a-MOLE-eh) — a thick sauce or paste made with a mix of mashed avocados and salsa.

hacienda (AH-see-EN-da) — a large estate, dwelling or plantation.

horno (OR-no) — beehive-shaped outdoor oven for the making of bread, originally brought from Spain.

huevos (WEH-vose) — eggs.

huevos rancheros (WEH-vose ran-CHEH-ros) — fried eggs with red chile sauce, cheese and lettuce.

jalapeño (HALL-a-PEN-yoh) — small hot pepper.

kachina doll (ka-CHEE-na) — a small wooden doll representing a Hopi spirit, usually carved from cottonwood.

kiva (KEE-va) — circular underground chamber used by the Pueblo Indians for ceremonial and other purposes.

kiva fireplace — traditional adobe fireplace, usually small, beehive-shaped and placed in a corner.

latillas (la-TEE-ahs) — network of thin wooden strips placed over beams or *vigas* just beneath the roof.

luminaria (loo-mi-NA-ree-ah) — hot, smoky bonfire made of pitchy piñon pine to celebrate the Christmas season.

nachos (NA-chos)— tortilla chips covered with a mix of beans, cheese and chile, baked and served as hors d'oeuvres.

natillas (na-TEE-ahs) — vanilla custard, a traditional northern New Mexican dessert.

nicho (NEE-cho) — recessed niche in an adobe wall for holding a statue or other ornament.

panocha (pan-OH-cha) — wheat flour pudding.

placita (pla-SEE-ta) — patio.

pollo (PO-yo) — chicken.

portal (por-TALL) — covered patio or sidewalk with supports and fixed roof.

posada (po-SA-da) — resting place or inn.

posole (po-SOLE-eh) — a hominy-like corn stew.

pueblo (PWEB-loh) — a Native American communal village of the Southwest consisting of multi-tiered adobe structures with flat roofs around a central plaza.

quesadillas (KEH-sa-DEE-yas) — lightly grilled tortillas stuffed with chicken, beef or beans.

reredo (reh-REH-doh) — carved altar screen for church.

retablo (reh-TAB-loh) — traditional Hispanic painting of a saint on a wooden plaque.

salsa (SAL-sa) — traditional northern New Mexican hot sauce composed of tomatoes, onions, peppers and spices.

santero (San-TEH-roh) — artist who depicts saints.

santo (SAN-toh) — a painted or carved representation of a saint.

sopaipilla (so-pie-PEE-ya) — Spanish popover. These "little pillows" puff up when fried, providing convenient hollows to fill with honey or butter.

taco (TA-koh) — folded corn tortilla usually filled with beans, meat, cheese, tomato and lettuce.

tamale (ta-MAL-eh) — corn meal stuffed with chicken or pork and red chile, wrapped in corn husks and steamed.

tapas (TAP-ahs) — appetizers.

tortilla (tor-TEE-ya) — thin pancake made of corn meal or wheat flour.

tostados (tos-TA-dos) — corn tortillas quartered and fried until crisp, usually eaten as hors d'oeuvres.

ristra (REES-tra) — string of dried red chiles, often hung on front porches.

trastero (tras-TER-oh) — wooden, free-standing closet or chest of drawers dating from the 17th century; usually ornately carved.

vigas (VEE-gas) — heavy ceiling beams usually made of rough-hewn treetrunks, traditional in Southwest architecture.

zaguan (zag-WAN) — long, covered porch.

Index

Index

LODGING BY PRICE

Price Codes

Inexpensive	Up to $50
Moderate	$50 - $80
Expensive	$80 - $120
Very Expensive	Over $120

Santa Fe

INEXPENSIVE
Alamo Lodge
Cottonwood Court
Park Inn
Pecos Trail Inn
Santa Fe Youth Hostel
Silver Saddle Motel
Stage Coach Motor Inn
Thunderbird Inn
Warren Inn

MODERATE
El Rey Inn
Garrett's Desert Inn
Inn on the Paseo
Santa Fe Motel

EXPENSIVE
Adobe Abode
Alexander's Inn

RESTAURANTS BY PRICE

EXPENSIVE
Como's Ristorante Italiano
E.K. Mas
El Farol
Fabio's
Garfield Grill
Japanese Kitchen
La Casa Sena
Rosedale

VERY EXPENSIVE
Coyote Cafe
Julian's
Pink Adobe
SantaCafe

Near Santa Fe
INEXPENSIVE
Angelina's
Cafe del Arroyo
Roadrunner Cafe
San Marcos Cafe
Tesuque Village Market

MODERATE

The Blue Window
Hot Shots
Rancho de Chimayó

EXPENSIVE
Anthony's at the Delta
El Nido

VERY EXPENSIVE
The Legal Tender

Taos
INEXPENSIVE
Floyd's Restaurant &
   Lounge
Golden Dragon Chinese
   Restaurant
Mainstreet Bakery
Michael's Kitchen
Pizza Emergency

MODERATE
Casa de Valdez
Double A Grill
El Patio de Taos

Garden Restaurant
La Cigale
Ogelvie's Bar & Grille

EXPENSIVE
Apple Tree Restaurant
Doc Martin's
Lambert's of Taos

Near Taos
INEXPENSIVE
Coyote Creek Cafe
L. Roberto's
The Outback
Northtown Restaurant

MODERATE
Andy's La Fiesta
Embudo Station

EXPENSIVE
Brett House
Carl's French Quarter
The Stakeout

RESTAURANTS BY CUISINE

For your convenience, we list here restaurants serving specific cuisines. Those places serving more than one type of cuisine are listed under more than one category. Keep in mind that restaurants featuring American and/or Continental cuisine are many in number, and that their definitions of cooking styles are difficult to categorize. Likewise, you may find little difference between Southwestern, New Mexican and Northern New Mexican cuisine; however, we list them separately because there <u>are</u> differences — especially in the use of chile and spices (see "Restaurants," page 134).

Santa Fe
AMERICAN
Cloud Cliff Bakery & Cafe
423
Garfield Grill
La Plazuela at La Fonda
Peppers Restaurant &
   Cantina
San Francisco Street Bar &
   Grill
Staab House
SantaCafe
Tecolote Cafe
Tiny's Restaurant &
   Lounge
Zia Diner

BARBECUE
Stephanie's Bones
Vickie Lee's Southern
   Barbeque

CHINESE
Peking Palace
Szechwan
Yin Yang

CONTINENTAL
Como's Ristorante Italiano
Garfield Grill
Grant Corner Inn
La Casa Sena
La Plazuela at La Fonda
Little Anita's

Pink Adobe
Zia Diner

EAST INDIAN
Delhi Palace

FRENCH
Santa Fe Gourmet

INTERNATIONAL
E.K. Mas
El Farol

ITALIAN
Como's Ristorante Italiano
Fabio's
Julian's
Pranzo Italian Grill

MAPS

A Note on the Author

Teresa Wright

Brandt Morgan has lived in the Santa Fe-Taos area since 1985. Born in Seattle, he graduated from the University of Washington in 1967 and spent two years with the Peace Corps in Brazil. He is the author of a guidebook to Seattle's parks (*Enjoying Seattle's Parks*, Greenwood Publications) and the co-author of four books in *Tom Brown's Field Guide* series on wilderness survival, animal tracking, nature observation and city survival (Berkley Publishing). He has also written for numerous national and local publications, including *Americana, Audubon, Mother Earth News, Pacific Northwest*, the *Albuquerque Journal* and the *Santa Fe Reporter*. In addition to freelance writing and editing, he has taught grade school, mountain climbing, wilderness survival and nature awareness skills. He presently lives in Santa Fe with Teresa Wright and their son Travis.

The pages of this book were composed on Quark Express by Berkshire Publication Services, Gt. Barrington, Massachusetts. The typeface, Palatino, created in the mid-20th century by Hermann Zapf, is named for the famous 16th-century calligrapher, Giambattista Palatino. Design of original text for the Great Destination series was by Janice Lindstrom, Stockbridge, Massachusetts.

Santa Fe and Taos Maps

SANTA FE AND TAOS RECREATIONAL SITES

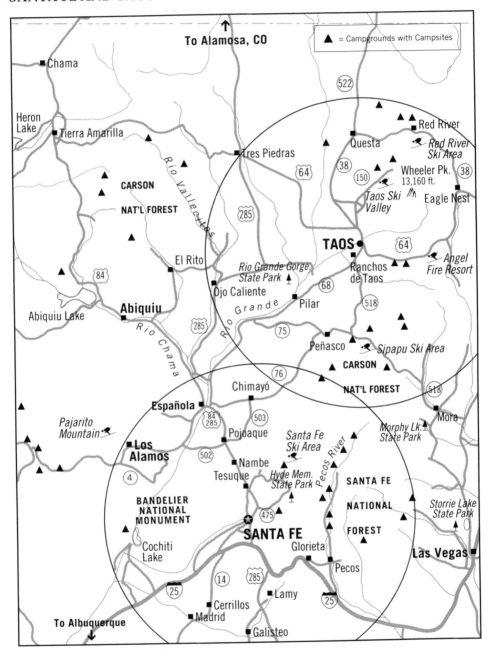

To Alamosa, CO

▲ = Campgrounds with Campsites

Chama

Heron Lake

Tierra Amarilla

Tres Piedras

522

Red River

Questa

Red River Ski Area

64

38

150

Wheeler Pk. 13,160 ft.

38

CARSON NAT'L FOREST

Rio Vallecitos

285

Taos Ski Valley

Eagle Nest

El Rito

Rio Grande Gorge State Park

TAOS

64

Angel Fire Resort

84

Abiquiu

Ojo Caliente

285

Abiquiu Lake

Rio Chama

Rio Grande

Pilar

68

Ranchos de Taos

518

75

Peñasco

Sipapu Ski Area

76

CARSON NAT'L FOREST

518

Chimayó

Española

Mora

Pajarito Mountain

84 285

503

Pojoaque

Santa Fe Ski Area

Morphy Lk. State Park

502

Nambe

Pecos River

Los Alamos

4

Tesuque

Hyde Mem. State Park

SANTA FE

Storrie Lake State Park

BANDELIER NATIONAL MONUMENT

475

NATIONAL

SANTA FE

Cochiti Lake

FOREST

Glorieta

Las Vegas

Pecos

25

14

285

Lamy

25

To Albuquerque

Cerrillos

Madrid

Galisteo

GREATER SANTA FE

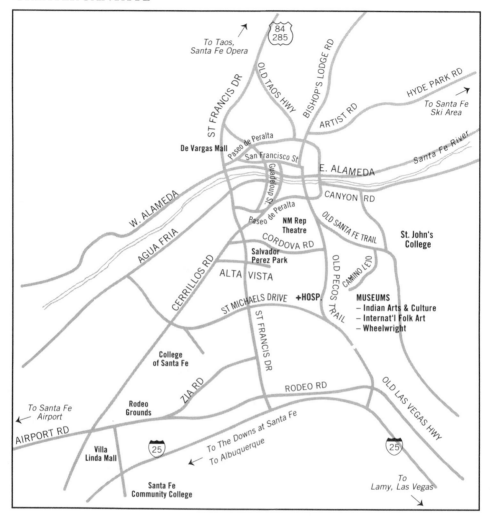

To Taos,
Santa Fe Opera

84
285

ST FRANCIS DR

OLD TAOS HWY

BISHOP'S LODGE RD

ARTIST RD

HYDE PARK RD

To Santa Fe
Ski Area

Paseo de Peralta

De Vargas Mall

San Francisco St

Guadeloup St

E. ALAMEDA

Santa Fe River

W. ALAMEDA

CANYON RD

AGUA FRIA

Paseo de Peralta

NM Rep
Theatre

OLD SANTA FE TRAIL

St. John's
College

CORDOVA RD

CERRILLOS RD

Salvador
Perez Park

ALTA VISTA

CAMINO LEJO

OLD PECOS TRAIL

ST MICHAELS DRIVE   +HOSP.

MUSEUMS
– Indian Arts & Culture
– Internat'l Folk Art
– Wheelwright

ST FRANCIS DR

College
of Santa Fe

ZIA RD

RODEO RD

OLD LAS VEGAS HWY

To Santa Fe
Airport

Rodeo
Grounds

AIRPORT RD

25

To The Downs at Santa Fe
To Albuquerque

25

Villa
Linda Mall

To
Lamy, Las Vegas

Santa Fe
Community College

DOWNTOWN SANTA FE

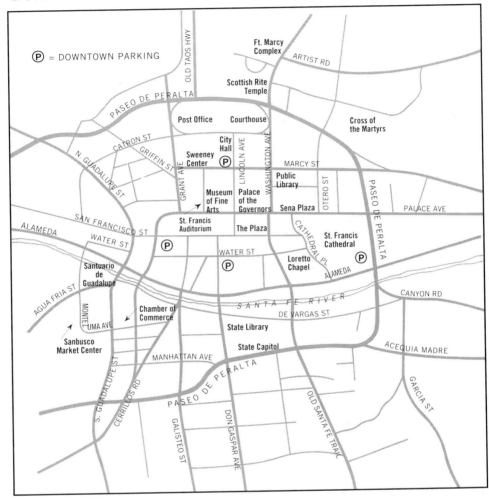

TAOS

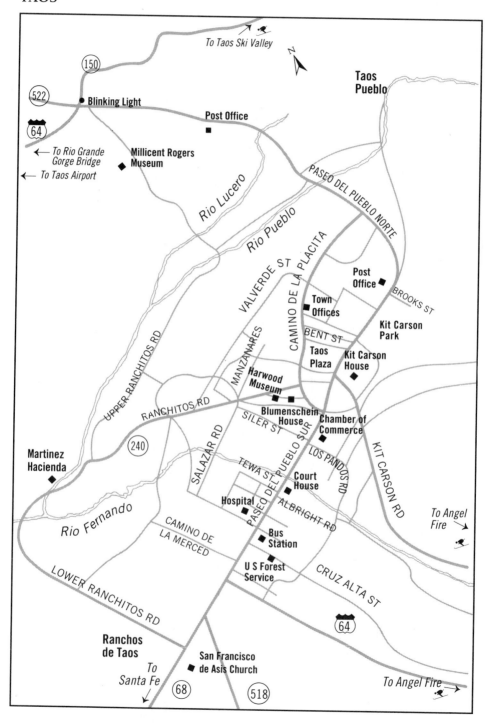

To Taos Ski Valley

Taos
Pueblo

150

522

64

Blinking Light

Post Office

← To Rio Grande
Gorge Bridge
← To Taos Airport

Millicent Rogers
Museum

Rio Lucero

Rio Pueblo

PASEO DEL PUEBLO NORTE

Post
Office

BROOKS ST

VALVERDE ST

CAMINO DE LA PLACITA

Town
Offices

BENT ST

Kit Carson
Park

MANZANARES

Taos
Plaza

Kit Carson
House

UPPER RANCHITOS RD

Harwood
Museum

RANCHITOS RD

Blumenschein
House

Chamber of
Commerce

240

SALAZAR RD

SILER ST

LOS PANDOS RD

KIT CARSON RD

Martinez
Hacienda

TEWA ST

Court
House

PASEO DEL PUEBLO SUR

Hospital

ALBRIGHT RD

To Angel
Fire →

Rio Fernando

CAMINO DE
LA MERCED

Bus
Station

U S Forest
Service

CRUZ ALTA ST

LOWER RANCHITOS RD

64

Ranchos
de Taos

To
Santa Fe

San Francisco
de Asis Church

To Angel Fire

68

518

THE ENCHANTED CIRCLE

COLORADO

NEW MEXICO

Costilla

Costilla Lake

522

196

Rio Grande

Latir Peak
12,723 ft

Molycorp
Mine

378

38

Red River

Baldy Mountain
12,441 ft

Questa

Bobcat
Pass

D.H. Lawrence
Ranch

Taos Ski
Valley

64

Arroyo
Hondo

150

Wheeler Peak
13,161 ft

Eagle Nest

64

To Cimarron
& I-25
(One Hour)

Arroyo Seco

Rio Grande
Gorge Bridge

Airport

Taos Pueblo

Vietnam Veterans
Memorial

Taos

Millicent Rogers Museum

Kit Carson
State Park

64

Angel Fire

Ranchos de Taos

Palo Flechado Pass

434

To Coyote Creek State Park,
Mora, & Las Vegas, NM

Rio Grande

68

518

To Santa Fe
via
High Road
(2 hours)

To Santa Fe
via River Route
(1 hour)

THE SANTA FE AND TAOS REGION

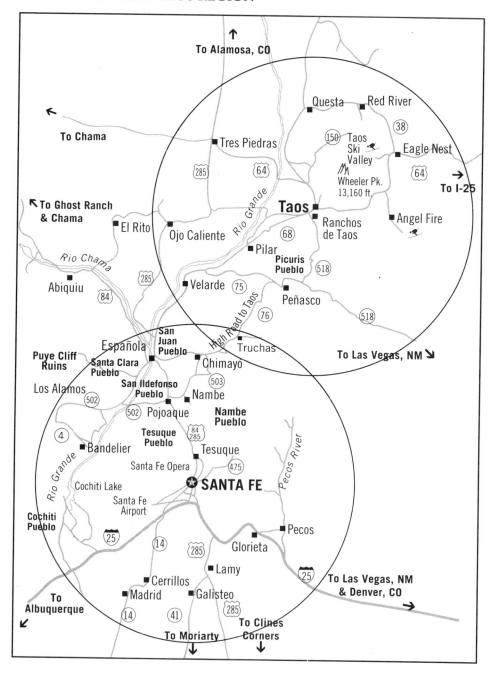

To Alamosa, CO

Questa   Red River

38

To Chama   Tres Piedras

150   Taos
Ski
Valley

Eagle Nest

285   64   Wheeler Pk.
13,160 ft.

64

To I-25

Rio Grande

Taos

To Ghost Ranch
& Chama

El Rito   Ojo Caliente   68   Ranchos
de Taos

Angel Fire

Pilar

Picuris
Pueblo   518

Rio Chama

285

Abiquiu

84   Velarde   75   Peñasco

518

High Road to Taos

76

San
Juan
Pueblo   Truchas

To Las Vegas, NM

Española

Puye Cliff
Ruins   Santa Clara
Pueblo   Chimayo

Los Alamos   San Ildefonso
Pueblo   503

502   502   Pojoaque   Nambe

Nambe
Pueblo

4   Bandelier   Tesuque
Pueblo   84
285

Tesuque

Rio Grande

Santa Fe Opera

Cochiti Lake

475

SANTA FE

Pecos River

Santa Fe
Airport

Cochiti
Pueblo   25   14   285   Glorieta

Pecos

25

To Las Vegas, NM
& Denver, CO

Lamy

To
Albuquerque   Cerrillos
Madrid   Galisteo

14   41   285

To Moriarty   To Clines
Corners